Pervasive Cloud Computing Technologies:

Future Outlooks and Interdisciplinary Perspectives

Lucio Grandinetti
University of Calabria, Italy

Ornella Pisacane
Polytechnic University of Marche, Italy

Mehdi Sheikhalishahi
University of Calabria, Italy

A volume in the Advances in Systems
Analysis, Software Engineering, and High
Performance Computing (ASASEHPC)
Book Series

Information Science
REFERENCE
An Imprint of IGI Global

Managing Director: Lindsay Johnston
Production Manager: Jennifer Yoder
Development Editor: Austin DeMarco
Acquisitions Editor: Kayla Wolfe
Typesetter: John Crodian
Cover Design: Jason Mull

Published in the United States of America by
     Information Science Reference (an imprint of IGI Global)
     701 E. Chocolate Avenue
     Hershey PA 17033
     Tel: 717-533-8845
     Fax: 717-533-8661
     E-mail: cust@igi-global.com
     Web site: http://www.igi-global.com

Library of Congress Cataloging-in-Publication Data

Grandinetti, Lucio, 1941-
 Pervasive cloud computing technologies : future outlooks and interdisciplinary perspectives / by Lucio Grandinetti, Ornella Pisacane and Mehdi Sheikhalishahi.
    pages cm
 Includes bibliographical references and index.
   ISBN 978-1-4666-4683-4 (hardcover) -- ISBN 978-1-4666-4684-1 (ebook) -- ISBN 978-1-4666-4685-8 (print & perpetual access) 1. Cloud computing--Case studies. I. Pisacane, Ornella. II. Sheikhalishahi, Mehdi. III. Title.
   QA76.585.G83 2013 004.67'82--dc23
                              2013025626

This book is published in the IGI Global book series Advances in Systems Analysis, Software Engineering, and High Performance Computing (ASASEHPC) (ISSN: 2327-3453; eISSN: 2327-3461)

British Cataloguing in Publication Data
A Cataloguing in Publication record for this book is available from the British Library.

For electronic access to this publication, please contact: eresources@igi-global.com.

Advances in Systems Analysis, Software Engineering, and High Performance Computing (ASASEHPC) Book Series

ISSN: 2327-3453
EISSN: 2327-3461

MISSION

The theory and practice of computing applications and distributed systems has emerged as one of the key areas of research driving innovations in business, engineering, and science. The fields of software engineering, systems analysis, and high performance computing offer a wide range of applications and solutions in solving computational problems for any modern organization.

The **Advances in Systems Analysis, Software Engineering, and High Performance Computing (ASASEHPC) Book Series** brings together research in the areas of distributed computing, systems and software engineering, high performance computing, and service science. This collection of publications is useful for academics, researchers, and practitioners seeking the latest practices and knowledge in this field.

COVERAGE

- Computer Graphics
- Computer Networking
- Computer System Analysis
- Distributed Cloud Computing
- Enterprise Information Systems
- Metadata and Semantic Web
- Parallel Architectures
- Performance Modeling
- Software Engineering
- Virtual Data Systems

IGI Global is currently accepting manuscripts for publication within this series. To submit a proposal for a volume in this series, please contact our Acquisition Editors at Acquisitions@igi-global.com or visit: http://www.igi-global.com/publish/.

Titles in this Series

For a list of additional titles in this series, please visit: www.igi-global.com

High Performance and Cloud Computing in Scientific Research and Education
Marijana Despotović-Zrakić (University of Belgrade, Serbia) Veljko Milutinović (University of Belgrade, Serbia) and Aleksandar Belić (Institute of Physics, Serbia)
Information Science Reference • copyright 2014 • 350pp • H/C (ISBN: 9781466657847) • US $195.00 (our price)

Agile Estimation Techniques and Innovative Approaches to Software Process Improvement
Ricardo Colomo-Palacios (Universidad Carlos III de Madrid, Spain) Jose Antonio Calvo-Manzano Villalón (Universidad Politécnica De Madrid, Spain) Antonio de Amescua Seco (Universidad Carlos III de Madrid, Spain) and Tomás San Feliu Gilabert (Universidad Politécnica De Madrid, Spain)
Information Science Reference • copyright 2014 • 312pp • H/C (ISBN: 9781466651821) • US $215.00 (our price)

Enabling the New Era of Cloud Computing Data Security, Transfer, and Management
Yushi Shen (Microsoft, USA) Yale Li (Microsoft, USA) Ling Wu (EMC, USA) Shaofeng Liu (Microsoft, USA) and Qian Wen (Endronic Corp, USA)
Information Science Reference • copyright 2014 • 336pp • H/C (ISBN: 9781466648012) • US $195.00 (our price)

Theory and Application of Multi-Formalism Modeling
Marco Gribaudo (Politecnico di Milano, Italy) and Mauro Iacono (Seconda Università degli Studi di Napoli, Italy)
Information Science Reference • copyright 2014 • 314pp • H/C (ISBN: 9781466646599) • US $195.00 (our price)

Pervasive Cloud Computing Technologies Future Outlooks and Interdisciplinary Perspectives
Lucio Grandinetti (University of Calabria, Italy) Ornella Pisacane (Polytechnic University of Marche, Italy) and Mehdi Sheikhalishahi (University of Calabria, Italy)
Information Science Reference • copyright 2014 • 292pp • H/C (ISBN: 9781466646834) • US $190.00 (our price)

Communication Infrastructures for Cloud Computing
Hussein T. Mouftah (University of Ottawa, Canada) and Burak Kantarci (University of Ottawa, Canada)
Information Science Reference • copyright 2014 • 583pp • H/C (ISBN: 9781466645226) • US $195.00 (our price)

Organizational, Legal, and Technological Dimensions of Information System Administration
Irene Maria Portela (Polytechnic Institute of Cávado and Ave, Portugal) and Fernando Almeida (Polytechnic Institute of Gaya, Portugal)
Information Science Reference • copyright 2014 • 321pp • H/C (ISBN: 9781466645264) • US $195.00 (our price)

www.igi-global.com

701 E. Chocolate Ave., Hershey, PA 17033
Order online at www.igi-global.com or call 717-533-8845 x100
To place a standing order for titles released in this series, contact: cust@igi-global.com
Mon-Fri 8:00 am - 5:00 pm (est) or fax 24 hours a day 717-533-8661

Dedication with love:

Lucio to Eleanor

Ornella to Salvino

Mehdi to his parents

Table of Contents

Chapter 4

Chapter 5

Chapter 6

Chapter 7

Preface

This book is addressed to a rather broad audience, encompassing anyone who is looking at cloud computing to use it, to learn more about it, or to apply it to her needs. Cloud computing is a buzzword in recent years, so diverse ranges of people need to understand it from different points of view.

This book aims to capture the interest of Information Technology practitioners, various engineers, managers, businesses, industries, and experimental scientific communities. More specifically, those who are in the grey area of usage, technical, and scientific profiles, and those practitioners (actual or potential end users) who need to attain the knowledge of novel and pervasive technologies. In addition, readers who want or need to learn essential but formal and rigorous technical materials of cloud computing may consider this book as a fruitful resource.

Very often it happens that as fast as IT-related technologies and their trends appear, they will disappear. In the computing landscape, "Application Service Provider," "Service-Oriented Architecture," "Services Architecture," and "Grid Computing" are a few technologies that appeared and disappeared quickly because of reasons like the emergence of contemporary and complementary technologies. How about cloud computing? Will this be true for this emerging technology? This is a question we are going to investigate in this book.

In this book, we consider cloud computing as a core topic and various things emerging around it such as its services and delivery models, its economic aspects, applications, usages, challenges, and so on.

Many design and architectural patterns are emerging around cloud computing that make it difficult to fit everything into a perfect definition. For instance, from the marketing point of view, the term cloud computing is vague and somewhat meaningless because of its extensive overuse and misuse. In recent years, whatever an IT vendor sold, it somehow called cloud computing.

In chapter 1, we describe cloud computing from different angles. We clear up some misconceptions and ambiguities about it to reach a sound understanding of the topic. Then, we enumerate cloud attributes and its essential characteristics. This chapter aims at all categories of audiences. Chapter 2 is devoted to the introduction of emerging technologies centered around cloud computing. From the technological point of view, cloud computing was born as a result of the emergence and the convergence of contemporary technologies. This chapter regards technological aspects of cloud. In the software area, Virtualization Technology and Web Services; in the hardware area, shared compute components (i.e., multicore processors); in networking, Security, Virtual Private Network (VPN), and Network Overlay are the promising and motivating technologies for the future complex computing infrastructures. In this chapter, we review these technologies and describe how they contribute to the anatomy and the characteristics of cloud computing. It addresses those readers who need to know about the technologies behind cloud computing such as Information Technology practitioners and computer engineers.

The term cloud computing covers a range of delivery and service models. In chapter 3, cloud service delivery models (i.e., Software-as-a-Service, Platform-as-a-Service and Infrastructure-as-a-Service) and cloud deployment models (private cloud, community cloud, public cloud, and hybrid cloud) are described. With the aforementioned themes, this chapter is devoted to cloud users like IT engineers, industrial users, and experimental scientists.

Standardization is a key answer and solution to our main question in this book (i.e., whether cloud computing will survive and remain on IT trends track or not). Standardization will bring interoperability, integration, and portability to the cloud computing landscape. Cloud standardization needs to be addressed at various layers of a cloud infrastructure such as: Virtual Machine Format, Data, Interface, Context, and Identity Layers. Chapter 4 reviews the emerging standards from the side of various organizations and standard bodies. It targets IT practitioners, managers, and IT engineers.

The other big challenge for adoption and survival of cloud computing is security. Although cloud computing has been widely accepted in the enterprise and its usage is growing exponentially, a worry still exists about the security risks. How can a company be sure that is getting a secure cloud computing solution whose implementation is secure in every possible aspect? Chapter 5 discusses this important issue and enumerates some initiatives to address it. This chapter has a broad audience from cloud users to managers and IT engineers who need to know about security aspects of cloud computing.

The huge amount of data generated from various environments represents a significant source of information and knowledge, and therefore, it needs to be efficiently managed and processed. For this purpose, high performance and advanced computing and scalable storage facilities and tools become essential. In chapter 6, the management of big data is analyzed and described with reference to the clouds, introducing some significant issues like data security and data integrity. Some specific data mining techniques are detailed and some real life applications are described. Therefore, its audience mainly consists of IT engineers and practitioners.

Economic benefits of cloud adoption are the main drivers and motivations of making cloud as ubiquitous an IT paradigm as it is becoming. Public cloud computing can avoid capital expenditures because no hardware, software, or network devices need to be purchased. Cloud usage is billed on actual use only and is therefore treated more as an expense. In turn, usage-based billing lowers the barrier to entry because the upfront costs are minimal. These economic aspects of cloud computing are discussed in chapter 7. We investigate whether cloud could be beneficial from economical points of view. Managers, economists, and IT decision makers are the main audience of this chapter.

Cloud computing is well-suited to support the multi-company business processes inherent in any supply chain of manufacturing, beginning with business applications as a service, followed by other cloud aspects such as development platforms. In chapter 8, the current usage of cloud in industry and manufacturing sectors are reviewed. This chapter gives useful information to business and industrial managers and practitioners.

Cloud computing is gaining consideration in the commercial world, with companies like Amazon, Google, and Yahoo! offering pay-to-play cycles to help organizations meet cyclical demands for extra computing power. Cloud computing technologies and service models are attractive to scientific computing users as well due to the ability to get on-demand access to resources, to replace or supplement existing systems, as well as the ability to control the software environment. Scientific computing researchers and resource providers servicing these users are considering the impact of these new models and technologies. Chapter 9 describes how cloud is helping researchers to accelerate scientific discovery by transforming manual and difficult tasks into the cloud. Thus, it particularly aims at experimental scientists.

Chapter 10 explores the connection between Operations Research and cloud computing. In particular, it demonstrates how the high intensive computational optimization tasks benefit from a cloud. For this purpose, some optimization problems that belong to linear programming, integer linear programming, stochastic programming, and logistics management are investigated. Then, it is shown how the optimization models and methods can support the process of designing and managing a cloud. For this purpose, the data center location problem, the workload distribution problem, the virtual machine allocation problem, and the partner provider selection problem are addressed. In addition, the relation between simulation-based optimization and cloud computing is highlighted.

Chapter 11 aims to discuss the intersection of cloud computing with healthcare. This is done by describing the advantages and benefits as well as the criticisms. The chapter also contains a useful and illustrative case study. In summary, the potential audience of this contribution mainly consists of medical experts, researchers, healthcare managers, and users.

Green computing is a research topic mostly developed in recent years to address climate and energy challenges of the world. Chapter 12 explores green computing. It envisions the duality of green computing with technological trends in other fields of computing such as High Performance Computing (HPC) and cloud computing on one hand and economy and business on the other hand. For instance, in order to provide electricity for large-scale cloud infrastructures and to reach exascale computing, we need huge amounts of energy. Thus, green computing is a challenge for the future of cloud computing and HPC. Alternatively, clouds and HPC provide solutions for green computing and climate change. In this chapter, we discuss this proposition by looking at the technology in detail.

Lucio Grandinetti
University of Calabria, Italy

Ornella Pisacane
Polytechnic University of Marche, Italy

Mehdi Sheikhalishahi
University of Calabria, Italy

Acknowledgment

The authors are very grateful to all outstanding individuals who have had an impact on this book. We were fortunate to have their perspective and insights during our book development.

We extend our appreciation and acknowledgment to those scientists who read the book chapters and made useful and constructive comments during the review process of our manuscript and to those who provided us with their materials and gave us permission to use them in our book in the form of images or quotes.

The first group includes Ankit Agrawal, Research Associate Professor, Department of Electrical Engineering and Computer Science, McCormick School of Engineering and Applied Science, Northwestern University; Patrizia Beraldi, Associate Professor, Department of Mechanical, Energy and Management Engineering, University of Calabria; Adamo Bosco, PhD; Ümit V. Çatalyürek, Professor, Department of Biomedical Informatics, Ohio State University; Geoffrey C. Fox, Professor, Informatics, Computing, and Physics, Indiana University Bloomington; Wolfgang Gentzsch, HPC and Cloud Projects Specialist, TheUberCloud, LLC; Vladimir Getov, Professor, School of Electronics and Computer Science, University of Westminster; Francesca Guerriero, Associate Professor, Department of Mechanical, Energy, and Management Engineering, University of Calabria; Patrick Martin, Professor, School of Computing, Queen's University; Rina Mary Mazza, PhD, Department of Computer Engineering, Electronics, and Systems, University of Calabria; Natalie Bates, Chair, the Energy Efficient HPC Working Group; Dana Petcu, Professor, Computer Science Department, West University of Timisoara; Alex Shafarenko, Professor, School of Computer Science, University of Hertfordshire; Domenico Talia, Full Professor, Department of Computer Engineering, Electronics, and Systems, University of Calabria; Yoshio Tanaka, National Institute of Advanced Industrial Science and Technology, Japan; Jose Luis Vazquez-Poletti, Assistant Professor, Universidad Complutense de Madrid; Richard Wallace, Universidad Complutense de Madrid.

The second group is Kes Wold, DMTF Executive Director; Troy Biegger, DMTF VP of Marketing; Stephanie Geary, Permissions, IDC; Kapil Bakshi, Cisco Systems Inc.; Geoff Brown, CEO and Founder of Machine-to-Machine Intelligence(m2mi) Corp.; Kiran Kamreddy, MBA, Product Marketing Manager, Darden; Miha Ahronovitz, "The Memories of Product Manager" blog; Bhumip Khasnabish, IEEE; Michael Weigelt, Living PlanIT SA; James R. Collins, Argonne National Laboratory; Mary R. Hale, Publications Relation Services, Argonne National Laboratory; Suma Boby, Group Manager-North America PR-AR, Avanade®; Stephen Vastagh, General Secretary, DICOM®; John Howie, Chief Operating Officer, Cloud SecurityAlliance; Wolfgang Gentzsch, HPC and Cloud Projects Specialist, TheUberCloud, LLC; Burak Yenier, VP of Operations at CashEdge; Keiichi Shima, Research Laboratory, IIJ Innovation Institute, Inc.; Marie Honorè-Grant, Ombudsman Specialist, Office of the Ombudsman, Gartner; Nate Odell, Director of Marketing, Skytap, Inc.

Moreover, the authors are very grateful to Francesco Pannuti, Founder and CEO, Nethical s.r.l., who provided the case study included in Chapter 11.

Lucio Grandinetti
University of Calabria, Italy

Ornella Pisacane
Polytechnic University of Marche, Italy

Mehdi Sheikhalishahi
University of Calabria, Italy

Chapter 1
A General Purpose and Hyperspecialization Model of Future Computing

ABSTRACT

In this chapter, the authors describe cloud computing from different angles. They clear up some misconceptions and ambiguities about it to reach a common understanding of the topic. Then, they enumerate cloud attributes and its essential characteristics. The authors consider cloud computing as a core topic and various things emerging around it such as its services and delivery models, its economic aspects, applications, usages, challenges, and so on. Cloud computing is a focal technological point for various technologies and shares its characteristics and features with them. Cloud is a dual technology for many emerging technologies such as Internet of Things, Smart Grid, Smart City, Green Computing, and Home Networking. On the other hand, cloud complements the growth and the development of these technologies. At the end, the authors explore these complementary technologies.

1. INTRODUCTION

On February 24, 2007, the term "cloud computing" was coined and that day Cloud Expo (Cloud Computing Expo, 2012) was announced. In 2007, the first Cloud Expo took place in New York City with 450 delegates. And in 2008, the number of delegates in Cloud Expo was with more than 10,000 and over 600 sponsors and exhibitors. This direct observation shows the importance and the rapid evolution of cloud computing.

DOI: 10.4018/978-1-4666-4683-4.ch001

Since the birth of TCP/IP, people have been drawing TCP/IP networks on diagrams like cloud metaphor. This metaphor resonates for the same reason the "electron cloud" is a useful metaphor for the behavior of electrons. A cloud represents a black-box: we do not have to know its internal details, just its behaviors or interfaces are needed by users. On the other hand, cloud computing is a new term to define and to represent infinity and utility computing in order to deliver elastic information technology (IT) over the Internet. However, the precise definition of cloud computing (Armbrust et al., 2009) varies widely and depends on the context, since clouds are not mature enough and they are in a rapid, continuous, and technological evolution stage.

In the cloud computing world, IT capabilities are delivered on the fly and on-demand through the Internet when the need arises instead of drawing from local and desktop computers. Many design and architectural patterns (Armbrust et al., 2010) are emerging around cloud computing that makes it difficult to fit everything into a perfect definition. For instance, from the marketing point of view (Buyya, Yeo, & Venugopal, 2008), the term "cloud computing" is vague and meaningless due to its widely misuse and extensive overuse. In the recent years of appearance of cloud computing, any software, service, tool, and product IT companies provide, offer, or sell, using Web technologies, are labeled 'cloud'. They are somehow in the cloud or are called "cloud computing."

The other face of cloud computing is outsourcing. Software companies are rapidly moving more and more of their services, software, and applications to cloud computing due to users' radical, urgent, growing, fluctuating, seasonal, competing, enormous, and economic demands. These number of demands cannot be met by running users' local and private infrastructures. On the other hand, if users invest in private infrastructures and buy lots of servers during falling and low demands times servers would be under-utilized; this would largely lead to wasting IT resources and energy. In addition, local infrastructures require IT system administration tasks such as installation, deployment, configuration, patching, upgrading, etc. With outsourcing, these all shift to cloud computing.

During the emergence and the evolution of computing models, we have seen computing technologies like time-sharing, mainframe, high performance computing (HPC), cluster computing, grid computing, and service oriented computing. We observe that some of these computing models are the building blocks of cloud computing such as time-sharing and service oriented computing while the others could be provided and be offered as a service from a right cloud provider. For example, there are many cloud offerings for HPC as a Service, Grid as a Service.

Again we ask this question: what is cloud computing and why should we care? We define it in simple terms from another angle: cloud computing simply means using remote, large and Internet-based data centers as if they belong to your own private infrastructure. This is similar to large pipes for computing, network, software, data, and information.

Large software and Internet companies including Salesforce.com, Google, Yahoo!

and Amazon are pushing forward to deliver information and software over the Internet (Armbrust et al., 2010). In accessing services, users do not know what is really happening and what is behind cloud infrastructures of these companies. It is like a Google search that we do not know anything about our search process like from where our search result is coming, what city the servers are located in, etc.

Salesforce.com is one of the best Software as a Service (SaaS) provider. It is a classic example of cloud computing. Salesforce.com has made cloud computing a reality by offering Customer Relationship Management (CRM) as a SaaS (CRM at Salesforce.com, Inc., 2012). SaaS is one of the categories of cloud computing that most industrial and manufacturing companies are interested in using. With CRM solutions of Salesforce based on SaaS "all you need is a browser and you have a CRM system."

In summary, we denote cloud computing as an extreme specialization (hyper-specialization) and at the same time a general purpose model of information technology to digest the flux of future IT.

The National Institute of Standards & Technology (NIST) definition of cloud computing includes five essential characteristics: on-demand self-service, broad network access, resource pooling, rapid elasticity, and measured service (Cloud Architecture Reference Models: A Survey, 2011). However, we connote the real definition of cloud computing as the convergence of the following essential and ideal characteristics of various distributed computing technologies that form the anatomy of cloud computing:

1. **Infinity:** Large scale data centers;
2. **Utility:** Pay per use;
3. **Elasticity:** Scalability, auto-scaling;
4. **Outsourcing:** Remote, over the Internet;
5. **On-demand;**
6. **Self-service:** Self-provisioning, on the fly;
7. **Federation;**
8. **Multi-tenancy;**
9. **Many-abilities:** Availability, reliability, scalability, sustainability, etc.

2. CHARACTERISTICS

Cloud computing has acquired special attention from both industry and research as it has emerged as a potential platform to address a broad array of computing needs and requirements such as custom software environments and increased utilization among others. Both private and public cloud services have demonstrated the ability to provide a scalable set of services that can be easily and cost-effectively utilized to tackle various enterprise and scientific workloads.

These benefits are a direct result of the anatomy of cloud computing: on-demand self-service resources that are pooled, can be accessed via a network, and can be elastically adjusted by the user. The pooling of resources across a large user base enables economies of scale (Armbrust et al., 2009), while the ability to easily provision and elastically expand the resources provides flexible capabilities.

Cloud computing attributes and characteristics make it a dream and an ideal IT delivery platform. Figure 1 illustrates the compelling features of a cloud. In this section, we describe the cloud's characteristics that establish and constitute the anatomy of cloud computing.

Figure 1. An illustration of cloud computing anatomy by its characteristics

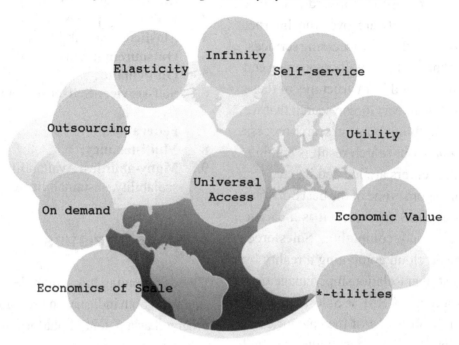

2.1 Infinity

According to International Data Corporation (IDC), "the cloud movement is about much more than the cloud." [1] Clouds rapidly approach infinity in terms of computation, storage capacity, services, and software (Armbrust et al., 2009), we observe this character from some statistics on computing, power, and software: (1) according to recent research by International Data Corporation (IDC), worldwide revenue from public IT cloud services exceeded $21.5 billion in 2010 and will reach $72.9 billion in 2015, representing a compound annual growth rate (CAGR) of 27.6%. [2] (2) According to Gartner, Inc., the public cloud services market is forecast to grow 18.5 percent in 2013 to total $131 billion worldwide, up from $111 billion in 2012 [3]. Gartner Press Release, "Gartner Says Worldwide Public Cloud Services Market to Total

$131 Billion," February 28, 2013, http://www.gartner.com/newsroom/id/2352816 (3) Power requirement for new megadata centers in 2011, according to Microsoft was 50 megawatts. In the dotcom era, it was 1 to 2 megawatts. (4) By 2015, one of every seven dollars spent on packaged software, server, and storage offerings will be through the public cloud model. (5) Maximum number of servers that Google says can be managed with its new software, will be 10 million. (6) Based on data from McKinsey and IDC, approximate number of servers in use globally is 60 million.

These numbers express the exponential growth of data center infrastructures and market for servers and cloud computing. According to these statistics, we predict an outsourcing shift to giant data centers in terms of everything in IT industry such as software, hardware, and IT economics.

2.2 Outsourcing: Remote, Over the Internet

In the early 2000s, hosting and "Software as a Service" companies like Salesforce.com pioneered the outsourcing concept by renting applications to customers by the month. With the advent of cloud computing, it is represented with a diagram that contains a cloud-like shape. This cloud shape denotes a layer where the responsibility for a service moves from user to provider. This is a service outsourcing from the user side to the provider side.

In Figure 2, outsourcing characteristics of cloud computing from technology and delivery points of view are illustrated. We may say everything in IT is offered via outsourcing like the electrical power drawing from electricity grid; a few of them are listed as follows; they provide access to a shared collection of computing resources:

- Networks for transfer
- Servers for storage and computation
- Applications or services for completing tasks

Figure 2. Outsourcing character of cloud computing: technological perspective and delivery point of view

2.3 Utility: Pay Per Use

In cloud computing, payment of resource consumption is just like utilities that are paid for by the hour. In other words, service consumption is metered and measured.

When demand for a service varies over time, and when demand is unknown in advance, the utility character of a cloud will definitely make it economically cost-saving.

In data center design provisioning a data center for the peak load that it must sustain a few days per month leads to under-utilization at other times. Instead, cloud computing lets an organization pay by the hour for computing resources, potentially leading to cost-savings even if the hourly rate to rent a machine from a cloud provider is higher than the rate to own one.

For instance, Web startups have usually an unknown demand initially. They will need to support a spike in demand when they become popular, followed potentially by a reduction once some of the visitors turn away.

Cost associativity is a direct consequence of pay-as-you-go model of cloud computing. It is defined as "using 1000 Amazon Elastic Computing Cloud (EC2) machines for 1 hour costs the same as using 1 machine for 1000 hours." Organizations that perform batch analytics or have parallel processing applications can benefit from cost-associativity to finish computations faster.

Currently, Web companies like Amazon sell their services on a utility basis. A company can start up hundreds or thousands of computers on the fly and turn them off when the peak is low or the work was done. Instead

of monthly or yearly contracts, customers pay only for what they use in computing cycles, bandwidth, and storage per hour. On the other hand, clouds should optimize resource use and control it for the level of service or type of servers such as storage or processing.

Figures 3 and 4 illustrate the current and the potential pay-per-use operational costs of three different industries, respectively. They illustrate the reduced amount of operational costs of each department with IBM cloud computing services [4].

2.4 Economies of Scale

The construction and operation of extremely large-scale, commodity-computer data centers at low-cost locations is the key necessary enabler of cloud computing (Armbrust et al., 2009). With the exception of very large enterprises, organizations, or governments, major cloud suppliers can purchase hardware, network equipment, bandwidth, etc. much cheaper than a regular business. For instance, the cost of electricity, hardware, network bandwidth, operations, software, and space is decreased in the factors of 5 to 7 at very large economies of scale. These factors combined with statistical multiplexing to increase utilization compared to a private cloud, meant that cloud computing could offer services below the costs of a medium-sized data center and yet still make a good profit (Armbrust et al., 2009).

In other words, the economies of scale means if you need more computational cycles, more server capacity, or more storage space it is just a matter of upping your subscription

Figure 3. Current operational costs

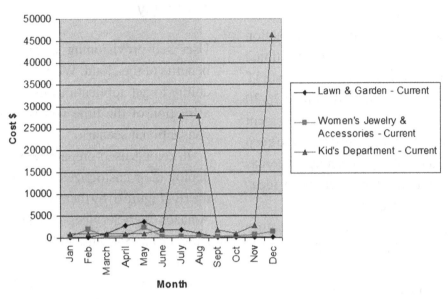

Figure 4. Potential pay-per-use operational costs [5]

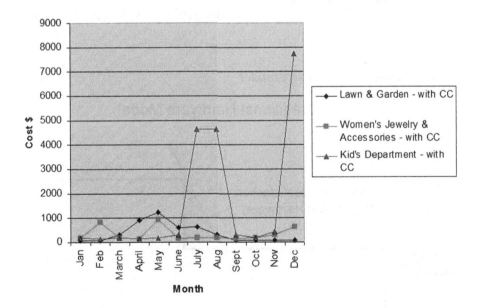

costs with your cloud provider, instead of buying new IT equipment.

With cloud computing, the most attraction is the potential to save money. In traditional computing models, the average corporate IT department has to deal with the dread 70/30 usage rule where they spend about 70 percent of their technology budgets just trying to keep IT products and service running, whereas leaving only 30 percent to develop new ideas and innovation (Vance, 2011).

Figure 5 illustrates how infrastructure costs change over time for a real case. That is how clouds can adapt to these changes to reduce costs compared to traditional computing model. The opportunity cost is defined as the benefit that could have been gained from an alternative use of the same resource. In the cloud economics model, there is no opportunity cost.

2.5 Self-Service: Self-Provisioning, on the Fly

User self-provisioning is one the greatest benefits of the cloud. With that, you have the ability to get applications up and running in a fraction of the time you would need in a conventional scenario.

In a cloud, users prepare their resources and deploy their customized IT environment on the fly (Figure 6) by themselves. For instance, Amazon Web Services (AWS) makes it possible for anyone with an Internet connection and a credit card to access the same world class computing systems that Amazon uses to run its $34 billion-a-year retail business and its operation.

Skytap Inc., a provider of self-service and self-provisioning cloud automation solutions (Figure7), provides cloud computing capabili-

Figure 5. Economic based infrastructure model

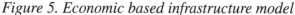

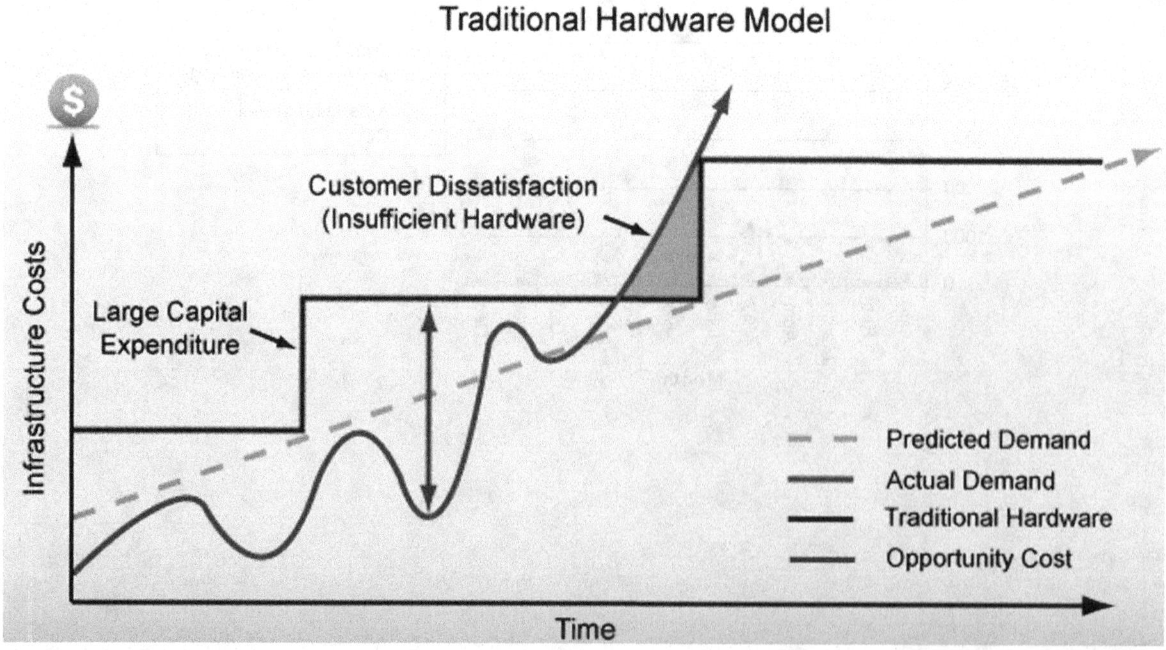

Figure 6. On the fly

ties for increased simplicity, security, visibility and control. Skytap's services make it easier for business users to tap into the Skytap Cloud [6], as well as offer the necessary visibility and control required by IT.

2.6 Elasticity: Scalability, Auto-Scaling

With elasticity, users can rapidly increase or decrease the capacity of their resources, companies can ramp capacity up and down; this is what comes in our mind when we think about elasticity.

Elasticity is not only at the compute layer; for instance, AWS offer elasticity at various layers of a cloud infrastructure such as computing (Amazon EC2), architecture: load balancing (Elastic Load Balancing), networking (Elastic IP addresses), and storage (Amazon Elastic Block Store).

Amazon EC2 enables users to increase or decrease capacity within minutes, not hours or

Figure 7. Self-service and self-provisioning cloud automation solutions in Skytap. Used with permission. [7]

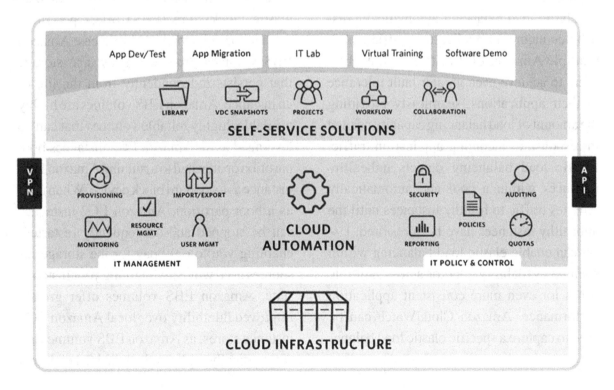

days. Users can commission one, hundreds or even thousands of server instances simultaneously. Since this is all controlled with Web service APIs, an application can automatically scale itself up and down depending on its needs. In other words, autoscaling for an application means that the application must be able to scale horizontally. For instance, if a company's Apache Web server is running out of capacity, the company just need to add more Web servers.

Amazon EC2 is at one end of the spectrum. An EC2 instance looks much like physical hardware, and users can control nearly the entire software stack, from the kernel upwards. This low level makes it inherently difficult for Amazon to offer automatic scalability and failover, because the semantics associated with replication and other state management issues are highly application-dependent (Vance, 2011).

Elastic load balancing automatically distributes incoming application traffic across multiple Amazon EC2 instances. It enables users to achieve even greater fault tolerance in their applications, seamlessly providing the amount of load balancing capacity needed in response to incoming application traffic. Elastic load balancing detects unhealthy instances within a pool and automatically reroutes traffic to healthy instances until the unhealthy instances have been restored. Users can enable elastic load balancing within a single availability zone or across multiple zones for even more consistent application performance. Amazon CloudWatch can be used to capture a specific elastic load balanc-

ers operational metrics, such as request count and request latency.

Elastic IP addresses are static IP addresses designed for dynamic cloud computing. An elastic IP address is associated with users' account rather than a particular instance, and users control that address until they choose to explicitly release it. Unlike traditional static IP addresses, however, elastic IP addresses allow users to mask instance or availability zone failures by programmatically remapping public IP addresses to any instance in users' account. Rather than waiting for a data technician to reconfigure or replace a host, or waiting for DNS to propagate to all of customers, Amazon EC2 enables users to engineer around problems with their instance or software by quickly remapping an elastic IP address to a replacement instance. In addition, users can optionally configure the reverse DNS record of any of their elastic IP addresses. Amazon elastic block store (EBS) offers persistent storage for Amazon EC2 instances. Amazon EBS volumes provide off-instance storage that persists independently from the life of an instance. Amazon EBS volumes are highly available, highly reliable volumes that can be leveraged as an Amazon EC2 instances boot partition or attached to a running Amazon EC2 instance as a standard block device. When used as a boot partition, Amazon EC2 instances can be stopped and subsequently restarted, enabling you to only pay for the storage resources used while maintaining your instance state. Amazon EBS volumes offer greatly improved durability over local Amazon EC2 instance stores, as Amazon EBS volumes are automatically replicated on the backend (in a single availability zone). For those wanting even more durability, Amazon EBS provides the ability to create point-in-time consistent snapshots of your volumes that are then stored in Amazon S3, and automatically replicated across multiple availability zones. These snapshots can be used as the starting point for new Amazon EBS volumes, and can protect your data for long term durability. You can also easily share these snapshots with co-workers and other AWS developers.

Application and domain-specific platforms such as Google App Engine are at the other extreme of the spectrum. Google App Engine is targeted exclusively at traditional Web applications, enforcing an application structure of clean separation between a stateless computation tier and a stateful storage tier.

Automatic scaling feature of Google App Engine and high availability mechanisms, and the proprietary MegaStore data storage available to Google App Engine applications (Armbrust et al., 2009), all rely on these constraints.

2.7 Federation

The word federation comes from foedus, foederis. A federation is the union of several smaller parts that perform a common action. In the politics it is known as "a federal state" that is a political entity characterized by a union of partially self-governing states or regions united by a central (federal) government. Moreover, the federation concept has been appeared in IT system of governments. For instance, the Federal Cloud Computing Initiative in the United States government

(cloud computing plan) is a plan to transition the US federal government's information technology infrastructure.

Cloud federation concept has been borrowed from the definition and the use of federation in important entities such as Fédération Internationale de Football Association (FIFA) in sport and Russian Federation in the political unit. Cloud federation is the management, interconnection, interoperation, deployment, and coordination of multiple public and private cloud computing services to function as a single entity, and to match business needs and spikes in demand. A federated cloud brings many benefits such as:

1. To load balance traffic and accommodate spikes in demand.
2. To gain economies of scale and an enlargement of the capabilities.
3. To enable providers to expand service footprint.
4. To build composite services by integrating multiple cloud computing.
5. To enable identity federation in the cloud.

Federated clouds are a future deployment model in which consumers can transparently acquire resources from multiple cloud resource providers or cloud service providers. Standardization is the big roadblock to this model.

2.8 On-Demand

Users can provision cloud infrastructure components such as servers and networks with little human intervention and through automation whenever they want. Provisioning is rapid and scales out or in (elasticity) based on the need (on-demand). For example, a project may need a large amount of computing capacity to complete a computation, but no longer need the computing power after completing the computation.

The other important difference between traditional computing model and cloud computing is the on-demand capability of clouds. In a cloud, if a user needs a service, she may connect to the cloud immediately; this is the on-demand character of cloud computing. While in the traditional model users have to plan in advance for any kind of service they need to have access to.

With clouds we get rid of the following operations and costs in IT landscape for stakeholders and users:

- **Managers' responsibilities:**
  - Ordering compute and storage infrastructure
  - Allocating space
  - Providing electricity
  - Providing cooling
  - Hiring administrators, and technicians to build IT infrastructure, etc.
- **Building IT infrastructure:**
  - Data center landscape
  - Providing virtualization
  - Providing networking
  - Providing security, etc.
- **End users and developers duties:**
  - Developing models, algorithms, tools, and software
  - Finding the right and the most efficient models, algorithms, tools and software
  - Installation of IT components
  - Configuration of IT components
  - Deployment and integration of IT components
  - Test
  - Reading user manuals, technical documents, etc.
  - Usage

All these difficulties, responsibilities, operations, and duties will be moved to Infrastructure as a Service (IaaS), Platform as a Service (PaaS), and Software as a Service (SaaS) service delivery models. These services will be delivered via public, hybrid, and federated deployment options of large scale cloud infrastructures through standard interfaces, standardized networking layers, and standard data formats. These all good things are the foundation of economics benefits of cloud computing.

2.9 Many-Abilities: Availability, Reliability, Scalability, Sustainability, Interoperability

A true cloud computing provides the main abilities in terms of availability, reliability, scalability, and sustainability in order to guarantee Service Level Agreements (SLAs) and provide the promised SLAs.

High availability of cloud computing makes accessibility to the cloud services and collaboration among users easier.

Interoperability is about the creation of an agreed-upon framework, ontology, open data format or open protocols/APIs that enable easy migration and integration of applications and data between different cloud service providers. With interoperability, users can move things between private and public clouds, and between clouds in general. This will help in the development of cloud federation. Services with interoperability allow applications to be ported between clouds, or to use multiple cloud infrastructures before business applications are delivered from the cloud.

Like many services on offer, Quality of Service (QoS) provides a guarantee of performance, availability, security, reliability and dependability. QoS requirements are associated with service providers and end-users. SLAs are an effective means for assuring QoS between service providers and end-users. QoS may entail systematic monitoring of resources, storage, network, virtual machine, service migration and fault-tolerance. In the context of a cloud service provider, QoS should emphasize the performance of virtualization and monitoring tools.

Fault-tolerance presents the ability of a system to continue to operate in the event of the failure of some of its components. Application-specific, self-healing, and self-diagnosis mechanisms are enabling tools for cloud providers to detect failure.

SLAs are mutual contracts between providers and users for the assurance of a cloud provider to deliver the services that are agreed upon. Currently, many cloud providers offer SLAs, but they are rather weak on user compensations on outages. Some of the important architectural issues are measurement of service delivery, method of monitoring performance, and improvement of SLA over time. Load balancing represents the mechanism of self-regulating the workloads within the clouds entities (e.g. servers, hard drives, network and IT resources). Load balancing is often used to implement failover in that the service components are monitored continually and when one becomes non-responsive, the load balancer stops sending traffic, de-provisions it and provisions a new service component. A load balancer is another key requirement to build dynamic and scalable cloud architecture.

2.10 Multi-Tenancy

In traditional data centers, computing systems suffer the same under-utilization in computing power, storage and networking bandwidth. Multi-tenant is a business model that provides a secure, exclusive virtualized computing environment in which servers, databases, and other resources are shared by multiple users in a cloud environment.

A multi-tenant cloud architecture allows the use of a cloud infrastructure (an application or a server) to provide cloud services for more than one customer.

On the other hand, multi-tenant cloud infrastructures can have intruders. In an unsecure multi-tenant environment, cloud users or providers settle on cloud land without right or title. That is they do not belong in the environment in which they are found.

3. CLOUD COMPUTING: A COMPLEMENTARY AND DUAL TECHNOLOGY FOR CONTEMPORARY AND UBIQUITOUS TECHNOLOGIES

Cloud computing is a focal technological point for various technologies and shares its characteristics and features with them. Cloud is a dual technology for many emerging technologies such as Internet of Things, Smart Grid, Smart City, Green Computing, and Home Networking. On the other hand, cloud complements the growth and the development of these technologies.

One of the main reasons for this duality is that cloud computing and all these technologies are ubiquitous. A ubiquitous technology is everywhere at any time for everyone. Thus, they meet each other everywhere. This omnipresent character introduces the prominent ubiquitous concepts such as in terms of space, time, size, and things.

In sum, Internet of Things, smart city, smart green, green computing, and cloud computing provide dual solutions to each other. Thus, these all provide complementary solutions to each other. This vision tells us that cloud computing does not only affect our computing and IT life, but also it will have a profound impact on the other aspects of our life that is being developed by other technologies. Cloud will be a building block of the new emerging and ubiquitous technologies.

On the other hand, computing technologies like time-sharing, mainframe, HPC, cluster computing, virtualization, grid computing, and service oriented computing have been exploited for the growth and the development of cloud computing. Some of these computing models are the building blocks of cloud computing such as virtualization and service oriented computing. However, they could be provided and be offered as a service from a right cloud provider like HPC as a Service and Grid as a Service.

3.1 The Internet of Things

The term Internet of Things was coined by Kevin Ashton in 1999 (Ashton, 2010). The Internet of Things is another breakthrough, omnipresent and transformative technology with a futuristic vision perhaps over a span of one thousand years. As the Internet of Things (IoT) is envisioned to be a platform for a new millennium various definitions for it have been appeared. This section lays out some basic definitions that are helpful for getting a quick grasp on the concepts of the IoT. The IoT refers to uniquely identifiable objects with their virtual representations in an Internet-like structure. Things such as devices can talk to each other. Every 'thing' in IoT is smart (Magrassi & Berg, 2002), just to name a few: Smart Instrumentation, Smart Interconnectivity, Smart Objects, Smart Devices, Embedded Intelligence, Virtual Objects (Avatars). In the IoT, 'things' are active participants in processes (business, information and social). They interact and communicate among themselves and with the environment by exchanging data and information 'sensed' about the environment. They react autonomously to the environment's events by triggering actions without direct human intervention.

In summary, the following list presents some important ICT and software based characteristics of IoT:

- Open network connectivity and interoperability.
- Dynamic global network infrastructure.
- Standard and interoperable communication protocols.
- High degree of autonomous data capture, event transfer.
- Having billions of parallel events.
- The exploitation of data capture and communication capabilities.
- Interfaces in the form of services.
- Self-configuring and auto-organized capabilities.
- Independent cooperative services and applications.
- Having intelligent software entities such as Web services, SOA components.
- Less failure tolerant, since interactions are machine-to-machine (M2M).

Furthermore, the IoT is omnipresent and highly ubiquitous. As we have mentioned earlier, this is one of the main reasons for being a dual technology for cloud computing. This omnipresent character brings very important ubiquitous concepts such as space, time, size, and things into the picture.

The IoT in terms of size is huge and almost infinite. It is estimated that the number of objects would encode 50 to 100 trillion objects. In another surveyed estimation, human beings in urban environments are each surrounded by 1000 to 5000 trackable objects.

The mathematics of time and time calculations will change in IoT. Since billions of parallel and simultaneous events occur in IoT, the time will not be like a common and linear dimension. The time will depend on entity, i.e., object, process, information system, etc. In addition, massive parallel computing systems have been exploited and will be used by the IoT to analyze these billions of parallel and simultaneous events.

The IoT covers infinite space, since it is huge and infinite in terms of size (100 trillion objects); in addition, because of its omnipresent character. Furthermore, time dimension changes in IoT, as a result space dimension also will change.

On the other hand, the precise geographic location of a thing is important and critical (OGC Abstract Specification, 2012) in IoT, since it is different from the Internet that only the information is processed by only human beings.

In IoT, everything is connected to the global network through IP-connected control systems. In addition, they use IP networks to report back information. From the networking perspective, there is a need of having ubiquitous IP addressability, like based on IPv6, to address the infinity needs of size and space. On the other hand, the steep growth of data volume flowing through IP networks will expand rapidly as well.

In sum, we can say everything in IoT in terms of size, space, IP addresses, and data will tend to infinity.

As we have mentioned earlier, everything in IoT in terms of size, space, IP addresses, and data approaches infinity; thus, this infinite weight increase of everything would result in prohibitively expensive computing capability requirements. Therefore, cloud computing as an infinite technology can address these requirements. The clouds will be the most suitable computing platform to affordably provide and manage ICT services to IoT.

A visionary keynote by Haller on "Internet of Things & Cloud: A Happy Marriage?" in Japan, addresses how the IoT, the cloud, and related services are "complementary aspects" of a real world Internet. IoT services can be widely dispersed and fine-grained. These services can provide streaming data and data communications.

On the other hand, IoT can address very large scale distributed communication and computing challenges and be exploited for the development of distributed applications.

Furthermore, IoT applications can address smart city needs such as waste management, urban planning, sustainable urban environment, continuous care, emergency response, intelligent shopping, smart product management, smart meters, home automation and smart events.

IoT products, applications and services are presented as follows. They all need cloud intelligence and support:

- The IoT connects refrigerators to supermarkets for automatic and intelligent shopping.
- Cars can communicate with other cars on the road to avoid collisions and to find the quickest route for destinations.
- Real-time data logging solutions like Pachube [8]: offering some basis to work with many "things" and have them

interact. The IoT relates to real-time cloud computing.

- Connectivity between devices using data points: Nimbits (Nimbits: free, social and open source Internet of things, 2012) is an open source data historian server built on cloud computing architecture that provides this service.
- The iDigiDeviceCloud™ (iDigi Device Cloud, 2012): allows users to connect a physical device to the cloud and use an online Web application for remote access. The application converts complex device data into simple and useful information for anyone, from business owners who want to get message when refrigerator temperatures fall below a specific threshold to farmers who want to measure soil quality. iDigi also creates Internet of Things content on their community site.

Through IoT all objects in the world will be connected; this has a transformative impact on our lives. The success of IoT depends strongly on standardization, which provides interoperability, compatibility, reliability, and effective operations on a global scale. The IEEE Standards Association (IEEE-SA) establishes many initiatives to address standardization challenges.

3.2 Smart City

As we enter the solid era of information and communication technology, cities with at least ten million inhabitants will double over the next ten to twenty years. It is expected that the amount of people living in urban areas will double until 2050. And 1.2 billion cars will be on the road by 2015 (Marit, 2010). With ICT, cities become more competitive. The concept of smart city highlights the importance of ICT in the last 20 years for enhancing the competitive profile of a city. In (Marit, 2010), a smart city is defined as "a city can be defined as smart when investments in human and social capital and traditional (transport) and modern (ICT) communication infrastructure fuel sustainable economic development and a high quality of life, with a wise management of natural resources, through participatory governance."

On the other hand, another definition of a smart city based on "philosophy of growth" of a traditional economist view, targets the aim of cities in competitiveness and economic performance and growth. One of the elements to reach this aim is quality of life.

In the definition of smart cities Council of European Municipalities and Regions (CEMR) proposes to replace growth by development and quantity by quality. The quality of life of our citizens must be the aim of our city policies. CEMR envisions a flexible and evolving strategy for improving our societies and the quality of life of all citizens with the help of ICT. Citizens are not just human capital or consumers. Cities, municipalities and regions are not enterprises (Marit, 2010).

In line with DG INFSO's definition: a smart city "makes a conscious effort to use innovative ICT based solutions to improve conditions of living and working and to support a more inclusive and sustainable urban environment (Marit, 2010)."

In sum, a really smart city develops the city to reach the aim of improving the quality of life. It needs sound and innovative economic development as a means to reach this aim. It uses ICT as a tool with a great potential to enhance quality of daily life, public services and the economy. Therefore, cloud computing will have a ubiquitous place in smart city development as part of ICT solutions. The main aim of smart cities and cloud computing is quality of life. A smart city has six main dimensions (Marit, 2010) (see also Figure 8).

Figure 8. Smart city components

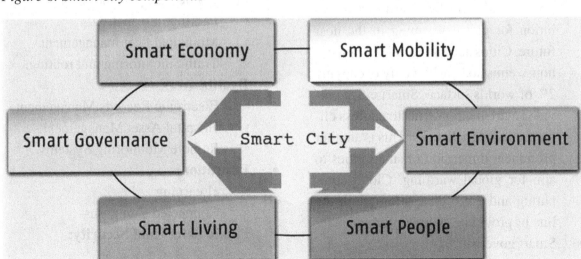

- **Smart economy:** Cloud computing with its economics characteristics can address some parts of economics aspects of smart cities to move towards better, more stable, and smarter economy;
- **Smart people:** Cloud provides a lot of services, products, and tools for individuals. In a smart city, these will be part of everybody life, therefore everyone can benefit from the knowledge provided from the cloud to make smart decision and do more intelligent actions. In conclusion, cloud computing makes people more intelligent and smarter; on the other hand, this can be controversial. The question would be it will make the people smarter, or more dependent on tools?
- **Smart mobility:** Includes smart transportation, and smart cars;
- **Smart living:** A good quality of life attracts high skilled human and social capital;
- **Smart environment:** Climate change needs a sustainable development. Smart cities will be a sustainable solution for global warming in the near future. Cities account for 75% of greenhouse emissions, while only occupying 2% of worlds surface. Smart cities provide smart environments to address climate change challenges. This is another prominent dimension of smart cities to aim for global warming. Cloud computing and green computing are in the line of providing smart environment;
- Smart governance;

- Smart communities.

According to Komninos (2002), intelligent cities become smarter:

- Applying a wide range of electronic and digital technologies to communities and cities. For instance, smartphone devices like iPhone, Android, and tablets are the means of instant communication.
- Using ICTs to transform life and work within a region.
- Embedding such ICTs in the city.
- The territorialisation of such practices in a way that bring ICTs and people together, so as to enhance the innovation, learning, knowledge and creative approach to problem solving which they offer.

In the following, various development areas of a city and their corresponding smart solutions are enumerated, respectively.

- **Transportation:**
  - Public transport monitoring.
  - Parking information.
  - Municipal fleet management.
  - Traffic monitoring and routing.
- **Healthcare:**
  - Electronic Records Management.
  - Hospital Asset Management.
  - Remote Monitoring Systems.
- **Education:**
  - eLearning.
  - Connected Campuses.
- **Public Safety and Security:**

- Video Surveillance: video analytics and workflow.
- Enhanced Emergency Systems.
- **Building Management:**
  - Smart-Meters.
  - Monitoring heating, lighting, security systems, water management.
- **Waste Management:**
  - Electronic sensors to detect toxicity in landfills.
  - Improve the efficiency of waste collection.
  - Waste-tracking.
- **City Administration:**
  - Facilitate automation of city processes.
  - eGovernment.

Heterogeneity, data mining, security, and power are some of the technological challenges of smart cities to be addressed by IT. In addition, there are other main and general challenges to be addressed:

- Legacy systems.
- Challenges over the limits of the departmental level.
- Privacy concerns.
- Politics.
- Security.
- Responsibility of businesses or government (public service).
- Open data.

Many cities are defining smart city projects, some of them are as follows: Masdar City Emirates, PlanIT Valley Portugal, Kochi India, and Songdo City South Korea.

PlanIT Valley [9] is ecosystem of large and small company partners that will focus on creating products and services for sustainable urbanization. This project attracts businesses and inhabitants. PlanIT Valley is developing Urban Operating System (UOS™). In UOS, data comes from an integrated Sensor Technology Network which connects every function of the urban environment. The collected data are analyzed and are inspected to derive knowledge and insight. Also, the collected data are aggregated to produce information. UOS can predict the outcomes of events. In addition, new applications and features can be added to UOS. This feature addresses Open Data challenge.

3.3 Green Computing

Climate change and global warming are the two most important challenging problems for the earth. These problems pertain to a general increase in world temperatures caused by increased amounts of carbon dioxide around the earth. Researchers in various fields of science and technology in recent years started to carry out research in order to address these problems by developing environmentally friendly solutions. Green IT and in particular green computing are two new terms introduced mainly in ICT community to address the aforementioned problems.

Green computing is a dual technology for computing and communication technologies such as HPC and cloud computing. This means that green computing solutions will drive the development of HPC and cloud computing; on the other hand, HPC solutions and cloud computing solutions will drive the development of green computing. Therefore, we envision green computing as a dual technology for HPC and cloud computing.

In chapter 12 of this book, we envision the duality of green computing with technological trends in other fields of computing such as cloud computing and HPC from one hand; and economy, and business, on the other hand. For instance, in order to reach exascale computing, we need huge amounts of energy to operate an exascale system. Thus, green computing is a challenge for the future of HPC. On the other hand, HPC provides solutions for green computing and climate change. In chapter 12, we discuss this proposition by looking at technologies in detail.

3.4 Smart Grid

The smart grid concept is emerging to address the electricity grid challenges. The smart grid is an intelligent electricity grid network to deliver sustainable, reliable, storage, ubiquitous, decentralized, flexible, economic, autonomic and secure electricity supplies (Smart Grid / Department of Energy, 2012). Green computing addresses energy consumption optimization at the energy consumer side, whereas smart grid addresses energy generation optimization and supply management at the energy producer side. The smart grid implementation requires smart technologies.

From the computing and communication perspective, smart grid exploits ICT (Smart Grid / Department of Energy, 2012) to deliver utility electricity of the new century through computer-based remote control and automation. The electricity grid is a large and global network composed of wires, substations, transformers, switches and much more physical components to carry electricity from the electricity plants to consumers through distribution of electricity. In traditional electricity grid, companies require operators to do the following mechanical tasks by workers to manage electricity distribution:

- Gather the data needed to provide electricity.
- Read meters.
- Look for broken equipment.
- Measure voltage.

In smart grid, these operations are automated and computerized. For that, devices in the grid are equipped with sensors and two-way digital communication technology. In addition, sensors collect data such as power meters, voltage sensors, fault detectors and send them to grid operations center. This automation via ICT in the smart grid facilitate the electricity utility management from a central location such as adjustment and control of each individual device or millions of devices.

The number of services and applications that can be used on the smart grid once the data communications technology is deployed is growing as fast as inventive companies can create and produce them.

Cloud computing providers such as Amazon, Microsoft, Google, Apple, Cisco, HP, Dell and VMware, provide IT cloud services for smart grid (1st International Workshop on High Performance Computing, Networking and Analytics for the Power Grid, 2010).

Currently, their main focus is on data network for smart meters, data management, standardization, and interoperability. The first four companies are building cloud computing standards and services for consumers and businesses whereas Cisco and VMware are more oriented to business users. By 2020, annual spending on smart grid data management could reach US$10 billion, according to Berg Insight and Bloomberg.

On the other hand, wide area and continent scale super grids transport large amounts of power from variable and intermittent renewable energy sources like wind farms and solar plants. These super grids require to store and manage big data. As a result, cloud computing is a vital option for their data management and services.

In addition, advantages of cloud computing such as cost-saving, pay-as-you-go, and infinity attracts smart grid industry. Although cloud adoption in utility industry is nascent, multiple cloud initiatives such as Green Button, home energy management, and smart grid network management are on the rise.

Cloud computing is an ideal platform for smart grid. The core advantages of cloud computing are lower costs and greater flexibility than traditional data centers, reducing mainframe computing costs and technological lock-in, that is lack of flexibility. On the other hand, the competition between smart grid cloud providers is making this key flexibility less certain.

Cloud computing suppliers for smart grid may decide to make it difficult for companies to move their software and data onto a competing cloud service, creating a new type of lock-in. This will create problems for smart grid operators wanting to cover large area networks. Hence, again standardization in cloud is a challenge for smart grid as well.

The United States needs a real-time demand response infrastructure to optimally manage and link electric supply- and demand-side systems. This smart grid infrastructure must be compatible with requirements of electric system grid operators and electric utility companies while serving the loads and needs of electricity customers. For that, the Demand Response Research Center [10] plans and conducts multi-disciplinary research to advance demand response within smart grid infrastructures in California, the nation, and abroad.

4. THE UBERCLOUD EXPERIMENT: A CASE STUDY PROJECT

Delivering high performance computing as a service comes with a set of challenges, both technical and social. The UberCloud experiment explores the various aspects of the service model, the people that need to be involved in the process, and the challenges faced when executing workloads on remote HPC resources (Gentzsch & Yenier, 2012b).

The UberCloud Experiment is an HPC Experiment with more than 160 participating organizations and individuals from 25 countries, working together in 25 teams. The Experiment has brought together four categories of participants: the industry end-users, the computing and storage resource providers, the software providers, and the experts. Participants have voluntary contribution to their individual teams and thus to the whole Experiment. This is an experimental research and study to address roadblocks on the way of transitioning to cloud solutions for industries. The Experiment kicked off on July 20, 2012. Wolfgang Gentzsch and Burak Yenier are the two main organizers of the project.

This case study is introduced in this chapter to set the stage for the discussion in the rest of the book and has been referred to throughout the book for specific real life examples. It would give practitioners a real-life example on the decision making process underlying the implementation of cloud computing projects.

The project answers the question of "how far are we from an ideal remote use of HPC or HPC-as-a-Service (HPCaaS) or HPC in the Cloud model?" At this point, we do not know, no one quite does. However, in the course of this experiment, following each team and monitoring its challenges and progress, there is an excellent insight into these roadblocks and how our 25 teams have tackled them (Gentzsch & Yenier, 2012b).

The first round of the Experiment presents the results of 3 months of work by the 25 teams and their members, their findings, challenges, lessons learned, and their recommendations. The organizers of the project were amazed by how engaged all participants moved forward, despite the fact that this was not their day job. The aim of the first round of the Experiment was to explore the end-to-end process of accessing remote computing resources and to study and overcome the potential roadblocks (Gentzsch & Yenier, 2012b).

The methodology of this project is based on collective actions. They have collectively selected the end-user projects to be worked on, assigning providers and experts to each project and finding ways to overcome the hurdles they were running into. Each team's goal was not only to complete the selected end-user project, but also to chart the way around the hurdles they identified. In addition, the findings and the results of the project are collective through sharing their detailed findings with all participants.

As the project gathers more information through building and following the progress of the teams it is also creating a positive feedback loop, where each team teaches the project's organizers and the new entrants how to build a stronger team for the next project. The future rounds of the experiment accumulates knowledge which will yield ever more successful projects.

Each team follows a common roadmap to keep the entire experiment consistent. The expert assigned to each team is the guide in following this roadmap. The roadmap calls for communication with the organizers at certain points, although generally the teams are autonomous and make their own decisions.

The roadmap defines six steps to be done by each team to reach their goal:

- Define the end-user project.
- Contact the assigned resources and set up the project environment.
- Initiate the end-user project execution.
- Monitor the project.
- Review results with the end-user.
- Document findings.

Intentionally, they performed the first round of this experiment manually not through an automated service, because the organizers believe the technology is not the challenge anymore; rather it is the people and their processes, and that is what they wanted to explore. They are continuously improving and better defining the roadmap to successful completion of projects.

The main roadblocks are: information security and privacy; unpredictable costs; lack of easy, intuitive self-service registration and administration; incompatible software licensing models; high expectations and disappointing results; reliability and availability of resource providers; and the need for a professional HPC Cloud Provider.

On the other hand, getting started was a challenge; a few teams struggled with figuring out which team member needs to do what and when. Team forming was one of the steps, which took the longest amount of time, each team member needed to exchange significant amounts of information about their background, capabilities, expectations, availability, and commitment levels with one another before the project could even kick off.

Furthermore, there were shortcomings in the course of the first round of the experiment which the UberCloud project has provided solutions for:

- Some resource providers run into resource crunches which delayed team projects;
- Some of our projects ran into long delays since the project and the resource provider were not the best match possible;
- Some resource providers struggled with installation of an application;
- Others had difficulties with providing network access through complex network connections;
- And resource providers differ in their service philosophies;
- And finally, manual processes are just slow, they consumed days, sometimes weeks especially because the various technology and people resources were inherently remote, each with different priorities.

Some of the aforementioned challenges and issues can be addressed by cloud technologies and cloud providers. However, choosing the right cloud provider is a key. "Resource crunches," "installation of applications," "network access," and "manual processes" are some of the challenges that can be addressed by cloud technologies. To address "network complexities," multi-cloud and federation characteristics of cloud technology can be used in some cases. "The matching" problem of resource providers and resource consumers, and providers' philosophies can be addressed by cloud providers and their SLAs.

The technology components of remote use of HPC that enable multi-tenant, remote access to centralized resources, and metered use are not unfamiliar to this community. However, as service-based delivery models take off, with its promise of easy access to pay-per-use computing, users in our community have been mostly on the fence, observing and discussing the potential hurdles to its adoption in HPC.

The day June 2, 2012 was the birth of the idea behind the project about "performing an open humanitarian experiment to explore the end-to-end process and challenges for end-users to access remote computing resources in HPC Centers and in HPC Clouds." This idea is something that is missing in the cloud computing landscape for different communities and being part of its main characteristics and anatomy.

A successful cloud computing model depends heavily on on-demand service availability through highly automated, intuitive, self-service registration and administration processes designed for mass public usage. Traditionally HPC systems are designed for repeated use by a small number of private users and sophisticated self service capabilities may not be such a strong need. Some of the HPC Experiment project teams ran into severe registration and administration related delays resulting from the lack of self service based systems.

The UberCloud experiment suggests the below recommendations:

- Some resource providers have bureaucratic registration and administration processes, where the end-users application for access to resources has to be reviewed and approved through manual means. We have noticed that such processes can be rather slow and present a roadblock, so we recommend the use of automated rules based instant decision making capabilities to be utilized.

- To speed up the resource allocation process, we recommend resource providers to consider setting up queues specific to the end-user needs and assign the queue during the registration process. From this point on relatively simple mechanisms such as tokens, coupon codes, and credit card based automated billing mechanisms can be used to track the usage per end-user without necessarily having to approve each resource allocation request manually.

- We have also noticed that resource providers may lack automation in customer support processes leading to potential delays in responding to end-user requests. Considering the highly technical nature of HPC, resource providers can invest in relatively inexpensive tools to develop self-service knowledge base tools which increase the efficiency of our support processes for the most common set of support requests. Similarly, an automated customer support ticketing system can be used to enforce service levels such as ticket resolution time.

- We recommend novice end users to start with a resource provider that offers an intuitive, mostly automated registration and administration processes even if this provider may not be the best selection to scale up in the long term.

Automation as one of the lessons learned from this experiment is in the line of cloud computing goals. The organizers instinctively believe in *Manual=Slow* equation that is manual processes are just slow. During the first round of the Experiment, it was confirmed to be true.

Each manual process consumed days, sometimes weeks especially because the various technology and people resources were inherently remote, each with different priorities. Manual processes will hinder the adoption of remote HPC technologies. Some of these manual steps can be reduced by developing self service portals, providing participants with knowledge bases, and other collaboration tools. Further process optimization can be achieved by investing in more sophisticated integration technologies. The organizers have decided to apply automation to remove steps from the process.

Two examples of this decision are:

- During the first round of the experiment the organizers treated the registration process and information gathering processes as two separate processes. In the second round of the experiment registrants will be able to register and provide information about their capabilities in one flow, removing a time consuming step from the overall process.

- The organizers are working closely with our resource and software providers to collect information on their registration processes. They are looking for opportunities to pre-register participants with the resources they will need access to eliminate yet another time consuming step.

Throughout the rest of this book we will refer to this case study in order to present an in-depth case study to explain the dilemmas, challenges, techniques, mechanisms, and ways to overcome them from the experience of a cloud project. This case study at the very beginning of the book set the stage for the discussion in the rest of the book and has been referred to throughout the book for specific real life examples. In addition, it would give practitioners a real-life example on the decision making process underlying the implementation of cloud computing projects.

REFERENCES

Armbrust, M., Fox, A., Griffith, R., Joseph, A. D., Katz, R., Konwinski, A., & Zaharia, M. (2010). A view of cloud computing. *Communications of the ACM*, *53*(4), 50–58. http://doi.acm.org/10.1145/1721654.1721672 doi:10.1145/1721654.1721672

Armbrust, M., Fox, A., Griffith, R., Joseph, A. D., Katz, R. H., Konwinski, A., & Zaharia, M. (2009). *Above the clouds: A Berkeley view of cloud computing* (Tech. Rep. No. UCB/EECS-2009-28). EECS Department, University of California, Berkeley. Retrieved from http://www.eecs.berkeley.edu/Pubs/TechRpts/2009/EECS-2009-28.html

Ashton, K. (2010). That 'internet of things' thing. *RFID Journal*, *53*(4), 50–58.

Buyya, R., Yeo, C. S., & Venugopal, S. (2008). Market-oriented cloud computing: Vision, hype, and reality for delivering it services as computing utilities. In *Proceedings of HPCC* (pp. 5-13). HPCC.

Cloud Architecture Reference Models: A Survey. (2011, January 25). (DRAFT NIST CCRATWG 004 v2).

Cloud Computing Expo. (2012). Retrieved from http://www.cloudcomputingexpo.com

CRM. (2012). Retrieved from http://www.salesforce.com

Gentzsch, W., & Yenier, B. (2012). *HPC experiment - Final report of round 1*. The UberCloud LLC.

IDIGI Device Cloud. (2012). Retrieved from http://www.idigi.com

Magrassi, P., & Berg, T. (2002). *A world of smart objects*. Retrieved from http://www.renewableenergyworld.com/

Marit, S. (2010, October 5). *Open days workshop 05a34 smart sustainable cities and regions*. Retrieved from http://ec.europa.eu/regional policy/conferences/od2010/

Nimbits: Free, Social and Open Source Internet of Things. (2012). Retrieved from http://www.nimbits.com

OGC Abstract Specification. (2012). Retrieved from http://www.opengeospatial.org/standards/as

Smart Grid / Department of Energy. (2012). Retrieved from http://energy.gov/oe/technologydevelopment/

1. *st International Workshop on High Performance Computing, Networking and Analytics for the Power Grid*. (2010). Retrieved from http://gridoptics.pnnl.gov/sc11/

Vance, A. (2011, March). The power of the cloud. *Bloomberg Business Week*, 68–75.

KEY TERMS AND DEFINITIONS

Elasticity: With elasticity, users can rapidly increase or decrease the capacity of their resources, companies can ramp capacity up and down.

Federated Clouds: A future deployment model in which consumers can transparently acquire resources from multiple cloud resource providers or cloud service providers.

Green Computing: Climate change and global warming are the two most important challenging problems for the earth. These problems pertain to a general increase in world temperatures caused by increased amounts of carbon dioxide around the earth. Researchers in various fields of science and technology in recent years started to carry out research in order to address these problems by developing environmentally friendly solutions. Green IT and in particular green computing are two new terms introduced mainly in ICT community to address these problems.

Grid Computing: Coordinated resource sharing and problem solving in dynamic, multi-institutional virtual organization. Grids have been the center of attention from scientific and High Performance Computing communities (HPC), especially for the distributed and large scale scientific applications, and also in collaborative style of work.

High Performance Computing (HPC): The use of advanced parallel processing systems (usually, above a teraflop or 1012 floating-point operations per second) for running complicated and huge processes quickly, efficiently, and reliably.

Internet of Things: Another breakthrough, omnipresent and transformative technology with a futuristic vision perhaps over a span of one thousand years. It is predicted that 50 to 100 billion things will be electronically connected by 2020. This Internet of Things (IoT) will fuel technology innovation by creating the means for machines to communicate many different types of information with one another.

Multi-Tenancy: A business model that provides a secure, exclusive virtualized computing environment in which servers, databases, and other resources are shared by multiple users in a cloud environment.

On-Demand: Users can provision cloud infrastructure components such as servers and networks with little human intervention and through automation whenever they want.

Outsourcing: Software companies are rapidly moving more and more of their services, software, and applications to cloud computing due to users' radical, urgent, growing, fluctuating, seasonal, competing, enormous, and economic demands.

Pay Per Use: Payment of resource consumption is like utilities that are paid for by the hour. With pay per use model, service consumption is metered and measured.

Salesforce.com: One of the best Software as a Service (SaaS) provider. It is a classic example of cloud computing. Salesforce.com has made cloud computing a reality by offering Customer Relationship Management (CRM) as a SaaS.

Smart City: Makes a conscious effort to use innovative ICT based solutions to improve conditions of living and working and to support a more inclusive and sustainable urban environment.

Smart Grid: Emerging to address the electricity grid challenges. The smart grid is an intelligent electricity grid network to deliver sustainable, reliable, storage, ubiquitous, decentralized, flexible, economic, autonomic and secure electricity supplies.

The UberCloud Experiment: Has brought together four categories of participants: the industry end-users, the computing and storage resource providers, the software providers, and the experts. Participants have voluntary contribution to their individual teams and thus to the whole experiment. This is an experimental research and study to address roadblocks on the way of transitioning to cloud solutions for industries.

ENDNOTES

1   http://www.idc.com/prodserv/idc_cloud.jsp

2   http://www.idc.com/prodserv/idc_cloud.jsp

3   http://www.gartner.com/newsroom/id/2352816

4   https://www.ibm.com/developer-works/mydeveloperworks/blogs/silverlining/?lang=en

5   https://www.ibm.com/developer-works/mydeveloperworks/blogs/silverlining/?lang=en

6   http://www.skytap.com/product/skytap-cloud

7   http://www.skytap.com/product/skytap-cloud

8   https://cosm.com/?pachube_redirect=true

9   http://www.living-planit.com/

10   http://drrc.lbl.gov/

Chapter 2
The Enabling Technologies for Cloud Computing

ABSTRACT

This chapter explores emerging technologies centered around cloud computing. From the technological point of view, cloud computing was born as a result of the emergence and the convergence of contemporary technologies. This chapter regards technological aspects of cloud. In the software area, Virtualization Technology and Web Services; in the hardware area, shared compute components (i.e., multicore processors); in networking, security, network virtualization, Virtual Private Network (VPN), virtual firewalls, and network overlay are the promising technologies for the future complex computing infrastructures. In this chapter, the authors review these technologies and describe how they contribute to the anatomy and the characteristics of cloud computing. These technologies constitute the building blocks of cloud computing technologies and infrastructures.

1. INTRODUCTION

From the technological perspective, cloud computing was born as a result of the emergence and the convergence of contemporary technologies. These technologies came from advances in software, hardware and networking.

Virtualization technology and Web services from the software domain, shared compute components such as symmetric multiprocessing (SMP), multicore processors and Non-Uniform Memory Access (NUMA) from the hardware domain, network virtualiza-

DOI: 10.4018/978-1-4666-4683-4.ch002

tion, and network overlay from the networking domain, virtual firewalls, and virtual private network (VPN) from network security are a few technologies that constitute the building blocks of cloud computing technologies and infrastructures.

In this chapter, we will review these technologies and describe how they contribute to the anatomy and the characteristics of cloud computing.

2. VIRTUALIZATION TECHNOLOGY

Virtualization is the primary enabler for cloud computing. Virtualization technology provides techniques and conditions to run multiple Virtual Machines (VMs) on top of a single physical machine (Barham et al., 2003) (See Figure 2).

Since about 1998 there has been an explosive increase in the use of VMs in addition to physical machines to offer many kinds of computer and communications services on local area networks and over the broader Internet. VMs can operate in isolation, for example as a guest operating system on a personal computer or under a unified virtualized environment overseen by a supervisory virtual machine monitor (VMM) or hypervisor process as shown in Figure 2.

Elasticity, scalability, auto-scaling, on-demand, and self-provisioning characteristics of cloud computing are the bonus of virtualization. Moreover, from the technical perspective to make more use of existing hardware by consolidation (Figure 1), virtualization technology is exploited in cloud computing.

Implementation of this technology is diverse; different approaches in the virtualization are developed:

- **Full-Virtualization:** VMware (VMware, 2010) (Figure 3), KVM, VirtualBox.
- **Para-Virtualization:** Amazon AMI, VMware, Xen (Figure 4), KVM, VirtualBox.
- **Operating System (OS) level virtualization:** OpenVZ (Figure 5), Linux-VServer and Linux Containers in the future Linux Kernel mainstream.
- **Hardware-assisted virtualization:** They are offered in various colors and flavors such as VT-x and NPT extensions on Intel, AMD-V and EPT extensions on AMD.

Virtualization offers the following features:

- **Isolation:** Computations running in a hardware virtualized environment do not interfere with one another and they are able to keep their computations separate from others. In (Kelem & Feiertag, 1991) there are arguments that the isolation provided by a hardware virtualization mechanism can be more easily mathematically abstracted than the isolation provided by a traditional time-sharing OS's security model. The sufficiency of the hardware virtualization security model can be evaluated by looking at the isolation at the hardware level. Since hardware virtualization is a simpler mechanism than an OS vir-

Figure 1. Consolidation with virtualization

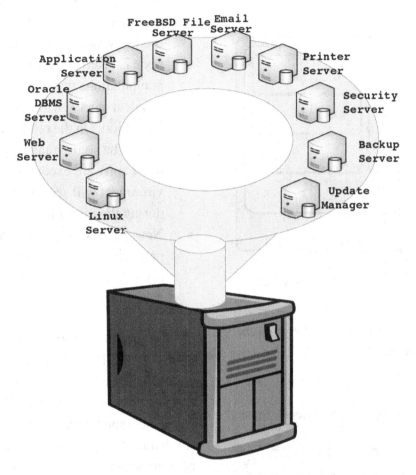

Figure 2. Virtualization technology: A general architecture

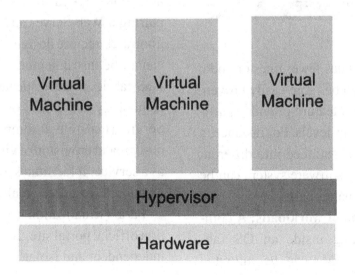

Figure 3. VMware: Full-Virtualization architecture

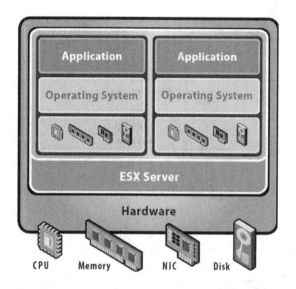

Figure 4. Xen: Para-Virtualization architecture (Barham et al., 2003)

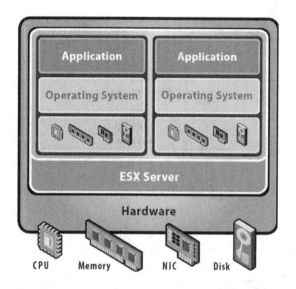

tualization and has fewer lines of code, its isolation can be more easily proven. In addition, this feature provides partitioning at various levels. For instance, a server can be partitioned into different pieces, or a big software system can be divided into smaller parts.

- **Live migration of workloads:** A computation running inside an OS (abstracted by a VM) can be migrated from one node in the virtualized setting to another while running. This allows the load on the nodes to be balanced more dynamically. Additionally, if a node is taken down for maintenance, its computations may be migrated to other physical nodes without significant interruption. On the other hand, there will always be some transitory interruption. Most software executing in a cloud environment will see an increased latency during the migration.

- **New class of sharing:** Virtualization provides the sharing of computing resources among several users more dynamically and securely.

Auto-scaling automates application scalability in the cloud. To accomplish this each component of an application (Web Server, RDBMS) is packaged in its own VM image; That is, each component must be a homogeneous, singleton deployable unit since the only unit of management (scalability) is the VM image. On the other hand, combining components and containers in the same VM image (i.e. pairing a Web Server and RDBMS) is not a good architecture design. This unit of scaling cannot be instrumented or controlled by the IaaS fabric. Briefly speaking, virtualization technology is the base of Infrastructure as a Service (IaaS) cloud computing model for the on-demand provision of virtualized resources as a service. It facilitates allocation and deallocation of resources really fast.

Para-Virtualization (Xen Paravirtualization official portal site, 2012) provides totally independent and isolated environments with maximum flexibility and security for VMs. In

Figure 5. Operating System (OS) Level Virtualization (Linux Containers project official portal site, 2012)

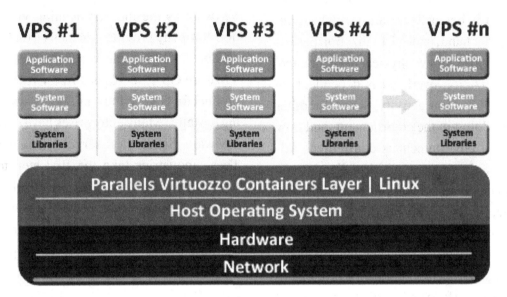

addition, they can run any operating system that is suitable for that physical hardware and any application software that can execute on that operating system. For instance, Windows XP, FreeBSD, and Fedora Core Linux distribution all can run as three isolated Virtual Machines on top of one physical machine.

In OS level virtualization (Linux Containers project official portal site, 2012), the operating system (kernel) runs multiple isolated instances (called containers or partitions) instead of just one. The OS kernel will run a single operating system and provides that operating system functionality to each instance. This creates isolated containers on a single physical server and OS instance to utilize hardware, software, data center, and management efforts with the best performance and efficiency. In addition to isolation mechanisms, the kernel provides resource management features to limit the impact of one

container's activities on the other containers. In other words, VMs on the same physical machine share the same kernel, but they are allowed to run different operating systems distributions from only one type such as only GNU/Linux-based distributions.

VT-x [1] and AMD-v [2] are the first generation of hardware-assisted virtualization extensions. Hypervisors use software to trap and simulate certain instructions, memory management and I/O in the host VMs. These two hardware extensions trapped these instructions in hardware to gain a significant speed improvement. NPT [3] and EPT [4] extensions are the second generation of hardware-assisted virtualization extensions. These two minimize the memory management bottleneck.

With OS level virtualization all VMs share the same kernel. As a result processes in containers use the same operating system's system call interface and do not need to be subject to emulation or run in an intermediate VM. Therefore, the performance of OS level implementation is better than para-virtualization. On the other hand, para-virtualization performance is close to raw physical performance.

Virtualization overhead is dependent on overall application activity, what the other VMs are doing in the environment, and how the overall environment is configured. Additionally, the impact of virtualization on performance varies by application type. For example, if all the VMs are doing something disk intensive, it is reasonable to think there will be some overhead in a application that is not related to what that application is doing. In general, the performance slowdown affected by virtualization is about 2%.

In the long term, the virtualization hypervisors as we know it today will not prevail. The microprocessors and all the controllers around them will embed more and more features that today are part of the hypervisors; this is as mainframes like IBM mainframe systems and high-end servers have been doing hardware partitioning for a long time. This market has become in a new industry and big hardware companies like Intel and AMD play the main roles.

The cloud needs this partitioning to be performed efficiently. In sum, some virtualization functionalities are increasingly implemented in hardware and firmware, however this simply means that virtualization can be implemented at different layers.

2.1 VMware

VMware as the industry-leading virtualization company provides various virtualization products. VMware Server as the successor to VMware GSX Server is a free virtualization product for GNU/Linux and Windows operating systems. Many enterprises have deployed VMware Server for server virtualization. These industries take the first step toward enterprise-wide virtual infrastructure by using this product. Users can provision new server capacity by partitioning a physical server into multiple VMs. VMware Server support 64-bit VMs architecture and Intel Virtualization Technology.

VMware virtual infrastructure products provide enterprise class suite of features for virtualization. It includes ESX Server with Virtual SMP and VirtualCluster with VMotion technology for large scale production server consolidation, business continuity, and enterprise-hosted desktop solutions. Mostly they are used in production server environments.

VMware VMotion is the main vehicle for live load migration. VMotion leverages the complete virtualization of servers, storage, and networking to move a running VM from one server to another on the fly. For that, the source and the target VMware ESX Servers need to have access to VM files concurrently. Thus, it works with vStorage VMFS cluster file system as a shared storage. The entire state of a VM is encapsulated by a set of files stored on shared storage. The active memory and precise execution state of a VM can be rapidly transmitted over a high speed network. Network identity and connections of the VM retains to ensure a seamless migration process through network virtualization of VMware ESX Servers. With VMotion there is no downtime and disruption, and it happens without administrators' intervention.

VMware Infrastructure is VMware's third generation, production-ready virtualization suite. It offers new capabilities for increased mobility and service availability. These features enable new use cases driving new customer adoption of virtualization within the industry. VMware infrastructure includes VMware Storage VMotion, VMware Update Manager, VMware Distributed Power Management, and VMware Guided Consolidation.

VMware Storage VMotion manages virtual infrastructure storage lifecycles more efficiently through transparent migration of workloads from storages needing downtime for maintenance, or dynamically rebalancing storage workloads without affecting VMs and services. Storage VMotion extends VMotion to storage resources of VMs, i.e. virtual disks. In other words, it enables live migration of VM disks from one storage system to another without disruption or downtime. This is an indispensable vehicle for administrators to dynamically balance their server workloads without planned downtime schedules for server maintenance. This addresses performance bottlenecks by migrating VM disks to the best available storage resource.

VMware Update Manager automates patch and update management for VMware ESX Server machines. Its integration with VMware DRS enables zero downtime of ESX Servers.

VMware Distributed Power Management (DPM) reduces energy consumption in data centers via intelligent workload balancing. In cooperation with VMware DRS, it is able to automatically power off servers where are not needed, and automatically power on servers as demand increases.

VMware Guided Consolidation is a feature of VMware VirtualCenter for server consolidation via an intelligent method. Through wizard steps, it discovers physical servers, identifies consolidation candidates, and places them onto the best ESX Server or VMware Server hosts. It makes the consolidation process quick and easy for any type of users.

Virtual Infrastructure is for purchase with different editions:

- **VMware ESX Server 3i:** Provides single server partitioning. It can be delivered embedded as firmware in server systems or as a standalone purchase for hard drive installation.
- **Virtual Infrastructure 3 Foundation (Starter):** Includes VMware ESX Server, VMware ESX Server 3i, VMware Consolidated Backup, and VMware Update Manager.
- **Virtual Infrastructure 3 Standard:** Brings higher levels of resiliency. It includes VMware HA in addition to the capabilities of Virtual Infrastructure 3 Foundation edition. VMware HA pro-

vides automated restart of VMs in case of hardware failures.

- **Virtual Infrastructure 3 Enterprise:** Has all capabilities of virtual infrastructure for resource management, workload mobility, and high availability. It includes VMware VMotion, VMware Storage VMotion, and VMware DRS with DPM in addition to the capabilities of Virtual Infrastructure 3 Standard edition.

- **VMotion, Storage VMotion, and DRS with DPM:** For standalone purchase with Virtual Infrastructure 3 Foundation and Standard.

3. WEB SERVICES

The other important technology that is currently the base of many technologies is Web Services as part of Service Oriented Architecture (SOA) (Figure 6). Web Services have Application Programming Interfaces (API) based on Internet protocols that can be accessed over a network. Often Web Services are executed on a remote system hosting the requested service. Interaction between services, resources and agents in a heterogeneous environment that is based on Web Services Technologies would be more interoperable. SOA is highly based on Web Services technologies.

Web Services (Web Services Architecture, 2012) is defined by the W3C "as a software system designed to support interoperable machine-to-machine interaction over a network. It has an interface described in a machine-processable format (specifically WSDL). Other systems interact with the Web Service in a manner prescribed by its description using SOAP messages, typically conveyed using HTTP with an XML serialization in conjunction with other Web-related standards."

Web services describe and deal with data transfer. REpresentational State Transfer (REST) and Simple Object Access Protocol (SOAP) are used in practice to transfer data. REST has been developed as an architectural

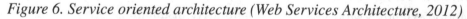

Figure 6. Service oriented architecture (Web Services Architecture, 2012)

style by Roy Fielding in his PhD dissertation. It uses Web technologies and protocols such as HTTP and XML. It is a way of getting information content from a Web site by reading a designated Web page that contains an XML file that describes and includes the desired content.

For its publishing, REST uses the same approach that many Web sites use with RDF Site Summary (RSS). RSS is based on Resource Description Framework (RDF), which is a standard way to describe a Web site.

SOAP allows the communication and the exchange of information between distributed applications and programs developed for different operating systems such as Linux, Windows, etc. SOAP uses HTTP and XML as Web technologies to exchange information; since these Web protocols are already installed for use by the major operating systems. Thus, HTTP and XML provide an easy solution to the problem of how programs running under different operating systems in a network can communicate with each other.

SOAP describes how to encode an HTTP header and an XML file so that a program on one computer can call a program in another computer and pass it information. Also, it explains how a called program can return a response.

REST and SOAP have the similar functionality. SOAP requires data server/client programs for its functionality, whereas REST is easier to use. Thus, SOAP provides more capability. It allows greater program interaction between the client and the server.

SOA unifies business processes by organizing large-scale applications as a collection of smaller modules known as "services." SOA's design framework realizes rapid and low-cost system development and total system quality.

4. NETWORKING

Networking and network security are essential and vital to uniting virtualized computing resources (such as CPU, IO, memory, network, and storage), and cloud resources (such as private clouds, public clouds) into operational information systems. Information systems cannot be flexibly built in a cloud environment without a flexible networking environment.

When many VMs operate under the same virtualized environment they might be connected together via a virtual network consisting of virtualized network switches between machines and virtualized network interfaces within machines. The resulting virtual network could then implement traditional network protocols like TCP or virtual network provisioning such as VLAN or VPN, though the latter while seems to be useful for their own reasons are in no way required. In this section, we present these networking concepts.

4.1 Network Virtualization

Flexibility is a key in the popularity of cloud computing. For instance, cloud providers that provide multi-tenant cloud services with virtualized computing resources deployed on physical computers in multiple data centers and in widely separated regions face restrictions due to physical networking cabling and complexities in network management due to routing configurations, network sub-address partitioning, and throughput limitations (aka throttling). Thus, they can become a bottleneck for flexible and scalable service provision and infrastructure expansion.

Virtual networks are logical networks that you can control to run on top of physical networks that you do not control. This gives the same flexibility as virtualization of compute elements. With virtual networking, networking virtual machines is done in the same way as physical machines building complex network configurations. Network virtualization includes virtual device adapter (Ethernet adapters), VLANs, and virtual switches. A VM can be configured with one or more virtual Ethernet adapters with their own IP addresses and MAC addresses. As a result, VMs have the same properties as physical machines from a networking point of view. We can build separate virtual network zones for production deployments, development and testing purposes and, virtual networks enable more functionalities than physical networks.

VMs are connected to each other by virtual switches. They allow VMs on the same physical host to communicate with each other using the same protocols that would be used over physical switches, without the need for additional networking hardware.

Amazon Virtual Private Cloud (VPC) (Amazon Virtual Private Cloud (Amazon VPC), 2012), VMware Infrastructure 3 (VMware Infrastructure 3, 2012), and the Open Network Foundation are examples of how virtual networks can enable new cloud computing techniques and alternatives.

Amazon VPC (Amazon Virtual Private Cloud (Amazon VPC), 2012) enables pro-

visioning of a private cloud as an isolated section of the Amazon Web Services (AWS) cloud where users can launch AWS resources in a virtual network that they define. Amazon VPC defines a virtual network topology that closely resembles a traditional network that operate in users' private data center. They have complete control over their virtual networking environment, including selection of IP address range, creation of subnets, and configuration of route tables and network gateways.

In addition, users can customize the network configuration for their Amazon VPC. For example, they can create a public facing subnet for Web servers that has access to the Internet, and place backend systems such as databases or application servers in a private facing subnet with no Internet access. They can leverage multiple layers of security, including security groups and network access control lists, to help control access to Amazon EC2 instances in each subnet. Moreover, users can create a hardware VPN connection between their corporate data center and their VPC and leverage the AWS cloud as an extension of corporate data center.

VMware Infrastructure 3 (VMware Infrastructure 3, 2012) provides a rich set of networking capabilities that integrate well with sophisticated enterprise networks. The key virtual networking components provided by Virtual Infrastructure 3 are virtual Ethernet adapters, used by individual VMs, and virtual switches, which connect VMs to each other and connect both VMs. The networking capabilities are provided by VMware ESX Server and managed by VMware VirtualCenter.

From the technical perspective, there are two different approaches to network virtualization, says Geoff Brown, CEO & Founder of Machine-To-Machine Intelligence (M2Mi) Corporation: (1) Virtualizing at the NIC level, mainly to remove Top of Rack Switch limitations and (2) Secure Network Virtualization that includes Orchestration and Automation across VMs, Power Management, Virtual and Physical Load Balancers, Firewalls, Access & Distribution Switches [5].

The second approach is much more desirable as it delivers end-to-end support for Service Level Agreements. Providers of private, public and hybrid clouds use Secure Network Virtualization to deliver SLAs.

Network virtualization at cloud scale is not easy. In a multi-tenant, multi-data-center cloud, its network architecture deals with at least six virtual network planes:

- The control plane for the fabric
- The shared service plane for storage, identity, and other services
- The intra-VPN plane inside each cloud customer's virtual network
- The inter-VPN plane, for SOA traffic that spans VPNs
- The inter-DC plane, for transit between DCs
- The edge plane for transit to/from the Internet

Undoubtedly, there are more network layers. For each of these planes, we have to consider the layer 2 (L2) fabric, and the various types of layer 3 (L3) networking that we layer on top such as IPv4, RFC1918, or IPv6.

Now if we scale all this up to tens of thousands of machines with several different generations of networking gear; it all is a tractable problem.

Lastly, Network Overlay (Network Overlay definition, 2012) is categorized as part of network virtualization in cloud computing. It provides facilities to build a network on top of another network. For example, many peer-to-peer networks are overlay networks on top of the Internet and dial-up Internet is an overlay upon the telephone network.

4.2 Software Defined Network

Software defined network (SDN) (OpenFlow, 2012) is a next generation network concept to address flexibility at network level in which the entire network is defined and controlled by software in order to dynamically configure the network structure. SDN is a new technology that enables network virtualization and automatic operation in a cloud environment.

The SDN concept resolves these issues by using software to control the configuration of virtual networks which connect multiple virtualized computing resources. With the SDN environment, an arbitrary number of VMs can be quickly created and deployed to any location with arbitrary network topologies. This allows construction of cloud environments that are more flexible than those currently in use.

Technologically speaking, OpenFlow (OpenFlow, 2012) is a core technology of SDN. OpenFlow is the next generation network control technology that enables the virtualization of the network. The OpenFlow Switch Consortium advocates for the technology and the Open Networking Foundation promotes standards for OpenFlow.

On April 5, 2012, Internet Initiative Japan Inc. and ACCESS Co. Ltd., announced the establishment of Stratosphere Inc. (Stratosphere Inc., 2012), a joint-venture company. Research is underway at Stratosphere Inc. to develop a suite of software to implement the software defined network concept.

4.3 Internet Protocol Version 6

Internet Protocol version 6 (IPv6) is the next generation network addressing. IPv6 was introduced fifteen years ago to deal with the long-anticipated depletion of IPv4 addresses, albeit remaining mostly experimental with small penetration. Recently, the transition to IPv6 has become a major concern to the network community with the exhaustion of IPv4 address space on the horizon. This pressure from IPv4 address scarcity has pushed regulatory bodies, network operators, software and hardware vendors to support IPv6.

In addition, the Internet of Things (Ashton, 2010) applications are in the need of IPv6 addressing. The next generation of Internet applications using IPv6 would be able to communicate with devices attached to virtually all human-made objects due to the extremely large address space of the IPv6 protocol. This system would therefore be able to identify any kind of object in the world.

However, the status of the Internet-wide deployment of IPv6 is in its infancy and replete with uncertainties. As the Internet network addressing is moving toward IPv6 from IPv4

addressing, cloud providers should support all Internet addressing, i.e., IPv4-only users, IPv4/IPv6 dual-stack users who will be a dominant users in near future, and IPv6-only users. Thus, future data centers (Shima et al., 2012) need to support and deal with IPv6 network addressing and protocols.

In (Shima et al., 2012), researchers proposed an operation model designed for IaaS systems operated with IPv6-only network with a wide area L2 network and IPv4-IPv6 translation software for backward compatibility.

The project based on (Shima et al., 2012) will focus on monitoring and understanding IPv6 adoption or its lack of. More specifically, they have focused on the following points:

- Collecting and processing topology and routing data for both IPv4 and IPv6 to track the evolution of IPv6 penetration;
- Developing models to capture the impact of different socio-economic factors. These models are envisioned to capture IPv6 adoption at the granularity of a single network and at regional levels as well;
- A crucial factor in determining whether IPv6 is widely adopted is the end-to-end performance achievable over IPv6. The project will also focus on measuring data-plane performance over IPv6;
- The first groups to adopt IPv6 will be mobile broadband (MBB) operators. Hence, this project will also work closely with local MBB operators to measure data plane performance over IPv6 in MBB networks.

5. NETWORK SECURITY

Cloud computing as an emerging technology, like any other IT infrastructure, needs special security services. There are four basic security services in use today: authentication and authorization; integrity; confidentiality; and non-repudiation which will have to be considered in cloud computing [6].

First, authentication and authorization services establish the validity of a transmission, message, and its originator. Second, integrity services address the unauthorized modification of data. To ensure data integrity, a system must be able to detect unauthorized data modification. Confidentiality service restricts access to the content of sensitive data to only those individuals who are authorized. Third, non-repudiation services prevent an individual from denying that previous actions had been performed [7].

Public Key Infrastructure (PKI) is a scalable and distributed approach to address these security needs. PKI uses public key cryptography technology. This form of cryptography has unique features that make it invaluable as a basis for security functions in distributed systems. Contemporary cloud computing is adopting PKI to provide scalable security services [8].

5.1 Virtual Private Network (VPN)

VPN is a private network that uses a public network such as the Internet to connect remote networks, sites, and users together. It uses virtual connections through the public network, instead of using dedicated connections such as leased or owned lines to connect private networks via tunneling and/or encryption over the public Internet, thus resulting in a much lower cost.

In addition, VPN provides individuals and remote offices with secure access to their organization's network. Therefore, VPN makes it easy to build wide-area virtual clusters in case of having firewalls and network address translation within networks. On the other side, VPN is an enabling technology for cloud federation and hybrid clouds. In addition, users can securely access to clouds with the help of VPN technology.

The granularity of a VPN implementation can be broken down further to a single end-to-end, one-to-one connectivity scenario. There are different types of VPN that reside in the different layers of the TCP/IP protocol suite; Link Layer, Network Layer, Transport Layer, and Application Layer. There are a few methods to construct VPNs within the network layer.

VPNs are either:

- **Remote-Access:** Connecting an individual computer to a network. In a corporate setting, remote-access VPNs allow employees to access their company's Intranet from home or while traveling outside the office.
- **Site-to-Site:** Connecting two networks together. This type of VPN allows employees in geographically separated offices to share one cohesive virtual network.

A VPN can also be used to interconnect two similar networks over a dissimilar middle network; for example, two IPv6 networks over an IPv4 network.

In addition, VPN systems can be classified by:

- The protocols used to tunnel the traffic.
- The tunnel's termination point, i.e., customer edge or network-provider edge.
- The connectivity type: site-to-site or remote-access.
- The levels of security provided.
- The OSI layer they present to the connecting network, such as Layer 2 circuits or Layer 3 network connectivity.

Secure Socket Layer (SSL) VPN is a secure remote access solution to access cloud services across the Internet. This type of VPN can be used with a Web browser; and unlike the IPsec VPN solution, it does not require specialized client software at the end user side. Of the note, SSL is a protocol for managing the security of message transmission on the Internet. Currently, SSL is included in Web browsers and Web server products. It is based on PKI security mechanism.

SSL VPN is used a lot in the cloud systems due to its ease of use for the end users on the client side. SSL VPN gateways provide an on-demand client mechanism, thus there is little management overhead on the client side, compared to IPsec-based VPN solutions.

Furthermore, SSL VPN provides better security practices through the use of endpoint security. For that, SSL VPN verifies that end users are compliant with your organization's security policies by:

- Requiring antivirus software to be running.
- Verifying that OS patches have been installed.
- Checking to see if malware or bots are running.

5.2 Virtual Firewall

Even though VMs are seen as sandboxed within the host operating system, they are not inherently secure. The host is not secured against exploitation from the VM and vice versa the host is threat to the VM.

As long as a computer network runs entirely over physical hardware and cabling, it is a physical network. Thus, it can be protected by physical firewalls. Instead, a virtual firewall (VF) is a network firewall service or appliance running entirely within a virtualized environment and which provides the usual packet filtering and monitoring provided via a physical network firewall. VFs are the core security components in cloud computing, particularly in IaaS.

Virtual networks are true networks, thus they may suffer the same kinds of vulnerabilities associated with a physical network:

- Users on machines within the virtual network have access to all other machines on the same virtual network.
- Compromising or misappropriating one VM on a virtual network is sufficient to provide a platform for addition-

al attacks against other machines on the same network segment.

- If a virtual network is Internetworked to the physical network or broader Internet then machines on the virtual network might have access to external resources (and external exploits) that could leave them open to exploitation.
- Network traffic that passes directly between machines without passing through security devices is unmonitored.

In brief, a VF can be realized as:

- A traditional software firewall on a guest VM already running
- A purpose-built virtual security appliance designed with virtual network security in mind
- A virtual switch with additional security capabilities
- Or a managed kernel process running within the host hypervisor

6. HARDWARE

Cloud computing infrastructures have been designed based on the appropriate and advanced hardware and networking infrastructures.

At the user end having the right equipment and environment like smartphones and tablets are important for the best interaction of users with the cloud. There are different types of clients with specific configurations to communicate with the cloud. Each client offers a different way to interact with applications and data in clouds. We categorize them as mobile devices, laptops, thin clients, and thick clients.

Mobile devices are like smartphones, PDAs, etc. They can connect to cloud servers where all processing and storage take place. Security and performance limits are drawbacks of mobile devices. In addition, they cannot support robust applications. However, there are applications that do not need high speed connections, and high performance computing; these applications do not deal with big data, or even gigabytes of data. In this case, cloud applications can be developed for mobile devices for accessing information like reading news.

Thin clients are computers without hard drives, DVD drives, etc. They simply display whatever coming from servers. Organizations with in-house cloud can use thin clients. It also depends on the type of applications and services that an organization uses. If clients only require to access cloud services or virtualized server, then thin clients are a good option. They are less expensive than thick clients, and much less expensive to maintain; and they consume less energy. They provide reduced maintenance costs and application updates, as well as higher security and energy efficiency. They are certainly more energy efficient than desktops with similar capabilities. Data security is high due to not having data on the thin client. All data resides in data centers of the clouds. Thus, the risk of a physical breach is small. An example of popular thin client is Sun Ray. It can display Windows, Linux, and Solaris desktops on the same device.

Thick clients are traditional personal computers that we use daily. Users have applications installed on their thick clients. In this model, mission-critical applications can stay in-house on thick clients. In addition, this type of clients can connect to cloud and virtualized server, and they are good choices if there are the needs of maintaining files on local machines and infrastructure, and run applications locally.

From the security point of view, thick clients are more vulnerable to attacks than thin clients. This is due to having data and applications locally. In addition, in the case of losing a thick client, everything on that client is lost, while this is not the case for thin client; there is just a need of a new thin client, and we all set.

Hewlett Packard (HP), Dell, and Sun are leaders in the world of client and virtual desktop development. Some of their products are: Sun Ray, Sun Virtual Desktop Infrastructure Software from Sun; HP Consolidated Client Infrastructure, HP Virtual Desktop Infrastructure, 6720t Mobile Thin Client, HP Compaq t5730, and t5735 Desktop Clients from HP; OptiPlex desktops from Dell.

At the cloud data center side, there are various hardware components including servers, processors, storage systems, networking equipments, etc.

SMP as the earliest style of multiprocessor machine architectures, multicore and NUMA are the technologies that put together more than one computing elements such as processor and memory inside one physical system.

SMP and multicore involve a multiprocessor computer architecture where two or more identical processors are connected to a single shared main memory. Today most common multiprocessor systems use SMP architecture. In multicore processors, the SMP architecture applies to the cores, treating them as separate processors. In the SMP systems, operating system would be able to move tasks between processors to balance the workload efficiently.

A single physical processor of multicore design type contains the core logic of more than one processor (Intel, 2010) (Figure 7). The multicore design puts several cores (multicore) together and packages them as a single physical processor. The main goal is to enable a system to run more tasks simultaneously and thereby achieve greater overall system performance.

In SMP architecture, when several processors attempt to access the same memory performance degrades. NUMA (NUMA: Definition and additional resources from ZDNet, 2012) attempts to address this problem by providing separate memory for each processor. NUMA systems dedicate different memory banks to different processors. Therefore, processors have access to their local memory quickly while it is slower for remote memory.

When more than one VM runs on a multicore or SMP system simultaneously, each VM runs independently of others and also in parallel with the others. In this case, a multiprocessor system like multicore architectures will have considerably better performance than a uni-processor since different VMs run on different processors simultaneously. This use case is the future computing model in clouds, thus multicore architecture is a perfect hardware technology for cloud computing.

Figure 7. Multicore: several cores in a processor (Intel, 2010)

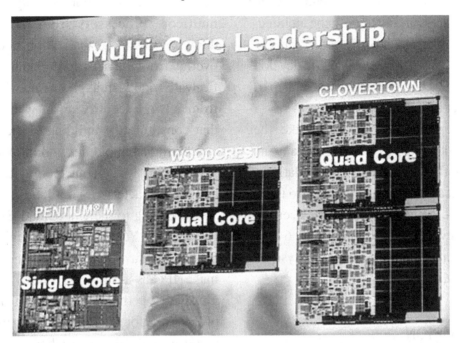

Moveover, future hardware designs are tailored towards specific cloud platforms. For example, Advanced Micro Devices (AMD) offers low-power, low-cost chips for Web hosting and cloud environments, which are looking for high-performance, energy-efficient servers for their data centers. Therefore, the Web hosting and cloud space is getting a lot of attention from chip and server makers.

The AMD Opteron 3200 family is AMD's latest effort to gain greater traction in the booming hosting and cloud markets, where businesses are looking for small, good-performing and highly energy-efficient servers. It includes three chips that offer four to eight cores, speeds ranging from 2.7GHz to 3.7GHz, thermal design power of 45 to 65 watts, and various AMD-developed power-saving technologies, such as Turbo Core and PowerNow, will give Web hosting companies a low-cost option when considering microservers, according to John Fruehe, director of product marketing for AMD's server group.

AMD has begun shipping the Opteron 3200 to systems makers, with platforms coming out from the likes of Dell, Fujitsu, MSI and Tyan.

On the other side, Intel already had been pushing the microserver segment including through its partnership with SeaMicro. However, after AMD announced its deal to buy the systems maker, Intel officials dismissed its importance, noting its own internal work as well as partnerships with the likes of Hewlett-Packard, Supermicro, NEC, Dell and Hitachi. Analysts also said recent Intel acquisitions of networking vendors give it the expertise to develop its own low-power fabric technology.

In addition, ARM Holdings, whose low-power non-x86 chip designs are found in most smartphones and tablets, and manufacturing partners such as Calxeda, Nvidia and Marvell Technology are working to push the architecture up the ladder and into low-power servers. HP already is working with Calxeda to develop ARM-based energy-efficient servers as part of its Project Moonshot initiative.

AMD's Fruehe said offerings like the Opteron 3200 chips give his company an edge over both Intel and ARM. The platform makes AMD a better cost alternative to Intel, he said, while ARM designs still lack certain enterprise-level features, including 64-bit capabilities and a strong server ecosystem, that both AMD and Intel offer.

7. CONCLUSION

In this chapter, contemporary technologies have been introduced. From the technological perspective, cloud computing was born as a result of the emergence and the convergence of these technologies. Virtualization technology and Web services from the software

domain, shared compute components like multicore processors from the hardware domain, network virtualization, and network overlay from the networking domain, virtual firewalls, and virtual private network (VPN) from network security are a few technologies that constitute the building blocks of cloud computing technologies and infrastructures. These technologies contribute to the anatomy and the characteristics of cloud computing.

According to the UberCloud Experiment (Gentzsch & Yenier, 2012b), it is fairly certain that we now have the technology ingredients to make HPC-as-a-Service (HPCaaS) happen. To glue it all together into a coherent end-to-end process, the founders of this experiment have come up with the "the UberCloud Experiment." Intentionally, the first round of this experiment has been performed manually, that is, not via an automated cloud service, because they believe the technology is not the challenge anymore; rather it is the people and their processes, and that is what they wanted to explore.

REFERENCES

Amazon Virtual Private Cloud (Amazon VPC). (2012). Retrieved from http://aws.amazon.com/vpc/

Ashton, K. (2010, April). That 'internet of things' thing. *RFID Journal*, *53*(4), 50–58.

Barham, P., et al. (2003). Xen and the art of virtualization. In *Proceedings of SOSP '03*. SOSP.

Gentzsch, W., & Yenier, B. (2012). *HPC experiment - Final report of round 1*. The UberCloud LLC.

Intel. (2010). Retrieved from http://www.intel.com/support/processors/xeon/sb/cs012641.htm

Kelem, N. L., & Feiertag, R. J. (1991). A separation model for virtual machine monitors. In *Proceedings of IEEE Symposium on Security and Privacy* (pp. 78-86). IEEE.

Linux Containers Project Official Portal Site. (2012). Retrieved from http://lxc.sourceforge.net/

Network Overlay Definition. (2012). Retrieved from http://en.wikipedia.org/wiki/Overlay network

Numa: Definition and Additional Resources from zdnet. (2012). Retrieved from http://dictionary.zdnet.com/definition/NUMA.html

Openflow. (2012). Retrieved from http://www.openflow.org/

Shima, K., Ishida, W., & Sekiya, Y. (2012). Design, implementation, and operation of ipv6-only iaas system with ipv4-ipv6 translator for transition toward the future internet datacenter. In *Proceedings of Closer 2012-2nd International Conference on Cloud Computing and Services Science* (pp. 306-314). Closer.

Stratosphere Inc. (2012). Retrieved from http://gl.accesscompany.com/newsevent/archives/2012/20120405 iij/

VMware. (2010). *Vmware dynamic resource scheduler.* Retrieved from http://www.vmware.com/files/pdf/drs datasheet.pdf

Vmware Infrastructure 3. (2012). Retrieved from http://www.vmware.com/products/vi/overview.html

Web Services Architecture. (2012). Retrieved from http://www.w3.org/TR/ws-arch/#whatis/

Xen Paravirtualization Official Portal Site. (2012). Retrieved from http://www.xen.org/about/paravirtualization.html

KEY TERMS AND DEFINITIONS

Multicore Processors: A single physical processor of multicore design type contains the core logic of more than one processor. The multicore design puts several cores (multicore) together and packages them as a single physical processor. The main goal is to enable a system to run more tasks simultaneously and thereby achieve greater overall system performance.

Network Overlay: Part of network virtualization in cloud computing. It provides facilities to build a network on top of another network. For example, many peer-to-peer networks are overlay networks on top of the Internet and dial-up Internet is an overlay upon the telephone network.

Network Virtualization: Includes virtual device adapter (Ethernet adapters), VLANs, and virtual switches. A VM can be configured with one or more virtual Ethernet adapters with their own IP addresses and MAC addresses. As a result, VMs have the same properties as physical machines from a networking point of view.

Virtual Firewall: A network firewall service or appliance running entirely within a virtualized environment and which provides the usual packet filtering and monitoring provided via a physical network firewall.

Virtualization: The primary enabler for cloud computing. Virtualization technology provides techniques and conditions to run multiple Virtual Machines (VMs) on top of a single physical machine.

Virtual Private Network (VPN): A private network that uses a public network such as the Internet to connect remote networks, sites, and users together. It uses virtual connections through the public network, instead of using dedicated connections such as leased or owned lines to connect private networks via

tunneling and/or encryption over the public Internet, thus resulting in a much lower cost.

Web Services: Services executed on a remote system hosting the requested service. Interaction between services, resources and agents in a heterogeneous environment that is based on Web Services Technologies would be more interoperable. SOA is highly based on Web Services technologies.

ENDNOTES

[1] http://www.intel.com/technology/itj/2006/v10i3/1-hardware/6-vt-x-vt-i-solutions.htm

[2] http://sites.amd.com/us/business/it-solutions/virtualization/Pages/virtualization.aspx

[3] http://www.developer.amd.com/assets/NPT-WP-1%201-final-TM.pdf

[4] http://www.vmware.com/pdf/Per_ESX_Intel-EPT-eval.pdf

[5] https://groups.google.com/forum/#!msg/cloud-computing/KNzitKrUjd8/9l7qDq4s2RMJ

[6] http://www.peterindia.net/ITSecurityView.html

[7] http://www.peterindia.net/ITSecurityView.html

[8] http://searchsecurity.techtarget.com/definition/PKI

Chapter 3
Service Delivery Models and Deployment Options

ABSTRACT

In this chapter, the authors consider cloud computing as a core topic and various models emerging around it such as its services and delivery models, its economic aspects, applications, usages, challenges, and so on. Cloud computing covers a range of delivery and service models. In this chapter, cloud service delivery models (i.e., Software-as-a-Service, Platform-as-a-Service and Infrastructure-as-a-Service) and cloud deployment models (private cloud, community cloud, public cloud, and hybrid cloud) are described. The right service delivery and deployment option have to be chosen for an organization's cloud application, according to organizational needs.

1. INTRODUCTION

Traditional software applications are based on a model with large and upfront licensing costs in addition to annual support costs. An enterprise software package requires software/hardware deployment, configuration, servers, backup and network provisioning to support the number of users mentioned in license agreement. In addition, software applications are highly customizable, which comes at a cost. These notes are about the traditional software model which were applicable when there were no cloud. Instead, the term cloud computing refers "to both the applications delivered as services over the Internet and the hardware and systems software in the datacenters that provide those services." (Armbrust et al., 2009)

Cloud computing covers a wide range of delivery and service models. The common

DOI: 10.4018/978-1-4666-4683-4.ch003

characteristics of these service models are pay-as-you-go, on-demand, outsourced, elasticity, and reliability. In conjunction with the growth of cloud computing new approaches to distributed computing and data analysis are also emerging. The aim of this chapter is to explore the current service delivery models and deployment options in cloud computing.

A public cloud is a cloud infrastructure made available to the public users in a pay-as-you-go model (Armbrust et al., 2009). In such a model, the service being sold is utility computing. Current examples of public utility computing include Amazon Web Services (AWS), Google App Engine, and Microsoft Azure. Instead, the term private cloud refers to internal data centers of a business or an organization that are not made available to the public.

Public cloud or private cloud terms refer to the deployment model of a cloud. A private cloud operates for a single organization, but can be managed on-premise or off-premise. On the other hand, a public cloud has an infrastructure that is available to the general public or a large industry group and is likely owned by a cloud based company.

On the other side, the services have long been referred to as Software as a Service (SaaS). The data center hardware and software is what we will call a cloud. Thus, generally speaking cloud computing is the sum of SaaS and utility computing, but does not normally include private clouds. We will generally use cloud computing, replacing it with one of the other terms only when clarity demands it.

To start the opening perspective of this chapter, a comparison between cloud services of Amazon and Google is illustrated in Figure 1.

2. SERVICE DELIVERY

Cloud offerings are typically categorized as Infrastructure as a Service (IaaS), Platform as a Service (PaaS), and Software as a Service (SaaS). The distinction between the service models is based on the service abstraction layer to the end user, e.g., hardware, development environment, system software, etc. The end user then has complete control over the software stack above the abstracted level. Thus, in IaaS a virtual machine or hardware is provided to the end user; the user controls the operating system and the entire software stack. We describe each of these service models and present existing examples in the commercial cloud space to understand their characteristics.

Currently, there are three main service delivery models in cloud computing: i.e. Software-as-a-Service, Infrastructure-as-a-Service, and Platform-as-a-Service. In Figure 2, a comparison between these three service delivery models are demonstrated. Figure 2 shows which parts of a cloud could be managed by a user based on the service delivery model.

SaaS provides the ability to use the software in a cloud environment, such as Web-based email or Customer Relationship Management (CRM) for the consumer.

PaaS is a variation of SaaS whereby the development environment is offered as a service. It provides the consumer the ability to deploy applications through a programming language or tools supported by the cloud platform provider. An example of platform as a service is an Eclipse/Java programming platform provided with no manual tasks or no downloads required.

Figure 1. Google versus Amazon cloud services

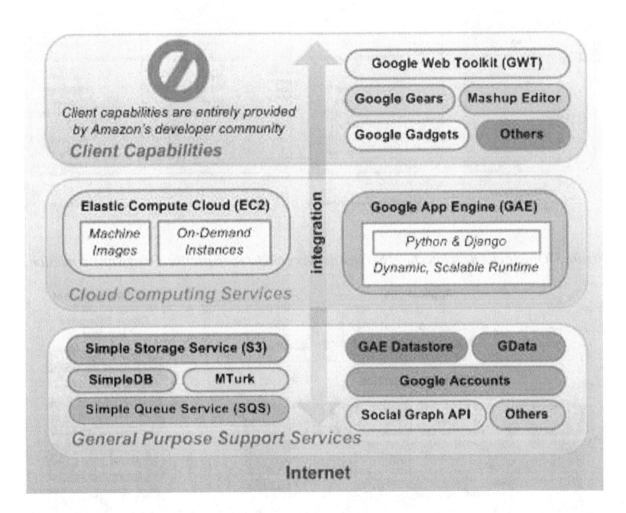

IaaS provides infrastructure such as compute instances, network bandwidth, and storage so that people can run any software or operating system.

Figure 3 illustrates Oracle cloud services based on service delivery models.

2.1 Software as a Service

In Software-as-a-Service, the capability provided to the consumer is to use the providers applications running on a cloud infrastructure. In a SaaS model, the customer does not purchase software, but rather rents it for use on

Figure 2. Cloud service delivery models

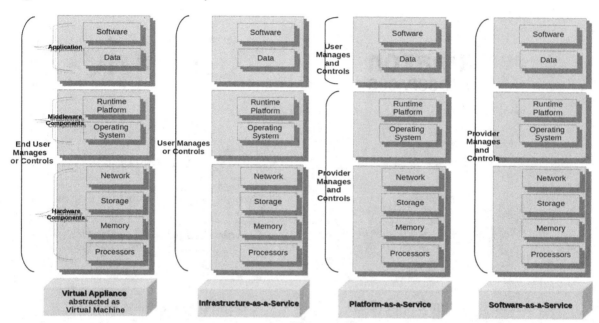

Figure 3. Oracle cloud architecture: Service delivery models perspective. Used with permission.

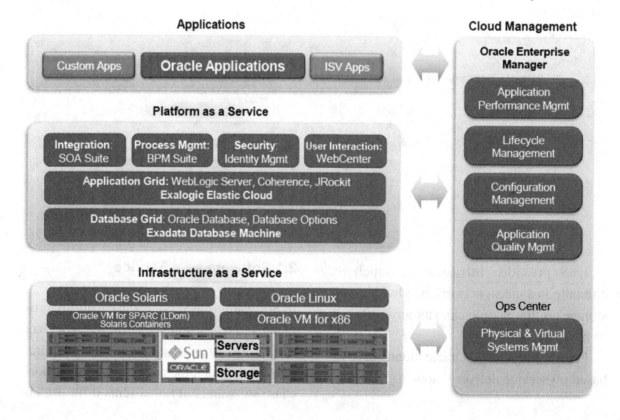

a subscription or pay-per-use model, i.e., an Operational Expense (OpEx).

Instead, traditional methods of purchasing software ask the customer loading the software onto his own hardware in return for a license fee that is a capital expense (CapEx). The customer could also purchase a maintenance agreement to receive patches to the software or other support services. Moreover, it was up to the customer the compatibility of operating systems, deployment, configuration, patch installations, and compliance with license agreements.

The applications are accessible from various client devices through a thin client and a user-friendly interface such as a Web browser. The consumers do not manage or control the underlying cloud infrastructure including network, servers, operating systems, storage, or even individual application capabilities. However, they may be able to define or to modify limited user-specific application configuration settings. The purchased service in this model includes the costs of hardware, software, and support.

Cloud services such as CRM (CRM at Salesforce.com, Inc., 2012), Social Networking (Facebook) (Social Networking (Facebook), 2012), Photo Sharing (Flicker) (Photo Sharing (Flicker), 2012) have been termed as SaaS.

In the following, some benefits and advantages of SaaS model versus the traditional software model are described:

- SaaS enables the organizations to outsource the hosting and management of applications to a third party (software vendor and service provider) as a means of reducing the cost of application software licensing, servers, and other infrastructure and personnel required to host the application internally.

- SaaS enables software vendors to control and limit the usage, prohibits copying and distribution, and facilitates the control of all derivative versions of their software. SaaS centralized control often allows the vendor or supplier to establish an ongoing revenue stream with multiple businesses and users without preloading software in each device in an organization.

- In SaaS, application delivery is one-to-many model approach. A user can access an application via a Web browser. Some SaaS vendors provide their own interface that is designed to support features that are unique to their applications.

- A typical SaaS deployment does not require any hardware and can run over the existing Internet access infrastructure. Sometimes changes to firewall rules and settings may be required to allow the SaaS application to run smoothly.

- Management of a SaaS application is supported by the vendor from the end user perspective, whereby a SaaS application can be configured using an API, but SaaS applications cannot be completely customized.

The most important architectural difference between the traditional software model and the SaaS model is the number of tenants the application supports. The traditional software model is an isolated, single-tenant model, which means a customer buys a software application and installs it on a server. The server runs only that specific application and only for that single customer's end user group. While SaaS model is a multi-tenant architecture model, which means the physical backend hardware infrastructure is shared among many different customers, but logically is unique for each customer.

Multi-tenant architecture design maximizes the sharing of resources across tenants, but is still able to securely differentiate data belonging to each tenant. For instance, when a user at one company accesses customer information by using a SaaS CRM application, the application instance that the user connects to can accommodate users from dozens, or even hundreds of other companies, all completely unbeknownst to any of the other users.

Furthermore, SaaS is different from Application Service Provider (ASP) from the following two perspectives:

- ASP applications are traditional, single-tenant applications, but are hosted by a third party. They are client/server applications.
- ASP applications are not written as network-native applications. Thus, their performance may be poor, and application updates are not better than self-managed premise-based applications.

In all, SaaS applications are multi-tenant applications that are hosted by a vendor with expertise in the applications. They have been designed as network-native applications and are updated on an ongoing basis.

On the other hand, the advantages of SaaS (Armbrust et al., 2009) to both end users and service providers are well understood. Service providers enjoy greatly simplified software installation and maintenance and centralized control over versioning; whereas end users can access the service anytime, anywhere, share data and collaborate more easily, and keep their data stored safely in the infrastructure.

Cloud computing does not change the above arguments, but it does give more application providers the choice of deploying their product as SaaS without provisioning a data center. It is the same as the emergence of semi-conductor foundries gave chip companies the opportunity to design and sell chips without owning a fab. Cloud computing allows deploying SaaS, and scaling on demand, without building or provisioning a data center. Analogously to how SaaS allows the user to offload some problems to the SaaS provider, the SaaS provider can now offload some of his problems to the cloud computing provider.

2.2 Platform as a Service

PaaS provides a computing platform as a service, supporting the complete life cycle of building and delivering applications. PaaS often includes facilities for application design, development, deployment and testing, and interfaces to manage security, scalability, storage, state, etc. Windows Azure, Hadoop, and Google App Engine are popular PaaS offerings in the commercial space.

Cloud mashups are a recent trend of PaaS solutions combining services from multiple clouds into a single service or application with on-premises data and services (client-side). Mashup service compositions offer new functionalities to clients at lower development costs. IBM's Mashup Center, Appirio Cloud Storage, and Forse.com are examples of cloud mashups and technologies.

In other words, PaaS is the purpose of clouds that provide on-demand Enterprise-class Web applications such as Force.com (CRM at Salesforce.com, Inc., 2012) or an application development environment and deployment container such as Google App Engine (Google App Engine, Google Code official portal site, 2012) without the cost of deploying infrastructure. Figure 4 illustrates Google App Engine's architecture.

In PaaS model, the vendor offers a development environment to application developers who develop applications and offer those services through the provider's platform. The provider develops toolkits and standards for development, and channels for distribution and payment. The provider receives a payment for offering the platform and the sales and distribution services.

PaaS solutions are development platforms for which the development tool itself is hosted in the cloud and accessed through a browser. With PaaS, developers can often build Web applications without installing any tools on their computer, and can then deploy those applications without any specialized system administration skill.

The developers use the building blocks, such as predefined blocks of code, of the vendor's development environment to create their own applications without having specialized expertise such as backend server development (e.g. Java/J2EE), frontend client development (e.g. JavaScript/Dojo), and Website administration.

Startup companies and developers can exploit PaaS to deploy Web applications without the cost and the complexity of buying servers and setting them up. With PaaS, the number of people who can develop, maintain, and deploy applications is increasing greatly. In all, PaaS offers to democratize the development of Web applications in much the same way that Microsoft Access democratized the development of client/server and database applications.

Traditional development tools are intended for a single user, while a cloud based studio supports multiple users i.e. multi-tenant development tools attribute of PaaS. In addition, in PaaS scalability of the application and data tiers is built-in; that is load balancing and failover are the basic elements of the developing platform, while in traditional model this attribute was left instead for the system administrators to handle when the project deploys. In sum, a PaaS solution provides the following elements:

- Development studio is browser based.
- An end-to-end PaaS solution provides a high productivity integrated development environment (IDE) running on the actual target delivery platform so that debugging and test scenarios run in the same environment as production deployment.

Figure 4. Google App Engine: Architecture. Google and the Google logo are registered trade-marks of Google Inc., used with permission.

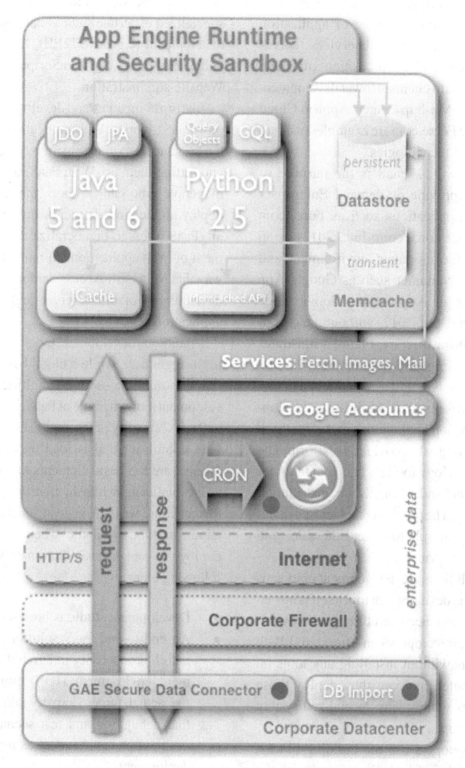

- Integration with external Web services and databases.
- Comprehensive monitoring of application and user activity to help developers understand their applications.
- Built-in multi-tenancy, scalability, reliability, and security, without requiring additional development, configuration, etc.
- A PaaS solution may support both formal and on-demand collaboration throughout the entire software life cycle (development, testing, documentation, and operations) while maintaining the security of source code and associated intellectual property.
- Pay-as-you-go metered billing.

True PaaS supports current programming models and applications, enables cloud portability, and provides the abstraction and management capabilities necessary to simplify application development and deployment. Most importantly, true PaaS systems have the flexibility and the portability designed into the architecture to prevent technology and vendor lock-in.

2.2.1 Google PaaS

Google Drive enables collaboration among various people on Google documents and other content from different computers.

The Google said at a conference that Google Drive is now available on Apple's iOS mobile operating system; it is already available on Windows, Mac and Chrome OS. Google executives shared updates on Google Apps for creating and managing documents, spreadsheets and presentations, all of which can now be stored in the cloud with Google Drive.

Google Drive is "deeply integrated" in Chrome OS, said Clay Bavor, director of product management for Google Apps, who also demonstrated the ability for a user to save a Google Doc on their device for offline viewing, such as when they are on a plane. They can edit the document offline and when they get reconnected to the Internet, the edited document automatically synchronizes with the earlier version in Drive. Google also announced a new SDK for creating applications in Drive.

2.2.2 Microsoft Windows Azure

Windows Azure is Microsoft's offering of a cloud services operating system. Azure provides a development, service hosting, and service management environment. Windows Azure provides on-demand compute and storage resources for hosting applications to scale costs. The Windows Azure platform supports two primary virtual machine instance types, the Web role instances and the Worker role instances. It also provides Blobs as a simple way to store data and access it from a virtual machine instance. Queues provide a way for worker role instances to access the work quantum from the Web role instance.

2.2.3 Akamai

Akamai introduces Terra Alta Application Acceleration Platform. Terra Alta is intended to map to the way enterprises are deploying and delivering business applications. Cloud platform provider Akamai Technologies introduced Terra Alta, an enterprise-class solution designed to address the evolving complexities of application acceleration in the cloud. Terra Alta helps simplify the process of developing and deploying applications in the cloud, making it easier to optimize hundreds or thousands of applications with greater flexibility and control. Terra Alta has also been designed to enable an increasingly mobile enterprise user base, and is available with packages supporting sets of three, five and ten applications.

As applications themselves evolve, Terra Alta helps accelerate complex applications that rely on multiple components, which may include business functions, modules or Web services from within other applications. Finally, Terra Alta can be deployed within an enterprises' existing network architecture, allowing IT decision makers to avoid making changes to network equipment investments already made.

"Enterprises are increasingly extending their IT infrastructure outside of the boundaries of their own data centers embracing cloud computing, as well as delivering content and applications over the Internet," said Lydia Leong, research vice president of IT analytics firm Gartner. "However, they face a new array of availability and performance challenges that may impact end-user adoption, acceptance and productivity, and need solutions for these challenges."

In the area of enterprise and cloud readiness, Terra Alta is intended to map to the way enterprises are deploying and delivering business applications. Features in this area include Enterprise Edge, a virtual machine running Akamai optimization technology within a customer's origin, which allows optimizations from the Akamai Intelligent Platform to be carried from the Internet into the data center.

For enterprises taking advantage of public cloud deployments, Edge load balancing is designed to ensure that application traffic can be load-balanced globally across the Web before traffic impacts an isolated single data center. Enterprise Domain Name System (DNS) mapping enables organizations to overcome the performance challenges caused by centralized DNS by dynamically adapting to user location and removing dependencies on enterprise DNS infrastructure redesigns.

Features designed to deliver acceleration capabilities across a broad set of Web applications include Web de-duplication, designed to ensure that only differences in the objects that have already been sent by the origin are delivered, reducing bandwidth consumption required for application delivery; Akamai Instant, which retrieves what are assessed as the most likely pages to be next requested by the user; and dynamic page caching, which allows pages that were previously considered dynamic and un-cacheable to be conditionally cached.

"Companies want to use the cloud as an enterprise application delivery environment because it's the most effective and efficient way to reach the broadest set of users. Unfortunately, controlling the cloud can seriously erode the promises and expectations of cloud computing," said Willie Tejada, senior vice president and general manager of the enterprise cloud division at Akamai. "With the release of Terra Alta, we are giving our customers solutions designed to provide the best possible performance for their portfolio of cloud-delivered business applications."

2.3 Infrastructure as a Service

In IaaS, the capability provided to the consumer is to provision processing, storage, networks, and other fundamental computing resources where the consumer is able to deploy and run arbitrary software, which can include operating systems and applications. The consumer does not manage or control the underlying cloud infrastructure but has control over operating systems, storage, deployed applications, and possibly limited control of selecting networking components (e.g., host firewalls).

In the IaaS provisioning model, an organization outsources equipment including storage, hardware, servers, and networking components. The service provider owns the equipment and is responsible for housing, running, and maintaining it. In the commercial space, the client typically pays on a per-use basis for use of the equipment.

AWS is the most widely used IaaS cloud computing platform today. Amazon provides a number of different levels of computational power for different pricing. The primary methods for data storage in Amazon EC2 are S3 and Elastic Block Storage (EBS). S3 is a highly scalable key-based storage system that transparently handles fault tolerance and data integrity. EBS provides a virtual storage device that can be associated with an elastic computing instance. S3 charges for space used

per month, the volume of data transferred, and the number of metadata operations in allotments of 1000. EBS charges for data stored per month. For both S3 and EBS, there is no charge for data transferred to and from EC2 within a domain (e.g., the U.S. or Europe). EC2 offers elastic and resizable computing capacity through Web service instances.

Eucalyptus (Nurmi et al., 2008), OpenStack, OpenNebula (OpenNebula, 2010), and Nimbus (Nimbus Toolkit Project, 2010) are open source software stacks that can be used to create a private or a public cloud IaaS service. These software stacks provide an array of services that mimic many of the services provided by Amazon EC2 including image management, persistent block storage, virtual machine control, etc. The interface for these services is often compatible with Amazon EC2 allowing the same set of tools and methods to be used.

The IaaS landscape is evolving and it is far from mature. Providers vary greatly in terms of the service, features, Service Level Agreement (SLA) and markets they serve. The leader in the market is Amazon AWS. Hosting.com has a unique feature to pay less for VMs that are not used. Rackspace is embracing the open source movement and they are on the right path to compete with the big cloud industries. Some providers are geared toward niches such as Disaster Recovery, Government, Compliance while others are general purpose.

The virtualization technology such as Citrix Xen (Xen Paravirtualization official portal site, 2012), open source KVM, and VMware are the predominant choices for

IaaS vendors. A public IaaS offers a Web services API to perform management functions such as provisioning, decommissioning, and replication of virtual servers on the IaaS platform. These system management functions when orchestrated appropriately can provide elasticity for resources to grow or shrink in line with workload demand.

Recently, Google has entered in the IaaS space by introducing Google Compute Engine for hosting applications on the company's massive computing infrastructure. Compute Engine, which Google said June 28, 2012 is available as a limited preview for now, was introduced on the second day of the Google I/O 2012 developer's conference in San Francisco.

Google already offers App Engine, which enables application developers to create their own applications and have Google host them in its data centers. App Engine currently hosts more than 1 million applications. Compute Engine is intended to serve a wider audience. Urs Holzle, senior vice president of technical infrastructure at Google, at the Google I/O 2012 developer's conference demonstrated Compute Engine's capabilities with the example of the Institute for Systems Biology, a research organization that tests potential new cancer drugs against the human genome. He explained that the Institute's own data center has only 1,000 compute cores for processing these tests, which is too slow. Access to Compute Engine increased that to 10,000 cores.

Google's Compute Engine has the technology to help in instances that are very computationally intensive, but do not need that much I/O. In that instance, the capacity for the Institute project could reach more

than 770,000 cores, of which the project used 600,000. That is how infrastructure-as-a-service is supposed to work.

2.4 Hardware as a Service

Hardware as a Service (HaaS) is also known as "bare-metal provisioning." The main distinction between this model and IaaS is that the user-provided operating system software stack is provisioned onto the raw hardware, allowing the users to provide their own custom hypervisor, or to avoid virtualization completely, along with the performance impact of virtualization of high-performance hardware such as InfiniBand. The other difference between HaaS and the other service models is that the user "leases" the entire resource; it is not shared with other users within a virtual space. With HaaS, the service provider owns the equipment and is responsible for housing, running, and maintaining it. HaaS provides many of the advantages of IaaS and enables greater levels of control on the hardware configuration.

3. DEPLOYMENT OPTIONS

According to the NIST definition, a cloud has one of the following deployment models, depending on how the cloud infrastructure is operated: (a) public, (b) private, (c) community, or (d) hybrid.

1. Public clouds refer to infrastructure provided to the general public by a large industry selling cloud services. Amazon's cloud offering would fall in

this category. These services are on a pay-as-you-go basis and can usually be purchased using a credit card.

2. A private cloud infrastructure is operated solely for a particular organization and has specific features that support a specific group of policies.

3. A community cloud infrastructure is shared by several organizations and serves the needs of a special community that has common goals. The NIST also defines community cloud as shared by several organizations supporting a specific community with shared concerns. FutureGrid (Future Grid Portal, 2012) can be considered a community cloud.

4. Hybrid clouds refer to two or more cloud infrastructures that operate independently but are bound together by technology compliance to enable application portability.

Private and public clouds are subsets of the Internet if we consider the term cloud as a metaphor for the Internet. They are also referred to as internal or external clouds.

3.1 Private

In private cloud, the cloud infrastructure is operated solely for an organization. It may be managed by the organization or a third party and may exist on premise or off premise. A private cloud is an offering of cloud computing on private sector. Private cloud delivers some benefits of cloud computing without its risks and threats such as security, governance and reliability concerns. Enterprises buy and manage private clouds, thus, perhaps they do

not benefit from lower upfront capital costs and less hands-on management. The operation of a private cloud is on the hands of the consumer. Therefore, in private cloud some operations and tasks are not outsourced and are managed by the client.

A private cloud differs from public cloud in which IT resources such as network, computing, and storage infrastructure associated with private cloud is dedicated to a single organization and is not shared with any other organizations that is a single organization tenant model. As a result, a variety of private cloud patterns have emerged:

- **Dedicated:** In this model, a private cloud is hosted within a client administrative domain (e.g. client's data center or at a collocation facility). In addition, it is administrated and operated by internal IT departments.

- **Managed:** In this pattern, cloud infrastructure owned by a customer and managed by a vendor.

- **Community:** In community cloud, the cloud infrastructure is shared by several organizations and supports a specific community that has shared concerns (e.g. mission, security requirements, policy, and compliance consideration). It may be managed by the organizations or a third party and may exist on premise or off premise.

In private cloud, security and operation of infrastructure, services and other things related to the cloud are managed by internal IT personnel or by a third party vendor with contractual SLAs. Therefore, a customer of a private cloud has a high degree of control and oversight of the physical and logical security aspects of the private cloud infrastructure such as the hypervisor and the hosted virtualized Operating Systems. With this high degree of control, it is easier for a customer to comply with established corporate security standards, policies, and regulatory compliance.

From the technological perspective, private clouds are not just virtualization, but rather the ability to use a resource on a "who needs it now" basis. There is elasticity in properly built private clouds just as there is in public clouds, how much is up to the customer. Private clouds may also be shared among a group of users (with the owner's permission). These could be partners, customers, geographically disperse users, etc. There are a number of government sponsored private clouds that are actually community clouds.

3.2 Public

Public cloud resembles the Internet and it is the main cloud computing model. Public cloud is hosted, operated and managed by a third-party vendor from one or more data centers. The service is offered to multiple customers, that we call it multiple tenants over a common infrastructure.

In public cloud, everything is outsourced to outside of a corporation administrative domain such as security management and day to day operations. These outsourced tasks are handled by the provider of public cloud

service offering. Hence, the customer of the public cloud service offering has much lower degree of control and oversight of the physical and logical security aspects of a private cloud.

3.3 Hybrid

Clouds can also be described as hybrid. A hybrid cloud is a deployment model, as a composition of both public and private clouds. A hybrid cloud consists of multiple internal and external providers. A hybrid model for cloud computing may involve both virtual and physical servers.

The concept of a hybrid cloud is attractive for many organizations. It allows an organization with an existing private cloud to alliance with a public cloud provider. This can be a valuable resource as it allows companies to keep some of their operation in-house, and benefit from the scalability and on-demand nature of the public cloud. However, there are a number of issues that organizations must consider before opting for a hybrid cloud setup.

With a hybrid cloud, an enterprise may run core applications and sensitive data in-house in private cloud, and run the other applications in a public cloud in case of a workload spike. Cloud bursting can be implemented by hybrid cloud model.

One of the reasons that the public cloud business has not picked up as much as it was expected is due to hybrid clouds. Most of the growth has been in the private clouds which is virtualization of existing applications as is.

3.4 Federated

Federated clouds are a future deployment model in which consumers can transparently acquire resources from multiple cloud resource providers or cloud service providers. Standardization is the big roadblock to this model.

Cloud federation is the management, interconnection, interoperation, deployment, and coordination of multiple public and private cloud computing services to function as a single entity, and to match business needs and spikes in demand. A federated cloud brings many benefits such as:

1. To load balance traffic and accommodate spikes in demand.
2. To gain economies of scale and an enlargement of the capabilities.
3. To enable providers to expand service footprint.
4. To build composite services by integrating multiple cloud computing.
5. To enable identity federation in the cloud.

3.5 Cloud Spot Markets

A couple more recent concepts being discussed in forums on the Web are cloud spot markets [1]. Spot markets are a concept that avoids the big resource providers like Amazon by combining resources from multiple providers under a single cloud. Resource providers can submit their resources for inclusion in the cloud and consumers can acquire the resources potentially from multiple providers.

Initially, cloud providers had only a fixed price for their service offerings (Chun et al., 2005) (Weng, Li, Lu, & Deng, 2005). As cloud systems grow larger and are partitioned into more unique configurations, this fixed price method becomes inefficient when total demand is much lower than data center capacity leading to under-use of the system so cloud providers need an incentive mechanism to encourage users to submit more jobs. When total demand rises over data center capacity, it is desirable to provide an incentive to users to reduce their demand through raising per-unit costs, decreasing performance, or decreasing system availability.

In 2009, Amazon introduced a new set of spot instances to sell its unused data center capacity based on a new market mechanism offering a variable pricing method. With this service, users are able to bid for unused capacity. The spot price mechanism for EC2 shares many similarities with the standard uniform price auction mechanism. The spot price charged for a request may fluctuate depending on the supply of, and demand for, spot instance capacity. Spot prices are a tuple of {*maximum price per hour the user wishes to pay for an instance type, the region desired, and the number of spot instances to run*}. If the maximum price bid exceeds the current spot price, the job(s) will run until termination by the user or the spot price increases above the user set maximum price. The cost of spot instance hours are billed based on the spot price at the start of each hour an instance executes. If the user spot instance is interrupted in the middle of an hour of instance use (because the spot price exceeded the user maximum bid price), the user is not billed for that partial hour of spot instance use. However, if the user terminates the spot instance a charge occurs for the partial hour of use [2].

Currently, Amazon EC2 spot instance services are available for 8 types of VMs. Each VM type has different resource capacities for CPU, memory and disk. Amazon EC2 runs one spot market for each VM type in each geographical availability zone. All spot markets share the free data center capacity. This capacity is the remaining resources after serving all the guaranteed (i.e., contracted) instances.

4. CLOUD APPLICATIONS, SERVICES, AND TOOLS

In this section, we introduce a list of cloud computing's applications, services, tools, and software for PaaS, IaaS, and SaaS. Then, we explore some of these applications in Governments and Public Administrations, Justice Administration, and e-Learning.

A list of free cloud computing services for application developers are provided in Table 1. This list enumerates developer tools including IDEs, source code management systems, and issue tracking tools.

Applications need to store data in databases. Installation, and configuration of a database and connecting an application to a database are time consuming and manual tasks for administrators. For that, a list of free cloud database services, open source databases,

CMSs and payment gateways for application and database developers are provided in Table 2.

In paper (Cattell, 2011), author give a nice survey of cloud data stores, in particular Scalable SQL versus NoSQL data stores. It introduces many products and services in the field and has links to the products.

The three major open source CMSs which are easy to set up on a cloud virtual machine as part of your application deployment are introduced in Table 3.

4.1 Governments and Public Administrations

The infrastructure, the services and the software on demand offered by cloud computing guarantee great advantages to the public administrations and to the governments. The recent work of (Wyld, 2010) pays attention on some of the most interesting and effective cloud solutions adopted by the governments and by the public administrations. Among them, the author describes a private cloud developed in Japan with the aim of improving the operating efficiency of the offered services and of reducing costs. This platform aims to provide a national digital archive. In addition, the author describes the cloud computing initiative launched by the city of Dongying (a region in the northern part of Shandong, China) with the aim of improving not only the efficiency of the offered services but also of promoting the economic development. In the foreseeable feature, more and more public organizations and governments are expected to adopt cloud-based solutions.

Table 1. A list of free cloud computing services for application developers

Name	Type	Description	Address
Koding	IDE	A free, fully featured Cloud Development environment. Create and edit code from anywhere.	http://koding.com/
Cloud9 IDE	IDE	Offers an online development environment for Javascript, Node.js applications, HTML, CSS, PHP, Java, Ruby and 23 other languages.	http://c9.io/http://c9.io/site/pricing/
eXo	DE	Multi-tenant, hosted development environment that enables social coding (the collaborative development of applications, gadgets and mashups), direct deployment to a PaaS	http://www.cloud-ide.com/
CloudForge	Source Code Management	By CollabNet Cloud Services, hosted self-service source code management, agile tools, integrations with popular cloud services, API integration services, and front-ends the deployment to PaaS and IaaS platforms like CloudFoundry.com, Force.com, and AWS, address the needs of Enterprise scalability and security.	http://www.cloudforge.com/
GitHub	Source Code Management	The best way to collaborate with others. Fork, send pull requests and manage all your public and private git repositories.	https://github.com/
BitBucket	Source Code Management	Store all Git and Mercurial source code in one place with unlimited private repositories. Includes issue tracking, wiki, and pull requests.	https://bitbucket.org/
Mercurial	Source Code Management	A free, distributed source control management tool. an easy and intuitive interface, for projects of any size	http://mercurial.selenic.com/
Fossil	Source Code Management	Simple, high-reliability, distributed software configuration management.	http://www.fossil-scm.org/download.html
Protecode	Source Code Management	Comprehensive solutions for managing open source software licenses. on-demand and on-premises solutions that enable lightning fast code scanning that works behind the scenes in real-time to detect and report open source licenses relative to company-defined policies.	Protecode.com
TrackStudio	Issue Tracking	is an ultra-configurable issue tracking system, workflow engine and document management system that can be used to track the progress of any kind of task such as issue resolution, requirements gathering, desktop support handling, project monitoring, hardware deployment and staff hiring.	TrackStudio.com
YouTrack	Issue Tracking	is an innovative, keyboard-centric issue tracking and project tracking tool. Customize your issue tracker to fit your workflow, not the other way around. Manipulate issues with just two simple controls and enjoy lightning-fast bug tracking and reporting!	http://www.jetbrains.com/youtrack/
Issue Tracking Anywhere	Issue Tracking	is a Web-based, bug and issue tracking system designed for work item tracking, project tracking, customer support and software development.	http://www.dynamsoft.com/Products/bug-tracking-issue-tracking-anywhere.aspx

Table 2. A list of free cloud database services

Name	Description	Address
Xeround	MySQL database replacement service, a seamless MySQL scalability and high availability. automatic database scalability, and maintain availability even in the event of failure. You can run your database on AWS and on Rackspace, on HP Cloud Services, as well as via the Heroku, Engine Yard, PHP Fog and AppHarbor platforms. Additional cloud service providers are being added on-going.	http://xeround.com/mysql-cloud-db-overview/
MySQL	Is the world's most popular open source database. Whether you are a fast growing Web property, technology ISV or large enterprise, MySQL can cost-effectively help you deliver high performance, scalable database applications.	http://www.mysql.com/products/ Setting Up on Amazon EC2 http://aws.amazon.com/articles/1663
CouchDB	Is a database that completely embraces the Web. Store your data with JSON documents. Access your documents with your Web browser via HTTP. Query, combine, and transform your documents with JavaScript. CouchDB works well with modern Web and mobile apps. You can even serve Web apps directly out of CouchDB. And you can distribute your data, or your apps, efficiently using CouchDB's incremental replication. CouchDB supports master-master setups with automatic conflict detection.	http://couchdb.apache.org/http://aws.amazon.com/amis/Community/2861
MongoDB	MongoDB (from "humongous") is a scalable, high-performance, open source NoSQL database. Written in C++, MongoDB features:	http://www.mongodb.org/ Setting Up on Amazon EC2 http://www.mongodb.org/display/DOCS/Amazon+EC2
The Apache Cassandra	Database is the right choice when you need scalability and high availability without compromising performance. Linear scalability and proven fault-tolerance on commodity hardware or cloud infrastructure make it the perfect platform for mission-critical data. Cassandra's support for replicating across multiple datacenters is best-in-class, providing lower latency for your users and the peace of mind of knowing that you can survive regional outages.	http://cassandra.apache.org/
Neo4j	A high-performance, NOSQL graph database with all the features of a mature and robust database. The programmer works with an object-oriented, flexible network structure rather than with strict and static tables, yet enjoys all the benefits of a fully transactional, enterprise-strength database. For many applications, Neo4j offers performance improvements on the order of 1000x or more compared to relational DBs.	http://neo4j.org/
The Apache Hadoop	Software library is a framework that allows for the distributed processing of large data sets across clusters of computers using a simple programming model. It is designed to scale up from single servers to thousands of machines, each offering local computation and storage. Rather than rely on hardware to deliver high-availability, the library itself is designed to detect and handle failures at the application layer, so delivering a highly-available service on top of a cluster of computers, each of which may be prone to failures.	http://hadoop.apache.org/

The private, public and community clouds can be adopted and adapted according to the specific needs. Some cloud platforms have been designed to develop and test military applications that are then distributed as services. Public organizations can offer services to small/medium enterprises. Some solutions have been also proposed with the aim to offer mail applications in a public cloud and to standardize the services.

Cloud computing offers advanced services that can be also used by the rural and

Table 3. A list of open source CMSs for cloud computing

Name	Description	Address
WordPress	Is an Open Source project, which means there are hundreds of people all over the world working on it. It also means you are free to use it for anything from your cat home page to a Fortune 500 Web site without paying anyone a license fee and a number of other important freedoms.	http://wordpress.org/about/
Drupal	Is a free software package that allows you to easily organize, manage and publish your content, with an endless variety of customization.	http://drupal.org/about
Joomla	Is an award-winning CMS, which enables you to build Web sites and powerful online applications. Many aspects, including its ease-of-use and extensibility, have made Joomla the most popular Web site software available. Best of all, Joomla is an open source solution that is freely available to everyone.	http://www.joomla.org/about-joomla.html

developing countries. As a consequence, they can guarantee higher service levels to their citizens without high costs. Also, the local governments can efficiently "work together" with the aim of accelerating their economic development.

In Liang (2012), the author illustrates the main advantages of using a cloud computing platform for managing governments. In particular, he highlights among them, the possibility to have *ubiquitous services*.

However, a full implementation of the cloud in the public sector is still limited by some challenging issues. Among the others, data security and interoperability among different systems represent two extremely significant concerns. Data security is a big concern due to the importance and relevance of the shared information. Therefore, it is extremely important that all the stored data are properly coded and protected by "robust" security mechanisms. Moreover, since data are geographically distributed (i.e., data in multiple jurisdictions), it is also necessary to take into account that they could be under different security and privacy norms.

The interoperability becomes an important and crucial requirement since the governments and the public administrations do not usually adopt common standards.

Moreover, it could be difficult to move from a cloud model to another and this could imply the "vendor lock-in." It means that public administrations, governments and small/middle enterprises have to select the providers also by taking in mind this risk. Then, they have properly to negotiate with them for instruments that can guarantee portability.

Despite these criticisms and disadvantages, the public authorities and governments can significantly benefit from a cloud in terms of a considerable cost saving since they pay for the used services, of a higher flexibility and elasticity, since the services and the applications can be easily deployed and provided on demand and finally, of sustainability, since the economies of scale offered by cloud computing guarantee significant reductions especially in terms of the energy consumptions.

Cloud computing gives to small and middle enterprises, that usually have not an internal "expertise," the opportunity to use advanced services on demand. In addition, the concept of "multi-tenancy" allows them to share the costs with other users that are in compliance with their aims and goals.

Public administrations, governments and small/middle enterprises can easily "re-use" software and applications "provided" by others according to their goals. However, it could not be always possible due to a poor software documentation and portability.

Small and middle organizations can access to "open data" provided by public administrations and governments and therefore, they can adapt applications and services according to the citizen needs. In addition, to migrate "open big data" to cloud data centers means also the possibility to use advanced data mining services and then, to properly process and analyze them.

Cloud computing can support governments and/or public organizations in delivering their services also to the citizens that live abroad (high social impact).

In conclusion, the clouds create *virtual organizations* in which the resources are provided on demand and users (such as public administrations and citizens) can interact with each other.

4.2 Justice Administration

A lot of the inefficiencies in justice administration are mainly due to a traditional distribution of the services. The adoption of cloud computing solutions in this specific sector can provide new advanced and efficient services and better support the collaboration among the different types of users.

Lawyers and judges could use more advanced services and then consult via Internet and in real time data and documents related to specific prosecutions. An electronic data repository, shared among the authorities, can contain several types of legal documents that can be consulted by the users. Instead, the legal documents on paper are usually consulted only few times after the conclusion of a trial. However, they could represent a significant source of knowledge since they could contain information useful and applicable to similar situations in the future.

Among the other things, cloud computing can offer advanced applications and services on demand to the lawyers, to the judges and to the legal authorities in order to efficiently manage the files from any device, to visualize some activities, to consult and share the digital archives, useful for the juridical searches.

The lawyers have the possibility to create a Web site of their law firm in order to provide useful functionalities to their clients. Moreover, a cloud application, by allowing the accesses from anywhere, can give to the law firms the possibility to quickly and easily share documents and information. It can also provide advanced software as services on demand in order to organize all the internal activities of a law firm. However, data security still remains a big concern that has to be taken into consideration especially for the importance and the relevance of the information shared in this sector. Therefore, it is extremely important that the lawyers choose the cloud providers that can better meet the security requirements.

Cloud computing can also be seen as a good solution to the problems that the traditional tools for the forensics analysis are facing. Among these, for example, they usually require very long computational times in order to examine data on the media. In the work of (Lee & Hong, 2011), a new cloud service concept is introduced. Then, the investigators are able to separate technology from the analysis process thanks to specific forensics techniques that are offered as services on demand. The authors propose a framework based on the integration of the mobile technologies and cloud computing in order to increase efficiency in the forensics investigations. However, they also highlight both security and privacy as the two big concerns that have to be addressed.

4.3 E-Learning

Nowadays, an e-learning platform plays a key role for education, training and academic purposes and creates a "virtual classroom environment" in which students and teachers are the two main types of users. In fact, the students can take on-line courses and develop new projects while the teachers can manage on-line courses, send in real-time useful feedbacks and communicate with students via forums. However, the e-learning systems are usually based on the traditional client/server architectures. Cloud computing can guarantee scalability and offer significant advantages to these systems (Phankokkruad, 2012). The videos, for instance, become services on demand and are stored on the cloud. In this way, they

can be downloaded by the users with the aim of reproducing a real classroom environment (Rajendran & Veilumuthu, 2011). Thus, the learning processes can be offered as services to all the users and this has a significant social and economic impact.

In Caminero et al. (2011), a cloud-based e-learning platform is proposed. The platform includes some virtual environments in which the students can pass on-line exams and perform exercises. In addition, specific techniques for managing the load of the platform are also used in order to improve the performances of the offered services. The main goal is to use cloud computing for improving the utilization of the academic resources and for minimizing the costs due to the energy consumption.

The work of Ghazizadeh (2012) highlights the main features of a cloud-based e-learning platform. The author identifies the main areas that benefit from a cloud-based e-learning solution: teaching, research and administrative area. Regarding teaching and research area, students and teachers can benefit from the advanced services provided by the cloud in terms of tools for managing materials and files. Regarding administrative area, the staff (the computer technicians, for example) can access services available all the day, anywhere and everywhere.

Cloud computing allows a better integration of the libraries that usually manage huge amounts of digital data (Abidi, Abidi, & Armani, 2012). In this way, it is also possible to considerably reduce the presence of duplicates, guaranteeing, among the other things, significant cost savings. In Abidi, Abidi, and Armani (2012), the authors conclude that cloud libraries mean "green libraries." In fact, an improved server utilization can mean, beyond the other aspects, a considerable reduction of the carbon emissions.

In the work of Srirama, Batrashev, Jakovits, and Vainikko (2011), the authors discuss the possibility of defining private clouds in academic contexts with the aim of providing the internal resources for running applications and solving challenging problems. Then, the authors identify the main benefit provided by the adoption of a such cloud in terms of virtual and infinite computational resources. The work continues with the discussion of the authors on the frameworks that are more suitable for running scientific applications on the cloud.

Moreover, in order to exploit the benefits and the advantages provided by both the mobile technologies and cloud computing, some systems integrate a mobile e-learning platform with the cloud. A mobile e-learning platform provides advanced services, accessible from any mobile device. Then, its integration with cloud computing allows, among the other things, to efficiently overcome the limits in terms of data storage and process capacity.

5. CONCLUSION

In this chapter, we have described the cloud service delivery models and deployment options. According to an organization needs and applications, the right service delivery and deployment option have to be chosen for an organization's cloud application.

Nonetheless, there are applications where cannot be moved to the cloud, while there are instances that have to be deployed in clouds. An organization can benefit from the cloud in different aspects.

In IaaS, users use cloud providers' machines. This service delivery model has been termed as *Everything as a Service* as well. In this model, users use a virtualized server and running software on it. Amazon EC2 is a de-facto standard and the most prevalent IaaS service in the world. EC2 allows users to obtain compute capacity with minimal effort and friction. It reduces the required time to boot compute instances to minutes, allowing quick scaling capacity up and down based on computing requirements fluctuation. This changes the computing economics by allowing users to pay only for their real usage of compute capacity.

On the other hand, PaaS offers the methods to build scalable applications in the cloud. PaaS providers like IaaS providers offer built-in redundancy, fault-tolerance, and geographical distribution of resources. Users and developers leverage PaaS management platform to automatically deploy and manage scalable cloud and Web applications. For example, Salesforce platform provides multi-tenant capabilities to build multiple sophisticated business applications within the same Salesforce instance to share a common security model, data model, and user interface. Users can create on-demand databases, on-demand workflow engine for users collaboration, building complex logic, mashups and integration with other applications and data through Salesforce.com Web services API. In addition, collaboration among multiple cloud services like cloud mashups opens up opportunities for providers to offer more sophisticated services that will benefit the next generation of clients.

In SaaS unlike PaaS, the cloud provider provides the applications for users. Traditional software model requires complex system and software installation, configuration, and administration, whereas SaaS digests these obstacles and needs only an advanced browser to function. This highly reduces time to value and time to market. In Software plus Services model, some software run locally but they can reach out to the cloud for additional services. In this model, data can be stored on-site, thus this model provides more security and reliability.

The cloud providers of Storage as a Service rent storage space to users. With this service users can outsource their data storing outside instead of their local storage system. These providers offer storage services such as backup, replication, disaster recovery, etc. Like other cloud services, users do not pay for the storage infrastructure and avoid capital investments for the storage and as a result this service is cost-saving. The cost models are per gigabytes stored, or per data transferred.

The UberCloud Experiment (Gentzsch & Yenier, 2012b) envision and investigates how far we are from an ideal remote use of HPC or HPC-as-a-Service (HPCaaS) or HPC in the Cloud model. At this point, nobody knows. However, in the course of this hands-on experiment, following each team and monitoring its challenges and progress, there is an excellent insight into these roadblocks and how 25 teams have tackled them.

HPC installations come in various shapes and sizes. With so many architectures, operating systems, queue managers there is staggering variability in the market. During the first round some of UberCloud experiment projects ran into long delays since the project and the resource provider were not the best match possible. Some resource providers struggled with installation of an application. Others had difficulties with providing network access through complex network connections.

Resource providers differ in their service philosophies. Some offer SaaS and are very specific in their offerings. Others can be more flexible since they offer generic IaaS. As an example, there was a project where the end-users request to access the computer resources directly to install software was not something the resource provider could easily accommodate, since they follow a SaaS model where the underlying resources are abstracted.

REFERENCES

Abidi, Abidi, & Armani. (2012). Cloud libraries: A novel application of cloud computing. In *Proceedings of 2012 International Conference on Education and e-Learning Innovations*. IEEE.

Armbrust, M., Fox, A., Griffith, R., Joseph, A. D., Katz, R. H., Konwinski, A., & Zaharia, M. (2009). *Above the clouds: A Berkeley view of cloud computing* (Tech. Rep. No. UCB/EECS-2009-28). EECS Department, University of California, Berkeley. Retrieved from http://www.eecs.berkeley.edu/Pubs/TechRpts/2009/EECS-2009-28.html

Caminero, A. C., Robles-Gomez, A., Ros, S., Hernandez, R., Pastor, R., Oliva, N., & Castro, M. (2011). Harnessing clouds for e-learning: New directions followed by UNED. In *Proceedings of Global Engineering Education Conference (EDUCON)*. IEEE.

Cattell, R. (2011). Scalable SQL and NOSQL data stores. *SIGMOD Record, 39*(4), 12–27. doi:10.1145/1978915.1978919

Chun, B. N., Buonadonna, P., Auyoung, A., Ng, C., Parkes, D. C., Shneidman, J., & Vahdat, A. (2005). Mirage: A microeconomic resource allocation system forsensornet testbeds. In *Proceedings of the 2nd IEEE Workshop on Embedded Networked Sensors*. IEEE. *CRM at salesforce.com, Inc.* (2012). Retrieved from http://www.salesforce.com

Future Grid Portal. (2012). Retrieved from https://portal.futuregrid.org/

Gentzsch, W., & Yenier, B. (2012). *HPC experiment - Final report of round 1*. The UberCloud LLC.

Ghazizadeh. (2012). Cloud computing benefits and architecture in e-learning. In *Proceedings of 17th IEEE International Conference on Wireless, Mobile and Ubiquitous Technology in Education*. IEEE.

Google App. Engine, Google Code Official Portal Site. (2012). Retrieved from http://code.google.com/appengine/

Lee & Hong. (2011). Pervasive forensic analysis based on mobile cloud computing. In *Proceedings of 2011 Third International Conference on Multimedia Information Networking and Security*. MINES.

Liang. (2012). Government cloud: Enhancing efficiency of e-government and providing better public services. In *Proceedings of 2012 International Joint Conference on Service Sciences* (IJCSS). IJCSS.

Nebula, O. (2010). *Opennebula cloud toolkit*. Retrieved from http://OpenNebula.org/

Nimbus Toolkit Project. (2010). Retrieved from http://nimbusproject.org/

Nurmi, D. etal. (2008). The eucalyptus open-source cloud-computing system. In *Proceedings of Cloud Computing and its Applications'08*. Academic Press.

Phankokkruad. (2012). Implement of cloud computing for e-learning system. In *Proceedings of Computer Information Science (ICCIS)*. ICCIS.

Photo Sharing (Flicker). (2012). Retrieved from http://www.Flicker.com

Rajendran & Veilumuthu. (2011). A cost-effective cloud service for e-learning video on demand. *European Journal of Scientific Research, 55,* 569–579.

Social Networking (Facebook). (2012). Retrieved from http://www.facebook.com

Srirama, Batrashev, Jakovits, & Vainikko. (2011). Scalability of parallel scientific applications on the cloud. *Science Progress, 19*(2-3), 91–105.

Weng, C., Li, M., Lu, X., & Deng, Q. (2005). An economic-based resource management framework in the grid context. In *Proceedings of the Fifth IEEE International Symposium on Cluster Computing and the Grid.* IEEE.

Wyld. (2010). The cloudy future of government it: Cloud computing and the public sector around the world. *International Journal of Web & Semantic Technology, 1*(1), 1–20.

Xen Paravirtualization Official Portal Site. (2012). Retrieved from http://www.xen.org/about/paravirtualization.html

KEY TERMS AND DEFINITIONS

Amazon EC2: A de-facto standard and the most prevalent IaaS service in the world. EC2 allows users to obtain compute capacity with minimal effort and friction.

Amazon Web Services (AWS): A public cloud infrastructure made available to the public users in a pay-as-you-go model. AWS is the most popular and the first public utility computing.

Deployment Options: Categorized as public, private, community, and hybrid. A cloud is deployed as one of them, depending on how the cloud infrastructure is operated.

Federated Cloud: The management, interconnection, interoperation, deployment, and coordination of multiple public and private cloud computing services to function as a single entity, and to match business needs and spikes in demand.

Google AppEngine: An application development environment and deployment container without the cost of deploying infrastructure.

Hybrid Cloud: A deployment model, as a composition of both public and private clouds. A hybrid cloud consists of multiple internal and external providers.

Microsoft Windows Azure: Provides a development, service hosting, and service management environment. Windows Azure provides on-demand compute and storage resources for hosting applications to scale costs.

Private Cloud: Operated for an organization. It may be managed by the organization or a third party and may exist on premise or off premise. A private cloud is an offering of cloud computing on private sector.

Public Cloud.: The main cloud computing model. Public cloud is hosted, operated and managed by a third-party vendor from one or more data centers. The service is offered to multiple customers, which is called multiple tenants over a common infrastructure.

Service Delivery: Cloud offerings are typically categorized as Infrastructure as a Service (IaaS), Platform as a Service (PaaS), and Software as a Service (SaaS). These are three main service delivery models in cloud computing.

ENDNOTES

[1] http://www.spotcloud.com

[2] http://aws.amazon.com/ec2/spot-instances

Chapter 4
Standardization

ABSTRACT

The importance of cloud computing standards is the same as the World Wide Web standardization. There are plenty of prevalent standards around cloud computing that make different aspects of cloud computing possible. Standardization is a key answer and solution to the main question in this book (i.e., whether cloud computing will survive and remain on IT trends track or not). Standardization will bring interoperability, integration, and portability to the cloud computing landscape. With these three features, the main elements of IT (i.e., computation and data) can move from one cloud provider to another. Therefore, it eliminates vendor lock-in that is one of the barriers in cloud adoption. In addition, cloud interoperability will minimize cloud fragmentation. We need interoperability and portability to achieve cloud federation and to build hybrid cloud. In addition, there is still no de facto standard for moving workloads or data among different clouds. Cloud standardization needs to be addressed at various layers of a cloud infrastructure such as: virtual machine format, data, interface, context, and identity layers. This chapter reviews the emerging standards from the perspective of various organizations and standard bodies.

DOI: 10.4018/978-1-4666-4683-4.ch004

1. INTRODUCTION

Unlike Internet protocols such as Hyper Text Transfer Protocol (HTTP), cloud protocols and APIs are not yet standardized, so currently each cloud provider has its own specific APIs for managing its services. This is the typical state of an industry in its infancy, where each vendor has its own proprietary technology that tends to lock in customers to their services because proprietary APIs make it difficult to change providers.

Standardization plays a key role in all areas of our life. In our IT life, we need it for the software, hardware, data formats, interfaces, and so on; and in our real life we can mention standardization for the house architecture, city organization, university structure, etc. In this chapter, we will review the emerging standards that make cloud computing possible.

Standards make the Internet go around, and by extension they are important to cloud computing. Standards are what make it possible to connect to the cloud. The current state of cloud computing is comparable to the nascent Internet. According to Institute of Electrical and Electronics Engineers (IEEE), cloud computing is primed for explosive growth, but "without a flexible, common framework for interoperability, innovation could become stifled, leaving users with a siloed ecosystem," the organization warns in a statement.

As cloud standards emerge, demonstrations of interoperability, integration and portability are important to show the value of standardization. In a more detailed view, cloud standardization need to be addressed at virtual machine format, data, interface, context, and identity layers.

A plethora of organizations, industries, companies and countries are working to standardize cloud computing. Among the continents, European Commission's digital agenda has put interoperability and standards at the forefront of the cloud computing agenda. In the US, National Institute of Standards and Technology (NIST) and IEEE have more importance than other standard bodies for cloud computing. International standardization efforts will have a huge impact on cloud computing. Open specifications are a key in creating competitive and flourishing markets that deliver what customers need. There are quite a lot of organizations, standard bodies and groups working on cloud standards. In this chapter, we introduce, enumerate, and categorize cloud standardization initiatives and their achievements.

2. STANDARDS LEAD BY THE INDUSTRY

The adoption level of an API make it a standard API in the industry. In this section, we go over Amazon EC2 interface and Open Virtualization Format (OVF) as the current standards in the real world of cloud computing. In addition, we introduce Venus-C project that supports Open Cloud Computing Interface (OCCI) and the Cloud Data Management Interface (CDMI) to have more discussion of standards use.

2.1 Amazon Interfaces

Amazon cloud interfaces are de facto standards in the cloud computing landscape. For instance, the EC2 API is a de facto standard in IaaS cloud while it was not designed as an industry-standard API. They have more impact than formal standards so far as everybody builds an EC2 interface to their IaaS.

The EC2 API was designed based on the needs of Amazon Web Services. Currently, many projects from Eucalyptus and Open-Nebula to OpenStack to enStratus to AWS, implement and use the EC2 APIs. This is due to the suitability of the EC2 API as a de facto standard. Thus, at least in the cloud industry, Amazon is the leader to push their cloud APIs.

In detail, the EC2 API consists of a SOAP API and a query API. Leveraging the SOAP API is not very common among the AWS ecosystem, it is common among the in-house applications. The query API is further divided into query by POST and GET. Thus, infrastructure level operations can be performed by using SOAP, HTTP GET, and HTTP POST.

The problem with Amazon interfaces is that services have different authentication and request signing mechanisms. For example, EC2 has three different versions of authentication.

ElasticFox, boto, jclouds, lib cloud, and Dasein Cloud are all using slightly different variants of EC2 APIs. Some use the HTTP GET while some use the HTTP post. Some use one timestamp format, others use different ones, etc.

2.2 Open Virtualization Format

With the rapid adoption of virtualization, there is a great need for a standard way to package and distribute virtual machines. VMware and other leaders in the virtualization field have created the Open Virtualization Format (OVF).

OVF specification [1] describes an open, secure, portable, efficient and extensible format for the packaging and distribution of software to be run in virtual machines. It is designed to address the portability and deployment of virtual appliances. Thus, OVF enables simplified and error-free deployment of virtual appliances across multiple virtualization platforms.

OVF is a common packaging format for independent software vendors (ISVs) to package and securely distribute virtual appliances, enabling cross-platform portability. By packaging virtual appliances in OVF, ISVs can create a single, pre-packaged appliance that can run on customers' virtualization platforms of choice.

OVF enables efficient, flexible, and secure distribution of enterprise software, facilitating the mobility of virtual machines and giving customers vendor and platform independence. Customers can deploy an OVF formatted virtual machine on the virtualization platform of their choice. With OVF, customers' experience with virtualization is greatly enhanced, with more portability, platform independence, verification, signing, versioning, and licensing terms.

VMware [2] collaborated closely with other virtualization vendors to develop this specification. OVF includes the following features that benefit both customers and solution providers:

1. **Optimized for Distribution:**
   a. Enables the portability and distribution of virtual appliances
   b. Supports industry standard content verification and integrity checking
   c. Provides a basic scheme for the management of software licensing

2. **A Simple, Automated User Experience:**
   a. Enables a robust and user-friendly approach to streamline the installation process
   b. Validates the entire package and confidently determines whether each virtual machine should be installed
   c. Verifies compatibility with the local virtual hardware

3. **Portable Virtual Machine Packaging:**
   a. Enables platform-specific enhancements to be captured
   b. Supports the full range of virtual hard disk formats used for virtual machines today, and is extensible to deal with future formats that are developed
   c. Captures virtual machine properties concisely and accurately

4. **Vendor and Platform Independent:** Does not rely on the use of a specific host platform, virtualization platform, or guest operating system

5. **Extensible**: Designed to be extended as the industry moves forward with virtual appliance technology

6. **Localizable:**
   a. Supports user visible descriptions in multiple locales
   b. Supports localization of the interactive processes during installation of an appliance
   c. Allows a single packaged appliance to serve multiple market opportunities

2.3 Venus-C Project

VENUS-C (Virtual Multidisciplinary EnviroNments USing Cloud Infrastructures) [3] is pioneering project for the European Commission's 7th Framework Programme that draws its strength from a joint cooperation between industry and scientific user communities.

VENUS-C aims to develop, test and deploy an industry-quality, highly-scalable and flexible cloud infrastructure to empower researchers through the easy deployment of end-user services.

VENUS-C takes advantages of interoperability and the current cloud standardization initiatives; this is a good example of using and demonstrating standards in cloud projects. This project has three main focus areas dealing with standards including VM Management (OCCI and OVF), Job Submission (BES) and cloud data storage (CDMI) along with other specifications like the SAGA connector for Azure.

The Engineering Group, as one of the partners of this project, focuses on OVF4ONE component in VENUS-C. In OVF4ONE, OCCI interface accepts rendering in OVF format; Standard management interface for OpenNebula; facilitating scaling, migration of services across OpenNebula and other cloud infrastructures.

Interoperability[4] in VENUS-C has focused on easing migration across different target platforms. Standards implementation for interoperability includes:

1. CDMI proxy and resource provisioning: contribution to EGI's Federated Cloud Test Bed.
2. OGF-BES: demonstrating the relevance of established OGF protocols in cloud infrastructures and identifying possible extensions to OGF-BES.
3. Standards for accounting and billing.
4. OGF and SNIA: exploring interoperability testing.

3. OPEN GRID FORUM

Open Grid Forum (OGF) is a leading standards development organization operating in the areas of grid, cloud and related forms of advanced distributed computing. The OGF community pursues these technologies through an open process for development, creation and promotion of relevant specifications and use cases.

OGF partners and participants throughout the international arena use these standards to champion architectural blueprints related to cloud and grid computing and the associated software development. This work enables the community to pursue the pervasive adoption of advanced distributed computing techniques for business and research worldwide. Organizations throughout the world use the resulting clouds and grids as distributed architectures built on these features to collaborate in areas as diverse as scientific data processing, drug discovery, cancer research, financial risk analysis, visualization and product design.

The OCCI specification (The Open Cloud Computing Interface (OCCI), 2012) set is a product of the OGF. OCCI comprises a set of open community-led specifications delivered through the OGF. OCCI is a general-purpose set of specifications for cloud-based interactions with resources in a way that is explicitly vendor-independent, platform-neutral and can be extended to solve a broad variety of problems in cloud computing. OCCI is a protocol and API for all kinds of management tasks such as deployment, autonomic scaling and monitoring. It is a flexible API with a strong focus on integration, portability, interoperability and innovation while still offering a high degree of extensibility. The current OCCI release is suitable to serve many other models in addition to IaaS, including PaaS and SaaS.

The current OCCI specification set consist of three documents, with others under preparation in the OGF standards pipeline. Future releases of OCCI may include additional rendering and extension specifications.

- **OCCI Core Specification:** The OCCI Core Model defines a representation of instance types which can be manipulated through an OCCI rendering implementation. It is an abstraction of real-world resources, including the means to identify, classify, associate and extend those resources. Through these core and model features, the Open Cloud Computing Interface provides a boundary protocol and API that acts as a service front-end to a providers internal management framework. Service consumers can be both end-users and other system instances. OCCI is suitable for both cases. The key feature is that OCCI can be used as a management API for all kinds of resources while at the same time maintaining a high level of interoperability.

- **OCCI Infrastructure Specification:** An OCCI implementation can model and implement an Infrastructure as a Service API offering by utilizing the OCCI Core Model. The OCCI Infrastructure specification contains the definition of the OCCI Infrastructure extension applicable for use in the IaaS domain. Such an API allows for the creation and management of typical resources associated with an IaaS service. These infrastructure types inherit the OCCI Core Model Resource base type and all of its attributes.
- **OCCI HTTP Rendering Specification:** OCCI HTTP Rendering defines how to interact with the OCCI Core Model using the RESTful OCCI API. The document defines how the OCCI Core Model can be communicated and thus serialized using the HTTP protocol.

OCCI has been successfully mapped and implemented upon the Amazon EC2 API. The work has been carried out by TU Dortmund University in cooperation with the compute and research center GWDG. The implementation uses the rOCCI framework.

4. STORAGE NETWORKING INDUSTRY ASSOCIATION

The Storage Networking Industry Association (SNIA) proposes a formal term for cloud storage, i.e. Data Storage as a Service (DaaS), defined as "delivery over a network of appropriately configured virtual storage and related data services, based on a request for a given service level." SNIA defines CDMI, the functional interface that applications may use to create, retrieve, update, and delete data elements from the cloud.

SNIA has created the Cloud Storage Technical Work Group (TWG) for the purpose of developing SNIA Architecture related to system implementations of cloud storage technology (Cloud Storage for Cloud Computing, 2012). The Cloud Storage TWG's tasks include:

- As the primary technical entity for the SNIA to identify, develop, and coordinate systems standards for cloud storage.
- A comprehensive set of specifications and drives consistency of interface standards and messages across the various cloud storage related efforts.
- Documents system level requirements and shares these with other cloud storage standards organizations under the guidance of the SNIA Technical Council and in cooperation with the SNIA Strategic Alliances Committee.

The SNIA Cloud Data Management Interface (CDMI) specification is a SNIA Architecture standard and will be submitted to the INCITS organization for approval as an ANSI and ISO standard as well. CDMI has a working draft reference implementation available at http://snia.org/cloud.

SNIA announced at SNW Spring 2010 the formal approval of CDMI as a SNIA Architecture Standard. This milestone marks the first industry developed open standard for cloud computing and will allow for interoperable cloud storage implementations from cloud service providers and storage vendors.

In addition, SNIA and OGF have collaborated on a cloud storage for cloud computing whitepaper. A demo of this architecture has been implemented and shown several times. More information can be found at the Cloud Demo Google Group.

5. IETF CLOUD REFERENCE FRAMEWORK

IETF published its Internet-draft on intra-cloud and inter-cloud reference frameworks (Khasnabish et al., 2012) on December 31, 2010. This reference framework documents basic functions or layers to support the general requirements of cloud applications and services. This framework, as it is illustrated in Figure 1, and Figure 2, can be used to standardize the interfaces between the functions or layers. Basically, the cloud framework can be divided into:

- **Four horizontal layers:** Application/ Service Layer (ASL), Resource Control Layer (RCL), Resource Abstract and Virtualization Layer (RAVL), Physical Resource Layer (PRL).
- **One stacked vertical layer to support:** Configuration management, registry, logging and auditing, security management, and service level agreement (SLA) management.

The Application/Service layer defines the requirements of the basic functional entities based on the virtual resources needed to perform any tasks. The tasks are classified according to three services models: IaaS, PaaS, and SaaS. Some cloud services are illustrated as an example of applications, such as:

- Server, desktop, database and VLAN for IaaS
- Development environment and test environment for PaaS
- Business, consumer, network and communication applications for SaaS

The Resources Control layer manages virtual resources, ensuring that the resources are efficient, secure and reliable. With the interface of virtual resources, the layer integrates the resources as a whole supplied to the layer above. The layer has the following responsibilities:

- **Resource security management:** Resources must be accessed and owned by the appropriate user. There are several function modules to fulfill this responsibility, including resource admission control, resource authentication, and authorization control.

Figure 1. Internet-Draft: Cloud reference framework (Khasnabish et al., 2012). Used with permission.

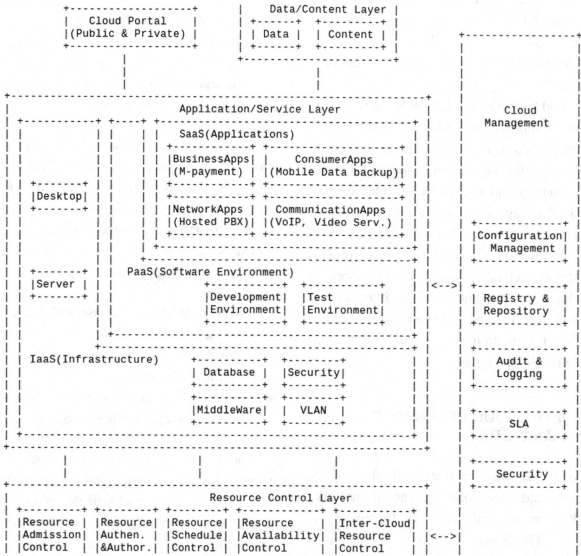

- **Resource schedule control:** This layer manages resources in the form of a resource pool. In a resource pool, the layer balances the virtual resources on physical equipment to achieve higher hardware utilization. Virtual resources can be migrated between physical

equipment if necessary and also can be allocated according to user's priority.

- **Inter-cloud resource control:** Resources in a cloud can be shared with another cloud in some circumstances, so a cloud must control resources in the other cloud and supply cloud services

Figure 2. Internet-Draft: Cloud reference framework (Khasnabish et al., 2012). Used with permission.

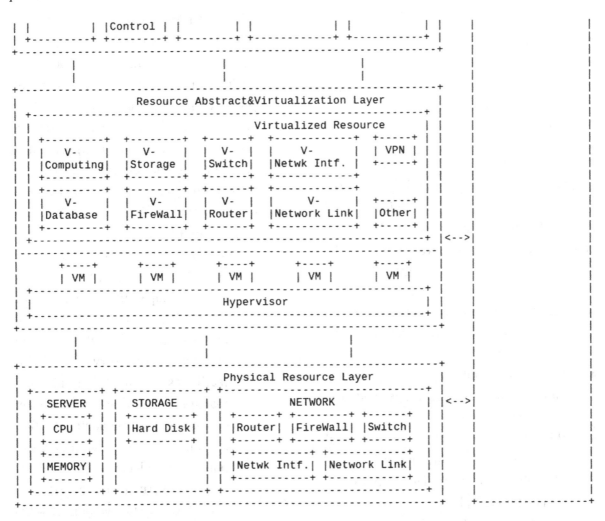

to end users. End users have no need to know where the resources are from.

- **Resource availability control:** This layer supports fault tolerance on resources. It can allocate another copy of resources as a backup, and switch over when some faults raised.

The function of the Resource Abstraction and Virtualization layer is to convert physical resources to virtual resources. Virtual resourc-

es are contained in a resource pool. Resources can be allocated to users from the resource pool and released back into the resource pool when they are no longer needed. Physical resources at the lowest level i.e. Resource Abstraction and Virtualization Layer are the most complex to share among multiple users. There are several hardware details that don't need to be visible to users, so we need a level of abstraction. In fact, these physical resources are abstracted first.

The Physical Resource Layer includes:

- CPU
- Memory
- Hard Disk
- Network Interface Card
- Network Link
- Ports
- Bandwidth

The Cloud Management Layer (CML) provides monitoring and administration of the cloud network platform to keep the whole cloud operating normally. Key features of the Cloud Management Layer include:

- Automatically deploying the cloud system based on the configuration data and policy;
- Real-time monitoring and alerting of cloud status, resource usage, and performance of cloud;
- Reporting and charting of historical events and performance metrics;
- Flexible IT management and operational status displays;
- Authenticating/Authorizing the published cloud service registry;
- Auditing the cloud environment to check whether its running smoothly;
- Controlling the SLA implemented in the cloud system;
- Maintenance concerned with performing repairs, upgrades, and joining new nodes into the Cloud;
- Providing a security mechanism for the Cloud.

Basically, CML includes four functions:

- **Cloud Configuration Management (CCM):** CCM is responsible for establishing and maintaining the consistent performance of the cloud system or product and its functional and physical attributes throughout its life-cycle. It mainly focuses on configuring the cloud system and retrieving the configuration information automatically.
- **Cloud Service Registry and Audit Management:**
  - The Service Registry/Repository provides management and governance capabilities that enable the published cloud service to be authenticated in the cloud system and accessed by service client. It facilitates storing, accessing and managing service information, called service metadata, so that the cloud service can be easily published, selected, invoked, enriched, governed, and reused.
  - Cloud Audit Management (CAM) provides an agent through which cloud providers and authorized consumers automate the Audit, Assertion, Assessment, and Assurance of the cloud infrastructure (IaaS), platform (PaaS), and application (SaaS) environments to reduce the risk. A common interface and namespace can be used by the CAM to facilitate these audit functions.

- **Cloud SLA Management:** Cloud SLA Management (CSM) is used to control the usage and receipt of resources from and by third parties. The strategy of CSM includes the negotiation of the contract and the monitoring of its realization in real time. Thus, CSM encompasses the SLA contract definition (basic schema within QoS parameters), the SLA negotiation, the SLA monitoring, and the SLA enforcement. CSM must also define rate reductions and discounts that are applied if a service provider fails to meet the desired service parameters or does not fulfill an agreement.

- **Cloud Service Security Management:** Cloud Service Security (CSS) provides a set of mechanisms (e.g. IP address filtering, message integrity and confidentiality, private key encryption, dynamic session key encryption, user authentication, and service certification) to protect cloud services and their operating environment from damage.

Inter-Cloud framework provides some Inter-Clouds interfaces such as Provisioning, Signaling, Control, Monitoring, Management, Transport, Security, Naming, Addressing and Translation.

6. DISTRIBUTED MANAGEMENT TASK FORCE (DMTF)

DMTF's Cloud Service Reference Architecture (Interoperable Clouds White Paper,11, November, 2009) as demonstrated in Figure 3 describes key components, such as actors, interfaces, data artifacts, profiles and the interrelationships among these components. This reference architecture is published in Interoperable Clouds White Paper on 11, November, 2009.

The Cloud Management Working Group (CMWG)[5] is developing a set of prescriptive specifications that deliver architectural semantics as well as implementation details to achieve interoperable management of clouds between service requestors/developers and providers. This WG is proposing a resource model that at minimum captures the key artifacts identified in the Use Cases and Interactions for Managing Clouds document produced by the Open Cloud Incubator.

The architecture has three primary actors: Cloud Service Provider, Cloud Service Consumer, and Cloud Service Developer. An organization may simultaneously play the roles of any combination of these actors.

The Cloud Service Provider makes services available to Cloud Service Consumers at agreed service levels and costs. The services may be of any type or complexity. The Cloud Service Provider manages the technical infrastructure required for providing the services and provides billing and other reports to consumers.

The Cloud Service Consumer represents an organization or individual who contracts for services with Cloud Service Providers and then uses those services. The Cloud Service Consumer could be another Cloud Service Provider. The Cloud Service Consumer is responsible for selecting the appropriate services, arranging payment for the services, and performing the administration necessary

Figure 3. Distributed Management Task Force (DMTF): Cloud service reference architecture (Interoperable Clouds White Paper,11, November, 2009). Used with permission

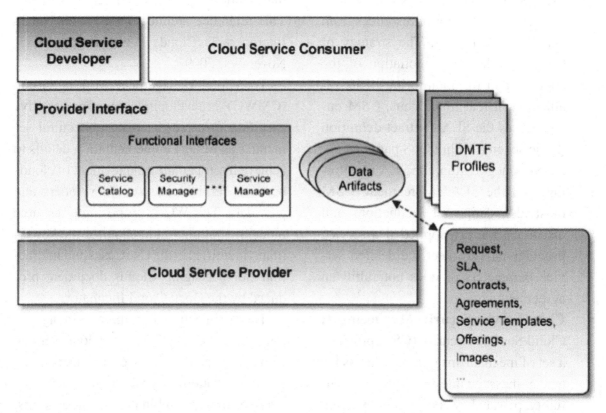

to use those services, such as managing user identities.

The Cloud Service Developer designs and implements the components of a service. The Cloud Service Developer describes the service in a service template. The Cloud Service Developer interacts with the Cloud Service Provider to deploy the service components based on the description in the templates that the Cloud Service Provider may customize before making them available as service offerings.

A provider interface defines how the developer and consumer interact with the provider. This architecture differentiates between

service endpoints that accept and respond to messages over a protocol based on some message exchange pattern (functional interfaces) and the data elements and operations that an interface can support (data artifacts). The interface comprises both functional interfaces and data artifacts.

Functional interfaces are programming interfaces (for example, APIs). Through these interfaces, Cloud Service Developers and Cloud Service Consumers interact with providers to request, deploy, administer, and use services. Examples of likely functional interfaces are:

- **A Service Catalog:** Through which service offerings are offered, requested, and managed;
- **A Security Manager:** Through which the security-related aspects of a cloud are managed;
- **A Service Manager:** Through which instances of deployed services are managed and modified.

Data artifacts are exchanged over the functional interfaces. In this context, a data artifact definition describes the semantic content and the specific format (for example, the XML schema definition that describes the XML payload). Examples of data artifact types include: service requests, service level agreements (SLAs) and other contracts, service templates, service offerings, and images that contain applications. For example, a customizable contract template that includes the customer request, SLA, and security requirements is needed to support the service catalog interface. SLA, security requirements, and resource specifications are used to build offerings.

DMTF profiles are normative specializations or extensions of the interfaces and artifacts, or combinations of them, which are useful in addressing certain contexts, such as those of interest to a security manager or a contract billing administrator. Profiles may be used to simplify the interactions and the potentially complex definitions and negotiation needed to request, manage, and use services. A profile may also specify the use of particular standards that are useful in the profile's target environment and use cases. A profile represents a view into the provider interface.

7. NATIONAL INSTITUTE OF STANDARDS AND TECHNOLOGY (NIST)

NIST is a non-regulatory federal agency whose mission is to promote the USA innovation and industrial competitiveness by advancing measurement science, standards, and technology. NIST has started a program to develop a set of cloud computing standards, with the first results being already published as NIST Cloud Computing Program. NIST is posting its working definition of cloud computing that serves as a foundation for its upcoming publication on the topic. Computer scientists at NIST developed this definition in collaboration with industry and government. It was developed as the foundation for a NIST special publication that will cover cloud architectures, security, and deployment strategies for the federal government.

8. INSTITUTE OF ELECTRICAL AND ELECTRONICS ENGINEERS

IEEE aims to drive cloud computing standards, starting with two development projects related to cloud interoperability. As part of its cloud push, IEEE has started two working groups, P2301 and P2302, which will look at a wide variety of areas. The P2301 Work Group will work on standardizing cloud portability and management, using a number of file formats and interfaces. While the P2302 Work Group will focus on cloud-to-cloud interoperability and federation.

At other side of spectrum, the IEEE Standards Association (IEEE SA) (IEEE Standards Association, 2012) establishes many initiatives to address standardization challenges in the Internet of Things.

It is predicted that 50 to 100 billion things will be electronically connected by 2020. This Internet of Things (IoT) will fuel technology innovation by creating the means for machines to communicate many different types of information with one another. Through IoT all objects in the world will be connected; this has a transformative impact on our lives. The success of IoT depends strongly on standardization, which provides interoperability, compatibility, reliability, and effective operations on a global scale.

Recognizing the value of IoT to industry and the benefits this technology innovation brings to the public, the IEEE Standards Association (IEEE SA) has a number of standards, projects and events that are directly related to creating the environment needed for a vibrant IoT.

This area provides a concise reference point for all things in SA related to IoT, including related fields such as the smart grid, cloud computing, and big data.

9. ORGANIZATION FOR THE ADVANCEMENT OF STRUCTURED INFORMATION STANDARDS

Organization for the Advancement of Structured Information Standards (OASIS) drives the development, convergence and adoption of open standards for the global information society. OASIS as the source of many of the foundational standards in use today sees cloud computing as a natural extension of SOA and network management models. The OASIS

technical agenda is set by members, many of whom are deeply committed to building cloud models, profiles, and extensions on existing standards, including [6]:

- **Security, access and identity policy standards:** OASIS SAML, XACML, SPML, WS-SecurityPolicy, WS-Trust, WS-Federation, KMIP, and ORMS.
- **Content, format control and data import/export standards:** OASIS ODF, DITA, CMIS, and SDD.
- **Registry, repository and directory standards:** vOASIS ebXML and UDDI.
- **SOA methods and models, network management, service quality and interoperability:** OASIS SCA, SDO, SOA-RM, and BPEL.
- **OASIS has founded three cloud specific or extended technical committees:**
  - **The OASIS Identity in the Cloud (IDCloud) TC:** The OASIS IDCloud TC works to address the serious security challenges posed by identity management in cloud computing. The TC identifies gaps in existing identity management standards and investigates the need for profiles to achieve interoperability within current standards. It performs risk and threat analyses on collected use cases and produces guidelines for mitigating vulnerabilities.
  - **OASIS Symptoms Automation Framework (SAF) TC:** Cloud computing in particular exacerbates the separation between consumer-based business requirements and provider-supplied IT responses. The SAF fa-

cilitates knowledge sharing across these domains, allowing consumer and provider to work cooperatively together to ensure adequate capacity, maximize quality of service, and reduce cost.

○ **OASIS Topology and Orchestration Specification for Cloud Applications (TOSCA):** The goal of TOSCA Technical Committee is to substantially enhance the portability of cloud applications and the IT services that comprise them running on complex software and hardware infrastructure. TOSCA will facilitate this goal by enabling the interoperable description of application and infrastructure cloud services, the relationships between parts of the service, and the operational behavior of these services (e.g., deploy, patch, shutdown) independent of the supplier creating the service, and any particular cloud provider or hosting technology. TOSCA will also enable the association of that higher level operational behavior with cloud infrastructure management. This capability will greatly facilitate much higher levels of cloud service/solution portability without lock-in, including:

- Portable deployment to any compliant cloud
- Easier migration of existing applications to the cloud
- Flexible bursting (consumer choice)
- Dynamic multi-cloud provider applications

Ultimately, this will benefit the consumers, developers, and providers of cloud-based solutions and provide an essential foundation for even higher-level TOSCA-based vocabularies that could be focused on specific solutions and domains.

10. THE OPEN GROUP

The Cloud Work Group within Open group[7] exists to create a common understanding among buyers and suppliers of how enterprises of all sizes and scales of operation can include cloud computing technology in a safe and secure way in their architectures to realize its significant cost, scalability and agility benefits. It includes some of the industry's leading cloud providers and end-user organizations, collaborating on standard models and frameworks aimed at eliminating vendor lock-in for enterprises looking to benefit from cloud products and services.

The Open Group Cloud Work Group has established several projects to enhance business understanding, analysis and uptake of cloud computing technologies, including: Cloud Business Use Cases, Cloud Business Artifacts, Cloud Computing Architecture, Service Oriented Cloud Computing Infrastructure, and Security in the Cloud.

Going forward, the group plans to provide a set of tools and templates to support business decisions on cloud computing, including: Cloud Business Use Case Template, Cloud Taxonomy for Buyers, Cloud Taxonomy for Sellers, CC Financial and ROI Templates, CC Business Adoption Strategies, Cloud definitions for business, Cloud Computing Business Scenario.

The Business Scenario technique of TOGAF can be used to gather and represent customer requirements in order for the supply side to better understand real needs of the customer side. The purpose of the Business Scenario is to gather customer views on the motivations for, and key requirements of, the use of cloud computing technologies.

The Cloud Business Artifacts (CBA) project produced "Building Return on Investment from Cloud Computing" whitepaper. This whitepaper presents the initial conclusions from The Open Group on how to build and measure return on investment (ROI) from cloud computing.

11. THE CLOUD STANDARDS CUSTOMER COUNCIL

The Cloud Standards Customer Council (CSCC) is an end user advocacy group dedicated to accelerating cloud's successful adoption, and drilling down into the standards, security and interoperability issues surrounding the transition to the cloud. The council will provide cloud users with the opportunity to drive client requirements into standards development organizations and deliver materials such as best practices and use cases to assist other enterprises.

On April 7th, 2012 CSCC released the Practical Guide for Service Level Agreements (The Practical Guide for Service Level Agreements, 2012). The guide highlights the critical elements of a service level agreement (SLA) for cloud computing and provides guidance on what to expect and what to be aware of when negotiating an SLA. The guide articulates a set of requirements from a consumer's perspective and identifies elements that need

to be addressed via open standards through CSCC's liaison partnerships with key standards development organizations.

12. OPEN CLOUD CONSORTIUM

The Open Cloud Consortium (OCC) supports the development of standards for cloud computing and frameworks for interoperating between clouds; they develop benchmarks for cloud computing; and support reference implementations for cloud computing, preferably open source reference implementations. The OCC has a particular focus in large data clouds. It has developed the MalStone Benchmark for large data clouds and is working on a reference model for large data clouds [8].

13. ENTERPRISE AND NETWORKING PERSPECTIVE

In this section, cloud standardization efforts from Elastra and Cisco companies are presented. As they are reflecting the review of particular companies, there is no proof that other companies will adopt their initiatives to become a de facto standard in enterprise and networking domain.

13.1 Elastra: A Cloud Technology Reference Model for Enterprise Clouds

Elastra is a Cloud Technology Reference Model for Enterprise Clouds (Charlton, 2012). Its main components and functionalities as illustrated in Figure 4 are enumerated as the following:

Figure 4. Cloud technology reference model for enterprise clouds. Used with permission.

- **Facilities & Logistics Management, Organizationally & Geographically Decentralized Software & Hardware:** The basic data center, which is now global and possibly cross-organizational and exposes power and cooling information.
- **Licensing, Security, Identity & Trust:** The control point for compliance and auditing, which adds trust, identity, and licensing.
- **Configuration Management:** Deals with hardware/software/network/storage settings, software packages, and dependencies.
- **Resource Management:** Deals with reservations from a pool of excess capacity in storage, computing, and network.

- **Hyperlinked Models & Metadata:** What uses or contains what other things.
- **System Lifecycles & Management Processes:** When and how can things change.
- **Governance:** Determining who has the authority or responsibility to make changes, and how those changes are made.
- **Constraints & Policies:** Describes how concerns are addressed in the design.
- **Testing, Monitoring & Operations:** Describes how changes are managed and verified.

13.2 Cisco Cloud Reference Architecture Framework

Cisco has developed a cloud reference architecture model (Bakshi, 2012) that portrays the architectural layers connected via APIs and repositories (Figure 5). According to the white paper entitled "Cisco Cloud Computing - Data Center Strategy, Architecture, and Solutions" authored by Kapil Bakshi from Cisco Systems Inc., the framework in a detailed view articulate the following aspects:

1. **Technology architecture:** This consists of three salient domains: network, computing, and storage. This layer hosts all the services that are delivered to a Cloud Service Consumer.

2. **Security layer:** The key takeaway in this layer is that security is blanketed as an end-to-end architecture across all aspects of the framework. Security is considered one of the key challenges to be solved in a cloud framework; hence, it has to be accounted for in a comprehensive sense.

3. **Service orchestration layer:** This is implemented with configuration repository enablers. The configuration repository stores key information such as the service catalogue, an asset inventory, and resource-to-service mapping. This layer is an important layer because it maps the technology components to the service components and serves as a reference point during service provisioning. The service orchestration layer is the glue

Figure 5. Cisco cloud reference architecture (Bakshi, 2012). Used with permission.

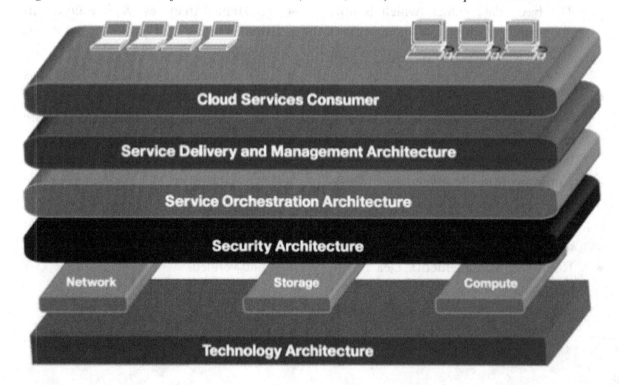

that integrates the lower layers to create a service for delivery.

4. **Service delivery and management layer:** This is the layer where the infrastructure and service management functions take place.

5. **Cloud services consumers layer:** The Cloud Service Consumer-facing layer, usually exposed via a portal-like solution. This is the layer where service is defined, requested, and managed by the Cloud Service Consumer.

The following is a use case scenario where this framework is utilized.

1. The Cloud Service Consumer logs on to a cloud portal and verifies/updates credentials and information.

2. Based on the consumer entitlement, a selected set of services are identified and presented for definition.

3. The end user selects the service for consumptions and triggers a service-provisioning request.

4. Resources are marked as reserved for service, and a new request is created for service provisioning.

5. The individual domains of compute, network, and storage are configured and provisioned with requested security and service level agreements (SLAs), for service delivery.

Hence, this framework provides a working structure to create, define, orchestrate, and deliver IT service via a cloud.

14. CONCLUSION

The importance of cloud computing standards is the same as the World Wide Web standardization. There are plenty of prevalent standards around cloud computing that make different aspects of cloud computing possible.

Standardization will bring interoperability, integration and portability to the cloud computing landscape. With these three features, the main elements of IT, i.e., computation and data, can move from one cloud provider to another. Therefore, it eliminates vendor lock-in that is one of the barriers in cloud adoption. In addition, cloud interoperability will minimize cloud fragmentation. We need interoperability and portability to achieve cloud federation and to build hybrid cloud. Currently, there is practically no way for cloud customers to avoid some degree of lock-in. In addition, there is still no de facto standard for moving workloads or data among different clouds.

In addition, since cloud computing is still in its infancy, there is also a risk that defining how things should work in detail could have an opposite effect and prevent innovation. Furthermore, there are many organizations developing standards but the risk is fragmentation or diffusion, which instead of strengthening cloud computing, may make everybody more watchful and cautious.

On the other hand, an ubiquitous and consistent cloud standard is a must to making cloud an ubiquitous technology and platform paradigm to be present everywhere at any time for everyone. Cloud standardization is a common language among all entities for the communication, negotiation, and agreement.

In order to provide ubiquitous cloud standards they must be based on the Web standards. HTTP is a stateless protocol for the communication on the Web, but it is not perfect for the cloud due to its polling behavior. The next generation of HTTP for cloud computing is called the Extensible Messaging and Presence Protocol (XMPP). XMPP is not based on HTTP, thus there is doubt about its widespread adoption. HTML and Dynamic HTML are standard presentation for the Web, they are also used in cloud computing.

Virtualization is another important dimension in standardization. A few companies like Citrix, VMware, AMD, Dell, HP, IBM, Intel, Broadcom, Cisco, Mellanox, and RedHat are working to advance open virtualization standards through collaborative development model. For that, VMware as the leader of this initiative provided a framework of interfaces as Virtual Machine Hypervisor Interfaces (VMHI) based on its virtualization products to accelerate the development of open standards in a neutral way.

On the security front, Secure Socket Layer (SSL) provides standard encryption and authentication for the communication. Currently, SSL is used in the cloud landscape as well.

REFERENCES

Bakshi, K. (2012). *Cisco cloud computing - Data center strategy, architecture, and solutions*. Cisco Systems Inc.

Charlton, S. (2012). *Cloud computing and the next generation of enterprise architecture*. Retrieved from http://www.slideshare.net/StuC/cloud-computing-and-thenextgeneration-of-enterprise-architecture-cloud-computing-expo-2008-presentation

Cloud Storage for Cloud Computing. (2012). Retrieved from www.snia.org/cloud/CloudStorageForCloudComputing.pdf

IEEE Standards Association. (2012). Retrieved from http://www.standardsinsight.com/ieeenews/iotworkshop-2

Interoperable Clouds White Paper. (2009). Retrieved from http://www.dmtf.org/about/cloud-incubator/DSPIS01011.0.0.pdf

Khasnabish, B., JunSheng, C., SuAn, M., So, N., Unbehagen, P., Morrow, M.,...Yu, M. (2012). *Cloud reference framework*. IETF Internet-draft.

Open Cloud Computing Interface (OCCI). (2012). Retrieved from http://occi-wg.org/

Practical Guide for Service Level Agreements. (2012). Retrieved from http://www.cloudcouncil.org/04102012.htm

KEY TERMS AND DEFINITIONS

Amazon EC2 Interface: A de facto standard in IaaS cloud while it was not designed as an industry-standard API.

Cloud Standardization: Will bring interoperability, integration and portability to the cloud computing landscape. With these three features, the main elements of IT, i.e., computation and data, can move from one cloud provider to another.

Extensible Messaging and Presence Protocol (XMPP): The next generation of HTTP for cloud computing. XMPP is not based on HTTP, thus there is doubt about its widespread adoption.

Interoperability: Will minimize cloud fragmentation. We need interoperability and portability to achieve cloud federation and to build hybrid cloud.

National Institute of Standards and Technology (NIST): A non-regulatory federal agency whose mission is to promote U.S. innovation and industrial competitiveness by advancing measurement science, standards, and technology. NIST has started a program to develop a set of cloud computing standards, with the first results being already published as NIST Cloud Computing Program.

Open Cloud Computing Interface (OCCI): A general-purpose set of specifications for cloud-based interactions with resources in a way that is explicitly vendor-independent, platform-neutral, and can be extended to solve a broad variety of problems in cloud computing.

Open Grid Forum (OGF): A leading standards development organization operating in the areas of grid, cloud, and related forms of advanced distributed computing. The OGF community pursues these technologies through an open process for development, creation, and promotion of relevant specifications and use cases.

Open Virtualization Format (OVF): An open, secure, portable, efficient and extensible format for the packaging and distribution of software to be run in virtual machines.

Organization for the Advancement of Structured Information Standards: Drives the development, convergence and adoption of open standards for the global information society. OASIS as the source of many of the foundational standards in use today sees cloud computing as a natural extension of SOA and network management models.

Secure Socket Layer (SSL): Provides standard encryption and authentication for the communication.

Vendor and Technology Lock-In: Standardization eliminates vendor and technology lock-in that is one of the barriers in cloud adoption.

VENUS-C (Virtual Multidisciplinary EnviroNments USing Cloud Infrastructures): Aims to develop, test and deploy an industry-quality, highly-scalable and flexible cloud infrastructure to empower researchers through the easy deployment of end-user services.

Virtual Machine Hypervisor Interfaces (VMHI): A framework of interfaces based on virtualization products to accelerate the development of open standards in a neutral way.

ENDNOTES

1. http://www.dmtf.org/standards/ovf
2. http://www.vmware.com/it/technical-resources/virtualization-topics/interfaces/ovf.html
3. http://www.venus-c.eu/
4. http://www.venus-c.eu/
5. http://cloud-standards.org/wiki/
6. https://www.oasis-open.org
7. http://www.opengroup.org/
8. http://opencloudconsortium.org/

Chapter 5
Cloud Security

ABSTRACT

Although cloud computing has been widely accepted in the enterprise, and its usage is growing exponentially, security and privacy are big challenges for adoption and survival of cloud computing. Security has two facets in the cloud computing landscape, that is there are pros and there are cons. Security is obligatory for all service delivery models of cloud computing. Additionally, cloud deployment options are another orthogonal dimension to the cloud service delivery models. With the adoption of cloud computing, a large part of network, system, applications, and data will move under provider control. The cloud service delivery model will create several virtual perimeters as well as a security model with responsibilities shared between the customer and the provider. This shared responsibility model will bring new security management challenges to the organization. This chapter discusses these issues and enumerates some initiatives to address them.

1. INTRODUCTION

Cloud computing introduces new dimensions in its computing model such as outsourcing which brings a lot of challenges and makes a great deal of uncertainty about how security at all levels can be achieved. This uncertainty

DOI: 10.4018/978-1-4666-4683-4.ch005

has led managers and chief technical officers to state that security is their number one concern in migrating to cloud computing.

There are specific and unique cloud security issues. From security point of view private clouds are not different from any other private distributed system and a traditional data center. The term 'private cloud' has mainly a marketing value and in some cases could be misleading as it does not follow the pay-per-use business model. On the contrary, public, federated, multi, and hybrid clouds are unique because many security problems originate from inside the cloud system. This is a completely new challenge and a very difficult one to tackle as for any other distributed computing system security problems normally originate from the outside environment.

The basic cloud middleware tools and technologies such as virtualization, Web services, distributed storage, distributed execution, data and computation migration, service definition and implementation, multicore processors have reached industry-standard engineering level. However, cloud computing is not yet widely adopted (Getov, 2012). This is due to several reasons, the most important one is related to security and privacy. There are unique security challenges for enterprises as well. Throughout this chapter we will present security aspects of cloud computing.

2. DEPLOYMENT OPTIONS SECURITY

This section reviews security aspects of clouds' deployment options. Depending on how the cloud infrastructure is operated, it can be categorized as: (a) public, (b) private, or (c) hybrid or federated.

2.1 Private Cloud

In comparison with the traditional IT infrastructure, private clouds do not impose new vulnerabilities, attacks, and threats to the infrastructure security. In addition, they do not require changes in risks specific to this deployment option.

With the implementation of a private cloud, an organization's IT architecture may change; however, its network topology will not change significantly. Moreover, there is no big difference between the traditional IT security model and a private cloud security model. That is the pervasive security considerations, strategies and measures can be kept in place for a private cloud. Thus, they are applicable to a private cloud infrastructure. In addition, the current security tools are necessary for a private cloud and they operate in the same way (Getov, 2012).

Security concerns for a private cloud's IT manager are almost the same as those associated with other distributed systems. However, when this private cloud is hosted by a third party, the security issues facing the customers become very complex and difficult to solve. Although in theory this cloud is still private, the fact that it relies on outsourced resources means that the users are no longer in control of their data. As a result, security remains a major adoption concern, as many cloud service providers (CSPs) put the burden of cloud security on the customer, leading some to explore costly ideas like third party insurance (Getov, 2012).

The security management processes that are relevant to cloud service delivery models in private clouds are enumerated as the following, these functions typically can be managed by IT department or managed services:

- Availability management
- Access control

- Vulnerability management
- Patch management
- Configuration management
- Incident response
- Monitoring system use and access

Hence, organizations that are looking to augment the public cloud for certain use cases can leverage and extend their internal security management practices and processes developed for their internal private cloud services.

2.2 Public Cloud

In private cloud and the traditional IT infrastructure everything is confined to a private network, but in a public cloud services, resources, and data are public to anyone; they are exposed to the Internet and to a shared public network of cloud provider.

The scope of infrastructure security in public cloud is limited to the layers of infrastructure that are outsourced to third-party service providers, that is moved beyond the organization's control and into the hands of service providers. In this deployment option, some security aspects are provided by cloud providers while the rest have to be provided by the customers. Public cloud security should address and incorporate how an organization's existing network topology interacts with public cloud provider's network topology.

Multi-tenancy feature of public clouds introduces data privacy concerns. In a public cloud applications face higher risks than the applications running on a private cloud or on a traditional IT infrastructure. Application-level security requirements are again worsened by cloud and are not specifically caused by it.

Certainly, there is an increased need for secure software development life cycles due to the public facing nature of public cloud applications, and the need to ensure that APIs have been thoroughly tested for security (Getov, 2012).

Network security has been based on security zones such as Intranet versus extranet and development versus production, to isolate and segregate network traffic for better security division. This model is based on exclusion, only individuals and systems in specific roles have access to specific zones. Similarly, systems within a specific tier often have only specific access within or across a specific tier. For instance, systems within a presentation tier are not allowed to communicate directly with systems in the database tier, but can communicate only with an authorized system within the application zone.

Nonetheless, in public clouds the isolation model of network security zones and tiers does not exist. The traditional model of network zones and tiers has been replaced in public cloud computing with security groups, security domains, and virtual data centers. They have logical separation between tiers but are less precise and afford less protection than the formerly established model. For instance, the security groups feature in AWS allows virtual machines to access each other using a virtual firewall that has the ability to filter traffic based on some parameters such as IP addresses, packet types, and ports. On the other hand, domain names based on DNS are used in various networking contexts and application-specific naming and addressing purposes. For example, Google App Engine provides a logical grouping of applications based on domain names such as *testapp.test. google.com* and *prodapp.prod.google.com.*

2.3 Hybrid Cloud

From the security point of view, hybrid, federated, and multi cloud models have the same security requirements as a public cloud. Like a public cloud service, a multi cloud service is never totally at users' realm, part of it is owned or operated by a third party which can lead to security concerns. The same security considerations, strategies and measures for public clouds can be used for hybrid cloud models.

The main issue in hybrid, federated, and multi clouds that organizations must consider is interoperability, that is internal and external systems must work together before security issues can be considered. It could be said that a true hybrid cloud is actually quite difficult to achieve when interoperability and security issues are considered. One solution might be a regulatory framework that would allow cloud subscribers to undergo a risk assessment prior to data migration, helping to make service CSPs accountable and provide transparency and assurance.

Specific security issues emerge during dynamic sharing and collaboration across multiple clouds. Particularly, trust, policy, and privacy concerns pertain to multi-cloud models. Some specific security concerns associated with collaboration among heterogeneous clouds include:

- Establishing trust among different cloud providers and secure delegation to encourage collaboration;
- Addressing policy heterogeneity among multiple clouds so that composite services will include effective monitoring of policy anomalies to minimize security breaches;
- Maintaining privacy of data and identity during collaboration.

3. SERVICE DELIVERY MODELS SECURITY

IaaS is the foundation of all cloud service delivery models, with PaaS building upon IaaS and SaaS in turn building upon PaaS, as illustrated in the Cloud Reference Model diagram (Figure 1).

SaaS clouds built upon public IaaS or PaaS clouds have similar characteristics. However, a public IaaS built on a private IaaS (e.g., Salesforce.com) may follow the traditional isolation model, but that topology information is not typically shared with customers. Understanding the relationships and dependencies between cloud computing models is critical to understanding of cloud computing security risks.

In the following, the security management processes that are relevant to cloud service delivery models in public clouds are enumerated:

1. **SaaS:**
    a. Access control
    b. Monitoring system use and access
    c. Incident response

2. **PaaS:** The following are limited to customer applications deployed in PaaS. Provider is responsible for the PaaS platform.

   a. Availability management

   b. Access control

   c. Vulnerability management

   d. Patch management

   e. Configuration management

   f. Incident response

   g. Monitoring system use and access

      1. **IaaS:**

   a. Availability management for virtual instances

   b. Access control (user and limited network)

   c. Vulnerability management (operating system and applications)

   d. Patch management (operating system and applications)

   e. Configuration management (operating system and applications)

   f. Incident response

Figure 1. Cloud Reference Model (Cloud Security Alliance, 2012)[1]. Used with permission.

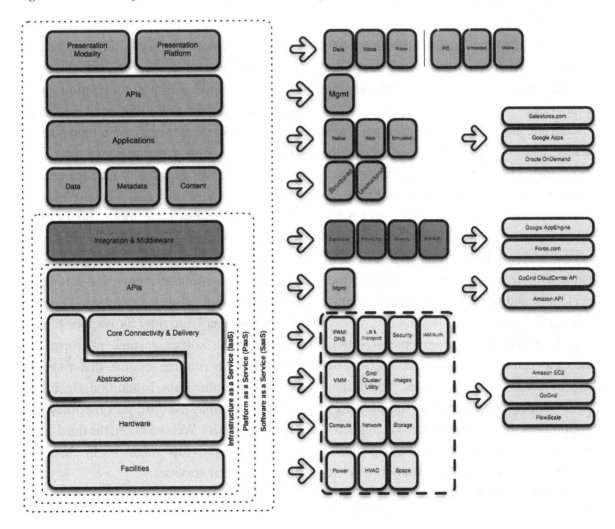

g. Monitoring system use and access (operating system and applications)

3.1 Software-as-a-Service

SaaS is built upon the underlying IaaS and PaaS stacks and provides a self-contained operating environment used to deliver the entire user experience including content, presentation, applications, and management capabilities.

The SaaS model dictates that the provider manages the entire suite of applications delivered to users. Therefore, SaaS providers are largely responsible for securing the applications and components they offer to customers. Customers are usually responsible for operational security functions, including user and access management as supported by the provider.

PaaS and SaaS platforms abstract and hide the host operating system from end users with a host abstraction layer. One key difference between PaaS and SaaS is the accessibility of the abstraction layer that hides the operating system services the applications consume. In the case of SaaS, the abstraction layer is not visible to users and is available only to the developers and the cloud provider's operations staff.

Under a non-disclosure agreement (NDA), customers can request information related to the provider's security practices. This information encompasses design, architecture, development, black- and white-box application security testing, and release management.

In short, SaaS and PaaS customers rely on the provider to offer a secure host platform on which the SaaS or PaaS application is developed and deployed by the provider and the customer, respectively.

3.2 Platform-as-a-Service

PaaS sits atop IaaS and adds an additional layer of integration with application development frameworks, middleware capabilities, and functions such as database, messaging, and queuing that allow developers to build applications upon the platform and whose programming languages and tools are supported by the cloud development stack.

With PaaS, developers can build applications on top of the platform. Providers offer to developers a set of security features including user authentication, single sign-on (SSO) using federation, authorization (privilege management), and SSL or TLS support. Thus, PaaS is more extensible than SaaS at the expense of customer-ready features. This tradeoff extends to security features and capabilities, where the built-in capabilities are less complete but have more flexibility to layer on additional security.

PaaS security includes security of the PaaS platform, i.e. runtime engine, and security of customer applications deployed on a PaaS platform. PaaS provider is responsible for securing the software stack platform that includes the runtime engine that runs the customer applications. In addition, since PaaS applications may use third-party applications, components, or Web services, the third-party application provider might be in charge of securing their services.

Providers are reluctant to share information pertaining to platform security using the argument that such security information could provide an advantage for hackers. However, customers should demand transparency from providers and seek information necessary to perform risk assessment and ongoing security management.

From the host security perspective, PaaS users are given indirect access to the host abstraction layer in the form of a PaaS API that in turn interacts with the host abstraction layer.

Currently, there is no PaaS security management standard; providers have unique security models, and security features vary from provider to provider. For example, with the Google App Engine a developer using Python or Java can configure the user profile and select HTTPs as a transport protocol. Similarly, Force.com offers an Apex API to configure security parameters, manipulate various runtime configurations, and assign certain TCP ports for application-to-application connection-type interactions using Apex objects.

3.3 Infrastructure-as-a-Service

IaaS includes the entire infrastructure resource stack from the facilities to the hardware platforms that reside in them. It incorporates the capability to abstract resources as well as to deliver physical and logical connectivity to those resources. IaaS provides a set of APIs which allow management and other forms of interaction with the infrastructure by consumers.

In IaaS, customers have full responsibility for securing their applications. Cloud providers do not offer any application security assistance to users other than basic guidance and features such as firewall policy that may affect the application's communications with other applications, users, or services within or outside the cloud. This model requires that operating systems, applications, and content be secured and managed by the consumers.

On the other hand, IaaS users are responsible for securing the hosts provisioned in the cloud. Given that IaaS services employ virtualization at the host layer, host security in IaaS can be categorized as the following:

- **Virtualization software security:** In a public IaaS service, customers do not have access to this software layer; it is managed by the provider only. As a result, its security is offered by the provider as well.

- **Customer guest OS or virtual server security:** The virtual instance of an operating system that is provisioned on top of the virtualization layer and is visible to customers from the Internet, e.g., various flavors of GNU/Linux, Microsoft Windows, etc. Customers have full access to virtual servers.

The integrity and availability of the hypervisor are of utmost importance and are key to guaranteeing the integrity and availability of a public cloud built on a virtualized environment. A vulnerable hypervisor might expose all user domains to malicious insiders. In addition, hypervisors are potentially susceptible to subversion attacks.

4. SECURITY ASPECTS OF CLOUD ANATOMY

The main security challenges in cloud computing have been emerged around the anatomy of cloud computing, that are public, elastic, and distributed nature of cloud computing.

4.1 Public and Outsourcing

In a public, cloud resources, services, and data are public to anyone; they are exposed to the Internet and to a shared public network of cloud provider. In addition, multi-tenancy feature of public clouds introduces data privacy concerns.

Reliance on network security has increased due to an increased amount of data and since an increased number of organizational personnel now depend on externally hosted devices to ensure the availability of cloud provided resources. Misconfiguration of network devices affect the availability of cloud resources. According to Boothe, Hiebert, and Bush (2006), several hundred of misconfigurations occur per month.

Attacks are other sources of unreliability, according to Boothe, Hiebert, and Bush (2006), attacks occur fewer than 100 times per month. However, with the rise of cloud computing, the number of attacks will increase; since as the use of cloud computing increases, the availability of cloud-based resources increases in value to customers. That increased value to customers translates to an increased risk of malicious activity to threaten that availability.

There are a wide range of attacks for resources on the Internet such as DNS attacks, denial of service (DoS) and distributed denial of service (DDoS) attacks. Although these attacks are not new and are not directly related to cloud computing, the issue with these attacks and cloud computing is an increase in an organization's risk at the network level due to some increased use of resources external to organization's network. For instance, there were DDoS attacks on AWS services (Walmart, 2012), making the services unavailable for hours at a time to AWS users.

Such attacks often originate from infected hosts as it is the case with network DoS. The DoS attack is a real threat in a cloud because of the real potential to access virtually unlimited resources. These attacks can range from repeatedly refreshing Web pages to loading the applications with specific tasks or protocol-specific requests supported by the cloud service.

4.2 Data Security

Data security is the main security challenge in cloud computing. There are several aspects of data security in the cloud: data regulations, data-in-transit, data-at-rest, data-processing including multi-tenancy, data lineage, data provenance, data remanence.

Companies are subject to regulations concerning the way the data they own should be dealt with, particularly important when the cloud adoption implies the disclosure of private, sensitive, and valuable data to the cloud service provider (CSP). There are a few critical questions for cloud users:

- Where will their data be stored?

- In which countries will the infrastructure be located?
- What are the security regulations in those countries?
- Is the data going to be stored in a single physical place or distributed across different sites?
- Are intermediate results of the computation secured/encrypted?
- Do the data storage and computation comply with the requirements expressed by the users?

As with other aspects of cloud computing and security, not all of these data security facets are of equal importance in all topologies, e.g., the use of a public cloud versus a private cloud, or non-sensitive data versus sensitive data. The only data protection technique for which there are recognized standards is encryption.

In some applications it might also be relevant to consider data provenance. Data provenance includes data integrity, and verifies that data is computationally accurate, i.e., the data was accurately calculated. Data integrity is to verify that data has not been changed in an unauthorized manner or by an unauthorized user. This information describes where and when data originated which is the first entry in the list of data lineage. If there is enough information describing where the information originated, the data can be considered as valid. A relevant example is an application that operates with currencies in which case the exchange rate should originate from a trustworthy source.

Data remanence is the residual representation of data that has been in some way nominally erased or removed. This residue may be due to data being left intact by a nominal delete operation, or through physical properties of the storage medium. Data remanence may make inadvertent disclosure of sensitive information possible, should the storage media be released into an uncontrolled environment. In this case, an organization's data can be inadvertently exposed to an unauthorized party.

4.2.1 Data in Transit

An organization's data-in-transit might be encrypted during transfer to and from a cloud provider for higher security, and its data-at-rest might be encrypted. For processing the data in the cloud, an organization's data is definitely not encrypted. Thus, for any application to process data, that data must be unencrypted.

A data-in-transit security vulnerability of Amazon Web Services reported in December 2008 (Percival, 2012), in which there was a flaw in the digital signature algorithm used when making REST query requests to Amazon SimpleDB, to Amazon Elastic Compute Cloud (EC2), and to Amazon Simple Queue Service (SQS) over HTTP.

With data-at-rest, the economics of cloud computing are such that PaaS-based applications and SaaS use a multi-tenancy architecture. In other words, when data processed by a cloud-based application or stored for use by a cloud-based application, is combined with other users' data. It is typically stored in a massive data store such as Google's BigTable.

4.2.2 Data Tagging

Although applications are often designed with features such as data tagging to prevent unauthorized access to commingled data, unauthorized access is still possible through some exploit of an application vulnerability such as Google's unauthorized data sharing [2] between users of Documents and Spreadsheets[3] in March, 2009.

4.2.3 Encryption

Although using encryption to protect data-at-rest might seem obvious, the reality is not that simple. If you are using an IaaS cloud service for simple storage (S3), encrypting data-at-rest is possible and is strongly suggested. However, encrypting data-at-rest that a PaaS or SaaS cloud-based application is using (e.g., Google Apps, Salesforce.com) as a compensating control is not always feasible. Generally, data-at-rest used by a cloud-based application is not encrypted, because encryption would prevent indexing or searching of that data.

The confidentiality risks can be mitigated by using encryption; specifically by using validated implementations of cryptography for data-in-transit. Secure digital signatures make it much more difficult for hackers to tamper with data, and this ensures data integrity.

Key management is very important in the cloud era. Users must isolate the decryption keys from the cloud where the data is hosted, unless they are necessary for decryption, and then only for the duration of an actual decryption activity. If an application requires a key to encrypt and decrypt for continuous data processing, it may not be possible to protect the key since it will be collocated with the application.

Until June 2009, there was no known method for fully processing encrypted data. In June 2009, IBM announced that one of its researchers who has been working with a graduate student from Stanford University had developed a fully homomorphic encryption scheme. This security scheme allows data to be processed without being decrypted. This is a huge advancement in cryptography, and it will have a significant positive impact on cloud computing as soon as it moves into deployment. Earlier work on fully homomorphic encryption [4], e.g. 2-DNF, was also conducted at Stanford University.

Though, the homomorphic scheme has broken the theoretical barrier to fully homomorphic encryption, it required immense computational effort. According to Ronald Rivest, coinventor of RSA encryption scheme, the steps to make it practical will not be far behind. Other cryptographic research efforts are underway to limit the amount of data that would need to be decrypted for processing in the cloud, such as predicate encryption. Predicate encryption is a form of asymmetric encryption whereby different individuals or groups can selectively decrypt encrypted data instead of decrypting all of it.

4.3 Elasticity and Dynamic

The cloud infrastructures harness the power of thousands of compute nodes, combined with the homogeneity of the operating system employed by hosts, means the threats can be increased quickly and easily that is called the velocity of attack in the cloud.

There are many reports of problems with non-aged IP addresses at one of the largest cloud providers. IP addresses are a finite quantity and a billable asset for cloud providers. Cloud providers do not sufficiently age IP addresses when they are no longer needed for one customer. Addresses are usually reassigned and reused by other customers as they become available. The persistence of IP addresses that are no longer in use can present a problem; a customer cannot assume that network access to its resources is terminated upon release of its IP address. There is necessarily a lag time between the change of an IP address in DNS and the clearing of that address in DNS caches. There is a similar lag time between when physical (i.e. MAC) addresses are changed in ARP tables and when old ARP addresses are cleared from cache; an old address persists in ARP caches until they are cleared. This means that even though addresses might have been changed, the old addresses are still available in cache, and therefore they still allow users to reach these supposedly non-existent resources. This type of security issue was likely an incentive for an AWS announcement of the Amazon Elastic IP capabilities in March 2008.

The issue of non-aged IP addresses and unauthorized network access to resources does not only apply to routable IP addresses, but also this issue applies to cloud provider's internal network for customer use and the assignment of non-routable IP addresses (Rekhter, et al., 1996) These resources are used for the management purposes within the cloud provider's network via private address-

ing. Every public or Internet-facing resource also has a private address. Other customers of a cloud provider may not be well intentioned and might be able to reach other customer's resources internally via the cloud provider's network. As reported in The Washington Post, AWS has had problems with abuses of its resources affecting the public and other customers (Amazon: Hey Spammers, Get Off My Cloud!, 2008).

4.4 Distributed

The application or the cloud service is inherently distributed. For instance, this typically happens in manufacturing and business domains, where different organizations interoperate and may to some extent share services or data. In these cases, the current tendency in addressing security and trust is to achieve security-by-obscurity (Getov, 2012), i.e. either the user trusts the CSP or the user owns the cloud itself. In other words, attempts to gain the users' trust are aimed mainly at avoiding the issue by privatizing or embedding the data and services (e.g. private clouds), rather than solving it.

Issues of the same nature also arise in more complex scenarios. Such that the application or the cloud service are inherently distributed. This typically happens in manufacturing and business domains, where different organizations interoperate and may to some extent share services or data. In these cases, the current tendency in addressing security and trust is to achieve security-by-obscurity (Getov, 2012), i.e. either the user trusts the CSP or the user owns the cloud itself. In other words, attempts to gain the users' trust are aimed mainly at avoiding the issue by privatizing or embedding the data and services (e.g. private clouds), rather than solving it.

4.5 Application Security

It has been a common practice to secure applications using perimeter security controls and access management. The cloud-based applications are based on the browser and rely on network technologies.

The Open Web Application Security Project (OWASP) is a 501(c) 3) worldwide not-for-profit charitable organization focused on improving the security of software. Its mission is to make software security visible, so that individuals and organizations worldwide can make informed decisions about true software security risks [5].

Developing cloud-based applications should take into consideration the common threats regarding Web applications such as OWASP's top 10. Of particular importance is the browser used to run the application. As all applications basically are run by the browser and not by the host's OS, it is not surprising that the browser can be seen as an OS for cloud applications. Therefore, the security policy should cover browser maintenance as well.

The DoS attack is a real threat in a cloud because of the real potential to access virtually unlimited resources. These attacks can range from repeatedly refreshing Web pages to loading the applications with specific tasks or protocol-specific requests supported by the cloud service.

The economic denial of sustainability (EDoS) is a specific type of attack for cloud computing. The elasticity of cloud computing allows users to scale servers up and up in order to service request demands. This opens a new avenue of approach for attackers, which originally was labeled an economic denial of sustainability attack by Christofer Hoff in November 2008. This type of attack is directly connected with a DoS attack, but its target is to inflate the cloud services budget [6]. Thus, a lengthy application DoS attack has financial implications due to the pay-per-use business model of cloud.

In short, if your cloud-based service is designed to scale up automatically (which some like Amazon EC2 are), then an attacker can grief you economically by sending a huge number of automated requests that appear on the surface to be legitimate, but are actually fake. Your costs will rise as you scale up, using more and larger servers automatically to service those fake requests. Ultimately, you will reach a point where your costs overtake your ability to pay.

The EDoS concept applies primarily to cloud-based services and not to people who own their own servers, because if you own your own servers and are the target of a DoS attack, you do not immediately and automatically scale your operation up to a larger size, so the attack does not immediately cost you money. It is only when the scaling-up is automated and there is no ceiling that you run the risk of economic damage.

4.6 Managed Security Services (MSSs)

Security-as-a-Service (SecaaS) [7] is relatively new approach to security in the cloud. Securing a cloud system is a complex and time consuming task. Some companies opted to outsource this process and the market experienced a necessity for such security services. A MSS provider (MSSP) assigns security personnel to its clients to administer the security mechanisms, in particular related to cloud services using a pay-per-use model. With this, the customer is in charge of the security policies and it is his responsibility to monitor the efficiency of the services provided by the MSSP.

The idea of security provisioning from the cloud arises as MSSPs considered ways to centralize the service due to the client pool. MSS is not the only factor that leads to the development of the SECaaS. Companies that do not outsource the security provisioning and individual cloud users were still an attractive target and opportunity for cloud security services. Cloud security within the cloud does have a strong advantage while harness the power of the cloud. Furthermore, due to the proliferation of endpoints and their dynamicity, it is attractive to protect the endpoints from within the cloud. A second benefit for this approach is a unified view over the threats, which can lead to better response times in the case of a new type of attack. However, SecaaS cannot achieve complete cloud security provisioning, there are still security measures which must be taken locally by each customer or their MSSP.

Vulnerability management represents the evolution of MSS. In an effort to alleviate the problems related to vulnerable VMs due to the shared environment, client vulnerabilities are managed from the cloud through the use of complex systems such as application firewalls (e.g. between VMs), virtual IDSs, cloud antivirus and VPNs over VMs. A recent study revealed that CloudAV (a cloud anti-virus solution) obtained a 35% improvement over endpoint-residing antivirus solutions (Oberheide, Cooke, & Jahanian, 2008). The centralization of vulnerability management activities could enable interoperation of increasingly complex security measures.

The identity management can be moved into the cloud too with simple adjustments to existing enterprise architectures. Such a move promises to be beneficial for customers because there is a centralized point from where identification requests are managed. This ensures standard compliance, interoperability in federations (using SSO) and removes the complexity of IAAA mechanisms from customers' management.

The SecaaS technology is still evolving with multiple and collective approaches. Some providers offer solutions that require traffic to be directed through their systems, whereas others offer specialized SaaS solutions which can be installed over the services that are already in use from other CSPs.

Currently, SecaaS providers come from two backgrounds. They are either new entrants specializing in niche zones and proposing novel solutions, or well-established anti-malware companies which extend their services in the cloud world. With time, the trust relationship between customers and CSPs on the one side and the SecaaS providers on the other side is expected to improve. This will lead to a proliferation of this type of services and a better penetration of these solutions.

4.7 Risk Governance, Regulatory, SLA, Privacy, Audit

Cloud computing adoption requires a change in approach to security, privacy, governance, regulatory, audit. Service providers and users must address a myriad of security, privacy, governance, and regulation.

Confidentiality, integrity, and availability should be encapsulated in a provider's service level agreement (SLA). In addition, many risks in cloud computing have to be addressed to realize its benefits. It is a huge risk as well as impractical to insure the expensive company data, potential losses from losing major trading or logistical applications are enormous. CSPs should offer greater assurance to reduce the idea that insurance is even needed. One solution might be a regulatory framework that would allow cloud subscribers to undergo a risk assessment prior to data migration, helping to make service CSPs accountable and provide transparency and assurance.

To mitigate data security risks, the first and the most important option is to ensure that any sensitive or regulated data is not placed into a public cloud or you encrypt data placed into the cloud for simple storage only. The confidentiality risks can be mitigated by using encryption; specifically by using validated implementations of cryptography for data-in-transit. Secure digital signatures make it much more difficult for hackers to tamper with your data, and this ensures data integrity.

Network level security issues exist regardless of what aspects of cloud computing delivery services are being used. The primary determination of risk level is related to which deployment model i.e. public, private or hybrid is used. Although some IaaS clouds offer virtual networking zone mechanism, they may not match an internal private cloud environment that performs stateful inspection and other network security measures.

Lastly, auditing process is important to both providers and customers in case of incident response and any digital forensics required for incident analysis.

5. SECURE CLOUD COMPUTING ARCHITECTURE

In this section, a secure cloud computing architecture that is proposed by Open Security Architecture (OSA) (Open Security Architecture, 2012) is described.

OSA provides free frameworks that are easily integrated in applications for the security architecture community. Its patterns are based on schematics that show the information traffic flow for a particular implementation as well as policies implemented at each step for security reasons.

The following description of the proposed cloud computing architecture, as illustrated in Figure 2, envisions the components of cloud computing platforms along with descriptions of elements that make them secure.

Figure 2. Cloud computing model: Open secure architecture (Open Security Architecture, 2012). Used with permission.

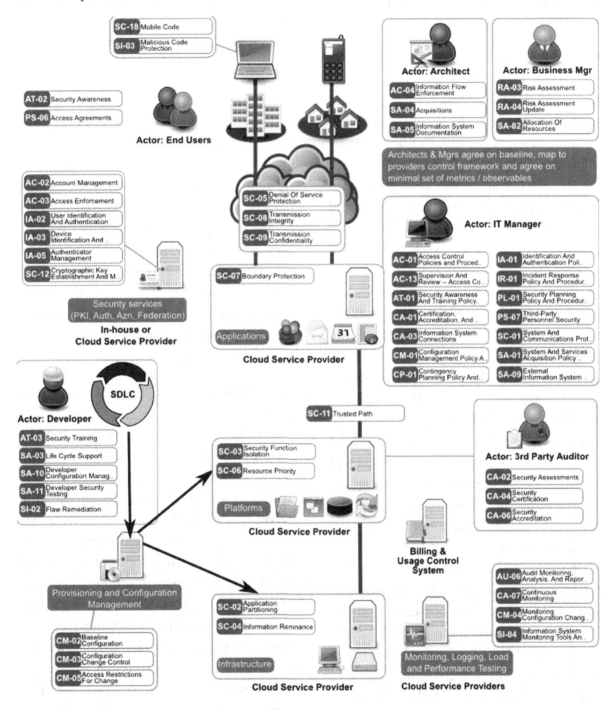

The important entities involved in the data flow are end users, developers, system architects, third party auditors, and the cloud itself.

5.1 End Users

End users need to access certain resources in the cloud and should be aware of access agreements such as acceptable use or conflict of interest. In this model, end user signatures may be used to confirm they are committed to such policies. The client organization should run mechanisms to detect vulnerable code or protocols at entry points such as firewalls, servers, or mobile devices and upload patches on the local systems as soon as they are found. Thus, this approach ensures security responsibilities fall on the end users and on the cloud alike.

However, the cloud needs to be secure from any user with malicious intent that may attempt to gain access to information or shut down a service. For this reason, the cloud should include DoS protection. One way of enforcing DoS protection is done by improving the infrastructure with more bandwidth and better computational power that the cloud has in abundance.

However, in the more traditional sense, it involves filtering certain packets that have similar IP source addresses or server requests. The next issue concerning providing cloud services to end users is transmission integrity. One way of implementing integrity is by using secure socket layer (SSL) or transport layer security (TLS) to ensure that sessions are not being altered by a man-in-the-middle attack. At a lower level, the network can be made secure by the use of the secure Internet protocol (IPsec). Lastly is transmission confidentiality, or the guarantee that no one is listening in on the conversation between authenticated users and the cloud. The same mechanisms mentioned above can also guarantee confidentiality.

5.2 System Architects

System architects write the policies that pertain to the installation and configuration of hardware components such as firewalls, servers, routers, and software such as operating systems, thin clients, etc. They designate control protocols to direct the information flow within the cloud such as router update/ queuing protocols, proxy server configurations or encrypted tunnels.

5.3 Developers

Developers building an application in the cloud need to access the infrastructure where the development environment is located. They also need to access some configuration server that allows them to test applications from various views. Cloud computing can improve software development by scaling the software environment through elasticity of resources. For example, one developer can get extra hard space as an on-demand resource instead of placing a work order and waiting for several days to get permission. Developers may desire extra virtual machines for time-consuming processes such as generating test data or performing data analysis. Also, using more processing power from the cloud can help catch up with development schedule. The cloud also helps developers create multiple evaluation environments for their applications, bypassing the need to incorporate additional security within the application and placing the burden on the cloud provider.

One significant drawback of cloud computing at the moment is its limitation to Intel x86 processor architecture. Even if this may very well change in the future, it is another stumbling block that developers and cloud computing experts need to overcome. Software monitoring may be done by monitoring API calls for server requests. With an architectural model where data is centralized, all eyes are focused in one direction, which implies better monitoring, although ultimately the issue rests with the developers/clients on how much effort will be directed in this regard. As applying security patches is easier with the SaaS approach, as they can be shared with everyone seamlessly rather than finding and patching every machine that has the software installed locally.

5.4 Third Party Auditors

Third party auditors are used by clients and providers alike to determine the security of the cloud implementation. Depending on the level of commitment to security and its usefulness in obtaining a competitive edge, a cloud vendor may choose to submit itself to regular security assessments in an attempt to obtain accreditation. The accreditation process needs to be undertaken every three years. In order to lower the constraints on the cloud vendor, some organizations may implement continuous monitoring of the cloud system.

5.5 Overview

The cloud is the resource that incorporates routers, firewalls, gateways, proxy and storage servers. The interaction among these entities needs to occur in a secure fashion. For this reason the cloud, just like any data center, implements a boundary protection also known as the demilitarized zone (DMZ).

The most sensitive information is stored behind the DMZ. Other policies that run in the cloud are resource priority and application partitioning. Resource priority allows processes or hardware requests in a higher priority queue to be serviced first. Application partitioning refers to the usage of one server or storage device for various clients that may have data encrypted differently. The cloud should have policies that divide the users' view of one application from the backend information storage. This may be solved by using virtualization, multiple processors, or network adaptors.

6. CLOUD SECURITY ALLIANCE

Cloud Security Alliance (Cloud Security Alliance, 2012) is "a not-for-profit organization with a mission to promote the use of best practices for providing security assurance within cloud computing, and to provide education on the uses of cloud computing to help secure all other forms of computing." The Cloud Security Alliance's Cloud Controls Matrix (CCM) is "specifically designed to provide fundamental security principles to guide cloud vendors and to assist prospective cloud customers in assessing the overall security risk of a cloud provider." The purpose of top threats to cloud computing is to provide needed context to assist organizations in making educated risk management decisions regarding their cloud adoption strategies.

Understanding the relationships and dependencies between cloud computing models is critical to understanding cloud computing security risks. IaaS is the foundation of all cloud services, with PaaS building upon IaaS and SaaS in turn building upon PaaS, as described in the Cloud Reference Model diagram (Figure 2). In this way, just as capabilities are inherited so are information security issues and risk. It is important to note that commercial cloud providers may not neatly fit into the layered service models.

Nevertheless, the reference model is important for relating real-world services to an architectural framework and understanding the resources and services requiring security analysis.

It should be clear that there are significant trade-offs to each model in terms of integrated features, complexity versus openness (extensibility), and security. Generally, SaaS provides the most integrated functionality built directly into the offering with the least consumer extensibility, and a relatively high level of integrated security (at least, the Cloud Service Provider bears a responsibility for security).

In the case of SaaS, service levels, security, governance, compliance, and liability expectations of the service and Cloud Service Provider are contractually stipulated, managed to, and enforced. In the case of PaaS or IaaS it is the responsibility of the Cloud Service Consumer's system administrators to effectively manage the same, with some expectation that the Cloud Service Provider will be responsible for securing the underlying platform and infrastructure components to ensure basic service availability and security. It should be clear in either case that one can assign or transfer responsibility but not necessarily accountability.

7. CONCLUSION

Although cloud computing has been widely accepted in the enterprise and its usage is growing exponentially, but still it is the first concern for managers; in particular, they are worried about the security risks. On the other hand, security has two facets in cloud computing landscape, that is there are pros and there are cons as well. The most obvious concern is for privacy considerations. Security is obligatory for all service delivery models of cloud computing. Additionally, cloud deployment options are another orthogonal dimension to the cloud service delivery models.

With the adoption of cloud computing, a large part of network, system, applications, and data will move under provider control. The cloud service delivery model will create several virtual perimeters as well as security model with responsibilities shared between the customer and the provider. This shared responsibility model will bring new security management challenges to the organization's IT operations staff. Security management is a constant process and will be very relevant to cloud security management.

Technically speaking, virtualization security threats such as VM escape, system configuration drift, and insider threats by way of weak access control to the hypervisor are part of the host level infrastructure security of cloud computing. It is important to understand how the provider is using virtualization technology and the provider's process for securing the virtualization layer. On the other hand, the elasticity of cloud computing introduces new operational challenges from a security management perspective. The operational model motivates rapid provisioning and fleeting instances of VMs.

From end user security point of view, users are responsible for end user security tasks such as security procedures to protect Internet-connected device. Protection measures include use of security software such as anti-malware, antivirus, personal firewalls, security patches, and Intrusion Prevention System (IPS) software on Internet-connected computers. The browser is an operating system in cloud computing, thus browsers have become the ubiquitous operating system for consuming cloud services. Hence, in the best practices cloud consumers take appropriate steps to protect browsers from attacks.

Although in the UberCloud Experiment (Gentzsch & Yenier, 2012b) information security is out of their goals, they have discovered that it is a requirement even for experimentation. Guarding the raw data, processing models and the resulting information is paramount to successful remote HPC. The end-user company (e.g. SME) should start with clearly documenting security and privacy requirements at the beginning of the project. This strongly influences the selection of the resource provider and the HPC experts who will be working on the project. They also recommend NDA's to be signed.

REFERENCES

Amazon: Hey Spammers, Get Off My Cloud! (2008). Retrieved from http://voices.washingtonpost.com/securityfix/2008/07/

Boothe, P., Hiebert, J., & Bush, R. (2006). Short-lived prefix hijacking on the internet. In *Proceedings of NANOG 36*. NANOG.

Cloud Security Alliance. (2012). Retrieved from http://www.CloudSecurityAlliance.org

Gentzsch, W., & Yenier, B. (2012). *HPC experiment - Final report of round 1*. The UberCloud LLC.

Getov, V. (2012). Security as a service in smart clouds - Opportunities and concerns. In *Proceedings of COMPSAC* (pp. 373-379). COMPSAC.

Oberheide, J., Cooke, E., & Jahanian, F. (2008). Cloudav: N-version antivirus in the network cloud. In *Proceedings of the 17th Conference on Security Symposium* (pp. 91–106). Berkeley, CA: USENIX Association. Retrieved from http://dl.acm.org/citation.cfm?id=1496711.1496718

Open Security Architecture. (2012). Retrieved from http://www.opensecurityarchitecture.org/cms/

Percival, C. (2012). *AWS signature version 1 is insecure*. Retrieved from http://www.daemonology.net/blog/2008-12-18-AWS-signature-version-1-is-insecure.html

Rekhter., et al. (1996). *RFC 1918: Address allocation for private internets*. Retrieved from http://tools.ietf.org/html/rfc1918

Walmart. (2012). *Amazon.com hit with denial of service attack*. Retrieved from http://www.techflash.com/seattle/2009/12/

KEY TERMS AND DEFINITIONS

Cloud Security Alliance: A not-for-profit organization with a mission to promote the use of best practices for providing security assurance within cloud computing, and to provide education on the uses of cloud computing to help secure all other forms of computing.

Data Privacy: Multi-tenancy feature of public clouds introduces data privacy concerns.

Dynamic Sharing and Collaboration: Specific security issues emerge during dynamic sharing and collaboration across multiple clouds. Particularly, trust, policy, and privacy concerns pertain to multi-cloud models.

Economic Denial of Sustainability (EDoS): A specific type of attack for cloud computing. The elasticity of cloud computing allows users to scale servers up and up in order to service request demands. This opens a new avenue of approach for attackers, which originally was labeled an economic denial of sustainability attack. This type of attack is directly connected with a DoS attack, but its target is to inflate the cloud services budget.

Homomorphic Encryption: This security scheme allows data to be processed without being decrypted. This is a huge advancement in cryptography, and it will have a significant positive impact on cloud computing as soon as it moves into deployment.

Infrastructure Security: The scope of infrastructure security in public cloud is limited to the layers of infrastructure that are outsourced to third-party service providers, that is moved beyond the organization's control and into the hands of service providers.

Managed Security Services (MSSs): An MSS provider (MSSP) assigns security personnel to its clients to administer the security mechanisms, in particular related to cloud services using a pay-per-use model. With this, the customer is in charge of the security policies and it is his responsibility to monitor the efficiency of the services provided by the MSSP.

Non-Disclosure Agreement (NDA): Under a non-disclosure agreement (NDA), customers can request information related to the provider's security practices. This information encompasses design, architecture, development, black- and white-box application security testing, and release management.

Public Cloud Security: In this deployment option, some security aspects are provided by cloud providers while the rest have to be provided by the customers. Public cloud security addresses and incorporates how an organization's existing network topology interacts with public cloud provider's network topology.

Security Groups: The traditional model of network zones and tiers has been replaced in public cloud computing with security groups, security domains, and virtual data centers. They have logical separation between tiers but are less precise and afford less protection than the formerly established model.

ENDNOTES

[1]   http://www.rationalsurvivability.com/blog/2009/03/update-on-the-cloud-ontologytaxonomy-model/

[2]   http://www.infosecurity-magazine.com/view/570/google-docs-leaks-out-private-data/

[3]   https://developers.google.com/google-apps/documents-list/

[4]   http://crypto.stanford.edu/dabo/papers/2dnf.pdf

[5]   https://www.owasp.org

[6]   http://blog.red7.com/edos-economic-denial-of-sustainability-attacks/

[7]   https://cloudsecurityalliance.org/research/secaas/

Chapter 6
Cloud Computing and Big Data

ABSTRACT

This chapter aims at exploring the intersection of cloud computing with big data. The big data analysis, mining, and privacy concerns are discussed. First, this chapter deals with the software framework, MapReduce™ that is commonly used for performing Big Data Analysis in the clouds. In addition, some of the most used techniques for performing Big Data Mining are detailed. For instance, Clustering, Co-Clustering, and Association Rules are described in detail. In particular, the k-center problem is described while with reference to the association rules beyond the basic definitions, the Apriori Algorithm is outlined and illustrated by some numerical examples. These techniques are also described with reference to their versions based on MapReduce. Finally, the description of some real applications conclude the chapter.

1. INTRODUCTION

Big data has become a buzzword like the situation of cloud computing a few years ago. The term *Big Data* denotes a *large data set* that is a data set with size greater than the capacity of the traditional databases. The large data sets represent a rich source of information. This data comes from everywhere, in particular from the Internet: sensors used to gather climate information, posts to social networks and social media sites, digital pictures and videos, purchase transaction records, and cell phone GPS signals to name a few. This data is big data. The sheer amount of data that is being collected by companies around the world is astonishing especially for business purposes, thus they have a high economic impact.

In addition, a huge amount of big data is generated from research in biology, medicine, and astrophysics to name a few. In 2010,

DOI: 10.4018/978-1-4666-4683-4.ch006

Avanade®, a global business technology solutions and managed services provider (www.avanade.com), published the results of a research survey on the business impact of big data. Figure 1 summarizes the top sources of data and highlights that e-mail with 72% is the major source of big data. It is worth nothing that the 543 involved respondents and IT decision-makers (from 17 countries across North America, Europe and Asia Pacific) were allowed to select up to 3 choices.

Figure 2 plots the results of the same survey with reference to the top big data producers. *Management* represents the top producer of big data that mostly concerns information on

Figure 1. Main big data sources. Source: (Avanade, 2010).

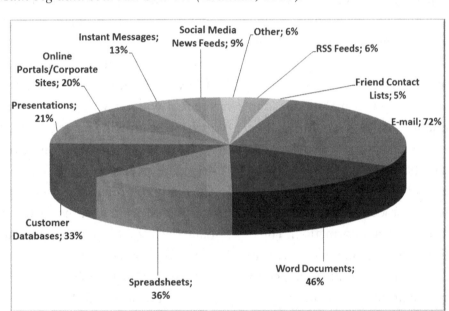

Figure 2. Main big data producers. Source: (Avanade, 2010).

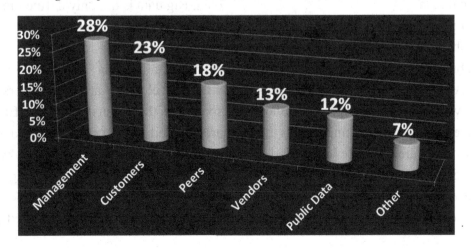

customers, on products, on services, and on activities. The big data stream generated from the public sector is instead expected to increase in the foreseeable future.

However, data in its raw form cannot increase knowledge. It needs to be properly processed in order to extract the relevant information such as structured data, and to acquire knowledge. For instance, the raw data generated from industry has to be properly analyzed by the managers in order to get the relevant information to forecast market, and to react to the customer needs quickly. Thus, the companies reach higher service levels, and as a result they are more competitive.

The higher the data availability is, the higher the quality analysis would be. For instance, in some simulation based applications, the quantity of inputs strongly affect the outcome quality. Some effective tools can be adopted to process the raw data and to consequently extract information. Thus, the availability of a huge amount of data is seen as a great advantage. With reference to the companies interested in making market forecasts the accuracy of the forecasting methods strongly depends on the quantity of the historical data.

Few companies besides the very biggest have been able to successfully mine their data resources, but this is a situation that is rapidly changing. As anticipation of big data opportunities grows, businesses today feel that they can no longer afford to do nothing; now is the time to act if they are not to be left behind.

Most organizations are still in the early stages, and few have thought through an enterprise approach or realized the profound impact that big data will have on their infrastructure, organizations and industries. Companies can no longer afford to ignore the opportunities that simply cannot be met with the traditional data streams and practices. Meanwhile, companies feel forced to act due to the never-ending media hype around big data.

For many industries, particularly government, education and manufacturing, the most immediate opportunities will lie in combining this data with the vast, underutilized reservoir of information from emails, multimedia files, transaction and other disparate sources. This fits with the belief that while much of the media hype has focused on storage and handling, the real winners will be those that can get a grip on the growing range of big data sources.

Nevertheless, big data initiatives introduce competition among IT and business leaders. Currently, big data ideas and opportunities are boundless, and some of the biggest big data ideas come from adopting and adapting ideas from other industries.

The challenge of big data is real, but most organizations do not differentiate big data from traditional data, and nearly use conventional databases as the primary means of handling data. Big data is not only defined in terms of size, but also there are numerous management challenges it poses.

Big data has four dimensions in terms of volume, velocity, variety, and veracity, and spans over these four dimensions. Enterprises are flooded with ever-growing data volume of all types, easily amassing terabytes even petabytes of information (Zheng, Zhu, & Lyu, 2013). This big data can be analyzed to turn terabytes of Tweets created each day into improved product sentiment analysis, or to convert 350 billion annual meter readings to better predict power consumption (Zheng, Zhu, & Lyu, 2013).

Velocity is another aspect of big data. Sometimes a few minutes is too late. For time-sensitive processes such as catching fraud, big data must be used as it streams into enterprises in order to maximize their value. Two examples of the importance of velocity of big data are: scrutinizing 5 million trade events created each day to identify potential fraud; analyzing 500 million daily call detail records in real-time to predict customer churn faster; catching terrorists activities through governments surveillance programs.

Big data is any type of data, structured and unstructured data such as text, sensor data, audio, video, click streams, log files and more. New insights are found when analyzing these data types together. For instance, monitoring 100's of live video feeds from surveillance cameras to target points of interest; exploiting the 80% data growth in images, video and documents to improve customer satisfaction (Zheng, Zhu, & Lyu, 2013).

Out of three business leaders, one does not trust the information they use to make decisions. It is impossible to act upon information if you do not trust it. Establishing trust in big data presents a huge challenge as the variety and number of sources grows. Nonetheless, big data is more than simply a matter of size; it is an opportunity to find insights in new and emerging types of data and content, to make businesses more agile, and to answer questions that were previously considered beyond reach.

Data processing and analyzing can be offered as a service and clouds can provide effective tools for efficiently managing, processing, interpreting and integrating them. This chapter is devoted to explore the benefits and advantages provided by the cloud for the big data management.

2. BIG DATA MANAGEMENT AND DATA CLOUD

Applications and experiments in all areas of science and industry are becoming increasingly complex and more demanding in terms of their computational and data requirements. Some applications generate data volumes reaching hundreds of terabytes and even petabytes. Analyzing, visualizing, and disseminating these large data sets has become a major challenge and data intensive computing is now considered as the "fourth paradigm" in scientific discovery after theoretical, experimental, and computational science.

As scientific and industrial applications become more data intensive, the technology of handling big data have gathered great importance. This necessity has made that applications have seen an increasing adoption on clouds infrastructures. The computing models, system software, programming models, analysis frameworks, and other clouds services need to evolve and accommodate them to face the challenge of big data applications.

The use of cloud technologies is a solution to meet the new data intensive challenges that are not well served by the current supercomputers, grids or compute-intensive clouds. For that, it is required to design new architectures and services for future clouds supporting data intensive computing. Special software and technology are needed to manipulate the mass of raw data in the digital world. Amazon, Google, and Microsoft use cloud computing technology and big data techniques:

- To acquire, record, store, amass, capture, collect, gather, and get big data.
- To handle, manage, manipulate, refine, and process huge data.
- To deal with hundreds of millions of people trying to access enormous volumes of raw data and information.
- To access, retrieve, analyze, examine, interpret, look at, and study information.
- To exchange, share, and transfer information and data.
- To spread data across the globe.
- To automate the command and control of big data centers and thousands of servers.
- To offer energy efficiency.

2.1 Database Management System

A *Database Management System* (DBMS) is a software system to handle an organized collection of intercorrelated data (*Database*-DB). A DBMS allows users to easily manage, process and analyze data and to reduce the presence of redundant information. For instance, it is extremely advantageous in the case in which the content of the large data set is processed and analyzed by the companies with the aim of achieving higher levels of competitiveness.

They can become more reactive to their customer needs by analyzing the data that usually describes the behavior and the requirements of the company. A higher data availability together with software tools contribute to give new perspectives and advantages.

Instead, a *Distributed Database* (DDB) is a DB with storage services distributed on a computer network. A *Distributed Database Management System* (DDBMS) provides the mechanisms for accessing and managing DDBs. Among the most significant features, *fault tolerance* is seen as a priority in this context; consequently, the servers in which data is stored have backup systems. However, a considerable disadvantage consists in a huge number of storage servers. As highlighted in Mathur, Mathur, and Upadhyay (2011), the database deployment to grid and to distributed environments becomes complex since the data needs to be replicated (or partitioned) among the nodes of the infrastructure. For instance, if a new node has to be added to the platform, the data has to be replicated also on it. And, especially in the presence of large databases, the data replication and partitioning are too time consuming processes.

Cloud virtualization together with the possibility to replicate data across large geographic distances guarantees *availability*, *scalability* and *reliability* over time. The cloud platforms are more dynamic and the storage components are provided or deallocated according to the real requirements.

The possibility to outsource the databases represents another great advantage since their management can be often committed to third parties at lower costs, exploiting the economies of scale (Gelogo & Lee, 2012). The DBMSs become cloud services, and with the economies of scale an overall efficiency and reduction in costs will be achieved.

However, beyond the advantages security remains an open issue, crucial in presence of multiple virtual machines that allow different applications to access data. Malicious attacks could potentially damage the database structure. In the work of Gelogo and Lee (2012), a continued control (such as a continued and/or periodic audit) of both the database and of the data accesses is proposed as a solution for this challenge. The system has to monitor, to register and to control each access and to notify the suspicious ones.

3. BIG DATA ANALYSIS

The traditional *business intelligence techniques* are suitable to analyze data and to take a picture of what happened in the past. However, this is not important for businesses. Instead they are interested in analyzing data in order to predict what will happen in the foreseen future, e.g., what type of customers will abandon and enter a specific market. In this context, it becomes significant to use different techniques that allow a predictive analysis on data. *Machine Learning* is the most widely used technique for this purpose. We refer the readers to the book of Alpaydin (2010) for an introduction to this topic. The goal is to understand why machine learning is important for big data. Machine learning is suitable to handle the complexity of dif-

ferent and various data that also comes from different sources. The major advantage of using machine learning for analyzing big data is due to its ability to constantly update the capacity of recognizing patterns as new data become available. Therefore, it is securely more efficient than the traditional techniques to analyze the increasing amount of big data.

In the remainder of this section, the MapReduce framework has been introduced. It has been developed by Google in 2004 as a programming model suitable for parallel processing of a large amount of data (Dean & Ghemawat, 2008) and provides two functions (*Map* and *Reduce*), both defined by the user. They are invoked to elaborate the data and to produce the final result. In particular, *Map* produces an intermediate set of couples of the type *(key, value)* from the input data. Instead, *Reduce* applies the specific operations defined by the user to an intermediate set in order to generate the final result. *Shuffle* is a built-in function that is automatically performed with the aim to "shuffle" the couples *<key, value>* returned by Map.

In particular, Map processes directly the input data and then, it produces a set of couples *<key, value>*. Shuffle properly groups these intermediate couples by *<key>* and returns to Reduce a set of couples *<key, list<value>>*. Finally, Reduce provides the final result.

Below, an illustrative example is described.

A user needs to know the titles of the scientific papers in the DB of a journal that present at least one keyword *key* in the list *kw* of his/her interest. The function Map reads the DB and, for each paper and its keyword *k*, emits a couple *<k, paper.title>*. Shuffle groups these couples by keyword *k* and therefore, returns couples $<k,L>$, where L is the list of titles associated to k. Reduce, for each keyword k of the aggregated couples that is contained in kw, emits couples $<k,L>$. In the following, a pseudo-code is proposed and Figure 3 illustrates it.

Map Input: DB
1. For each paper *pap* in DB:
   a. For each keyword k in *pap.keywords*: emit $<k,pap.title>$.

Reduce Input: kw, $<k,L>$
   1. For each aggregated couple $<k,L>|k\epsilon kw:$ emit$<k,L>$.

Several implementations of this framework are described in literature. For instance, a large document can be divided into X no overlapped portions, and then several copies of the program are started. The approach is based on Master/ Workers paradigm and a copy represents the master, responsible to select the workers that execute a Map process (*Map workers*) and the ones that run a Reduce process (*Reduce workers*). Each Map worker generates the couples $<key,value>$ on its portion and stores them in a local memory. The master accesses these couples, and then it assigns a subset to each Reduce worker for determining the final results. Each Reduce worker stores its final couples in the output file. More details can be found in the scientific paper of Dean and Ghemawat (2008).

Some parallel solutions are often adopted in many research fields since they guarantee the fault tolerance breaking up a task into subtasks, each of them assigned to a different node. When a node fails, its subtask is immediately reassigned to another.

Figure 3. An example

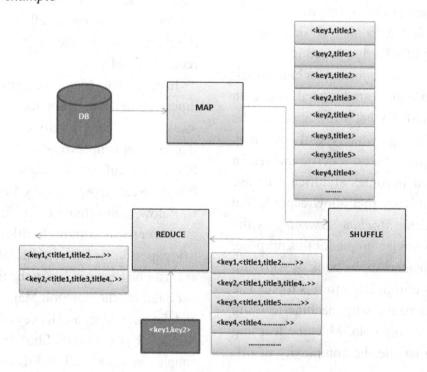

Professionals and developers are referred to Dean and Ghemawat (2008).

4. DISCOVERING AND CLUSTERING FROM DATA MINING

Data Mining denotes the process of analyzing databases with the aim of extracting the relevant and useful information. Several data mining techniques are described in literature. However, in the following, the attention is mainly focused on the two most used data mining techniques since an exhaustive treatment is beyond the scope of this book. Moreover, the interested readers are referred to the book of Han (2005).

One of the most popular data mining techniques is based on the *Association Rules*. It aims to "find" the "hidden" associations among the "items" that belong to a large data set. It is usually adopted in the case of financial applications, payment procedures and purchases. In these cases, each *transaction* denotes the set of items that are bought together and generates a list that contains a lot of valuable information. For instance, in the case of a purchase this list could contain the *price* and the *date*.

In order to introduce the association rules, some basic concepts and definitions are given in the following. However, a detailed study and analysis on this topic can be found in Zhang and Zhang (2002).

Definition: Itemset

An itemset is a collection of one or more items.

Definition: Support of an itemset

Given a set T of τ transactions, the support $sup(I)$ of an itemset I is the number of transactions $T_i \in T$ that contain I, mathematically expressed as:

$$sup(I) = |\{T_i : I \subseteq T_i, T_i \in T\}|.$$

where $|.|$ returns the number of transactions that satisfy the specified condition.

Definition: Frequent Itemset

An itemset I is *frequent* if its *support* ($sup(I)$) is greater or equal to a minimum fixed threshold.

Definition: Association Rule

$L \Rightarrow H$ is an association rule, where L and H are two disjointed itemsets such that $L \bigcap H = \varnothing$.

According to this last definition, it is possible to deduce that an association rule is an implication. For instance, in the case in which the transaction is a purchase, the association rule $L{\Rightarrow}H$ implies that if the item L is bought, then the item H is also bought.

Definition: Rule's Support

The support RS of the rule $L{\Rightarrow}H$ is mathematically defined as:

$$RS(L \Rightarrow H) = \frac{sup(L \bigcup H)}{\tau}$$

Definition: Rule's Confidence

The confidence RC of the rule $L \Rightarrow H$ is mathematically defined as:

$$RC(L \Rightarrow H) = \frac{sup(L \bigcup H)}{sup(L)}$$

Definition: Strong rule

Given a minimum threshold c_{min} of confidence, a *strong rule* is an association rule with a confidence c greater or equal than c_{min}.

The strong rules are the association rules of interest and, in order to generate them, the frequent itemsets have to be found. For this purpose, the *Apriori Algorithm*, described in (Agrawal & Srikant, 1994), is analyzed. It starts generating the 1-itemsets from T. For each 1-itemset i, it computes the related support sup_i and compares it with a minimum threshold t_{min}. If $sup_i \geq t_{min}$, the 1-itemset i is included in the list L^I of the frequent itemsets. Starting from the frequent 1-itemsets, it generates all the 2-itemsets and includes in L^I only the frequent ones. This is iteratively repeated. Therefore, the algorithm ends when all the η − itemsets, generated from a generic iteration η, are not frequent.

This algorithm is based on the *Apriori Principle* such that if an itemset is frequent, then all its subsets are also frequent. This allows to optimize the phase of generating the frequent itemsets. For this purpose, the following numerical example better illustrates these steps.

The set of transactions related to the purchase of four items (a, b, c and d, respectively) is summarized in Table 1. The support

of each item is reported in Table 2. By fixing the minimum threshold t_{min} to 0.25, the 1-itemsets are {a,b,c,d} and since all have a support greater than 0.25, they are put into L^I.

The 2-itemsets can be generated from the frequent 1-itemsets: {{a,b}, {a,c}, {a,d}, {b,c}, {b,d}, {c,d}}. The support of each of these is 0.5, 0.25, 0.25, 0.25, 0 and 0.25, respectively. Then, the itemset {b,d} is not put into L^I.

The 3-itemsets can be generated from the frequent 2-itemsets: {{a,b,c},{a,c,d}} with support equal to 0.25 and 0, respectively. Then, {a,c,d} is discarded.

The algorithm ends and therefore, the list of the frequent itemsets is $L^I =${{a}, {b}, {c}, {d},{a,b},{a,c},{a,d},{b,c},{c,d},{a,b,c}}. For instance, the support of the rule {a,b}$\Rightarrow$c (such as L={a,b} and H={c}) is

$$RS(\{a,b\} \Rightarrow c) = \frac{sup(L = \{a,b\} \bigcup H = \{c\})}{\tau} = 0.25$$

Table 1. Set of transactions

ID	Description
1	{a,b}
2	{a,b,c}
3	{c,d}
4	{a,d}

Table 2. Support of each item

Item ID	Support
a	3/4=0.75
b	2/4=0.5
c	2/4=0.5
d	2/4=0.5

When all the frequent itemsets are generated, the strong rules can be identified. Each of them is individuated by partitioning a frequent itemset I in two subsets (both no empty) L and H, such that $H = I - L$ and by verifying if the rule's confidence $RC(L \Rightarrow H)$ is greater or equal than a minimum threshold c_{min}.

By setting $c_{min}=0.5$ and considering the itemset {a,b,c} of the previous example, the confidence of the rule {a,b}$\Rightarrow${c} can be computed as in the following:

$$RC(\{a,b\} \Rightarrow \{c\}) = \frac{sup(\{a,b,c\})}{sup(\{a,b\})} = 0.5$$

Since the rule {a,b}$\Rightarrow${c} has a confidence equal to $c_{min}=0.5$, it can be considered a strong rule.

Instead, the confidence of the rule {a}$\Rightarrow${b,c} is the following:

$$RC(\{a\} \Rightarrow \{b,c\}) = \frac{sup(\{a,b,c\})}{sup(\{a\})} = 0.33$$

Therefore, the rule {a}$\Rightarrow${b,c} is not strong since its confidence is less than 0.5.

In the Apriori algorithm, the data sets are scanned several times as well as a lot of itemsets are generated with the aim of identifying the frequent ones. This is a time consuming phase especially in the presence of large databases and in literature, several improved versions of the algorithm exist. In particular, in the work of (L. Li & Zhang, 2011), the authors present an improved version of the Apriori algorithm based on MapReduce with the aim of improving its efficiency. Their experiments show that it can be efficiently adopted under cloud computing environments.

Clustering is another data mining technique. It mainly aims to group the data/objects into *clusters* according to their similarities and features. Each cluster contains objects that differ from the objects of the other clusters. In a data mining process, clustering can be used especially for determining the distributions followed by the data and then, for focusing the attention on the more interesting ones. For this purpose, it is usually adopted in a *pre-processing phase* since the individuated clusters can be used for different other purposes such as for data classification. The clustering algorithms usually work on data that are organized into a matrix in which the rows are associated to the objects and the columns represent the related variables.

The k-center problem represents one of the most studied and analyzed clustering problems. In particular, k points are selected from a given set. Each of them represents the *center* of a cluster. The problem consists in assigning each of no selected points to a specific cluster in order to minimize its maximum distance from the related *center*. In literature, several faster MapReduce clustering algorithms have been proposed. In a very general approach (see Ene, Im, and Moseley (2011)), the data points are properly partitioned and each partition is assigned to one machine. Each partition is then clustered and one point is finally selected from each machine. All the selected points are then sent to a unique machine that collects them. Then, these points are clustered and the final result is given in output.

In the presence of large data sets, the attributes/variables related to the objects have to be considerably reduced without damaging the data representation. One of the most used data pre-processing techniques is the *co-clustering* (Hartigan, 1972). It is used in a lot of contexts such as *text mining* and *bio-informatics* and performs a simultaneous clustering along the dimensions of a given matrix. In the case of bi-dimensional matrices, the co-clustering (also known in literature as *Bi-clustering*) simultaneously clusters the rows (objects) and the columns (attributes/variables). Then, it aims to generate a subset of rows with similar features across a subset of columns (or vice versa). Since this technique is successfully adopted in a lot of applications, a distributed framework for co-clustering applied to large matrices and based on MapReduce has been proposed in Papadimitriou and Sun (2008).

5. BIG DATA APPLICATIONS

The importance of using clouds for data management is evident in the presence of high performance applications that analyze a huge amount of data. An example is represented by the scientific research analysis conducted on genetic and neuroimaging data. In fact, it is usually requested to process huge data repositories with the aim of discovering the variabilities between individuals. In this case, big data becomes a very challenging issue especially from the computational point of view. For this purpose, in Tudoran, Costan, Da Mota, Antoniu, and Thirion (2012), the authors describe a cloud platform for addressing this computational problem.

In the HPC landscape, the UberCloud Experiment is paving the way to High Performance Computing as a Service. Hundreds of participants including Intel, Nimbix, Simulia, Amazon, Bull, ANSYS, SGI, San Diego Supercomputer Center, and many others came together to prove the benefits of High Performance Computing as a Service. A similar experiment with the focus on data would address big data challenges of this community. Another example is the sensors of the GPS systems installed on the mobile phones/vehicles that collect data from networks of data centers to be properly processed by specific analysis tools. Other illustrative examples are the in-vehicle sensors that collect the traffic information. This information is sent to cloud data centers in order to generate optimized routes for drivers. In this way, the traffic information is constantly updated and dynamic planners results manage more efficiently the routes of the vehicles.

Some systems have been also developed for storing and accessing large data sets on the clouds by using the wireless networks. In the scientific field, the researchers use the cloud as a tool for running their experiments and their computations on large datasets. In the literature, several examples have been explored. For example, a graph is a data structure that is used for representing the road networks, the relationships and so on. Almost all the analysis procedures on a graph could be efficiently run on a cloud. The applications that estimate the graph diameter and the vertex centrality are other examples. In particular, the vertex centrality can be evaluated by a mathematical metric, i.e., the *Betweenness*.

Given a graph $G = (V, E)$, where V is the set of vertexes and E is the set of edges, the

Betweenness $B(v)$ associated to a vertex $v \in V$ is computed as in the following (Freeman, 1977):

$$B(v) = \sum_{v_1, v_2 \in V | v_1 \neq v_2 \neq v} \frac{\rho_{(v_1, v_2)}(v)}{\rho_{(v_1, v_2)}}$$

where $\rho_{(v_1, v_2)}$ denotes the number of geodetics that connect v_1 to v_2 while $\rho_{(v_1, v_2)}(v)$ represents the number of geodetics that connect v_1 to v_2 and that pass through v. The graph can be direct or undirected. A cloud implementation of a distributed, loosely-coupled graph processing framework in order to measure the Betweenness on large scale graphs is proposed in Redekopp, Simmhan, and Prasanna (2011).

Another application is related to turbulence, a phenomenon that appears in fluids and characterized by a lot of chaotic fluctuations. The traditional modeling approach is not always suitable to take into consideration all these fluctuations. Simulation is then seen as a solution. However, the numerical simulations usually require a considerable computing power. The cloud can provide improved computing power at lower costs, and running the experiments on the clouds, the researchers can also expand the feasible range for their simulations.

Seismology is another application field that can benefit from a cloud. The data related to an earthquake is usually collected, analyzed, and processed in order to identify global events. When an anomaly is identified, the seismic data collected by sensors can be sent to a central cloud system. Specific algorithms are run to investigate the nature of anomaly. For example, *Prestack Kirchhoff Time Migration* algorithm is one of the most used and famous seismic imaging algorithm. In Rizvandi, Boloori, Kamyabpour, and Zomaya (2011), the authors propose a version of the *Prestack Kirchhoff Time Migration* algorithm in order to be run on the cloud.

6. BIG DATA PRIVACY

The privacy concerns impact big data. Big data may include a variety of different data owners, providers and customers, and its information must be aggregated and disseminated inside the context of a formal, understandable agreement with those owners.

The Cloud Security Alliance (CSA) launched the Big Data Working Group to establish best practices for big data security and privacy, and to help businesses and governments to adopt these practices (Cloud Security Alliance, 2012). According to Arnab Roy, a research staff member with Fujitsu Laboratories of America and Big Data Working Group member, "there are fundamental ways in which big data science differs from current technology."

Individuals have serious concerns on personal data and how it is used, they generally do not like surprises. For instance, the ongoing sudden outburst and uproar over leaks of several National Security Agency (NSA) surveillance programs is a good example of this, even though the American public is split over whether the NSA activities are good or bad.

It is fair to say that limited disclosure of personal data usage or no disclosure at all usually creates distrust among consumers, and that is something that big data advocates should strive to avoid. The promises of a data-driven society will fail to resonate with the public if they fear the result will be more unpleasant than ideal perfection. The goal of data usage should be to deliver benefit to both the collector of information that is typically a business or government and the provider, according to Hunter Albright, chief executive officer for North America and global head of consulting for Beyond Analysis, a consumer analytics consulting firm.

As demonstrated by the NSA controversy, and by Facebook's seemingly endless series of privacy mishandling, many organizations are not doing a good job of stating their data-usage intentions, which in some cases (e.g., national security, law enforcement, or general nefariousness) may be intentional.

The growth of big data presents a greater need for data collectors to provide full disclosure about the fate of personal data like what a cloud provide can do with individuals' data. But even that approach will not solve every privacy issue. For instance, if a consumer grants one company permission to use his or her data, what rules, if any, will regulate how that information is shared across multiple companies?

It is also important for data collectors to make it easier for customers to opt in or out of having their information used, like users who subscribed to mailing lists they can use an unsubscribe option to opt out. In collecting data based on the opt-in approach there is a contract between the consumer brand and the consumer in terms of the collection of data. On the other hand, loyalty and rewards programs are a good example of how companies persuade customers to reveal more details about things like shopping habits.

7. CONCLUSION

With Websites and devices gathering petabytes of data on a daily basis, many large corporations today are sitting on a veritable gold mine of information that is just waiting to be analyzed for insights.

This chapter was devoted to emphasize the importance of cloud computing for efficiently managing big data. It introduced some basic concepts and definitions with the aim of providing the readers with a general framework. The theoretical aspects were also supported by some illustrative numerical examples. Some application examples and privacy concerns discussion concluded the chapter.

REFERENCES

Agrawal & Srikant. (1994). Fast algorithms for mining association rules in large databases. In *Proceedings of the 20th International Conference on Very Large Data Bases*. Morgan Kaufmann Publishers Inc.

Alpaydin. (2010). *Introduction to machine learning* (2nd ed.). Cambridge, MA: The MIT Press.

Avanade. (2010). *Global survey: The business impact of big data.* Academic Press.

Cloud Security Alliance. (2012). Retrieved from http://www.CloudSecurityAlliance.org

Dean & Ghemawat. (2008). Mapreduce: Simplified data processing on large clusters. *Communications of the ACM, 51*(1), 107–113. doi:10.1145/1327452.1327492

Ene, Im, & Moseley. (2011). Fast clustering using mapreduce. In *Proceedings of the 17th ACM SIGKDD International Conference on Knowledge Discovery and Data Mining*. ACM.

Freeman. (1977). A set of measures of centrality based on betweenness. *Sociometry, 40*(1), 35–41.

Gelogo & Lee. (2012). Database management system as a cloud service. *International Journal of Future Generation Communication and Networking, 5*(2), 71–76.

Han. (2005). *Data mining: Concepts and techniques.* San Francisco: Morgan Kaufmann Publishers Inc.

Hartigan. (1972). Direct clustering of a data matrix. *Journal of the American Statistical Association, 67*(337), 123–129.

Li & Zhang. (2011). The strategy of mining association rule based on cloud computing. In *Proceedings of 2011 International Conference on Business Computing and Global Informatization (BCGIN)*. BCGIN.

Mathur, Mathur, & Upadhyay. (2011). Cloud based distributed databases: The future ahead. *International Journal on Computer Science and Engineering, 3*(6), 2477–2481.

Papadimitriou & Sun. (2008). Disco: Distributed co-clustering with map-reduce: A case study towards petabyte-scale end-to-end mining. In *Proceedings of Eighth IEEE International Conference on Data Mining*. IEEE.

Redekopp, Simmhan, & Prasanna. (2011). Performance analysis of vertex-centric graph algorithms on the azure cloud platform. In *Proceedings of Workshop on Parallel Algorithms and Software for Analysis of Massive Graphs*. Academic Press.

Rizvandi, B. Kamyabpour, & Zomaya. (2011). Mapreduce implementation of prestack kirchhoff time migration (PKTM) on seismic data. In Proceedings of Parallel and Distributed Computing, Applications and Technologies. PDCAT.

Tudoran, Costan, Da Mota, Antoniu, & Thirion. (2012). A-brain: Using the cloud to understand the impact of genetic variability on the brain. In *CloudFutures*. Berkeley, CA: Microsoft.

Zhang & Zhang. (2002). *Association rule mining: models and algorithms*. Berlin: Springer-Verlag.

Zheng, Z., Zhu, J., & Lyu, M. R. (2013). Service-generated big data and big data-as-a-service: An overview. In *Proceedings of 2013 IEEE International Congress on Big Data (BigData Congress)* (pp. 403–410). IEEE. doi:10.1109/BigData.Congress.2013.60

KEY TERMS AND DEFINITIONS

Big Data: A large data set that is a data set with size greater than the capacity of the traditional databases.

Clustering: A data mining technique that mainly aims to group the data/objects into clusters according to their similarities and features.

Database Management System: A software system to handle an organized collection of intercorrelated data (database).

Data Mining: The process of analyzing databases with the aim of extracting the relevant and useful information.

Distributed Database: A database with storage services distributed on a computer network.

Distributed Database Management System: Provides the mechanisms for accessing and managing the distributed databases.

Chapter 7
Economics of Cloud Computing

ABSTRACT

Economic benefits of cloud adoption are the main drivers and motivations of making cloud as ubiquitous an IT paradigm as it is becoming. The authors believe cloud computing has the potential to transform a large part of the IT industry; this large transformation of IT has big impact on the economy of IT and the global economy. Public cloud computing can avoid capital expenditures because no hardware, software, or network devices need to be purchased. Cloud usage is billed on actual use only and is therefore treated more as an expense. In turn, usage-based billing lowers the barrier to entry because the upfront costs are minimal. In this chapter, the authors describe the business and economics aspects of cloud computing. They then discuss why cloud computing could be economically beneficial by enumerating its characteristics and giving a few examples. This chapter addresses when and how these economic benefits appear.

1. INTRODUCTION

Cloud computing is becoming an ubiquitous technology and platform. When something is or becomes ubiquitous, it is or will be beneficial from different aspects, since it is everywhere at any time for everyone. We may call cloud computing technology, God computing technology as a metaphor of its omnipresent.

On the other hand, economic benefits of cloud adoption are one of the main drivers and motivations of making cloud a ubiquitous IT paradigm as it is becoming. We believe cloud computing has the potential to transform a large part of the IT industry; this large transformation of IT has big impact on the economy of IT, and the global economy.

DOI: 10.4018/978-1-4666-4683-4.ch007

In this chapter, we describe the business and economics aspects of cloud computing. We discuss why cloud computing could be economically beneficial by enumerating its characteristics and giving a few examples. This chapter addresses when and how this economical benefits appear.

2. BUSINESS MODEL

User self-provisioning of resources in virtualized form, economies of scale, pay-as-you-go basis of consumption and payment are important features and characteristics of adopting a cloud model.

The cloud business model brings in substantial or small profit for cloud providers. They can develop money making services, i.e., there are applications where each $1 invested in development pays off $10 in services. Cloud computing's goal is not only to reduce costs but also to make more money with better and better return on investments (ROIs).

Business management is always seeking ways to better capture customer loyalty. For example, selling something that the customer need, but including a hook in the product or service that more or less involuntarily tied the customer to the company. As long as a customer is using the product, she has to keep coming back. Printers need ink cartridges just like as razors need blades. Cloud computing inherently has these business management strategies in itself. When an organization's applications, data, and services move into the cloud gradually that organization will be dependent on the cloud provider offerings.

On the other hand, standardization is an effort to address vendor and technology lock-in and dependency on a cloud provider; hence it seems it is against business management strategies of a cloud provider, but it will bring competition among cloud providers. As a result, since standardization addresses vendor lock-in but provides competition, it is good for the global business management strategies of and global economy of all cloud providers. Thus, more customers will enter to the cloud since there is no vendor lock-in barrier, and providers will provide and guarantee better services to keep their customers up.

Amazon, Microsoft, and Google are frequently dropping prices. The cloud services are not a primary business for any of these companies. Once any of them serve a customer, they have a good chance of holding on to the customer for a long period of time because it is difficult for users to switch cloud service providers.

"The myth is that cloud computing is always cost-effective," said David Linthicum, Chief Technical Officer (CTO) of Blue Mountain Labs, a company that advises businesses on moving to the cloud.

Clouds bill every user of services, including the internal users in private clouds. No one collects the actual money from internal users, but the Chief Information Officer (CIO) has a clear record of how much they would have paid if they were using a public cloud.

2.1 Cost Analysis of In-House Versus Public Iaas Cloud

Art Wittmann, Managing Director of InformationWeek Reports, wrote an article (Wittmann, 2012) entitled "Why Infrastructure As A Service Is A Bad Deal" in InformationWeek magazine, to question the value of

Infrastructure-as-a-Service offerings based on their lack of adherence to Moore's Law; that is while CPU performance and drive storage capacity continue to climb at logarithmic rates, IaaS vendors are not providing those implied cost savings back to their customers.

This article shows that in-house hardware has lower cost than using IaaS services and uses only Amazon storage as illustration. In this article, there are mostly theoretical arguments. Author's argument is that the cost of on-premise storage has dropped a lot over the past five years, much more than S3 and we can take advantage of today's prices every day. From that, he concludes that on-premise is a better model.

Some of the points in the article that IaaS does not make sense in all the situations are right. It is not that the author is wrong that compute and storage can take advantage of cheaper hardware prices today, that is true. Instead, it is not taking into account normal hardware replacement policies and labor costs. Also the author underestimates the labor, cooling, space, and other costs.

The main point is that this article takes into account one aspect of service (bandwidth, storage), scaling it to other levels, looking at it in isolation, and then drawing conclusions about cloud providers. We really need to look at a complete and realistic solution, and compare total costs. In direct hosting, there is a fixed cost for box/rack unit/cage for the month. There may be some variance on electrical bills if a provider meters its users, but in general users have some fairly consistent month-to-month costs.

Amazon S3 service is not always more cost effective than on-premise, one has to look at the scale and growth of S3 storage to recognize that a large user base finds it a compelling value proposition. Amazon has 0.75 trillion objects in storage as of Q411 and S3 is growing at well over 100% per year. This is enormous demand. From that real-world perspective, we conclude:

- First, as a provider If one of your major challenges is just installing enough equipment to keep up with demand, reducing prices significantly is a poor strategy. It is obvious that the market sees what you are offering and the price you are offering it at as attractive. There is no need to reduce price to attract customers.

- Moreover, reducing prices would only increase demand. Since you are having trouble keeping up with the demand you see, why would you want to increase it further, especially as an inability to offer the service would affect all customers and impose market dissatisfaction with your service. This would require Access Control mechanisms like the ones proposed in (Vazquez-Poletti, Moreno-Vozmediano, & Llorente, 2011). Public cloud infrastructures have experimented a great increase in their demand. Therefore, cloud service providers need to choose wisely which services they should accept for provisioning via admission control mechanisms. The impact from faults due to unprovisioned resources has to be minimized and the net income of provisioning has to be maximized at the same time. A proposal for a service model which allows to define easily SLAs has been given in Vazquez-Poletti, Moreno-Vozmediano, and Llorente (2011).

- Third, with such a large user base one should accept the market's judgment that S3 offers a valuable service at its current price points to make it more attractive than the other options, which include on-premise storage.

All in all, in the recent years hardware cost has reduced and in future it will go down further. This is an advantage shared by both technology and business. Whether cloud providers pass on the cost benefit to consumer is a question of business and not technology.

In another study by Kiran Kamreddy, Darden MBA, a product marketing manager at a technology company, pricing of Amazon and Rackspace offerings are compared. They found that the yearly cost was at least more than 7-8 times the cost of maintaining on premise infrastructure. Some findings of that economical research on cloud are as the following:

- IaaS makes more sense when there are economies of scale. For example, the environment that they were looking at had only 150 servers. They also had free licenses from Microsoft for operating system and database servers. These freebies are lost if they move to IaaS. The vendors which they evaluated refused to offer bare bones infrastructure.

- There is not much variability in terms of server usage in the current IT environment. Even by factoring 75% as the most pessimistic usage, the costs of Amazon/Rackspace were to the tune of 6X.

- The server sizes offered by vendors are often restrictive, they are sometimes too small and sometimes too large. For example, Rackspace has only four sizes of server offerings and often they are not exactly met by the usage servers.

- The IT environment has a small team of IT management team, like 6 in total, and they do not see it changing for various reasons, even if they move to IaaS.

- The network and backup costs are considered in the ROI calculations which will even skew the numbers in favor of on premise. Also, the transition costs (training, culture change, etc.) to cloud from existing environments were another considerations which will only add to IaaS costs.

- Since not all applications can be moved to external environment, there is additional overhead in developing and maintaining applications which will talk to private and public environments.

Now let us land in the Google cloud to evaluate network costs. Network cost is huge in cloud computing. If we take a look at the price calculations of Google.com services at Google Apps for Business (2012), we see a bill of $8.2K for storage and $6.5K for network costs. This observation shows that about 50% or more of total cost of operating a cloud is network costs. Miha Ahronovitz, in his blog "The Memories of a Product Manager"[1], wrote an article on the cost comparison between Google and Amazon offerings, and network costs.

If we assume that Google charges a promotion of $0 (zilch) for storage, there is still a charge of $6.5K for network. Charlie Oppenheimer from Matrix Partners has a similar observation, but much more thorough calculation.

The conclusion is that in some cases Amazon (or Google) is better and in others the in-house private cloud is better (Ahronovitz, 2012). As it is illustrated in Figure 1, the deciding factor is data-transfer fees over the network. If workload distribution is flat, choose in-house hosting. Otherwise, if workload distribution is spiky, go to cloud providers. In between these two extremes, where actually every institutional user sits, we have a wide space where the cost of the networking (bandwidth cost) can tilt the balance either way. The cost of the network is the decisive factor, everything else is just a small change.

Also, Amazon Web Services (AWS) offers a Free Tier for Elastic Compute Cloud (EC2) consisting in micro instances and a few given images[2]. Other services such as S3, RDS are included as well.

The other decisive parameter is the performance of a public cloud offering versus a private hosting. In the big data analytics space the rule of thumb that is passed around is that AWS is circa 2.5x more expensive than doing

Figure 1. Cost analysis of public cloud versus in-house services

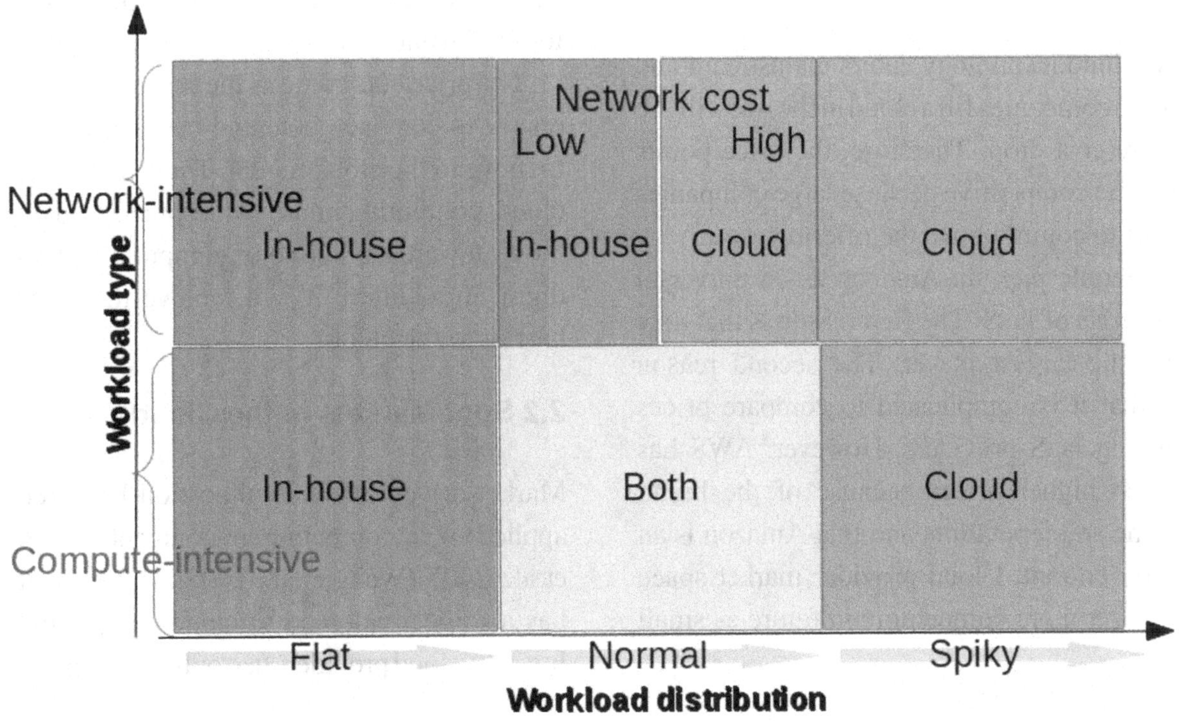

it in a private hosting. While this ignores that AWS offerings are providing quite poor performance for some types of analytic usage patterns or offer very inconsistent performance. As a result, it is not uncommon for a lot of testing to be done on AWS but production systems run in private clouds. AWS can be very expensive for the kind of performance you get out of it.

All in all, these researches highlight the importance of cost analysis and evaluation about when a cloud solution could be economically beneficial and profitable respect to a private hosting. There will be a need to carefully balance all costs and benefits associated with cloud computing, in both the short and the long terms. This is a challenging question for organizations that would like to move towards cloud solutions, whether it will be cost-effective to reduce their costs?

2.1.1 Price Drops

As cloud technology enters mainstream and more companies fill a cloud niche, we will see more cost drop. Therefore, the price points will be competitive because large companies start to commoditize the offering.

People pick up Amazon as an universal example of IaaS. The first reason is that they are the largest player. The second reason is that it is complicated to compare prices among IaaS providers. However, AWS has much higher prices because of the brand name and reputation, and that Amazon is an early entrant. Cloud provider market space will get more competitors in future as small

players emerge, and as a result will lead to cost reduction.

On the other hand, cloud computing price cuts by Google, Amazon, and Microsoft may indicate that businesses are discovering that moving to the cloud does not always save costs.

Service providers like Amazon are likely hearing this from potential customers that: they are losing on deals where people are going to buy hardware and software because it is cheaper than leasing their services. They are reacting by reducing prices to capture market.

Recently, Microsoft dropped the price on its Azure Storage pay-as-you-go service and lowered the price of its six-month storage plan. The cost to use Azure Extra Small Compute has dropped in half. In addition, Google cut the price of its Cloud Storage service and AWS dropped prices on EC2, S3, Relational Database Service, ElastiCache, and Elastic Map Reduce. Amazon highlighted how the new price cuts will particularly reduce costs for big businesses.

The price cuts come as the service providers try to convince potential new customers to move to the cloud model. Thus, that make cloud computing more widespread and to move towards ubiquitous computing paradigm. In addition, it will remove the entry barrier to the cloud.

2.2 Spot Markets in the Cloud

Market driven resource allocation has been applied to grid computing environments (Chun et al., 2005)(Weng et al., 2005). Recently, it has also been adopted to cloud computing. Initially, cloud providers had only a fixed price for each type of service offerings. As clouds approach infinity (Armbrust et al., 2009), this fixed pricing scheme is inefficient when total demand is lower than data center capacity, so that the data center becomes under-utilized. In this case the cloud provider would need an incentive mechanism to encourage customers to submit more requests. On the other hand, when total demand rises over the data center capacity, it is desirable for the cloud provider to incentivize the customers to reduce their demand.

Motivated by this variable data center resource utilization, an incentive mechanism to address this problem is a variable pricing scheme. Thus, with this incentive pricing scheme, cloud service prices may change over time according to resource utilization to rationalize demand. This market economy reshapes the demand by dynamically adjusting the price of services.

More specifically, when total demand is high, the mechanism increases the price to ensure resources are allocated to users who value them the most. On the other hand, when total demand is low, the mechanism lowers the prices and provides incentive for customers to increase their demand.

In December 2009, Amazon EC2 introduced a new instance so-called spot instances to sell its unused data center capacity based on a new market mechanism to offer variable pricing scheme.

2.2.1 Amazon EC2 Spot Service

With the spot instance service, users bid for unused Amazon EC2 capacity (Amazon,2010). Amazon EC2's spot instance mechanism shares many similarities with the standard uniform price auction mechanism. The provider assigns resources to bidders in decreasing order of their bids until all available resources have been allocated or all resource requests have been satisfied. Based on the provider's spot pricing policy, the selling price, i.e. the spot price, is equal to the lowest winning bid, or the selling price depends on the supply and the demand. You get the instance only when your bid exceeds the spot price. A seal-bid uniform price auction is a truthful auction, providing the supply level is adjustable ex post, i.e., after the bids have been decided.

Amazon provides the price history to help customers decide their bids. Figure 2 shows an example of price history graph obtained from Barr (2012).

Currently, Amazon EC2 spot services are available for 8 types of VMs, each VM type has different resource capacity for CPU, memory and disk. Amazon EC2 runs one spot market for each VM type in each availability zone. All spot markets share the free data center capacity, which is the remaining capacity after serving all the guaranteed instances.

3. ECONOMICS BENEFITS OF MOVING INTO THE CLOUD

In this section, we enumerate economics benefits of moving into the cloud. This list focuses on human and financial capitals for economy. With cloud computing end users should not pay for operational costs such as electricity, cooling, human resources, installation, deployment, and configuration, in addition for hidden costs of operating our IT

Figure 2. Amazon EC2 spot instance price history (Barr, 2012)

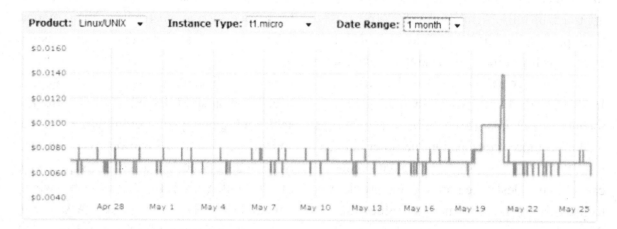

environment such as support, disaster recovery, application modification, security, and data loss insurance.

The growth of cloud computing is predicted on the return on investment that grows. It seems intuitive that by sharing resources to smooth out peaks, paying only for what is used, and cutting upfront capital investment in deploying IT solutions, the economic value will be there.

With public clouds, a user can apply a large cluster of servers to a problem for a few hours or a few days a month at a price that most companies can afford. This is an unforeseen and revolutionary change in the IT business landscape, one that applies a global competition, and its consequences have yet to be fully understood.

3.1 Hardware and IT Staff

In traditional computing model, we use the same hardware for on average of three years or more in corporate environments. Then, there is the labor cost of doing the upgrades.

In addition, most organizations are not really in the IT business, and IT is not in their core strength realm. Their business is business, not IT, thus they cannot really be expected to deliver to the degree of assurance and security that they should be meeting. One of the most basic business values that the cloud will tend to overturn is the perception that major computer resources are expensive and are reserved for a specially trained IT administrators and business intelligence experts that know how to use them.

On the other hand, in large organizations that are not technology focused we can see billions of funds being spent on IT. While IT is not the core business, it gets the core business done, thus it is a competitive advantage. Therefore, we might say cloud does have a place in IT budget of enterprises and organizations. The questions are around what level of risk do you wish to assume for your IT needs: 'in-house' or 'outsource'.

Unless your business IT footprint is large enough to allow for appropriate investment, your security and IT operations costs will be out of your needs. In contrast, a public cloud services provider can do exactly that, like a community-service.

Small businesses and startups have faced this decision and have decided against making investments in both people and IT and elected to spend their IT funds with public cloud services, thus leaving IT in the hands of a professional staff they never need to hire or manage. Therefore, on the human resources front, by moving to the cloud, you will rely on fewer staffers.

3.2 Capital Expenditures

Public cloud computing can avoid capital expenditures because no hardware, software, or network devices need to be purchased. Cloud usage is billed on actual use only, and is therefore treated more as an expense. In turn, usage-based billing lowers the barrier to entry because the upfront costs are minimal.

Cloud providers purchase hardware, network equipment, and bandwidth much cheaper than a regular business; this means they would sell it cheap to their customers as well. As a result, if you need more storage, it is just a matter of upping your subscription costs with your provider, instead of buying new equipment. If you need more computational cycles, you need not buy more servers; rather you just buy more from your cloud provider.

3.3 Time to Market

One of the greatest benefits of the cloud is the ability to get applications up and running in a fraction of the time you would need in a conventional scenario. This feature of cloud reduces the time to solutions substantially, therefore from this point of view also cloud computing is economically vital.

Moreover, companies with large batch-oriented tasks can get their results as quickly as their programs can scale, since using 1000 servers for one hour costs no more than using one server for 1000 hours. This elasticity of resources, without paying a premium for large scale, is unprecedented in the history of IT.

According to the UberCloud experiment (Gentzsch & Yenier, 2012c), "end users can achieve many benefits by gaining access to additional compute resources beyond their current internal resources (e.g. workstations)," the most important two are:

- The benefit of agility gained by speeding up product design cycles through shorter simulation run times.
- The benefit of superior quality achieved by simulating more sophisticated geometries or physics, or by running many more iterations to look for the best product design.

3.4 Economies of Scale

The construction and operation of extremely large-scale, commodity-computer data centers at low-cost locations is the key necessary enabler of cloud computing (Armbrust et al., 2009). With the exception of very large enterprises, organizations, or governments, major cloud suppliers can purchase hardware, network equipment, bandwidth, etc. much cheaper than a regular business. For instance, the cost of electricity, hardware, network bandwidth, operations, software, and space is decreased in the factors of 5 to 7 at very large economies of scale. These factors combined with statistical multiplexing to increase utilization compared to a private cloud, meant that cloud computing could offer services below the costs of a medium-sized data center and yet still make a good profit (Armbrust et al., 2009).

In other words, the economies of scale means if you need more computational cycles, more server capacity, or more storage space it is just a matter of upping your subscription costs with your cloud provider, instead of buying new IT equipment.

On the other hand, when a resource gets shared and the volume of service is huge, it will always be better than own infrastructure. The economies of scale of very large-scale data centers combined with "pay-as-you-go" resource usage has recognized the rise of cloud computing.

3.5 Elasticity

Most development projects have a sizing phase during which one attempts to calculate the storage, processing power, and memory requirements during development, testing, and production. It is often difficult to make accurate estimates: underestimation or over-estimation of these calculations is typical. With the flexibility that cloud computing solutions offer, companies can acquire computing and development services as needed and on-demand, which means development projects are less at risk of missing deadlines and dealing with the unknown.

It is now attractive to deploy an innovative new Internet service on a third party's Internet data center rather than your own infrastructure, and to gracefully scale its resources as it grows or declines in popularity and revenue. Expanding and shrinking daily in response to normal diurnal patterns could lower costs even further. Cloud computing transfers the risks of over-provisioning or under-provisioning to the cloud provider, who mitigates that risk by statistical multiplexing over a much larger set of users and who offers relatively low prices due to better utilization and from the economy of purchasing at a larger scale.

4. SPOT PRICING MECHANISM

This section covers the basics of spot pricing mechanism. Spot pricing is all about random variables. Thus, spot price itself is a random variable to customers. Nobody knows if spot price is going to go up or down next, exactly when it will happen and by how much. In this section, we go over the details of a spot pricing algorithm.

In spot market everyone pays the same price. Due to that spot pricing could be one of the easiest to implement dynamic pricing schemes. In order to design spot pricing algorithm, we assume the following variables:

- *SpotPrice* is a spot price
- N: There are N instance slots available for spot instances of some type at some point in time
- *Bids* and M: At the same time, there are M single-instance bids, i.e.

$Bids = [B_1, B_2, ..., B_m]$. We assume this array is sorted as $B_i \leq B_{i+1}$

- The spot pricing algorithm steps are as follows:

- *SpotPrice initialization*: Provider starts with knowing only N and setting some initial spot price.

- *Bids submission:* In response to spot price, customers submit their bids, which cumulatively are a random variable to provider because it cannot know what they will be.

- *SpotPrice recalculation*: Once the bids are in, spot price is recalculated and the cycle continues.

4.1 More Free Instance Slots Than Bids

We assume the number of free instance slots is bigger than the number of bids, i.e. $N \geq M$. In this case, information above is not sufficient for provider to set the spot price; it can vary quite a bit depending on optimization.

In order to maximize the number of running spot instances, the provider would set spot price at or below B_1.

On the other hand, if the provider would like to maximize its revenue, it would set the spot price quite differently, depending on specific values of B_i. For instance, with $N = 10$ if *bids* are $Bids = [1,2,5,50]$, then we have $N \geq M$, so that revenue maximization spot price would be *50*; on the other hand, if *bids* are $Bids = [1,2,5,45,50]$, it would be *45*.

The below algorithm presents a spot pricing algorithm based on revenue maximization pol-icy: def SpotPriceRevenueMaximization(N, Bids): assert len(Bids) <= N, "does not work when the number of bids exceeds N"

Revenue, SpotPrice = max([(sum([p for x in Bids if x >= p]), p) for p in Bids])

return SpotPrice, Revenue The above spot price algorithm for $N = 10$ and the following bids would provide the following *SpotPrice* and *Revenue*:

- With *bids* as $Bids = [1,2,5,50]$, then the function call is

$SpotPriceRevenueMaximization(10, [1,2,5,50])$;

it provides $SpotPrice = 50$ and $Revenue = 50$

- With *bids* as $Bids = [1,2,5,45,50]$, then the function call is

$SpotPriceRevenueMaximization(10, [1,2,5,45,50])$;

it provides $SpotPrice = 45$ and $Revenue = 90$

- With *bids* as $Bids = [1,2,25,45,50]$, then the function call is

$SpotPriceRevenueMaximization(10, [1,2,25,45,50])$;

it provides $SpotPrice = 45$ and $Revenue = 90$

This exercise shows that bids placed on the lower end of the spectrum have a very little chance of getting an instance.

For a bid of *2* to run, spot price must not exceed *2*. Since all users pay the spot price and not their bid, a provider stands to lose quite a bit of revenue if it were to do it. At spot price *45*, revenues are *90*. On the other hand, at spot price *2*, revenues will be only *8*, even though more customers will get their instances.

4.2 More Bids than Free Instance Slots

In case the number of free instance slots is less than the number of bids, i.e. $N \leq M$. Then, bid B_1 cannot be allowed to run; therefore, spot price is going to be greater than B_1. This highlights another weakness of spot pricing from provider's point of view.

For example, with $N = 3$, if bids are $[10, 20, 30, 40]$, spot price with revenue maximization policy is *20* or *30*, both yield a revenue of 60. However, if bids are $[10, 10, 10, 40]$, $[20, 20, 20, 40]$, $[30, 30, 30, 40]$ or even $[39, 39, 39, 40]$, spot price is *40* with only *40* of revenue. What if $B_1 = B_2 = B_3 = ... = B_k$, in this condition none of them can be allowed to run and spot price must be set at a higher level.

With bids as $[40, 40, 40]$, and $N = 2$, spot price cannot be set at or below *40*; as a result despite available slots there will be no spot instances running at all.

Therefore, a provider would benefit from diversity of bids, especially at the low end, and so should potentially encourage it.

4.3 Bids Diversity

A provider can measure degree of correlation between bids and current spot price. We need effective techniques to deliver diverse bids. How could a provider influence bids submitted by users to achieve desired diversity?

One method is through the use of price anchoring. One obvious anchor is a regular price for a specific product. For example, Amazon prices $0.085 per hour for *m1.small Linux/UNIX* in *us-east-1*. Another hook is current spot price.

In Amazon, a single spot price is set for the entire region and each region has two or more availability zones. If a submitted bid exceeds a spot price and requests a specific zone which has no spot capacity, the provider faces a dilemma. There are three mechanisms to handle this dilemma:

- It could raise the spot price for entire region to the level above this bid.
- It could set individual spot prices for each zone instead of each region.
- It could make an exception and let the bid in without getting an instance until capacity becomes available.

Amazon seems to have chosen the latter approach, even though the second approach would have been cleaner but would allow users to match zones between AWS accounts.

5. APPLICATION MIGRATION CONSIDERATIONS

Developers with innovative ideas for new interactive Internet services no longer require the large capital outlays in hardware to deploy their service or the human expense to operate it (see Section 3.1). They need not be concerned about over-provisioning for a service whose popularity does not meet their predictions, thus wasting costly resources, or under-provisioning for one that becomes wildly popular, thus missing potential customers and revenue.

All workloads are not appropriate for cloud hosting. Several parameters and factors should be taken into account in order to evaluate whether to use cloud or physical hosting. It may not make sense to just pick up an existing enterprise application and forklift it to the cloud. Some of these economical parameters that need to be factored in are: (1) time to market (2) how long did it take to order and install those in-house infrastructure? (3) cost-savings from automation.

Additionally, in transition to the cloud old data center centric tools likely will not work very well anymore so users have to explore and deploy cloud centric management and monitoring. Thus, the additional effort to master those tools should be considered as well.

Some applications cost more in a utility pricing model than in direct hosting. Migration to the cloud does come with its own unique challenges related directly to application:

- **Resource consumption:** Now when you move to a full utility model where you are charged for any and all access to resources you open up the door to a resource-promiscuous bad application, particularly ones with large amounts of disk access, to cost you a bundle. You also have some arbitration overhead from the virtualization hypervisor, even where very light in some situations, which adds some brokering overhead to access to the resources. We have observed some not well sorted applications which huge resource access both slowing because of the hypervisor brokerage on access and costing a mint to run because of the large amounts of access being charged for.

- Before you move to a full utility model you may want to take the time to look at the architecture of your application and how it makes use of resources to satisfy your business efforts. If you have a very resource promiscuous application then you may want to consider maintaining some level of physical hosting and colocation, even if it is for a piece of the architecture which is dirtier than the rest.

- **Full cloud resource utilization:** As you pay for a resource usage, application should use the whole resource not a fraction of it. Second, for many applications the AWS instances available are poor matches for workload such that you only really use a fraction of what you are paying for. This can add up to AWS being integer factors more expensive than what you could build yourself, all in.

- **Bad architecture:** There are some applications that are sufficiently badly matched to something like AWS that you really cannot run them there at all.

- **Performance:** AWS can be very expensive for the kind of performance you get out of it.

The costs between cloud or hosted is not a big enough factor alone to justify moving to the cloud. There are lots of hidden advantages and costs. Hidden costs could include support, maintenance, disaster recovery, application modification, security, and data loss insurance. We have to make sure that we understand them all before using or moving to the cloud.

6. CONCLUSION

This chapter went over business, economic, and operational benefits and advantages of cloud computing. Due to these cloud technology is the recent big advancement in the computing landscape.

Cloud computing changes business processes by providing applications, services, and storage out of the box. Reduced cost, automation, flexibility, better mobility, increased storage, and better use of human resources are some of the operational benefits which brings cloud. In the cloud, services are paid incrementally, due to that it is cost effective in the long run.

Nonetheless, cloud advantages are not only in equipment savings, but also they are realized throughout an organization. Economic benefits involve people, hardware, pay-as-you-go model, and time to market. There is a cut in human resources budget by using cloud computing technologies due to reliance on fewer staffers. The same is true for hardware infrastructure, and pay-as-you-use model of payment. They are provided off the shelf and out of the box. Time to market is another benefit of cloud computing in which it greatly brings profit to industries and busi-

nesses faster. This is due to having required services ready for businesses in seconds.

With economies of scale, projects can acquire IT infrastructure like computing and development services on demand and as required. Thus, this means there is no sizing phase to calculate IT infrastructure requirements for computing, storage, and memory for the different phases of a project. In addition, projects are less at the risk of missing deadlines and dealing with the unknown.

All in all, cloud computing is an economic approach to the computer systems. Considering the cloud transformation should be the first priority of managers and stakeholders of information technology systems; whether you are a small shop or a big market chain, or a large international organization, cloud technologies are beneficial to your different departments for different purposes such as marketing, development, etc.

In the UberCloud Experiment (Gentzsch & Yenier, 2012b), each category of users has its own characteristics, requirements, and benefits. End users can achieve many benefits by gaining access to additional compute resources beyond their current internal resources (e.g. workstations), arguably the most important two are: the benefit of agility gained by speeding up product design cycles through shorter simulation run times; the benefit of superior quality achieved by simulating more sophisticated geometries or physics, or by running many more iterations to look for the best product design. Tangible benefits like these make HPC and more specifically HPC-as-a-Service quite attractive.

The Software and Service Provider participants include software owners of all stripes, including ISVs, public domain organizations and individual developers. Using rock-solid software has the potential to be used on a wider scale. For the purpose of this experiment, on-demand license usage has been tracked in order to determine the feasibility of using the service model as a revenue stream.

Application software and service provider participants supported the experiment in multiple ways. Other than contributing their software licenses or services to the experiment, they have been an escalation point for the experts, in case they ran into hurdles they could not cross. The software and service providers started by filling in an online information gathering form to provide information about their software and expertise to the experiment organizers.

Businesses operate around budgets and HPC projects are not any different. Unpredictable costs can be a major problem in securing a budget for a given project. During the first round of the UberCloud Experiment multiple projects ran out of budget and had to terminate before reaching the desired goals confirming unpredictable costs as a roadblock is real.

Unpredictable cost structures originate from not monitoring closely pay per use billing. According to the first round final report automated, policy driven monitoring of usage and billing is essential to keep costs under control. The recommendation is to select a monitoring system early on and do not scale up without configuring it to match your needs.

"Resource providers may find limiting the usage of their resources to a budget to be to their disadvantage. However, since unpredictable costs are a roadblock to implementation of a remote HPC at scale, we believe building this feature into their offering is a wise decision."

"We've noted third party monitoring solutions built over resource provider API's and/or usage report data. Such solutions can be used as long as they satisfy data privacy requirements of the end-user."

In the HPC market, software licensing costs may be connected to usage, such as amount of data processed, CPU core hours used. In such scenarios the monitoring and billing solutions must be flexible enough to monitor and account for the cost of software licenses to be able to provide a complete view of the cost structure.

REFERENCES

Ahronovitz, M. (2012). *The memories of a product manager: Amazon or self-hosted?* Retrieved from http://my-inner-voice.blogspot.it/2012/02/amazon-or-selfhosted.html

Amazon. (2010). *Amazon ec2 spot instances.* Retrieved from http://aws.amazon.com/

Armbrust, M., Fox, A., Griffith, R., Joseph, A. D., Katz, R. H., Konwinski, A., & Zaharia, M. (2009). *Above the clouds: A Berkeley view of cloud computing* (Tech. Rep. No. UCB/EECS-2009-28). EECS Department, University of California, Berkeley. Retrieved from http://www.eecs.berkeley.edu/Pubs/TechRpts/2009/EECS-2009-28.html

Barr, J. (2012). *Amazon ec2 spot price history.* Retrieved from http://aws.typepad.com/aws/2011/07/ec2-spot-pricing-now-specific-toeach-availability-zone.html

Chun, B. N., Buonadonna, P., Auyoung, A., Ng, C., Parkes, D. C., Shneidman, J., & Vahdat, A. (2005). Mirage: A microeconomic resource allocation system for sensornet testbeds. In *Proceedings of the 2nd IEEE Workshop on Embedded Networked Sensors.* IEEE.

Gentzsch, W., & Yenier, B. (2012a). *HPC experiment - Final report of round 1.* The UberCloud LLC.

Gentzsch, W., & Yenier, B. (2012b). *HPC experiment - Final report of round 2.* The UberCloud LLC.

Google Apps for Business. (2012). Retrieved from http://www.google.com/enterprise/apps/business/pricing.html

V'azquez-Poletti, J. L., Moreno-Vozmediano, R., & Llorente, I. M. (2011). Comparison of admission control policies for service provision in public clouds. In K. D. Bosschere, E. H. D'Hollander, G. R. Joubert, D. A. Padua, F. J. Peters, & M. Sawyer (Eds.), *Parco* (Vol. 22, pp. 19–28). IOS Press.

Weng, C., Li, M., Lu, X., & Deng, Q. (2005). An economic-based resource management framework in the grid context. In *Proceedings of the Fifth IEEE International Symposium on Cluster Computing and the Grid* (pp. 542–549). Washington, DC: IEEE Computer Society. Retrieved from http://dl.acm.org/citation.cfm?id=1169222.1169513

Wittmann, A. (2012). *Why infrastructure as a service is a bad deal.* Retrieved from http://www.informationweek.com/cloud-computing/infrastructure/whyinfrastructure-as-a-service-is-a-bad/232601889

KEY TERMS AND DEFINITIONS

Amazon EC2's Spot Instance Mechanism: Shares many similarities with the standard uniform price auction mechanism. The provider assigns resources to bidders in decreasing order of their bids until all available resources have been allocated or all resource requests have been satisfied.

Economies of Scale: When a resource gets shared and the volume of service is huge, it will always be better than own infrastructure.

Over-Provisioning: Cloud computing transfers the risks of over-provisioning or under-provisioning to the cloud provider, who mitigates that risk by statistical multiplexing over a much larger set of users and who offers relatively low prices due to better utilization and from the economy of purchasing at a larger scale.

A Seal-Bid Uniform Price Auction: A truthful auction, providing the supply level is adjustable ex post, i.e., after the bids have been decided.

Spot Markets: Amazon EC2 runs one spot market for each VM type in each availability zone. All spot markets share the free data center capacity, which is the remaining capacity after serving all the guaranteed instances.

Spot Price: Based on the provider's spot pricing policy, the selling price, i.e. the spot price, is equal to the lowest winning bid, or the selling price depends on the supply and the demand. You get the instance only when your bid exceeds the spot price.

Vendor and Technology Lock-In: Standardization eliminates vendor lock-in that is one of the barriers in cloud adoption.

ENDNOTES

[1] http://my-inner-voice.blogspot.it/
[2] http://aws.amazon.com/free/

Chapter 8
Cloud in Enterprises and Manufacturing

ABSTRACT

Cloud computing has the potential to transform a large part of industry and manufacturing. This large transformation will have a big impact on the global economy and business in almost all industries. Industries will produce innovative products and services through this transformation enabled by cloud computing. Cloud computing is well suited to support business processes in any supply chain of manufacturing. With the help of new technologies, manufacturing processes can be done faster than before. A group of collaborators in a manufacturing sector could share their work, collaborate, and communicate through distributed infrastructure and services. In this chapter, the current trend and practice of cloud computing in industry and manufacturing sectors are presented. Then, by exploring the role of cloud computing in industry, the authors envision how cloud computing in these areas will evolve in the future.

1. INTRODUCTION

Collaborative work via innovative distributed computing paradigms among multiple entities and organizations is the key for future business success. We cannot work on the traditional basis of two decades ago when there was not any ICT solution connecting people and offering high performance computing and high quality services via the Internet. Nowadays with the help of new technologies manufacturing processes could be done faster than before; a group of collaborators in a manufacturing sector could share their work, collaborate, and

DOI: 10.4018/978-1-4666-4683-4.ch008

communicate through distributed infrastructure and services; no need to travel.

Cloud computing has the potential to transform a large part of the industry and manufacturing. This large transformation will have big impact on the global economy and business in almost all industries. Industries will produce innovative products and services through this transformation enabled by cloud computing.

Nonetheless, we need to address some barriers which make access to cloud services difficult for industry. The aim is reducing or eliminating these barriers to make cloud services a pervasive technology in industry.

We believe innovative and ubiquitous ICT solutions and services will be applied to all kinds of industries and especially the manufacturing sectors. In this chapter, by exploring the role of cloud computing in industry, we envision how cloud computing in these areas will evolve in the future.

2. EMERGENCE OF CLOUD INDUSTRIALIZATION

Still with high performance computing (HPC) and with the advent of advanced high-end computing systems, most manufacturers such as small and medium businesses (SMBs) are using just their workstations for R&D work (Gentzsch & Yenier, 2012a).

According to the UberCloud experiment[1], "the most severe barriers to HPC adoption of workstation users are: lack of application software, lack of sufficient talent, and cost constraints. Therefore, buying their own high-performance server systems and HPC

software to speed up each simulation run, do more frequent CAE (Computer Aided Engineering) simulation runs, or to analyze larger geometries, finer meshes/more cells, or better physics, are simply out of reach for many companies." HPC in the Cloud solution addresses these requirements and constraints.

In Gentzsch and Yenier (2012a), researchers investigated how breaking the CAE jobs free from the restrictions of the workstation environment and moving them to the cloud could benefit the CAE engineers as well as the CAE software vendors.

According to a Microsoft survey[2], cloud computing and social computing are transforming manufacturing industry value chains. This 2011 survey polled 152 IT and business decision-makers within automotive, aerospace, high-tech, electronics, and industrial equipment manufacturing companies in Germany, France and the United States, with 42.1% respondents from the United States, 30.3% from France and 27.6% from Germany.

According to 48.3% of respondents, the biggest benefit of cloud computing is lowered cost of optimizing infrastructure; this was followed closely by efficient collaboration across geographies (47.7%) and the ability to respond quickly to business demands (38.4%).

In addition, the survey results revealed a need (47.4%) to better integrate collaboration tools with business systems and to improve access to unstructured data and processes (36.2%). Almost 60% predict an industry-wide collaboration that includes manufacturing products and services providers, IT providers, systems integrators and in-house business analysts as most capable of bringing about these improvements.

In brief, according to the survey results, the biggest benefits with cloud computing technology in the order of importance are:

- Infrastructure cost-reduction
- Better collaboration
- Agile response to business demands
- Innovation and strategy improvements
- New business opportunities

In summary, cloud computing is emerging as one of the major enablers for the manufacturing industry to transform the traditional manufacturing business model.

3. INDUSTRIAL TRANSFORMATION TO THE CLOUD

The anatomy and ubiquity of cloud computing make it a key technology to advance and accelerate innovations in industry and manufacturing sectors.

Current IT infrastructure of industries cannot address global trends such as globalization and ubiquity. Instead, cloud computing addresses both IT requirements and marketing objectives of industries. In key areas of manufacturing, such as IT, the key benefits of clouds have been pay-by-the-usage business models, production scaling up and down per demand, and flexibility in deploying and customizing solutions (Xu, 2011).

Other benefits of clouds are:

1. Creating new lines of business
2. Increasing competition
3. Reducing product lifecycle and time to market (example: PING Golf cut its design cycle time by 68% (Gentzsch & Yenier, 2012a))
4. Dynamic and fragmented global supply chains
5. Changing customer demographics
6. Aligning product innovation with business strategy
7. Creating intelligent factory networks
8. Effective collaboration
9. Economic benefits (example: Alcoa reported a 98% cost reduction in product testing (Gentzsch & Yenier, 2012a))
10. Optimizing processes (example: Procter & Gamble saved millions by optimizing its Pringles line (Gentzsch & Yenier, 2012a))
11. Simplifying access to information and tasks in one place across multiple enterprise applications tailored to job role
12. Reducing capital expenditure
13. Reducing the need for software development and HPC expertise

For private end users and Small to Medium Enterprises (SME) the risk versus reward of moving to the cloud is strongly in favor of adopting relevant new cloud services as they become available, while working to reducing the risks. On the other hand, for large organizations, especially those in regulated sectors, the decision to remove the legacy environments is not simple; however, IT staff, C-level, and business IT decision makers are driving the adoption of cloud computing within industries.

The following are a few manufacturing and industry software components that if moved to the cloud will have a good return on investment (ROI):

- Line of business (LoB) software applications in Enterprise Resource Planning (ERP)
- Manufacturing Execution Systems
- Supply Chain Management (SCM)
- Product Lifecycle Management
- Customer Relationships Management (CRM)

There are a number of control areas that must be considered carefully before moving computing operations to cloud services:

- Contractual agreements
- Certification and third party audits
- Compliance requirements
- Availability, reliability and resilience
- Backup and recovery
- Service levels and performance
- Decommissioning

3.1 Supply Chain

A supply chain is a network of interdependent trading partners who are geographically dispersed. Each trading partner has many upstream and downstream trading partners with whom they need to coordinate plans, schedules, deliveries, etc. Cloud computing provides a geographically dispersed network approach that is much better aligned to serve all these trading partners trying to communicate with each other through different systems. Supply chains are networks; cloud computing comprises networks for delivering business applications anywhere, anytime, therefore significantly improving supply chain capabilities, communication and coordination.

Cloud computing is well suited to support the multi-company business processes inherent in any supply chain of manufacturing, beginning with business applications as a service, followed by other cloud aspects such as development platforms and ongoing integration on an outsourced subscription basis. Market analysts at IDC (Parker, 2011) predict that cloud computing will be part of an expanding portfolio of options for the Chief Information Officer (CIO), with the biggest growth in collaborative applications, growing 46.3%.

Within the organization, demand planning and supply chain organization can be tied into a cloud-based system, allowing different parts of the organization to see the opportunities that their sales teams are working on. In a more traditional environment, that would involve a few real meetings, several face-to-face discussions, or phone conversations (Xu, 2011).

The following functional areas within supply chain of industries will most benefit from this transformation (see Table 1).

1. Sales and marketing
2. Product design and engineering
3. Logistics and transportation
4. Manufacturing operations and processes
5. Supply chain and distribution networks

3.2 Commerce as a Service

Cloud technology provides a considerable support for e-commerce. With that, the sale volumes can increase, and enterprises can use new and advanced software and hardware

Table 1.

Example 1	Accellos Inc. is a provider of supply chain execution software solutions. They announced the launch of its *AccellosOne warehouse management system* (WMS) in a cloud deployment option. The offering has been presented for review at Microsoft Dynamics Convergence 2012 [3] The platform offers warehouse management capability in a hosted model using enterprise cloud technology.
Example 2	"A historic number of small and midsized businesses are turning to cloud software applications to support their operations because of the flexible pricing, speed of deployment and simplicity it brings the IT team," said Chad Collins, Accellos chief marketing officer. "We expect this deployment option will allow even more SMBs (small and midsize businesses) to take advantage of full-featured WMS." Key features of AccellosOne Cloud WMS are as follows: • Flexible subscription pricing • Technical administration such as backup • Disaster recovery and system availability monitoring provided by Accellos • Software updates included as part of the service • Elastic computing resources • The ability to personalize systems to meet the needs of specific distribution centers • Standard integration of many accounting and enterprise resource planning (ERP) packages, including Microsoft Dynamics, Sage, and SAP BusinessOne In addition, the AccellosOne Cloud WMS offers features designed to ensure efficient performance of distribution centers, including inbound order processing, inventory control, optimized tasking, wave planning and outbound order fulfillment.
Example 3	Furthermore, additional modules from the AccellosOne platform can be added to the AccellosOne Cloud WMS such as dock door scheduling, supply chain business intelligence, document management and third-party logistics (3PL) billing.
Example 4	"The AccellosOne platform is perfectly suited for operating in an enterprise cloud due to the rich user interface which runs in a Web browser and the inherent multitenancy of the platform," said Ross Elliott, Accellos chief technology officer. "Additionally, our ERP connectors are available to ensure seamless communication between the WMS and ERP even if the ERP is deployed on-premise."
Example 5	The Accellos Inc. also has made AccellosOne electronic data interchange (EDI) product for Microsoft Dynamics GP and AccellosOne Collect for Microsoft Dynamics GP available in Data Resolutions' enterprise cloud. This allows customers to run their ERP, EDI and bar-coding solutions in a single cloud environment. The EDI and bar-coding solutions are available for sale through a network of VARs who provide the software, hosting and support for a single subscription fee.
Example 6	Similar to the EDI product, AccellosOne Collect for Microsoft Dynamics GP was built and integrated specifically for companies running Microsoft Dynamics GP as a single, embedded system. AccellosOne Collect for Microsoft Dynamics GP enables companies with manufacturing and distribution needs to automate their manual warehouse processes, while providing the user with real-time information to keep track of inventory.

infrastructures as services on demand. An enterprise can outsource its services without the need of creating physical presences in the other geographical areas with a consequent increment of competitiveness and of cost savings. It is possible to manage and/or to create new commercial Websites at lower costs and without having specific technical skills. Therefore, the companies can keep in contact with the customers and to easily promote the new products/services.

Cloud computing supports e-commerce in terms of scalability. In fact, the enterprises can easily extend their services, make use of additional ones during some periods and, on the contrary, easily cut them as demand slows. In this way, also the middle and the small companies can use advanced software systems for analyzing the market trends. The companies can perform predictive analysis on data by adopting specific software tools as services and then, they can be able to quickly react according to the market changes.

The use of a cloud for hosting the e-commerce Web sites is securely an advantage in terms of elasticity, for example, but it could also become a criticism. In fact, the number of data center locations of a cloud provider is usually limited (Hao, Walden, & Trenkamp, 2013). With that, an e-commerce Web site could be placed very far from its users with a consequent increment of the client perceived response times. Companies could lose their money and customers, consequently. For this purpose, (Hao, Walden, & Trenkamp, 2013) propose a virtual proxy platform together with a k-means table partitioning algorithm with the aim of accelerating these e-commerce sites.

Today, e-Commerce customers not only buy through Websites but also via their smartphones, social media and in-store kiosks. Thus, e-Commerce services need to handle all types of transactions [4].

In addition, cloud computing can be an effective solution in offering business-to-business (B2B) solutions for commerce transactions between businesses, such as between a manufacturer and a wholesaler, or between a wholesaler and a retailer. See Table 2 for examples.

Customers who decide to use third-party tools to build out user interfaces for their e-Commerce efforts can still use these services, Nelson said.

And companies that already have an ERP system from the likes of Oracle and SAP can deploy SuiteCommerce as a stand-alone system, and then integrate its data back to their core ERP, according to Nelson.

Table 2.

Example 1	SuiteCommerce is being touted as a unified hub for all e-Commerce activity. NetSuite is going up against vendors such as Demandware in the market for cloud-based e-Commerce platforms, announcing a new product, Suit-eCommerce, during the SuiteWorld conference in San Francisco.
Example 2	While NetSuite has offered e-Commerce technologies for some time, this product aims to up the ante and replace first-generation e-Commerce platforms, which largely revolve around purchases made through company Websites. Some of the latter may come through machine-to-machine purchasing scenarios, Nelson said. For example, a surgical robot could automatically order new surgical needles it uses as supplies run low, he said.
Example 3	SuiteCommerce, under development for several years, consists of two main new pieces. One, called SuiteCommerce Experience, is used for building user interfaces across multiple device types. The other is a set of services for connecting interfaces built with SuiteCommerce Experience to back-end components in the core NetSuite system, such as for payment processing and order management.

3.3 Business Intelligence and Automation

A major use of computing power in business that will be furthered by adoption of the cloud is the use of business intelligence by analytical systems.

With wider cloud adoption, access to business-critical data and analytics will not just help enterprises stay ahead, it will also be crucial to their existence.

If a project's information is located on a small set of similar servers, tapping into and analyzing information will be easier than when it is spread across incompatible systems. On the other hand, when a project's information is tied to product sales activity on the company Web site, and both are powered by the internal cloud, then that information can be analyzed and cross-referenced more easily than when it must be drawn from disparate systems.

The cloud has to address the following business intelligence and data requirements for the success of industries:

- Get real-time information on the business through the process of data warehousing and complex event processing or other techniques
- Consolidating data across enterprise data stores to improve business intelligence and collaboration
- Simplified access to information across functional silos
- Architecture that combines unstructured and structured data and processes
- Real-time issue resolution in context with improved collaboration and communication
- Incorporating a cloud computing foundation alongside data center optimization

3.4 Pay by the Usage

Cloud computing has the potential to be a game-changing technology in manufacturing for everyone from small shops to extremely large manufacturing plants. The key is understanding the process, and making wise provider decisions.

This is a tremendous change from what manufacturers had to do just five to ten years ago. Instead of having to buy large computers and purchase lots of software, with these large information flows and Internet server farms

you can simply pay for the services you need on a "pay by the usage" basis.

This "pay by the usage" scenario will revolutionize manufacturing in the same way that the Internet has already revolutionized our everyday and business lives. Manufacturers are starting to take advantage of cloud computing because it simply makes good economic sense. You pay for what you use and do not have the additional costs and burden of managing your own data center. Instead of large capital expenses (CapEx) for new computer systems and infrastructure, the costs will move to operating expenses (OpEx) and you will pay for only what you actually use. This could be achieved without requiring a large CapEx investment upfront and came as a relief to many.

3.5 Standardization and Data

Standardization and data challenges are also present in manufacturing and industry sectors.

Manufacturers have been influenced by the Information Technology Infrastructure Library (ITIL) best practices and similar approaches (Parker, 2011), which call for building catalogs of services that can be replicated and shared throughout an organization. They are slightly more likely than companies in other industries to see cloud computing technology as a way to standardize IT services. "There is a movement among manufacturers to do this kind of catalog of services," Parker said (Parker, 2011).

On the other hand, manufacturing's dramatic shift toward outsourcing comes at a time when companies are de-emphasizing traditional IT jobs and hiring more data scientists. In manufacturing there is a transformation in terms of the IT experts who work in IT. This transformation has moved IT experts from building systems that drive processes to analyzing data to drive better decisions. For instance, anthropologists trained to analyze human behavior in social media, and others with the hybrid IT and business skills to perform analytics on "big data," Parker said (Parker, 2011).

From the point of view of software issues, manufacturers more than other industries have software license challenges. Incompatible software licensing models are a roadblock in the UberCloud experiment. Without the participation of the software vendors in developing compatible software licensing models, the adoption of HPC in the Cloud will be significantly slower.

In the UberCloud experiment, on-demand license usage has been tracked in order to determine the feasibility of using the service model as a revenue stream (Gentzsch & Yenier, 2012b). According to the first round report, "In the HPC market software licensing costs may be connected to usage, such as amount of data processed, CPU core hours used. In such scenarios the monitoring and billing solutions must be flexible enough to monitor and account for the cost of software licenses to be able to provide a complete view of the cost structure" (Gentzsch & Yenier, 2012b).

"Although many software providers are diligently working on making on-demand licenses available, the landscape is difficult to navigate. It is hard to predict which software provider has on-demand licensing models fully developed and it is even more difficult

to know how to work with their significantly different models. Many of our teams ran into license management challenges and required extra help to move forward.," reported in the first round report of the UberCloud experiment.

Furthermore, interoperability is an essential requirement for service providers, industries, manufacturers, and enterprises. At the other end, data portability at the application layer is another important challenge. Open data format and open APIs have been proposed to address these challenges (Xu, 2011).

Industry vendors and users have been seeking a common language to be used for the entire product development life cycle that can describe design, manufacturing, and other data pertaining to a product. Many solutions were proposed, the most successful is the Standard for Exchange of Product data (STEP) (Nee, 2009; Kim, Pratt, Iyer, & Sriram, 2008).

STEP provides a mechanism that is capable of describing product data, independent of any particular system. The nature of this description makes it suitable not only for neutral file exchange, but also as a basis for implementing, sharing and archiving product data over a cloud manufacturing system. ISO 10303-AP203 (Kim, Pratt, Iyer, & Sriram, 2008) is the first and perhaps the most successful AP (Application Protocol) developed to exchange design data between different CAD systems.

STEP-based data models are utilized as the central data schema in manufacturing and industry sectors. With coupling technologies, STEP-based data models can be connected to commercial CAD/CAM software suites, giving the system much needed portability.

4. CLOUD MANUFACTURING

Two types of cloud computing in the manufacturing sector have been proposed (Xu, 2011): manufacturing with direct adoption of cloud computing technologies and cloud manufacturing that is the manufacturing version of cloud computing.

Although the concept of cloud manufacturing is relatively new, virtual enterprise, and distributed manufacturing concepts have been around for a while and some of the proposed systems and frameworks bear the trace of cloud manufacturing, e.g. development of a service-oriented manufacturing environment and different SaaS for engineering applications. In cloud manufacturing (Xu, 2011), distributed resources are encapsulated as cloud services and managed in a centralized way. Users can use cloud services according to their requirements. They can request services ranging from product design, manufacturing, testing, to management, and all other stages of a product life cycle.

Cloud manufacturing is a multi-disciplinary domain and a computing and service oriented manufacturing model developed from existing advanced manufacturing technologies and models such as networked manufacturing (NM), virtual manufacturing, agile manufacturing (AM), Application Service Provider (ASP), Manufacturing Grid (MGrid), and enterprise information technologies under the support of cloud computing, Internet of Things (IoT), virtualization, service oriented technologies, and advanced computing technologies.

In a cloud manufacturing system, various manufacturing resources and abilities are intelligently sensed and connected into the Internet. In addition, they are automatically managed and controlled using IoT technologies such as RFID (Radio-Frequency IDentification), wired and wireless sensor network, and embedded system. The manufacturing resources and abilities are virtualized and encapsulated into different manufacturing cloud services (MCSs), that can be accessed, invoked, and deployed by using virtualization technologies, service-oriented technologies, and cloud computing technologies.

The MCSs are classified and aggregated according to specific rules and algorithms, and different kinds of manufacturing clouds are constructed. Different users can search and invoke the qualified MCSs from related manufacturing cloud according to their needs, and assemble them to establish a virtual manufacturing environment or solution to complete their manufacturing task involved in the whole life cycle of manufacturing processes.

Three categories of users play a key role in the cloud manufacturing:

- **Providers:** As persons or organizations who provide the resources involved in the life cycle of the manufacturing processes;
- **Consumers:** Subscribing the manufacturing cloud services provided in the platform and paying for the use of the platform according to their needs;
- **Operators or experts:** Operating on the platform for providing specific services and functions to both consumers and providers themselves;

Table 3.

Example 1	A very recent example of cloud manufacturing platform is the one provided by Scala, Inc., in March, 2012. It is a cloud-based predictive analytics platform that can transform information on the flows of goods into important messages that can help retailers to better understand *when* and *how much* to order. The platform is suitable to manage millions of data records about sales; products information; customer behaviors; pricing changes; marketing trends; time of day; day of week; seasonality effects and so on. By using predictive analytics, the system is able to determine the probability of what might happen next in a retail environment. It is a Software as a Service (SaaS) cloud application. The most relevant functionalities of the Scala cloud manufacturing platform are: • Increasing product or category sales; • Managing inventory to reduce stock-outs; • Increasing the effectiveness of in-store promotions and improving customer satisfaction with higher service levels;
Example 2	**The time-to-value:** "We see the DIRA Framework, combined with the unparalleled discrete manufacturing content and application solutions from Rockwell FactoryTalk, as an opportunity to help our customers leverage their IT investment by accelerating the integration of manufacturing and enterprise information to reduce the time-to-value for the enterprise," said Doug Lawson, chief software strategist at Rockwell Automation.
Example 3	**Automation:** "Siemens welcomes the new DIRA Framework which is a good fit to its own industry software offering and Totally Integrated Automation approach," said Ralf-Michael Franke, CEO Industrial Automation Systems, Siemens. "We expect this architecture to lever an improved interoperability information flow between the shop floor and the enterprise functions, as well as increase efficiency between enterprise systems and enterprises throughout the supplier network. The Siemens MES product, SIMATIC IT, is just one example that aligns well with this reference architecture."
Example 4	"Apriso supports the DIRA Framework initiative because it echoes many of the architectural principles that we currently practice; it is essentially an extension of the global platform for manufacturing operations that Apriso's customers currently utilize," said Tom Comstock, executive vice president of Apriso."
Example 5	**Data-driven and complex business problems:** "A comprehensive reference architecture is essential for dynamic, data-driven applications to meet current and future challenges, said Scott Jones, chief technology officer and vice president of R&D at Camstar Systems. "Customers will benefit from these technologies to assist in solving complex business problems and meeting today's industry needs."
Example 6	**Competitiveness:** "At Tata Consultancy Services, we help the manufacturing industry improve competitiveness with best-of-breed solutions that deliver business functionality, integration and data synchronization. Our solution uses industry best practices for all manufacturing enterprise roles," said Kalpan Raval, practice director, Enterprise Solutions, Tata Consultancy Services. "The solution ensures full integration between shop floor systems, Siemens MES, enterprise resource planning and other data sources, which enable lean and traditional scheduling principles to be readily applied. Using this newly released reference architecture, we expect to accelerate value realization for our customers due to asset-leveraged, shorter implementation cycles."
Example 7	"ICONICS provides to the discrete manufacturing industry HMI/SCADA solutions and manufacturing intelligence solutions that assist our customers in maximizing their productivity and efficiency," said Gary Kohrt, vice president, Marketing and Product Marketing for ICONICS. "ICONICS supports the DIRA Framework and utilizes many of the technologies referenced by it. For example, by utilizing Microsoft Silverlight and Microsoft SharePoint Technologies, our GENESIS64 and PortalWorX products are able to deliver user interfaces that are not only graphically rich, natural to use and role-based to the many different users in our customers' enterprise, but also often 'excite' those that use and share information with them. By utilizing Microsoft's mobile technologies, we can deliver information to our customers' ever-shifting, on-the-go workforces, with no loss in functionality."
Example 8	"The principles of discrete manufacturing reference architecture align well with key offerings from Infosys, such as Supply Chain Visibility and Collaboration product suite and manufacturing collaboration accelerators," said Sanjay Jalona, vice president and head of Manufacturing North America, Infosys Technologies Ltd. "These offerings take advantage of Microsoft technologies to solve business challenges like supplier collaboration, innovation management and knowledge management."

At the other side, the organization of a cloud manufacturing architecture is divided into different layers as follows (Xu, 2011):

- The layer of the resources involved in the manufacturing process;
- The perception layer enabling resources to be connected inside the network and processing the data and results;
- The layer for virtualizing resources to encapsulate them inside the cloud services;
- The layer for cloud services providing the specific services that support the infrastructure;
- The layer of applications developing an application system on the base of the consumer needs;
- The portal layer providing user-friendly interfaces for the cloud services;
- The enterprise cooperation application layer providing commerce, business cooperation, collaborative design and manufacturing cooperation;
- The knowledge layer developing manufacturing domain knowledge, process knowledge, model knowledge, etc., useful for the other layers of the architecture;
- The cloud security layer offering different security mechanisms and strategies;
- And finally, the Internet layer, the base communication environment for resources, service, consumers and operations;

4.1 Reference Architecture Framework for Discrete Manufacturers Initiative

According to Microsoft, new technology advancements such as cloud computing and social computing, are transforming manufacturing industry value chains in cloud manufacturing (see Table 3).

Microsoft has created a Reference Architecture Framework for Discrete Manufacturers Initiative, called DIRA Framework [5], to drive solutions based on cloud computing across manufacturing networks.

Stakeholders in an industry-wide collaboration include: manufacturer's end-users, manufacturing products and services providers, IT providers, systems integrators and in-house business analysts.

Microsoft partners involved in the initiative including industry solution vendors and systems integrators are Apriso Corp., Camstar Systems Inc., ICONICS Inc., Rockwell Automation Inc., Siemens MES and Tata Consultancy Services Ltd.

The initiative follows the following goals:

- Integrate processes within and across the enterprise;
- Extend the reach of the network to more companies globally;
- Connect smart devices to the cloud;

In addition, the initiative defines six key themes:

- Natural user interfaces
- Role-based productivity and insights
- Social business
- Dynamic value networks
- Smart connected devices
- Security-enhanced, scalable and adaptive infrastructure

5. CONCLUSION

The UberCloud experiment is a successful project in accelerating the adoption of cloud computing in industries. During the course of the first round of the UberCloud experiment, over 160 active participants and observers from 25 countries have registered at the experiment Website. This healthy pool of participants allowed the organizers to break this group into 25 teams, which were working in parallel (Gentzsch & Yenier, 2012b).

HPC Experiment's purpose is to help end-users from industry and research to use cloud computing technologies for their HPC and CFD experiments. The experiment has been designed in a way that each team can work autonomously but follow a common methodology, a common documentation standard and a common calendar. Participants include end-users from industry and research, computing resource providers, software providers, and HPC & CAE experts.

The inner workings of the Experiment is an example for many industries in their transition to cloud computing. The problem statement is as follows: the end-user is in need of additional compute resources to speed up a product design cycle, say for simulating more sophisticated geometry or physics, or for

running many more simulations for a higher quality result. That suggests a specific software stack, domain expertise, and even hardware configuration. The general idea is to look at the end-user task and select the appropriate resources, software and expertise that match its requirements. Then, with modest guidance from the Experiment organizers, the user, resource providers, and HPC experts will implement and run the task and deliver the results. The hardware and software providers will measure resource usage; the HPC expert will summarize the steps of analysis and implementation; the end user will evaluate the quality of the process and of the results and the degree of user-friendliness this process provided. The experiment organizers will analyze the feedback received. Finally, the team will get together, extract lessons learned, and present further recommendations as input for the corresponding case study.

To make service-based HPC come together the organizers have defined four stakeholders for four roles. Stakeholders consist of industrial end users, resource providers, software providers, and high performance computing experts.

A typical example of industrial end users is a small or medium size manufacturer in the process of designing and prototyping its next product. These users are candidates for remote HPC or HPC-as-a-Service when in-house computation on workstations has become too lengthy a process, but acquiring additional computing power in the form of HPC is too cumbersome or is not in line with budgets. HPC is not likely to be the core expertise of this group. The end-users started the process by filling in an online information gathering form to provide information about their projects to the experiment organizers.

Incompatible software licensing models is one of the main roadblocks in this experiment. Without the participation of the software vendors in developing compatible software licensing models, the adoption of HPC in the Cloud will be significantly slower.

As a case in point, there was one project where the software provider was not willing to participate in the Experiment with their end-user customer. Since the requirements of the end-user were tightly coupled with the software they were using the end-user needed to terminate the project.

"We looked closely at how much friction was caused by software licensing models of the providers which were willing to participate in the Experiment. Although many software providers are diligently working on making on-demand licenses available, the landscape is difficult to navigate. It is hard to predict which software provider has on-demand licensing models fully developed and it is even more difficult to know how to work with their significantly different models. Many of our teams ran into license management challenges and required extra help to move forward."

"Many software providers are already working on compatible licensing models. We recommend end-users to contact their software providers early on and include them in their HPC initiatives. Alternatively, the HPC Experiment is a great way to work hand-in-hand with a resource provider on testing an HPC in the Cloud compatible licensing model. There are already existing successful on-demand licensing models from some forward looking

ISVs (also part of our experiment) which we believe the others can learn from." is recommendations from the experiment.

One end-user after experience in the first round requested to work with a professional HPC Cloud services provider, for several good reasons (Gentzsch & Yenier, 2012b):

"The primary interest to participate in HPC experiment is to be able to continue using the resource provider after the experiments are done, through a commercial arrangement. We are not sure how this works with our current HPC center team partner and if it fits into their modus operandi. We assume that it is not possible in the near term.

The HPC center uses the traditional beowulf cluster architecture. Although this is very suitable for many HPC scientific problems, it is not suitable for us as we are interested in using MapReduce with our code. Additionally, we are already running our code in a beowulf cluster at our premises.

We don't have the permission to install new packages or (re)configure existing ones at the HPC Center, basically root/administrative access. This is totally understandable from their perspective. For example, we wanted to compile our code using some little used configuration to see if it gives better performance. We were not able to do at the HPC center resource.

We are interested in doing several experiments with different architectures like n nodes, n+4 nodes, n+8 nodes and so on. Each of them may require the (re)installation of application software and/or OS. This is easily possible in a cloud environment and less on a traditional beowulf cluster setup."

REFERENCES

Gentzsch, W., & Yenier, B. (2012a). *CAE in the cloud- New business opportunities for manufacturers and ISVS*. Retrieved from http://www.hpcinthecloud.com/hpc-cloud/2012-07-19/cae-in-the-cloud

Gentzsch, W., & Yenier, B. (2012b). *HPC experiment - Final report of round 1*. The UberCloud LLC.

Hao, Walden, & Trenkamp. (2013). Accelerating e-commerce sites in the cloud. In *Proceedings of 2013 IEEE 10th Consumer Communications and Networking Conference*. IEEE.

Kim, J., Pratt, M. J., Iyer, R. G., & Sriram, R. D. (2008). Standardized data exchange of CAD models with design intent. *Computer Aided Design, 40*(7), 760–777. doi:10.1016/j.cad.2007.06.014

Nee, A. Y. C. (2009). *Advanced design and manufacturing based on step*. London: Springer London.

Parker, R. (2011). *Business strategy: Cloud computing in manufacturing*. Academic Press.

Xu, X. (2011, July). From cloud computing to cloud manufacturing. *Robotics and Computer-integrated Manufacturing*, 1–12. doi: doi:10.1016/j.rcim.2011.07.002

KEY TERMS AND DEFINITIONS

Cloud Industrialization: The anatomy and ubiquity of cloud computing make it a key technology to advance and accelerate innovations in industry and manufacturing sectors.

Cloud Manufacturing: The manufacturing version of cloud computing. In cloud manufacturing, distributed resources are encapsulated as cloud services and managed in a centralized way. Users can use cloud services according to their requirements. They can request services ranging from product design, manufacturing, testing, to management, and all other stages of a product life cycle.

Manufacturing Industry: Cloud computing is emerging as one of the major enablers for the manufacturing industry to transform the traditional manufacturing business model.

Networked Manufacturing (NM): Cloud manufacturing is a multi-disciplinary domain and a computing and service oriented manufacturing model developed from existing advanced manufacturing technologies and models such as networked manufacturing (NM), virtual manufacturing, agile manufacturing (AM), Application Service Provider (ASP), Manufacturing Grid (MGrid), and enterprise information technologies under the support of cloud computing, Internet of Things (IoT), virtualization, service oriented technologies, and advanced computing technologies.

Supply Chain: A network of interdependent trading partners who are geographically dispersed. Each trading partner has many upstream and downstream trading partners with whom they need to coordinate plans, schedules, deliveries, etc.

ENDNOTES

1   http://www.hpcexperiment.com/

2   http://decisivconnect.com/tag/micro-soft-discrete-manufacturing-cloud-computing-survey/

3   http://www.microsoft.com/presspass/press/2011/apr11/04-03mscloudfrag-mentspr.mspx.

4   http://www.netsuite.com/portal/prod-ucts/commerce/main.shtml

5   http://www.microsoft.com/en-us/news/press/2011/apr11/04-03mscloudfrag-mentspr.aspx

Chapter 9
Cloud in Science

ABSTRACT

Cloud computing technologies and service models are attractive to scientific computing users due to the ability to get on-demand access to resources as well as the ability to control the software environment. Scientific computing researchers and resource providers servicing these users are considering the impact of new models and technologies. SaaS solutions like Globus Online and IaaS solutions such as Nimbus Infrastructure and OpenNebula accelerate the discovery of science by helping scientists to conduct advanced and large-scale science. This chapter describes how cloud is helping researchers to accelerate scientific discovery by transforming manual and difficult tasks into the cloud.

1. INTRODUCTION

Computation and data are considered the third and the fourth mode of science, respectively, where the previous modes or paradigms were experimentation, observation and theory. With the introduction of high performance supercomputers, the methods of scientific

research could include mathematical models and simulation of phenomenon that are too expensive or beyond our experiment's reach. With the advent of cloud computing, a fifth mode of science is on the horizon.

In 1998 and later in 2001, Foster, Kesselman and Tuecke (Foster, Kesselman,& Tuecke, 2001) introduced Grid Computing as "coordinated resource sharing and problem solving in dynamic, multi-institutional virtual

DOI: 10.4018/978-1-4666-4683-4.ch009

organization." Grids have been the center of attention from scientific and High Performance Computing communities (HPC) (Grandinetti, 2008) and (Gentzsch, Grandinetti, & Joubert, 2010), especially for the distributed and large scale scientific applications, and also in collaborative style of work.

Grid is the first technology that is developed to address scientific needs. A huge number of projects within countries (e.g. National Grid Projects) such as TeraGrid (2012) and Italian Grid Infrastructure (2012), within continents and industries in various areas were defined around Grid during these years. These projects all are initiated to address scientific needs. For instance, in Europe, the European Grid Initiative (EGI) (European Grid Initiative, 2012) is the latest project that represents a new effort to establish a sustainable Grid infrastructure in Europe after EGEE-III project. National Grid Initiatives (NGI) (Italian Grid Infrastructure, 2012) within EGI operate the Grid infrastructures in each country. In principle, NGI is the main foundations of EGI.

On the other hand, cloud computing is gaining traction in the commercial world, with companies like Amazon, Google, and Yahoo! offering pay-to-play cycles to help organizations meet cyclical demands for extra computing power. Cloud computing technologies and service models are attractive to scientific computing users due to the ability to get on-demand access to resources and to replace or supplement existing systems, as well as the ability to control the software environment. Scientific computing users and resource providers servicing these users are considering the impact of these new models and technologies.

Cloud service delivery models play different roles in scientific computing. For instance, the IaaS model enables users to control their own software stack that is useful to scientists that might have complex software stacks.

Instead, SaaS provides access to an end user for an application or software that has a specific function. Examples in the commercial space include services like Salesforce.com and Gmail. This model can be attractive since it allows the user to transfer the responsibility of installing, configuring, and maintaining an application and shields the end-user from the complexity of the underlying software. On the other hand, science portals can also be viewed as providing a Software as a Service, since they typically allow remote users to perform analysis or browse data sets through a Web interface.

In this chapter, we review current practices of cloud computing in various scientific fields. We see what services and capabilities cloud introduces for accelerating the discovery of science.

2. COMPLEXITY OF SCIENTIFIC APPLICATIONS

The Large Hadron Collider (LHC), as shown in Figure 1, is a gigantic scientific instrument (particle accelerator) constructed near Geneva, Switzerland (CERN - The Large Hadron Collider, 2012). It spans the border between Switzerland and France about 100m underground. Physicists will use the LHC to study the smallest known particles, the fun-

Figure 1. ALICE detector (CERN - The Large Hadron Collider, 2012)

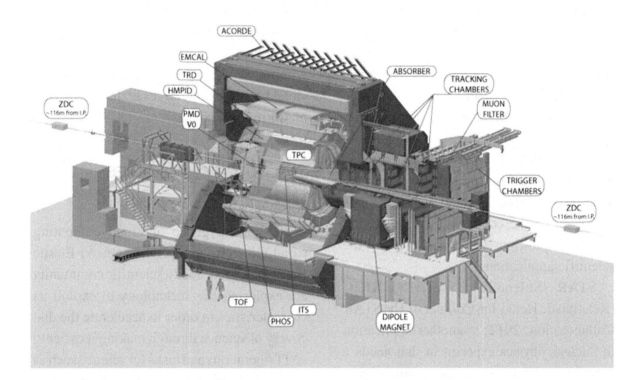

damental building blocks of all things, and to recreate the conditions just after the Big Bang. Physicists from around the globe will analyze the particles created in the collisions using special detectors in a number of experiments dedicated to the LHC: ALICE (A Large Ion Collider Experiment), ATLAS (A Toroidal LHC Apparatus), CMS (Compact Muon Solenoid), LHCb (Large Hadron Collider beauty), TOTEM (TOTal Elastic and diffractive cross section Measurement), LHCf (Large Hadron Collider forward). These six experiments at the LHC are all run by the international collaborations bringing together scientists and individuals from institutes all over the world.

In brief, the LHC was built to help scientists to find the answer of a few important unresolved questions in particle physics. From these prominent experiments in the world the need of having a standard scientific computing infrastructure such as Grid arises.

Particularly, the scientific questions are very complicated, so the technologies in physics and computer science behind them also are becoming very complex. In the field of computer science, the computing infrastructure and applications for the scientific problems have to address the challenges of storing the data generated by these instruments, also the issues related to analyzing these huge amounts of data.

If we research on the scientific applications, we will find out they are becoming more and more complicated. They are developed by different groups and individuals, build around various components and technologies and often need a heterogeneous execution environment. More importantly, they likely require a custom execution environment, with specific operating system, software libraries, compilers, binaries and so on. Even some scientific applications need to work with a specific version and release of software. In addition, usually these applications process large amounts of input data and produce huge amounts of output data and results. This is the result of the complexity of underlying scientific questions to be answered by the scientific applications.

STAR (Solenoidal Tracker At RHIC (Relativistic Heavy Ion Collider)) (The STAR Collaboration, 2012) is another application in nuclear physics experiment that needs a specific version of operating system and precise specific software environment, libraries, tools and compilers with right configuration to work correctly. Usually, there is no such environment in current Grid infrastructure and it is not easy to be deployed on Grid resources immediately. According to Douglas Olson, a staff scientist at Lawrence Berkeley National Laboratory: "even just validating a new platform is a big job even when it all compiles.," "STAR is using rarely used features of the language" and "It tends to push the boundaries on what will actually compile." STAR also requires some Grid components such as Open Science Grid (OSG) Compute Element CE as a headnode, OSG Worker Nodes (WNs) as worker nodes with STAR configuration, gridmap files, host certificates, NSF for shared filesystem and PBS as Local

Resource Manager to be deployed and configured properly.

In sum, for a scientific application like STAR only a virtual machine based solution will provide a right execution environment, without virtualization technique it is impossible to provision large scale production platform for scientists.

3. CLOUD TECHNOLOGIES FOR SCIENCE

With the emergence of cloud computing paradigm from enterprise (Amazon Elastic Compute Cloud, 2012), scientific community are exploring this technology to exploit its characteristics in order to accelerate the discovery of science through making it easier to do IT operations and tasks for science such as conducting simulation experiments, file transfer, etc. For instance, computer scientists who are developing technologies for scientists, have defined cloud based projects such as Globus Online (Globus Online Project, 2011), Nimbus Toolkit (Nimbus Toolkit Project, 2010), and Cumulus [1] within Globus community.

If we consider the advantages and the benefits of cloud computing, we conclude that with the appearance of cloud models, the number of scientific users with different demands and strict software environments will be increased significantly. Moreover, scientific applications will benefit from reliability, accuracy and efficiency of running their computations on Science Clouds (Keahey, 2008).

Cloud platform such as Open Source Nimbus Toolkit (Nimbus Toolkit Project, 2010)

is one of the first attempts to complement grid and cloud. Nimbus is like Commercial Amazon Elastic Compute Cloud (EC2) that provides computational capabilities for computing in Enterprise sector; they are often referred as Infrastructure-as-a-Service (IaaS).

3.1 Nimbus Toolkit, OpenNebula, and Haizea

Nimbus is an Infrastructure-as-a-Service (Nimbus Toolkit Project, 2010) cloud computing for science. Nimbus platform is an integrated set of tools that deliver the power and versatility of infrastructure clouds to scientific users. Nimbus platform allows you to combine Nimbus, OpenStack, Amazon, and other clouds.

Nimbus Infrastructure is an open source EC2/S3-compatible Infrastructure-as-a-Service implementation specifically targeting features of interest to the scientific community such as support for proxy credentials, batch schedulers, best-effort allocations and others.

Nimbus has been developed within Globus Toolkit community, a de facto standard for Grids, so that it seems it can bring IaaS cloud into the Grid with some straightforward efforts. Nimbus makes it easy for scientific projects to experiment with cloud computing. With the help of Nimbus, scientists can do new jobs in e-Science context:

- Launch one-click, auto-configuring clusters: Leasing on-demand resources (as VMs) to build turnkey virtual clusters (with Context Broker of Nimbus)
- Finding the right environment in distributed systems

- Deploying network gateways on infrastructures
- Using IaaS features
- Leveraging external Infrastructures with IaaS Gateway

With Nimbus you can launch virtual clusters with one command. There is no need to configure anything, cluster configurations are automated with the workspace context broker. Technically, each VM launches a very lightweight agent that greatly simplifies dealing with changing cluster topologies, identities, and credentials (no secrets need to reside on the image before booting).

Nimbus and OpenNebula (OpenNebula, 2010) are considered as a local infrastructure manager (LIM) since they operate at the local level. Thus, from the architecture point of view Nimbus and OpenNebula services appear in the resource layer of Grid architecture.

In addition, multi-cloud feature of Nimbus allows users to get resources over multiple geographically distributed cloud resource. This feature supports contextualizing across multiple clouds. This is also true for OpenNebula by its hybrid clouds capability. In this case we can say, Nimbus and OpenNebula (Sotomayor, Montero, Llorente, & Foster, 2009) are in the class of global infrastructure managers (GIM) and offer some global services. Moreover, there are attempts to use OpenNebula (OpenNebula, 2010) within EGI Grid.

Haizea (Sotomayor, 2010) is an open source lease management system which supports pluggable scheduling policies, various scheduling algorithms, etc. Leases in Haizea are implemented as virtual machines. It is an open and general-purpose VM-based scheduler, flexible and modular for further extensions and enhancements. Nimbus uses Haizea as a scheduling back-end; thus, Haizea is an LIM's scheduler. In addition, OpenNebula can use Haizea for its scheduler back-end.

Instead, RESERVOIR (Reservoir project, 2012) is an GIM to provide deployment and management of IT services across a number of geographically distributed data centers, federating infrastructures or hybrid clouds, with high quality of service, high productivity, high availability and competitive costs. It was an European Union FP7 funded project to reach the goal of Service-Oriented Computing's visionary promise by leveraging Virtualization, Grid Computing and business service management techniques.

The other Open Source cloud middleware tools are Cumulus, EUCALYPTUS (Nurmi et al., 2008), Nimrod [2], openQRM [3] and Enomaly [4]. EUCALYPTUS stands for Elastic Utility Computing Architecture for Linking Your Programs To Useful Systems. Its interface is compatible with Amazon's EC2 interface. EUCALYPTUS is implemented using commonly available Linux tools and basic Web Service technologies making it easy to install and maintain. In sum, its functionalities are like Nimbus. Instead, Cumulus is an Open Source Storage Cloud for Science; it is like Amazon S3.

3.2 Globus Online

Globus Online is a hosted service to automate the tasks associated with moving files between sites. It does not require custom infrastructure,

Globus Online is software-as-a-service that can be used today without building these features yourself.

Globus Online (Globus Online Project, 2011) is among the first cloud solutions for scientists, it makes robust file transfer capabilities accessible to any researcher with an Internet connection and a laptop. Globus manages the entire file transfer operation: monitoring performance, retrying failed transfers, recovering from faults automatically whenever possible, and reporting status. Users cite Globus Online as their preferred service since it is easy, fast, secure, reliable and research-focused.

4. SCIENCE CLOUDS

Science Clouds (Keahey, 2008) have been emerged as a result of scientific application needs for outsourced compute and storage infrastructures. Science Clouds (Science clouds project, 2012) provided by Open Source Nimbus Toolkit, and Commercial Amazon Elastic Compute Cloud (EC2) that provide computational capabilities for computing are often referred as IaaS. They provide compute cycles in the cloud for scientific communities using Nimbus.

The Science Clouds (Science clouds project, 2012) are an informal group of small clouds made available by various institutions on a voluntary basis. The Science Clouds started in mid-2008 and roughly speaking have two goals: (1) to make it easy for scientific projects to experiment with IaaS-style cloud computing, (2) to enable projects developing infrastructure for such clouds to learn from user requirements.

Marketplace in cloud computing is a place to find virtual appliances encapsulated as VMs. The Science Clouds marketplace is like the virtual machine marketplaces that are becoming popular but is specifically for scientific applications and VMs that are useful for grid computing. For example, at (Nimbus Toolkit Project, 2010) there are some useful and popular virtual machines customized for Nimbus environment. Each is accompanied by a populated workspace metadata file for quick deployment on resources running the Workspace Service. Each image is annotated with its requirements.

Access to Science Clouds is provided by each site on a voluntary basis. If you have a research or scientific project you should have no problem getting access, however site policies may vary. Unlike the Amazon's EC2 service, the Science Clouds like Nimbus do not require users to directly pay for usage. Their usage is based on asking from the scientist to provide some information about: an email account with the sponsoring institution, Web pages, pointers to papers and asking for a short write-up of the scientific project.

5. CLOUD PROJECTS FOR SCIENCE

With the advent of cloud computing, many projects and initiatives have been proposed to use cloud services and solutions in science. The Magellan project (Mallegan project, 2012) is one of the first projects to conduct an exhaustive evaluation of the use of cloud computing for science in the US. The Magellan project is funded through the U.S. Department of Energy (DOE) Office of Advanced Scientific Computing Research (ASCR). Instead, HelixNebula is a recent cloud computing project for Science Clouds; it has been launched by some of Europe's biggest research such as CERN along with European IT companies.

In addition, there are smaller scale and shorter term initiatives and projects to study the use of cloud for science and scientific applications. For instance, since 2003 a collaboration between two big energy departments, Brookhaven and Argonne National Laboratory (ANL), in the US has been started for building a middleware to facilitate execution of STAR application. The goal of this particular analysis is to sift through collisions searching for the missing spin. This collaboration initiated due to the difficulties behind production running of STAR application. The result of this collaboration (The STAR Collaboration, 2012) was that STAR scientists with the help of Nimbus Toolkit (developed at ANL) were able to dynamically provision compute resources to build a cluster on TeraPort at ANL and on Amazon's EC2 resources quickly in an order of minutes to run STAR applications at the scale of one hundred nodes.

5.1 Magellan

Magellan (Mallegan project, 2012) is a research and development effort to establish a nationwide scientific mid-range distributed computing and data analysis testbed. The Magellan's goal was to investigate the potential role of cloud computing in addressing the computing needs for the DOE Office of Science, particularly related to serving the needs of mid-range computing and future data-intensive computing workloads.

Specifically, Magellan objectives are as the following:

- Understand which science applications and user communities are best suited for cloud computing.
- Understand the deployment and support issues required to build large science clouds. Is it cost effective and practical to operate science clouds? How could commercial clouds be leveraged?
- How does existing cloud software meet the needs of science and could extending or enhancing current cloud software improve utility?
- How well does cloud computing support data-intensive scientific applications?
- What are the challenges to addressing security in a virtualized cloud environment?

For that, a set of research questions was formed to probe various aspects of cloud computing from performance, usability, and cost. More specifically, Magellan was charged with answering the following research questions:

- Are the open source cloud software stacks ready for DOE HPC science?
- Can DOE cyber security requirements be met within a cloud?
- Are the new cloud programming models useful for scientific computing?
- Can DOE HPC applications run efficiently in the cloud? What applications are suitable for clouds?

- How usable are cloud environments for scientific applications?
- When is it cost effective to run DOE HPC science in a cloud?

To address these questions, a distributed testbed infrastructure was deployed at the Argonne Leadership Computing Facility (ALCF) and the National Energy Research Scientific Computing Center (NERSC). It has two sites at NERSC and ALCF with multiple 10's of teraflops and multiple petabytes of storage, as well as appropriate cloud software tuned for moderate concurrency.

Magellan Software Architecture is illustrated in Figure 2. In this context, Magellan can be considered a private cloud that provides its services to DOE Office of Science users.

Magellan evaluation methodology covered various dimensions: cloud models such as Infrastructure as a Service (IaaS) and Platform as a Service (PaaS), virtual software stacks, MapReduce and its open source implementation (Hadoop), resource provider and user perspectives.

Results from both sites has been compared to existing mid-range resources in the Office of Science labs. These results has generated data for a cost-benefit analysis of various mid-range computing options for the Office of Science. Magellan project promotes open interface specifications for clouds.

Magellan allocation policy is the same as Science Clouds policy. They take requests for users interested in conducting exciting research on Magellan. Scientists seeking a project allocation on the Magellan machines

Figure 2. Magellan software architecture (Mallegan project, 2012). Courtesy of Argonne National Laboratory. Used with permission.

Argonne Magellan Software Architecture

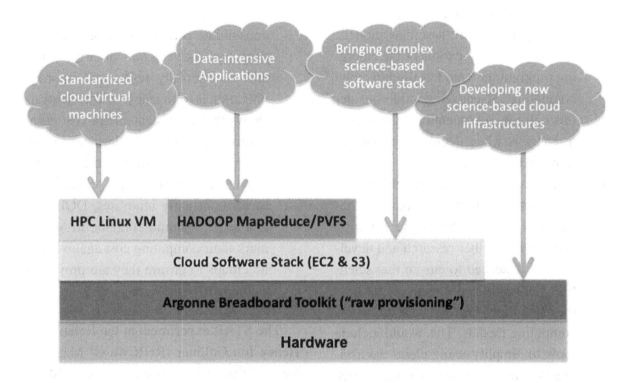

have to provide the following information as per the request of Science Cloud policy:

- Project name and title
- Project description
- Description of the science and expected achievements
- Requested allocation amount and duration

The key findings and recommendations of the Magellan project are summarized as the following:

- Cloud approaches provide many advantages, including customized environments that enable users to bring their own software stack and try out new computing environments without significant administration overhead, the ability to quickly surge resources to address larger problems, and the advantages that come from increased economies of scale. Virtualization is the primary strategy of providing these capabilities. Experience of working with application scientists using the cloud demonstrated the power of virtualization to enable fully customized

- environments and flexible resource management, and their potential value to scientists.

- Cloud computing may require significant initial effort and skills in order to port applications to these new models. This is also true for some of the emerging programming models used in cloud computing. Scientists should consider this upfront investment in any economic analysis when deciding whether to move to the cloud.

- Significant gaps and challenges exist in the areas of managing virtual environments, workflows, data, cyber security, and others. Further research and development is needed to ensure that scientists can easily and effectively harness the capabilities exposed with these new computing models. This would include tools to simplify using cloud environments, improvements to open source clouds software stacks, providing base images that help bootstrap users while allowing them flexibility to customize these stacks, investigation of new security techniques and approaches, and enhancements to MapReduce models to better fit scientific data and workflows. In addition, there are opportunities in exploring ways to enable these capabilities in traditional HPC platforms, thus combining the flexibility of cloud models with the performance of HPC systems.

- The key economic benefit of clouds comes from the consolidation of resources across a broad community, which results in higher utilization, economies of scale, and operational efficiency. Existing DOE centers already achieve many of the benefits of cloud computing since these centers consolidate computing across multiple program offices, deploy at large scales, and continuously refine and improve operational efficiency. Cost analysis shows that DOE centers are cost competitive, typically 3-7x less expensive, when compared to commercial cloud providers. Because the commercial sector constantly innovates, DOE labs and centers should continue to benchmark their computing cost against public clouds to ensure they are providing a competitive service.

The STAR experiment at the Relativistic Heavy Ion Collider (RHIC) used Magellan for real-time data processing. In addition, Biologists used the ALCF Magellan cloud to quickly analyze strains suspected in the E. coli[5] outbreak in Europe in summer 2011.

5.2 HelixNebula

A new cloud computing project called HelixNebula for Science Clouds has been launched by some of Europe's biggest research powerhouses along with European IT companies (HelixNebula project for Science Cloud, 2012). Three leading European research centers, the European Space Agency (ESA), along with the CERN physics laboratory and the European Molecular Biology Laboratory (EMBL), are teaming with commercial service providers to create a European cloud computing platform that can provide data storage and processing power for some of the region's major scientific research projects, beginning with the LHC at CERN.

"CERN's computing capacity needs to keep up with the enormous amount of data coming from the Large Hadron Collider and we see HelixNebula as a great way of working with industry to meet this challenge," Frédéric Hemmer, head of CERN's IT department, said in a statement.

The project's commercial partners include Atos, Capgemini, CloudSigma, Interoute, Logica, Orange Business Services, SAP, SixSq, Telefonica, Terradue, Thales, The Server Labs and T Systems, along with the Cloud Security Alliance, the OpenNebula project and the European Grid Infrastructure.

HelixNebula will allow European research organizations to carry out large complicated calculations probing some of the biggest mysteries of the universe, and to access additional cloud computing power to analyze huge sets of data.

During two years, pilot organizations CERN, ESA, and EMBL will use the Science Clouds for research projects and providing infrastructure on demand to their scientists; in particular, they will exploit HelixNebula for the following purposes, respectively:

- CERN plans to use the Science Clouds to sift through the reams of data being generated by particle collisions inside its ATLAS experiment on the LHC, which is searching for new particles never seen before, such as the rumored

Higgs boson thought to give other particles mass.

- The ESA, headquartered in Paris, plans to use the extra computing power to create a system that analyzes satellite observations of Earth to study earthquakes and volcanoes. ESA will collaborate with other science institutions on the project.

- The EMBL, based in Heidelberg, Germany, aims to utilize the cloud to analyze large genomes, such as those of mammals, to study evolution and biodiversity.

The Science Clouds will be tested by these three organizations during a two-year pilot phase, but welcomes other scientific organizations and industry partners to join the collaboration. Furthermore, HelixNebula will become available to governmental organizations and industry after an initial pilot phase.

5.3 VENUS-C

VENUS-C (Virtual Multidisciplinary EnviroNments USing Cloud Infrastructures)[6] is a project funded under the European Commission's 7th Framework Programme drawing its strength from a joint co-operation between computing service providers and scientific user communities to develop, test and deploy a large cloud computing infrastructure for science and SMEs in Europe.

VENUS-C provides innovative cloud solutions for individual and small research groups across diverse disciplines, with the aim of accelerating discovery. End-users are typical of the vast majority of researchers that have never had access to supercomputing networks and have relied on desktop resources.

The VENUS-C platform is underpinned by Windows Azure, resources from the Royal Institute of Technology (KTH, Sweden) and the Barcelona Supercomputing Center (BSC, Spain), Microsoft European data centers and the data center of the Engineering Group. Azure offers a multi-layer solution, including computing and storage power, a development environment and immediate services, together with a wide range of services that can be consumed from either on-premises environments or over the Internet. From an Open Source perspective, EMOTIVE and OpenNebula solutions are being implemented.

VENUS-C user scenarios stem from seven partner affiliations developing applications for the cloud across four thematic areas: Biomedicine, Architecture and Civil Engineering, Civil Protection and Emergencies, and Marine Biodiversity Data. VENUS-C has also provided seed funds for 15 pilots with applications spanning biology, bioinformatics, chemistry, earth sciences, maritime surveillance, mathematics, medicine and healthcare, physics and social media.

VENUS-C is co-funded by the GÉANT and e-Infrastructure Unit, DG Information Society and Media of the European Commission, as one of six European Distributed Computing Infrastructures (DCIs). It is committed to working in synergy with these initiatives, combining experiences in Grid infrastructures and cloud computing to capitalize on EU investments. This project brings together 14 European partners. Microsoft invests in Azure resources and manpower through Redmond and its European research centers.

According to Andrea Manieri, Engineering & VENUS-C Co-ordinator: "VENUS-C has a compelling range of applications that has grown over time with the on-boarding of 15 new pilots, helping to capture the benefits of cloud across diverse scientific settings and small businesses."

"Impressive second year results, positioning cloud as an effective paradigm not only for the research community, but also to small companies for which HPC systems are not economically affordable."

6. OPERATIONS RESEARCH AS A SERVICE

We have defined cloud computing as outsourcing of IT resources (software, hardware, etc.) in which dynamically scalable and often virtualized resources are provided as a service over the Internet. It means an infrastructure that provides on-demand, on the fly, instant and elastic resources or services over the Internet, usually at the scale and reliability of a data center.

In Software-as-a-Service (SaaS) model, software resides on a server accessed by numerous client machines over a network, as opposed to software residing in multiple copies on its users' machines. The future of software is in the cloud.

In this section, we envision how Operations Research as a scientific field can take advantages of cloud computing to provide more efficient and better services to users and scientific community. It is our vision that by combining Operations Research (OR) and cloud computing technologies, OR cloud will make a wider audience able to easily access and benefit from the increasing number of OR services. Researchers are familiar with OR tools, but with OR cloud we can offer a much simpler and faster method for doing Operations Research.

Operations Research (OR) is an important tool in engineering, science, economics, and business. But to be a practical tool, it needs to be integrated into modern corporate information technology (IT). Mike Trick in his blog (Trick, 2008) wrote, "Within OR, we often don't track IT concepts such as SOA or business intelligence, but we should: it can have a great effect on how our work is used in organizations." This statement says that exploiting cloud computing for OR is a must. In this section, we go over this special topic.

OR cloud mission is similar to Globus Online that is a hosted service to automate the tasks associated with moving files between sites. It does not require custom infrastructure, Globus Online is software-as-a-service that can be used by users without having to build these features. However, Operations Research is a much more complex science than file transfer, thus to develop a general-purpose and complete solution, PaaS and IaaS cloud models should be exploited.

Obtaining, configuring, and maintaining solvers for numerous optimization classes is an expensive and time consuming proposition. Additionally, optimization problems often require significant computing time. Running multiple problem instances, each requiring substantial CPU resources on a client machine such as a laptop is not practical. The ability to solve optimization problems in a distributed environment is an ideal solution.

Lack of standardization in OR world, makes the development of OR as a service more difficult. In OR world, there are numerous modeling languages with their own format, diverse problem instances with their own representation, various solvers with different APIs, results, etc.

In all, with OR in the cloud, scientists would benefit from the following advantages:

- No IT Required: requires no software installs or complex IT infrastructures
- Give users a tool that simplifies dealing with OR
- Automates the time-consuming and error-prone activity of doing OR, so users can stay focused on what is most important: their research
- Provide users with direct access to a wide variety of OR tools and services without the need to install, configure, or upgrade software on her computer.
- Enable better collaboration among users
- Reduce the time they have to spend on manual tasks
- Get the service up and running in minutes
- Provide a better solution for end users
- Handling and managing of users' dataset such as Graph, Matrix, Network, etc.
- Validating users' dataset
- Converting users' dataset into other data structures

177

With OR cloud, users simply specify their OR problem and some other information, e.g., which math programming model they would like to use, which methods, etc. They will do this through a few questions. Then, the OR cloud will provision the customized and the optimized OR environment for that OR problem.

Next parts of this special topic are organized as follows. Section 6.1 presents some background information on the topic. Then, Section 6.2 goes over related work. Section 6.3 presents operations research landscape. Section 6.4 discusses operations research cloud solution.

6.1 Background

Currently, if a researcher wants to solve an specific problem of her research area, she would need to pass through the following steps: (1) developing or finding the right and the most efficient model, algorithm, tool and software (2) installation (3) configuration (4) deployment (5) test (6) usage. In this special topic, we consider operations research and we provide cloud solutions to address the aforementioned challenges in solving OR problems for OR community.

Consider the following scenario as part of the first step. You read about an optimization algorithm in the literature and you get an idea on how to improve it. Testing your new idea typically requires re-implementing (and re-debugging and re-testing) the original algorithm. Often, clever implementation details are not published. It can be difficult to replicate reported performance. Now imagine the scenario if the original algorithm was publicly available in a community repository. Weeks of re-implementing would no longer be required. You would simply check out a copy of it for yourself and modify it. Imagine the productivity gains from software reuse. This part is addressed by OR free software such as COIN-OR (COmputational INfrastructure for Operations Research) [7]. The COIN-OR project is an initiative to spur the development of open source software for the operations research community. The Open Source Initiative explains it well. When people can read, redistribute, and modify the source code, software evolves. People improve it, people adapt it, people fix bugs. The results of open source development have been remarkable. Community-based efforts to develop software under open source licenses have produced high-quality, high-performance code. They are building an open source community for operations research software in order to speed development and deployment of models, algorithms, and cutting-edge computational research, as well as provide a forum for peer review of software similar to that provided by archival journals for theoretical research. This is a lofty goal, but we believe it's a worthwhile one. We have ideas, but we don't have all the answers. Only the community of users and contributors can define what is needed to make it a reality. In addition to free software resources, there are many enterprise OR tools such as CPLEX [8] that can be hosted in the cloud. With these rich set of OR resources that are hosted in the cloud, OR cloud will be able to intelligently offer OR services for OR community.

The first and the main obstacle in usage of software, tools, and source code repositories is their installation and then their configuration management. Users need to install and deploy them in order to use them. This is a big challenge for user community of any scientific field. The second difficulty of scientists is the usage of a software and a service. In addition, some questions such as whether a software is a good one for a problem, whether a software is optimized for a problem, etc. are very important for scientists in order to solve their problems with the most efficient and optimal methods. In addition, installation, configuration, and deployment of these OR tools, software and services is a time-consuming task. By transforming all these bundles in the cloud we can instantiate them faster and users will get rid of all the difficult tasks. As a result, time to solutions will be faster than before.

There are many tools, software and services in the market and open source software in free software to offer appropriate solutions for various OR community. We have diverse set of OR problems, diverse set of models, methods, etc., etc. One solution, one piece of software, one interface, one tools, one math programming model does not suit the needs of all operations research users. Thus, if for an OR department we only use one OR software tool such as CPLEX, we cannot say that all OR users will be able to use it to solve their problems, also in the future perhaps will be more problems which cannot be solved by CPLEX. Therefore, we need to provide to an OR user a suitable and customized OR environment in order to model their problems with the most appropriate and optimized math programming model (e.g. algebraic language), and then select the best and the most efficient method to solve their problems. This OR environment depends on the focus of research activity. In sum, the OR cloud should be general-purpose and rich enough in order to address the needs of all OR user community or a large part of them.

In order to provide customized OR environment to a user according to its need, problem, and so on, we need to develop an OR-aware interface as an abstraction layer over OR tools, software, mathematical programming models, methods, algorithms, etc. An OR-aware interface at the highest level of cloud will determine the user needs based on a few questions and then will prepare the most efficient OR environment for that user. In cases that there are more than an option, this interface will suggest to the user the best possible options. This abstraction layer will be implemented as part of SaaS solution of OR.

In order to implement an OR cloud system with the aforementioned features, IaaS and SaaS cloud paradigms should be exploited as well.

6.2 State of the Art

Globus Online (Globus Online Project, 2011) is among the first cloud solutions for scientists, it makes robust file transfer capabilities accessible to any researcher with an Internet connection and a laptop. Globus manages the entire file transfer operation automatically: monitoring performance, retrying failed transfers, recovering from faults automatically whenever possible, and reporting status. Users cite Globus Online as their preferred service since it is easy, fast, secure, reliable and research-focused.

NEOS (Network-Enabled Optimization System) (Czyzyk, Mesnier, & Mor´e, 1998) is an online optimization service which has been widely used by the OR community for over a decade. A central server maintains and queues job submissions for solvers that run on a variety of workstations scattered around the Internet. The main drawback of NEOS is its central server paradigm.

At first, submissions were MPS-format files for linear problems and C or Fortran programs for nonlinear ones, but in the recent versions the great majority of submissions are in high-level modeling languages, predominantly AMPL (AMPL, 2011) and GAMS (GAMS, 2011).

Submissions through the NEOS Web portal[9] remain popular, and they can also be made by sending XML text files through email. The latest NEOS release features a NEOS API that permits all server functions to be accessed through remote function calls using the XML-RPC protocols (www.xmlrpc.com). This has brought NEOS more in line with the precepts of SOA and has made it much easier to integrate into optimization modeling environments. Nevertheless, its design still adheres in many respect to the central server paradigm. Also NEOS employs whatever file formats are supported by the various solvers; the over 40 solvers in the NEOS lineup require instance inputs of about a dozen different kinds. Similarly there is no NEOS standard

format for communicating options to solvers or communicating results from solvers.

In Fourer, Ma, and Martin (2010), authors present a distributed optimization environment (Optimization Services or OS) in which solvers, modeling languages, registries, analyzers, and simulation engines are implemented as services. It defines standards for decentralized optimization on the Internet: representation of optimization instances, results, and solver options; communication between clients and solvers; and discovery and registration of optimization-related software using Web Services. The OS project addresses NEOS weaknesses.

In all, while OS provides online distributed optimization services as a SaaS cloud, but it is not a complete cloud solution. Users will not be able to build their own OR applications if they cannot be offered by SaaS solution. In order to approach a more complete solution, IaaS and PaaS cloud paradigms are suggested to be used in this special.

6.3 Operations Research Landscape

In this section, we review Operations Research landscape that includes everything in Operations Research world to model and to solve OR problems such as all types of OR software, mathematical programming models, methods, algorithms, etc. In COmputational INfrastructure for Operations Research (2011), there are various OR projects, therefore it shows that OR is not only LP and IP algorithms. The COIN-OR OS libraries currently support the commercial solvers CPLEX and LINDO, in addition to the open source COIN-OR solvers

Bonmin, Cbc, Clp, Couenne, DyLP, Ipopt, SYMPHONY, and Vol. The GNU GLPK solver is also supported by the OS libraries. These OR projects are categorized into the following:

- **Developer tools:** At this category, there are developer tools such as BuildTools, CoinBazaar, CoinBinary, CoinWeb and so on to build new OR applications based on them. They provide compilation, configuration, build, test, integration and distribution of OR applications. The corresponding cloud solution for this category is a PaaS paradigm.

- **Documentation:** By transforming everything to the cloud, we do not need documentation any more. To help and support users how to use OR tools, etc. For instance, CoinEasy provides information for new users of COIN-OR. Its objective is to make it easy to use COIN-OR projects. Different users have different objectives and it is important to provide information on how to get up and running easily depending upon objective. OR-aware interface as an abstraction layer over OR tools will ask a few question to the user and will provide the most straightforward solution and environment.

- **Graphs:** Problem's data can be represented as a matrix, vector, graph, directed graph, directed acyclic graph(DAG), undirected graph, network, etc. Even some data structures may exploit random distributions (continuous), e.g., in

stochastic problems. There are various tools to make the process of input data preparation much easier. Tools such as data structure conversion would be very helpful. COIN-OR Graph Classes (CGC) provides a collection of network representations and algorithms. Library of Efficient Models and Optimization in Networks (LEMON) is a C++ template library aimed at combinatorial optimization tasks, especially those working with graphs and networks. An OR cloud service such as "OR Data as a Service" can be developed to provide various data services for OR community.

- **Interfaces:** In OR world, we need some interfaces to link different components in order to build a customized OR environment such as links, APIs, and Web Services. For example, AIMMSlinks provides interfaces to link the modeling language AIMMS and COIN-OR solvers. And GAMSlinks links between GAMS (General Algebraic Modeling System) and solvers that are hosted at COIN-OR. Also, APIs are categorized as interfaces, for example CoinMP is a lightweight API and DLL for CLP, CBC, and CGL. NLPAPI is Nonlinear Programming API, a subroutine interface for defining and solving nonlinear programming problems. OSI (Open Solver Interface) is an uniform API for calling embedded linear and mixed-integer programming solvers. OS (Optimization Services) offers standards for representing optimization instances, results, solver options, and communication between clients and solvers in a distributed environment using Web Services.

- **Metaheuristics:** Algorithms and methods are the main engine of OR world to solve problems. Djinni is a templatized C++ framework with Python bindings for heuristic search. METSlib is an object oriented metaheuristics optimization framework and toolkit in C++. Open Tabu Search(OTS) is a framework for constructing tabu search algorithms.

- **Modeling systems:** An OR problem should be formulated by a mathematical programming model. There are various mathematical programming models. CMPL(Coin Mathematical Programming Language) is a mathematical programming language and a system for modeling. Coopr(A COmmon Optimization Python Repository) integrates a variety of Python optimization-related packages. Coopr supports a diverse set of optimization capabilities that can be used to formulate and analyze optimization applications. FLOPC++ is an algebraic modeling language embedded in C++. PuLP is Python library for modeling linear and integer programs. ROSE, Reformulation-Optimization Software Engine, is a software for performing symbolic reformulations to Mathematical Programs (MP).

In addition, there are specific projects in Open Source community for specific problems. There are numerous optimization problem classes including linear, nonlinear, mixed-integer linear and nonlinear, stochastic, cone, etc.

- **Optimization convex non-differentiable:** OBOE(Oracle Based Optimization Engine) is optimization of convex problems with user-supplied methods delivering key first order information (like support to the feasible set, support to the objective function)

- **Optimization deterministic linear continuous:** CLP (COIN-OR LP) is a simplex solver. DyLP(Dynamic LP) is an implementation of the dynamic simplex methods. VOL (Volume Algorithm) is a subgradient algorithm that also computes approximate primal solutions.

- **Optimization deterministic linear discrete:** There are many methods to solve this type of problems. ABACUS, A Branch-And-CUt System, is an LP-based branch-and-cut framework. BCP, Branch-Cut-Price Framework, is a framework for constructing parallel branch-cut-price algorithms for mixed-integer linear programs. CBC, COIN-OR Branch and Cut, is an LP-based branch-and-cut library.

- **Optimization deterministic non-linear:** DFO: Derivative-Free Optimization, a package for solving general nonlinear optimization problems when derivatives are unavailable.

filterSD: Subroutines for nonlinear optimization, a library for nonlinear optimization written in Fortran. Ipopt: Interior-Point Optimizer, for general large-scale nonlinear optimization. MOCHA: Matroid Optimization: Combinatorial Heuristics and Algorithms, heuristics and algorithms for multicriteria matroid optimization

- **Optimization deterministic nonlinear discrete:** Bonmin: Basic Open-source Nonlinear Mixed INteger programming, an experimental open-source C++ code for solving general MINLP (Mixed Integer NonLinear Programming) problems Couenne: Couenne, a branch-and-bound algorithm for mixed integer nonlinear programming problems LaGO: Lagrangian Global Optimizer, for the global optimization of nonconvex mixed-integer nonlinear programs.

- **Optimization deterministic semidefinite continuous:** CSDP, an interior-point method for semidefinite programming

- **Optimization stochastic:** SMI: Stochastic Modeling Interface, for optimization under uncertainty

- **Optimization utility:** ADOL-C is a package for the automatic differentiation of C and C++ programs. CHiPPS, COIN-OR High Performance Parallel Search Framework, a framework for constructing parallel tree search algorithms (includes an LP-based branch-cut-price implementation). CppAD, a tool for differentiation of C++ func-

tions. PFunc: Parallel Functions, is a lightweight and portable library that provides C and C++ APIs to express task parallelism.

6.4 Operations Research Cloud Solutions

In the previous section we enumerated various OR projects, tools, software packages, libraries, etc. in OR world. OR cloud solutions should reuse and exploit already available solutions in OR world with the help of IaaS, PaaS and SaaS cloud paradigms. SaaS paradigm suits to reuse software without significant changes such as tuning configuration parameters, while when we want to build new OR applications based on available OR solutions and our development, IaaS and PaaS paradigms are the right choice, for example to link a model to an interface and exploit our specific OR algorithm for a specific OR problem.

Table 1 provides some information on the corresponding cloud solution for each category of the aforementioned OR projects in the previous section, and compare the provisioning time and actions of traditional OR projects versus OR cloud solutions.

In addition to free software resources, there are many enterprise OR tools such as CPLEX that can be hosted in the cloud. With these rich set of OR resources that are hosted in the cloud, OR cloud will be able to intelligently offer OR services to OR community. In the provisioning column we use the first letter of provisioning actions to represent them i.e. I. for installation, C. for configuration, D. for deployment, T. for test, and B. for boot.

Table 1. Traditional OR solution vs. its corresponding OR cloud solution

Traditional OR solution	Provisioning actions and time	OR cloud solution	Provisioning actions and time
Developer tools	I.C.D.T.B long	IaaS, SaaS	B short
Documentation	B short	SaaS:OR-aware cloud interface	B short
Graphs	I.C.D.T.B long	IaaS, PaaS	B short
Interfaces	I.C.D.T.B long	IaaS, PaaS, SaaS	B short
Modeling systems	I.C.D.T.B long	IaaS, PaaS	B short
Metaheuristics	I.C.D.T.B long	IaaS, PaaS	B short
Optimization utility	I.C.D.T.B long	IaaS, PaaS	B short

Table 1 demonstrates applicability of cloud paradigms to OR world. Unlike traditional OR solution with this, OR world would be available online without significant attempt to provision OR environment.

Figure 3 presents a high level architecture of OR cloud.

OR-aware interface is an abstraction layer over OR tools, software, mathematical programming models, methods, algorithms, etc. An OR-aware interface at the highest level of cloud will determine the user needs based on a few questions and then will provide the most efficient OR environment for that user, like in (Fourer, Ma, & Martin, 2010) that optimization problems are solved automatically with minimal input from the user. Users only need to provide a definition of the optimization problem; all additional information required by the optimization solver is determined automatically. In cases that there are more than an option, this interface will suggest to the user the best possible options. This abstraction layer might be implemented as part of SaaS solution.

In Fourer, Ma, and Martin (2010), if users are not sure of the type of optimization problem, they should consult the Optimization Tree of the NEOS Guide for information on optimization problems. The choice of solver is then dictated by the language used to define the optimization problem. However, we move this action to the cloud i.e. OR-aware interface layer.

At IaaS we have a number of Virtual Appliances abstracted as Virtual Machines (VM). IaaS VMs are developed by reusing available OR tools. They are prepared by OR experts of various fields. These VMs contain customized OR environments for different OR problems. We reuse OR tools, software, services, open source software, etc. in order to build these VMs.

With development environment (Platform-as-a-Service) on the cloud, users will be able to develop their own OR applications by exploiting already available OR tools, algorithms, methods in the cloud.

Like any cloud effort, standardization at the interface and data levels are very important, for example open standards for data interchange.

Figure 3. Operations Research cloud architecture

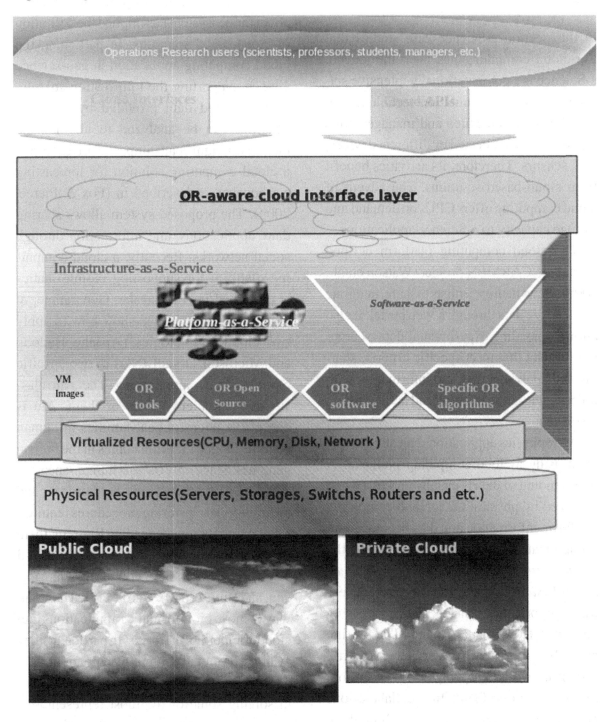

7. E-SCIENCE

In this section e-Science case studies that use cloud computing has been introduced. e-Science is a computationally intensive science that adopts simulation techniques on distributed architectures and manages huge amount of data collected by different devices, e.g., sensors. Therefore, its activities benefit from cloud-based solutions. The advent of cloud computing offers CPUs on demand and storage capacity to e-Science applications.

The cloud computing platform defined within the CARMEN project (Watson et. al., 2008) allows neuroscientists to share, integrate and analyze data through a Web portal. It also allows uploading experimental data, searching for data that meet specific criteria, sharing and analyzing data and information with others using authentication and authorization mechanisms.

Astrophysics applications can also benefit from using a cloud computing platform. A huge amount of data is usually processed and analyzed by physics. On a cloud computing platform, information and data become input for applications and codes. For example, the *Computational Infrastructure for Nuclear Astrophysics* represents the first experiment that supports file sharing, data processing and workflow management. The online cloud based approach described in (Smith, 2011) allows accelerating tasks execution, removing errors, facilitating collaborations and providing new ways to analyze data. The author shows how this approach can be used for integrating nuclear data with some astrophysical simulation codes.

The increasing need of getting information about the ecosystem has implied the definition of cloud-based solutions. In particular, the cloud computing application in geo-science aims at supporting the information sharing. The collected data provided by different satellites can be analyzed to identify the ones with significant impact. For example, a cloud computing solution for forecasting earthquakes is described in (Fox & Pierce, 2009). The proposed system allows sharing data, applications, and information through social networks. Recently, a cloud computing platform for supporting bioinformatics is described in (Ekanayake, Gunarathne, & Qiu, 2010). The authors show how to apply two cloud technologies (Apache Hadoop and Microsoft DryadLINQ) to two specific bioinformatics applications. The Alu classification problem is one of them. Alu is one of the largest repeat families in human genome (about 1 million copies in the human genome). Since only 0.7% is human-specific, Alu classification is a very hard process and the traditional clustering procedures require a lot of computational capacity. Running them on cloud architectures can guarantee useful advantages. In Dudley, Pouliot, Chen, Morgan, and Butte (2010), it is described how and why to move bioinformatics applications into cloud computing platforms. In particular, they evaluate the cloud computing potentialities in performing a large-scale data integration and in solving some of the most representative research problems in genomics. In fact, fast and large-scale comparative genomic strategies can be run on cloud computing architectures. For example, in Wall et al. (2010), it is shown how to adapt the comparative algorithm (Reciprocal Smallest Distance, RSD) to be executed on Amazon's Elastic Computing Cloud (EC2). In (Wall et al., 2010), the authors show the economic benefits in defining a cloud computing platform in genomics. In particular, they optimize the computation of a large-scale resource (Roundup) using cloud computing and some cost-effectiveness procedures are also detailed.

Recently, in Chang, Wills, and Walters (2011), a general framework for implementing cloud solutions (*Cloud Computing Business Framework*-CCBF) is adapted for addressing bioinformatics issues. The authors present a PaaS model to simulate dynamic three-dimensional modeling and visualization of proteins, genes, molecules and medical imaging.

The lack of appropriate tools to efficiently manage a huge amount of data is a bottleneck for scientific research. Data management as cloud services is a solution. In this way, the researchers can use SaaS models and the applications can be remotely hosted and accessed via Web. However, a relevant problem that still remains in using cloud-based e-science solutions is related to data transition. The Argonne team is currently working on the definition of *GlobusOnline*, a data movement service for researchers (see Table 2).

Many efforts are currently addressed to the definition of cloud computing platforms for supporting simulations in Computational Fluid Dynamics (CFD). In fact, in March 2012, Nimbis Services, Inc. has presented an on-demand *Caedium CFD Accelerator* cloud product. Some examples of possible CFD models analyzed with Caedium are: airflow

Table 2.

Example 1	In 2011, the Kyoto University (Japan) within the *GenomeNet* project designed a cloud computing platform. Life science research generates a huge amount of data to be stored (and not only managed) also for a long period of time. The Kyoto University Bio-informatics center focused on the definition of a high performance cloud for handling genomics and other research projects. The system was equipped with two servers: one for the computational chemistry and one for the GenomeNet computations.
Exmaple 2	In 2012, the University of Missouri, one of the most important centers for genomics in the Midwest, has involved the St.Louis-based analytics company (Appistry) in order to provide solutions for life sciences, financial services and intelligence markets. The center has leveraged Appistry's platform (*Ayrris/BIO*) for managing big data related to plant and animal genomes. This platform transforms the traditional analytic applications into high-performance distributed ones and the responsibility for data management passes from the researcher to an automatic system. Then, researchers can focus their efforts only on detecting scientific results analyzing data thanks to advanced software, hardware and storage.

over a moving car, water flow around watercraft and through pipes. The goal is to provide a cloud platform to make CFD simulations and support users that can access to virtually unlimited computing resources, consider more options in less time. This allows significantly reducing costs and improving performances (see Table 3)

Table 3.

Example 1	*DNAnexus*, an important American company, defines cloud-based systems for supporting biotechnology and e-Science. In particular, it aims to provide large genomic datasets to all scientific researches and communities. The company has recently worked with Google Cloud Storage to define a public repository of DNA sequencing data from some research institutions.

Many of the experiments in e-Science are also called *in-silico experiments*. An in-silico experiment, frequently used in bio-informatics, adopts local applications and remote services to verify and test hypothesis and demonstrate facts ((Addis et al.,2003)). A cloud platform for these types of experiments is described in Table 4.

Table 4.

Example 1	University of Florida and University of Chicago have proposed *CloudBLAST* (Matsunaga, Tsugawa, & Fortes, 2008). BLAST (*Basic Local Alignment Search Tool*) is a tool used for individuating regions of local similarities between nucleotide or protein sequences. Given a set Q of q sequences, BLAST compares each of them with a database of s sequences. Then, it calculates the statistical significance of matches. The platform parallelizes, deploys and manages these bio-informatics applications combining distributed computing technologies. It adopts the MapReduce paradigm for parallelizing and better managing the application executions. According to parallel paradigms, Q is partitioned and each BLAST instance (worker) looks for similarities in a subset of Q.
Example 2	In 2012, the project *HelixNebula - the science cloud* has been launched and supported by the European Union. Companies like Atos, CloudSigma and T-Systems cooperate with three European research centers: the European organization for Nuclear Research, the European Molecular Biology Laboratory and the European Space Agency. The aim is to allow the scientific organizations to acquire, elaborate, store and analyze big data using the new ICTs. Cloud computing can offer efficiency and innovation. The three centers have already defined distributed scientific applications involving and using the data centers provided by Atos, Cloud Sigma and T-Systems. The Higgs boson identification, a significant result announced by the CERN, has been possible thanks to this cloud platform that allows the center to perform a large number of simulations with reasonable computational efforts.

8. CONCLUSION

The UberCloud Experiment has demonstrated how cloud computing is being adopted in science. The second round of the experiment started on November 15th, 2012 with the kick-off in the Intel Booth Theater at SC'12 in Salt Lake City, together with a live Webinar broadcasted to all participants around the world. This time the project has extended the application areas to more scientific disciplines: HPC, CAE, and Life Sciences communities (Gentzsch & Yenier, 2012c).

They have applied the cloud computing service model to challenging CAE workloads. With the capacity of their current workstations often unable to provide enough memory, simulations taking too long, and the number of jobs too small to get quality results, CAE engineers and their organizations are looking to increase their available computing power beyond the workstations. The problem statement for them is: Should they buy or rent? Buying additional compute power leads to all kinds of challenges in the context of a high-performance compute cluster acquisition. With the advent of cloud computing the other option is to use remote resources from cloud providers.

SaaS solutions like Globus Online, IaaS solutions such as Nimbus Infrastructure and OpenNebula, and services provided by the UberCloud experiment all hands-in-hands accelerate the discovery of science by helping the endpoints get together and conduct advanced and large scale science.

REFERENCES

Addis, M., Ferris, J., Greenwood, M., Li, P., Marvin, D., Oinn, T., & Wipat, A. (2003). Experiences with e-science workflow specification and enactment in bioinformatics. In *All hands meeting*. Academic Press.

Amazon Elastic Compute Cloud. (2012). Retrieved from http://aws.amazon.com/ec2

AMPL. (2011). Retrieved from http://www.ampl.com

CERN - The Large Hadron Collider. (2012). Retrieved from http://public.Web.cern.ch/public/en/LHC/LHC-en.html

Chang, V., Wills, G., & Walters, R. (2011). The positive impacts offered by healthcare cloud and 3D bioinformatics. In *Proceedings of 10th E-Science all Hands Meeting 2011*. Academic Press.

Computational Infrastructure for Operations Research. (2011). Retrieved from http://www.coinor.org

Czyzyk, J., Mesnier, M. P., & Mor'e, J. J. (1998). The neos server. *IEEE Computational Science & Engineering*, *5*, 68–75. doi:10.1109/99.714603

Dudley, J. T., Pouliot, Y., Chen, R., Morgan, A. A., & Butte, A. J. (2010). Translational bioinformatics in the cloud: An affordable alternative. *Genome Medicine*, *2*(8), 51. doi:10.1186/gm172 PMID:20691073

Ekanayake, J., Gunarathne, T., & Qiu, J. (2010). *Cloud technologies for bioinformatics applications*. Academic Press.

European Grid Initiative. (2012). Retrieved from http://www.egi.eu/

Foster, I., Kesselman, C., & Tuecke, S. (2001). The anatomy of the grid – Enabling scalable virtual organizations. *The International Journal of Supercomputer Applications*, *15*, 200–222. doi:10.1177/109434200101500302

Fourer, R., Ma, J., & Martin, R. K. (2010). Optimization services: A framework for distributed optimization. *Operations Research*, *58*(6), 1624–1636. doi:10.1287/opre.1100.0880

Fox, G. C., & Pierce, M. (2009). *Web 2.0, cloud computing, and earthquake forecasting*. Retrieved from http://grids.ucs.indiana.edu/ptliupages/publications/CloudWeb-20Quakesim.pdf

Gams. (2011). Retrieved from http://www.gams.com

Gentzsch, W., Grandinetti, L., & Joubert, G. (2010). *High speed and large scale scientific computing*. IOS Press Inc. Retrieved from http://books.google.it/books?id=c6xc-nhMXSsC

Gentzsch, W., & Yenier, B. (2012). *HPC experiment - Final report of round 2*.

Globus Online Project. (2011). Retrieved from http://www.globusonline.org/

Grandinetti, L. (2008). *High performance computing and grids in action*. IOS Press Inc. Retrieved from http://books.google.it/books?id=zNmZLutAXA8C

Helixnebula Project for Science Cloud. (2012). Retrieved from http://www.HelixNebula.org

Italian Grid Infrastructure. (2012). Retrieved from http://www.italiangrid.org/

Keahey. (2008). Science clouds: Early experiences in cloud computing for scientific applications. In *Proceedings of Cloud Computing and its Applications 2008 (CCA-08).* Chicago, IL: CCA.

Mallegan Project. (2012). Retrieved from http://magellan.alcf.anl.gov/architecture/

Matsunaga, A., Tsugawa, M., & Fortes, J. (2008). CloudBLAST: Combining MapReduce and virtualization on distributed resources for bioinformatics applications. In *Proceedings of IEEE International Conference on eScience.* IEEE.

Nimbus Toolkit Project. (2010). Retrieved from http://nimbusproject.org/

Nurmi, D. et al. (2008). The eucalyptus open-source cloud-computing system. In *Proceedings of Cloud Computing and its Applications'08.* CCA.

OpenNebula. (2010). *Opennebula cloud toolkit.* Retrieved from http://OpenNebula.org/

Reservoir Project. (2012). Retrieved from http://www.reservoir-fp7.eu/

Science Clouds Project. (2012). Retrieved from http://www.scienceclouds.org/

Smith, M. S. (2011). Nuclear data for astrophysics research: A new online paradigm. *Journal of the Korean Physical Society, 59*(2), 761–766.

Sotomayor, B. (2010). *Haizea.* Retrieved from http://haizea.cs.uchicago.edu/

Sotomayor, B., Montero, R., Llorente, I., & Foster, I. (2009). Virtual infrastructure management in private and hybrid clouds. *IEEE Internet Computing, 13*(5), 14–22. doi:10.1109/MIC.2009.119

Teragrid. (2012). Retrieved from http://www.teragrid.org/

The Star Collaboration. (2012). Retrieved from http://www.star.bnl.gov

Trick, M. (2008). *Operations research blog: Don Ratliff at IFORS.* Retrieved from http://mat.tepper.cmu.edu/blog/?p=301

Wall, D., Kudtarkar, P., Fusaro, V., Pivovarov, R., Patil, P., & Tonellato, P. (2010). Cloud computing for comparative genomics. *BMC Bioinformatics, 11*(1), 259. doi:10.1186/1471-2105-11-259 PMID:20482786

Watson, P., Lord, P., Gibson, F., Periorellis, P., & Pitsilis, G. (2008). Cloud computing for e-science with Carmen. In *Proceedings of 2nd Iberian Grid Infrastructure Conference* (pp. 3–14). Academic Press.

KEY TERMS AND DEFINITIONS

Cumulus: An Open Source Storage Cloud for Science; it is like Amazon S3.

Globus Online: A hosted service to automate the tasks associated with moving files between sites. It does not require custom infrastructure; Globus Online is software-as-a-service that can be used today without building these features yourself.

Grid Computing: Coordinated resource sharing and problem solving in dynamic, multi-institutional virtual organization. Grids have been the center of attention from scientific and High Performance Computing communities (HPC), especially for the distributed and large scale scientific applications, and also in collaborative style of work.

HelixNebula: A recent cloud computing project for Science Clouds; it has been launched by some of Europe's biggest research such as CERN along with European IT companies.

High Performance Computing: The use of advanced parallel processing systems (usually, above a teraflop or 1012 floating-point operations per second) for running complicated and huge processes quickly, efficiently, and reliably.

Magellan: One of the first projects to conduct an exhaustive evaluation of the use of cloud computing for science in the US. The Magellan project is funded through the U.S. Department of Energy (DOE) Office of Advanced Scientific Computing Research (ASCR).

Nimbus Infrastructure: An open source EC2/S3-compatible Infrastructure-as-a-Service implementation specifically targeting features of interest to the scientific community such as support for proxy credentials, batch schedulers, best-effort allocations, and others.

Nimbus Toolkit: An Infrastructure-as-a-Service cloud computing for science. Nimbus platform is an integrated set of tools that deliver the power and versatility of infrastructure clouds to scientific users. Nimbus platform allows you to combine Nimbus, OpenStack, Amazon, and other clouds.

Science Clouds: Have emerged as a result of scientific application needs for outsourced compute and storage infrastructures. Science Clouds provided by Open Source Nimbus Toolkit, and Commercial Amazon Elastic Compute Cloud (EC2) that provide computational capabilities for computing are often referred as IaaS. They provide compute cycles in the cloud for scientific communities using Nimbus.

ENDNOTES

[1] http://scienceclouds.org/blog/cumulus-open-source-storage-cloud-for-science/

[2] http://messagelab.monash.edu.au/News/NimrodCloud

[3] http://www.openqrm-enterprise.com/community/

[4] http://www.enomaly.com/

[5] http://www.cdc.gov/ecoli/outbreaks.html

[6] http://www.venus-c.eu/

[7] http://www.coin-or.org/

[8] http://www-01.ibm.com/software/integration/optimization/cplex-optimizer/

[9] www.mcs.anl.gov/neos/solvers

Chapter 10
Cloud Computing and Operations Research

ABSTRACT

The aim of this chapter is twofold. On one hand, it shows how some classes of optimization problems can be efficiently solved on a cloud platform, especially in terms of storage capacity and computing power. Since an exhaustive treatment of this topic is beyond the purpose of the book, the attention is focused on the following classes of optimization problems: Linear Programming, Integer Linear Programming, Stochastic Optimization, and Logistics Management. On the other hand, the chapter also shows how some problems that arise in designing and managing the clouds can be mathematically formulated as optimization problems. Among these, the attention is focused on the Data Center Location Problem, the Virtual Machines Allocation Problem, and the Partner Provider Selection Problem. Finally, some useful conclusions are derived on the relation between Simulation-based Optimization and cloud computing.

1. INTRODUCTION

Operations Research (OR) aims to define theoretical foundation and mathematical methods for modeling and simulation, of complex, challenging optimization, organization, management, planning problems and to devise the relevant computational algorithms and software for their numerical solution.

This chapter shows the close relation between cloud computing and OR. For this purpose, it is mainly organized in two parts.

The first part (Section 2) highlights how some classes of optimization problems can

DOI: 10.4018/978-1-4666-4683-4.ch010

be efficiently solved by running the related algorithms on a cloud. However, since an exhaustive treatment of this topic lies outside the scope of this book, particular attention is given to the following classes of optimization problems: *Linear Programming*, *Integer Linear Programming*, *Stochastic Optimization* and *Logistics Management*. For a detailed introduction to Operations Research, we refer the interested readers to specific books. For each of the aforementioned classes, after introducing some basic concepts, major emphasis is then given to how they can be efficiently solved on a cloud by also providing application examples taken from literature. Finally, among the advantages, the possibility to use advanced optimization solvers and software tools as cloud services is also considered.

The second part of the chapter (Section 3), instead, describes how some issues that arise in designing and managing a cloud can be mathematically modeled as optimization problems. Particular attention will be given to some problems such as the *Data Center Location Problem* and the *Virtual Machine Allocation Problem*. Finally, the last two paragraphs of the chapter will be devoted to present some useful considerations on the problem of selecting the partner providers of a cloud and on the relation between Simulation-based Optimization approaches and cloud computing.

2. OPERATIONS RESEARCH ON CLOUDS

Generally speaking, the *optimization problems* aim to find the optimal solution (or a suboptimal one) among a set of feasible alternatives with reference to an objective function to be minimized or maximized. An example is to find the best resources utilization in order to reach a desired optimization objective (to minimize the total cost or maximize the service levels, for instance).

More precisely, the optimization problems are mathematically formulated by identifying the variables that represent the decisions to be determined and by defining the objective to be minimized or maximized, as well as the constraints on the decision variables, by functions on the variables domain.

Depending on the mathematical formulation, we can have different classes of optimization problems. After individuating the specific class, one can adopt the related solution approaches for the problem under investigation.

This section is mainly devoted to show how some of the most interesting classes of optimization problems can be efficiently solved by running the related solution algorithms on a cloud.

The optimization solvers are usually run on local computers that could not have the sufficient storage capability, for instance. To overcome these limitations, cloud computing can be seen as an effective solution. Among the other significant advantages, cloud computing can also provide the decision makers with the most advanced optimizers to be used as services.

The advantages provided by the adoption of a cloud platform can be more evident especially in the case of large scale optimization problems. It is worth noting that the term large scale is here referred not only to the optimization problems with a considerable number of variables and constraints but also to the ones that exhibit challenging structures for the currently available solution methods.

2.1 Linear Programming

A Linear Programming problem can be mathematically formulated in the following *standard form*:

Min

$$z = c^T x$$

subject to

$$Ax = b$$

$$x \geq 0$$

where: $x \in \Re^n$ represents the column vector of the *decision variables*, A is a $m \times n$ matrix of the *technological coefficients*, $c \in \Re^n$ denotes the column vector of the *cost coefficients* and $b \in \Re^m$ is the column vector of the *right hand side terms*. The constraints of the model as well as the objective are assumed to be defined by linear functions.

A solution $\bar{x}$ that satisfies all the constraints (such that: $A\bar{x} = b$ and $\bar{x} \geq 0$) is a *feasible solution* of the model. The *feasible region* of the model ($\Omega \subseteq \Re^n$) consists of only the feasible solutions.

An optimal solution (x^*) of the model is a feasible solution (such that $x^* \in \Omega$) and, in addition,

$$z^* = c^T x^* \leq z(\bar{x}) = c^T \bar{x}, \forall \bar{x} \in \Omega.$$

When a solution is found, the values of the components of x become known and then, all the required information is deducted.

However, in the presence of many realistic applications, the required computational efforts could be high and also the needed storage capability could be significant. These issues can be efficiently addressed by moving to a cloud. A linear programming problem could become a large scale optimization problem if formulated on realistic scenarios that require, for instance, to introduce a lot of constraints and decision variables. In these contexts, cloud computing provides the decision makers with an advanced computing environment and the required storage capability.

The *Simplex Method* (introduced by George Dantzig in 1947), the most popular solution method for the linear programming models in their standard form, has been efficiently implemented in a distributed version. The scientific contribution of (Yarmish & Van Slyke, 2009) proposes a scalable and distributed version of the simplex implementation for large linear programs. The authors implement the standard form of the method in order to reach a higher level of scalability and their proposed version is shown to be efficient and effective also in the presence of dense problems.

Cloud computing provides the decision makers, that usually have very limited computing resources to run large scale linear optimization tasks, with considerable computing power and advanced software tools as services. However, data security still limits the adoption of cloud computing especially in all the cases in which the performed computations process and/or generate confidential information. Robust security mechanisms become a need in order to protect the users data and to prevent malicious attacks that could also misrepresent the final results. For example, in the work proposed in Wang, Ren, and Wang (2011), the authors address these security issues with particular attention to the outsourcing of linear programming computations. The proposed security mechanism explicitly decomposes the linear programming computations into *public linear programming solvers*, that can be run on a cloud, and into *private linear programming parameters*, that contain the confidential data. Then, the authors develop an appropriate set of transformation techniques with the aim of preserving the private information. The readers interested to get more details on this topic are referred to their work.

2.2 Integer Linear Programming

In the case in which some or all the decision variables of a mathematical model are constrained to be integer, the related optimization problem belongs to the class of (*Mixed*) *Integer Linear Programming*. If the n components of the vector (x) of the decision variables have to be integer, the feasible region Π of the problem is defined as $\Pi = \Omega \bigcap \mathbb{Z}^\nu$. Therefore, a feasible solution $\bar{x} \in \Pi$ belongs to Ω and its components are integer. The mathematical model is in the following:

Min

$c^T x$

subject to

$$Ax = b$$

$$x_i \geq 0, integer \quad \forall i = 1, \ldots, n$$

The *Branch and Bound* (B&B) method is certainly the most widely used one in that it allows to specify exact solution algorithms for this class of optimization problems. It is based on a *divide and conquer* approach for exploring the feasible region Π. But, instead of performing a complete and exhaustive exploration of the region, it applies a bounding technique with the aim of exploring only some parts of Π.

The basic principles of the method are discussed in the following:

Branching: the problem P is decomposed into k distinct sub-problems $P_j, j = 1, \ldots, k$ and Π is divided in k disjointed sub-regions $\Pi_1, \Pi_2, \cdots, \Pi_k$ such that

$$\Pi_i \bigcap \Pi_j = \varnothing, \forall i, j = 1, \ldots, k, i \neq j,$$

and

$$\bigcup_{j=1}^{k} \Pi_j = \Pi .$$

Each of these subproblems is separately solved. The branching phase is performed by using two or more exhaustive and mutually exclusive constraints. Denoting by $z_{P_j}^*$ and z^* the optimal value of the objective function of a sub-problem P_j and P, respectively, the following condition holds:

$$z^* = \min\left\{z_{P_j}^*, j = 1, \ldots, k\right\}.$$

Therefore, the optimal solution of P is the best solution among the ones found by solving each sub-problem $P_j, j = 1, \ldots, k$. The set of all the sub-problems defines the so called *branch-and-bound tree* (T).

Bounding: in order to explore only the most promising parts of the set of feasible integer solutions, a lower bound on the optimal value of the objective function of each sub-problem is determined. For this purpose, one of the widely used methods consists of solving its associated linear programming problem, obtained by removing the integer constraints on the decision variables. Therefore, the linear programming problem P'

Min

$c^T x$

subject to

$Ax = b$

$x \geq 0$

is the relaxed linear problem of an integer linear programming problem P. Then, the optimal value of the objective function of P' is a lower bound on the optimal value of the objective function of P.

Pruning: denoting by $\underline{z}_{P_j}$ a lower bound of $z_{P_j}^*$ and by $\bar{z}$ an upper bound of z^*, if $\underline{z}_{P_j} \geq \bar{z}$, the sub-problem P_j is "pruned."

If the bound on the optimal value of the objective function of each sub-problem is determined by solving its linear program-

ming relaxation, a pseudo code of the B&B algorithm is described in the following:

- **Step 0:** Set the list of the active problems to solve $L = \{P\}$ and the best current upper bound $z = +\infty$;
- **Step 1:** If $L = \varnothing$, then set $z^* = \bar{z}$ and return the optimal solution x^*. Otherwise, go to **Step 2**;
- **Step 2:** Select and remove from L an problem P_j. Solve its linear programming relaxation P_j'. Go to **Step 3**;
- **Step 3**:
  ○ **Step 3.1:** If $\Omega_{P_j'} = \varnothing$, the problem is infeasible and go to **Step 1**;
  ○ **Step 3.2:** If $z_{P_j'}^* \geq \bar{z}$, go to **Step 1**;
  ○ **Step 3.3:** If $z_{P_j'}^* < \bar{z}$ and the optimal solution of P_j' ($x^{*(P_j')}$) has all integer components, set $\bar{z} = z_{P_j'}^*$, $x^* = x^{*(P_j')}$ and go to **Step 1**;
  ○ **Step 3.4:** If $z_{P_j'}^* < \bar{z}$ and $x^{*(P_j')}$ has at least one not integer component, go to **Step 4**;
- **Step 4:** Perform the branching phase on P_j, put its sub-problems in L and go to **Step 1**.

The readers are referred to specific books on this topic and also on all the possible policies for selecting an active problem from L.

However, due to the computationally intensive nature of this class of problems, the algorithm can benefit from a parallel/distributed implementation that can be run on a grid/cloud platform (see Drummond et al. (2006) for example).

One of the most used paradigms for implementing parallel B&B algorithms is the master/workers paradigm. For example, in the work described in Aida, Natsume, and Futakata (2003), the master subdivides the problem in sub-problems and therefore, it maintains *T*. It distributes each of these sub-problems to the workers. Each worker divides the sub-problem in other sub-problems (branching phase), performs on each of them a bounding step and then a pruning phase. It will return to the master the only sub-problems that are not pruned together with the best bound on the objective function.

However, the authors show that this parallel implementation of the B&B algorithm is affected by several significant factors and therefore, it is usually not suitable for distributed environments as grids/clouds.

Among the other things, it requires high communication overheads and the single master process can easily become a bottleneck for the computation, especially in the presence of many worker processes. In conclusion, the B&B algorithm based on the traditional implementation of the master/workers paradigm is affected by scalability problems.

In order to overcome these issues, in literature, several advanced implementations of the B&B algorithm, suitable to be run on grids/clouds, have been proposed. Among these, some implementations of the B&B algorithm based on the hierarchical master/workers paradigm have been described and analyzed.

In the hierarchical master/workers paradigm, a single process is the *coordinator* and it is responsible to dispatch the tasks to a set of master processes that consequently distribute them to their workers. Therefore, when a worker ends, it sends its final solution to its master process. In the same work of Aida, Natsume, and Futakata (2003), the authors propose an alternative and more efficient parallel implementation of the B&B algorithm by using the hierarchical master/workers paradigm. In the proposed version, the coordinator divides the problem in sub-problems and dispatches them to the master processes. Its main task is to perform a load balancing among the master processes of the hierarchy. Each master process divides the sub-problem in other sub-problems and each of them is sent to a worker together with a bound. The worker performs a branching step, a bounding phase and then it prunes the no promising sub-problems. Each worker will send to its master the list of no discarded sub-problems together with the best bound. Each master process, instead, will send the best bound and the list of no discarded sub-problems to the coordinator. It is also responsible to eventually update its best bound when a new bound is sent by the coordinator. The readers are referred to the scientific work of Aida, Natsume, and Futakata (2003) for more details.

A hierarchical B&B algorithm is also proposed in Bendjoudi, Melab, and Talbi (2012). The coordinator (*root master node*)

Cloud Computing and Operations Research

is responsible of an initial branching of the problem into sub-problems and of an initial pruning of the no promising ones. Then, it distributes the sub-problems to the masters of the second level (*inner master nodes*). Each of these receives a set of sub-problems to solve, branches each its sub-problem, prunes the no promising ones and then, sends sub-sets to the inner master nodes of the underlying level. This is done until fine-grained sub-problems are reached that are explored sequentially by the *worker nodes*. When a worker finds a better bound, it shares this information with the others of its level and with its inner master node that eventually updates its current best bound. Then, the inner master node shares the new best bound with the other inner master nodes of its level. This mechanism allows to propagate the solution. When all the processes of the same level terminate, the processes of all the underlying levels terminate consequently.

The innovative contribution of this proposed approach consists in a well balanced workload distribution. For this purpose, the authors distinguish the *Free Workers* (FWs) and the *Pending Workers* (PWs). Each FW aims to explore a smaller sub-problem, associated to a sub-problem of a PW. The master manages the pending sub-problems related to the PWs. When a FW ends its computations, the master divides a pending sub-problem into smaller sub-problems and assigns each of them to a FW. When the pending sub-problem associated to a PW is definitively explored, the related PW becomes FW. The authors apply this framework to a Flow-Shop scheduling problem using a real computational grid and demonstrating the features of scal-

ability and of efficiency. Therefore, the readers are referred to this scientific contribution to get more details on the proposed approach.

2.3 Stochastic Optimization

Stochastic Programming (SP) is an important OR branch and allows to explicitly deal with the random nature that characterizes a lot of the real world applications.

Uncertainty is represented in terms of random variables defined on a given and known probability space. Therefore, a mathematical SP model can be derived starting from the standard formulation of a Linear Programming Problem under uncertainty:

Min

$$z = c(\theta)^T x$$

subject to

$$A(\theta)x = b(\theta)$$

$$x \geq 0$$

where c, b and A depend on θ that represents the random event.

A familiar and commonly used technique to deal with this more involved class of mathematical problems would trivially rely on replacing the random functions with a nominal value. Although appealing and numerically efficient, this generic approach suffers from serious limitations, which have long been recognized in literature. In fact, by trivially replacing the random constraints with their expected values does not account

198

for the variability in the parameter levels, making the nominal solution useless, or even worse, misdealing.

The readers are referred to the introductory scientific work of Dantzig (2004) in which an alternative approach, the *SP with recourse*, is also described. Roughly speaking, the recourse can be viewed as a solution strategy adopted for managing the infeasible solutions that could be generated due to the presence of random parameters. In particular, in the two-stage framework, it is assumed that two types of decision variables are involved: a set of first-stage variables (x) that represent the *anticipative decisions* and a set of second-stage variables (y) that correspond to the *adaptive decisions* performed after observing the realizations of the random variables. The y variables strongly depend on x and therefore, the aim is to find an optimal first stage solution that can be adjusted (*recourse*) in the second stage at a minimum cost i.e., minimizing the cost of the initial solution plus the expected second stage cost.

Under the assumption of discrete distributions, the two-stage model can be formulated as in the following (see also Linderoth and Wright (2003)):

Min

$$c^T x + \sum_{s=1}^{N} p_s q_s y_s$$

subject to

$$Ax = b$$

$$T_s x + W_s y_s = h_s \, \forall s = 1,...,N$$

$$x \geq 0, y_s \geq 0 \; \forall s = 1,...,N$$

where q_s, T_s, W_s and h_s are vectors and matrices of proper size associated with the realization (*scenario*) s which occurs with a given probability p_s. The value of N denotes the total number of scenarios.

The SP models are more flexible and accurate than their deterministic counterpart. However, their size exponentially grows according to the number of scenarios used to mathematically represent uncertainty. A larger number of scenarios guarantees a more faithful representation of uncertainty, calling, on the other side, for the design of advanced solution approaches which can better exploit the problem structure.

A traditional approach for solving SP problems with recourse is based on a *Decomposition Method* that defines as many sub-problems as the number of scenarios according to the adaptive decisions. The anticipative decisions, instead, assume parametric values. By iteratively adding cuts (i.e., specific constraints) to the formulation, optimality (or feasibility) can be reached.

One significant literary contribution is the work of Linderoth and Wright (2003). The authors introduce some advanced distributed algorithms for the two-stage stochastic linear programming with recourse taking into consideration two asynchronous solution approaches: the *L-shaped* and a *trust-region method*. The implemented paradigm is the master/workers. In particular, the master solves the first-stage problem while the workers find solutions for the second-stage problems. The proposed versions have then been run on a heterogeneous grid and tested on large-scale problems.

In Langer, Venkataraman, Palekar, Kale, and Baker (2012), the authors describe a parallel decomposition approach based on the master/workers paradigm and they also include a work assignment scheme for balancing the workloads. The solution approach has been successfully applied to the problem of allocating US military aircraft to various cargo and personnel movement missions under uncertain demands.

An improved distributed dual decomposition algorithm for stochastic integer programming is proposed in Lubin, Martin, Petra, and Sandikçi (2013) by exploiting the structure of the interior-point solvers.

A complete literature review of the stochastic strategies based on the *Benders decomposition algorithm* is instead presented in Latorre, Cerisola, Ramos, and Palacios (2009). The authors describe the implementation of these strategies on the computational grids. Particular attention is given to reduce dependency among the sub-problems.

In the work of Beraldi, Grandinetti, Musmanno, and Triki (2000), the authors design a parallel method for solving two-stage stochastic linear programs with restricted recourse. The importance of this scientific contribution is related to the fact that the proposed mathematical model is suitable to represent several real-world applications such as the financial and the production planning problems. The described parallel method basically adopts a primal-dual path-following interior point algorithm.

In the work of Triki and Grandinetti (2001), the authors present a parallel algorithm suitable to be run on grids for solving large scale optimization problems under uncertain data. Their attention is especially focused on the class of large scale stochastic optimization problems that requires to achieve a real-time solution. In particular, they present a path-following algorithm suitable to be run on grids.

On a cloud, these kind of algorithms can be efficiently run and/or provided as a service in order to solve many SP applications (such as the ones of financial optimization).

2.4 Logistics Management

Advanced decision support systems are usually designed in logistic contexts with the aim, among the other things, of efficiently managing the supply chains. Usually, the defined optimization models aim to minimize the total costs and to maximize the total revenue under the service level constrains. The customer satisfaction plays, in fact, a key role for the competitiveness of a logistic system.

The mathematical models and the solution approaches dealt with the most challenging issues that concern the activities of a supply chain such as the provision of the raw materials, the selection of the suppliers, the transportation of the finite products and the inventory management.

A *supply chain* can be modeled as a graph in which the first set of nodes represents the *suppliers* of the *raw materials* that have to be transformed into the *finite products*. This transformation is performed by the *plants* such as by the second set of nodes of the graph. The finite products are then distributed to the *warehouses* (third set) in which they are temporarily stocked. Then, the warehouses send them to the *customers* according to their requests. Figure 1 illustrates a simple representation of supply chain with *n* suppliers, *m* plants, *r* warehouses and *t* customers. However, in some realistic situations, this scheme can become more complex. For example, it could be also possible that the plants provide both the customers and the warehouses with the finite products.

A bottleneck of this scenario is represented by the distribution of both the raw materials and the finite products. It is worth noting, in fact, that the distribution activities considerably impact on the total logistic cost of a company and they require, among the other things, the efficient management of the fleet and of the routes of the vehicles. The routes are usually determined with the aim of minimizing the total transportation cost and of handling the customer demands in time.

The process of defining the routes can be efficiently supported by an automatic system suitable to find good quality solutions. These automatic decision systems are typically based on appropriate interactive software that can be run by the managers on their computers. The managers can interactively modify the proposed solution (such as adding or removing the customers). However, the daily demand fluctuations as well as the time windows within the customers have to be served, for instance, introduce new complexities that cannot be under the manager control. Good quality routes cannot be found under the assumption to have enough capacity to satisfy the daily demands such as without considering the demand fluctuations. In summary, the route planners have to dynamically adapt themselves to the external continuous changes.

Cloud computing can support this planning process and can provide new advanced software as services that receive the orders in

Figure 1. An illustrative example of supply chain

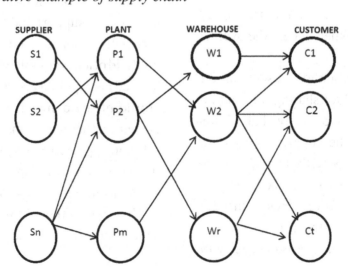

real time and transmit the optimized routes. In particular, the traffic information and the customer demands can be gathered in real time and then, the routes of the vehicles can be updated consequently.

In Povidaiko, Fernandes, Moreira, and Filho (2010), it is described a cloud for supporting a urban network with the aim to route the vehicles also including information on traffic congestion. The decision process identifies the best route for handling the customer needs. In addition, the traffic congestion is an information available over time on the contrary of the traditional planners that do not include it during the decision process. The authors propose a routing meta-heuristic that includes the traffic congestion and determines good quality solutions with reasonable computational overheads. An application hosted on the cloud provides information on the traffic congestion.

In Rossetti and Chen (2012), the authors propose a cloud for simulating the large scale supply chains. The designed simulator allows users to specify the network structure, the inventory management policies and the characteristics of the demand in order to estimate, among the other things, the average inventory levels.

In Li (2011), the author presents an advanced cloud model for sharing information among the partners of a supply chain. Information sharing in the supply chains plays a significant role especially to improve the quality of the offered services. A cloud platform provides information services that can be easily used by the partners. These services could be also provided by third parties with a substantial cost reduction. In this way, also

the small and medium companies can use secure and advanced information systems at low costs.

In Leukel, Kirn, and Schlegel (2011), it is shown an advanced cloud perspective on the supply chain management. The supply chain is here represented by a set of provided services and by a set of service requests (such as customer demands) that can be coordinated by optimally determining the services composition. The authors experiment their proposal in the context of the airport service supply chains.

In conclusion, cloud computing allows to redefine the traditional logistic services that can be offered more efficiently.

3. OPERATIONS RESEARCH FOR CLOUDS

This section describes some mathematical models proposed in literature for efficiently designing and managing a cloud.

All is offered as a service on demand in a cloud platform. Therefore, quantitative techniques for market forecasts can be adopted in order to support the decision processes especially under uncertainty. The literature in this field offers a complete set of techniques to be used and applied according to the specific profile of the demand. In addition, sophisticated mathematical models and advanced solution approaches could be also offered by stochastic programming in order to support the decisions in this context of high uncertainty.

However, in the following, the attention is paid to some of the most interesting problems such as the *Data Center Location Problem* and the *Virtual Machines Allocation Problem*.

Emphasis is also given to the *Partner Provider Selection Problem* and to the relation between *Simulation-based Optimization* and cloud computing.

3.1 Data Center Location Problem

A challenging issue for the cloud providers consists in deciding, among the other things, where to place the data centers taking into consideration the user demands.

From the OR point of view, this problem could share some features with the *Facility Location* problems (Iyoob, Zarifoglu, & Dieker, 2013). They represent some of the most significant strategic decisions in logistics and there is, in fact, an extensive literature on this topic. However, in the following, the attention is focused on one of the simplest mathematical formulations presented in literature that could share some features with the problem under investigation (Love, Morris, & Wesolowsky, 1988; Mirchandani & Francis, 1990) on the facility location problems).

The problem can be represented by a bipartite graph $G = \langle L_1 \bigcup L_2, A \rangle$, where the set L_1 consists of the potential facilities to open and L_2 contains the sites in which the users are assumed to be placed. Moreover, for each $i \in L_1$ and $j \in L_2$, an arc $(i, j) \in A$ exists whose weight c_{ij} could denote, for instance, a unitary transportation cost. A fix cost $f_i, i \in L_1$, is also incurred for opening the

facility i. Each user $j \in L_2$ has a demand d_j and each facility $i \in L_1$ has a maximum technological capacity q_i.

Under the hypothesis that each user has to be handled by only one facility, the mathematical formulation is the following:

Min

$$\sum_{i \in L_1} \sum_{j \in L_2} c_{ij} x_{ij} + \sum_{i \in L_1} f_i z_i$$

subject to

$$\sum_{i \in L_1} x_{ij} = 1 \quad \forall j \in L_2$$

$$\sum_{j \in L_2} d_j x_{ij} \leq q_i z_i \quad \forall i \in L_1$$

$$x_{ij} \in \{0,1\} \quad \forall i \in L_1, j \in L_2$$

$$z_i \in \{0,1\} \quad \forall i \in L_1$$

where, $x_{ij}, i \in L_1, j \in L_2$ is a binary decision variable equal to 1 if the facility i handles the user placed at the site j, 0 otherwise. The binary decision variable $z_i, i \in L_1$ is equal to 1 if the facility i is open, 0 otherwise.

The first component of the objective function denotes the assignment costs while the second one represents the fixed costs for opening the facilities.

The first group of constraints assures that each user is handled by only one site while the second group imposes that the capacity of a facility is never exceeded.

The decision maker could also fix the total number of facilities ($\bar{p}$) to open by introducing the following constraint:

$$\sum_{i \in L_1} z_i = \bar{p}$$

In cloud computing, the set of the "facilities" to open is represented by the data centers while the total "transportation cost" could be replaced by the total latency (Iyoob, Zarifoglu, & Dieker, 2013). In the presence, for instance, of a constraint on the minimum service level offered to the users, it could be possible to remove from A the arcs that do not guarantee this condition.

However, the problem is usually more complex than the one described above. For example, one should also include the demand variabilities and additional considerations have to be done in order to model the dependencies among the services of the data centers that can affect the performances in terms of latency (Greenberg, Hamilton, Maltz, & Patel, 2008).

Recently, the problem of finding the best server placement has been formulated in Kreinovich (2013). The author addresses the problem under different hypothesis. However, in the following, we present only one of these formulations and we refer the interested readers to this scientific work.

Under the hypothesis to know the number of requests per time and per area around the location x, expressed by a density function $\rho_u(x)$, and also the maximum number of potential servers to be placed (B), the author formulates the optimization problem with the aim of minimizing the average communication delay (assumed to be expressed in terms of average travel distance). The decision variable of the problem is denoted by $\rho_s(x)$ such as the storage density function. Then, the author formulates the following constraint optimization problem:

Min

$$\int (\rho_s(x))^{-1/2} \rho_u(x) dx$$

subject to

$$\int \rho_s(x) dx = B$$

For such a problem, he illustrates a standard solution approach based on the Lagrangian multiplier method.

3.2 Workload Distribution Problem

The workload distribution problem is a challenging issue in the context of the clouds since the workload can significantly vary over the time (all is offered as a service on demand).

In this section, we focus the attention on the scientific work proposed by Borovskiy, Wust, Schwarz, Koch, and Zeier (2011) in which it is assumed that each task is characterized by a workload. The workloads are not assumed to considerably vary over time and therefore, it is possible to estimate their value. The problem aims to find a distribution of these workloads among the servers of the platform in order to minimize the total number of used servers. Each workload w_i of each task i is usually expressed in the same units of the server capacity (in terms of CPU time, for example).

In Borovskiy, Wust, Schwarz, Koch, and Zeier (2011), the problem is formulated as a classic *Set Partitioning Problem*. They firstly group the tasks into all the possible combinations, each of them is denoted as *block* and it can be potentially assigned to one server. Then, they identify the *feasible* partitions. A partition represents a composition of blocks in order to handle all the workloads and it is *feasible* if it satisfies the capacity constraint. Therefore, a feasible partition is a potential solution of the problem.

In a homogeneous platform, all the servers have the same capacity, here denoted by C, while the total workload C_b of the block b is expressed as the sum of the workloads of its tasks.

Therefore, the feasibility condition on a partition Pa can be mathematically formulated as in the following:

$$C \geq C_b, \forall b \in Pa$$

Under the hypothesis that a block is assigned to one server of the platform, to minimize the total number of used servers means to minimize the total number of blocks in the final partition. The decision variable y_j is equal to 1 if the block j belongs to the optimal partition and 0 otherwise. By assuming that all the blocks have been gener-

ated, since a task could belong to more than one block, a binary matrix A is introduced where a_{ij} is equal to 1 if the task i belongs to the block j, 0 otherwise. Therefore, A has a number of rows equal to the number of tasks (n) and a number of columns equal to the number of total blocks (m). The mathematical model proposed by the authors is the following:

Min

$$\sum_{j=1}^{m} y_j$$

subject to

$$\sum_{j=1}^{m} a_{ij} y_j = 1 \quad \forall i = 1, \ldots, n$$

$$y_j \in \{0,1\} \, \forall \, j = 1, \ldots, m$$

where the objective function to minimize denotes the total number of blocks used in the optimal partition under the constraint that each task is processed in exactly one block. In the following, we illustrate a numerical example.

A set of 3 tasks is characterized by the following workloads $w_1 = 50, w_2 = 40$ and $w_3 = 60$. The capacity C of each server is equal to 100. All the possible blocks are shown in Figure 2.

The last two blocks in this figure are not feasible. Therefore, the mathematical model has 5 decision variables (y_1, y_2, y_3, y_4, y_5 one

Figure 2. All possible blocks in the example

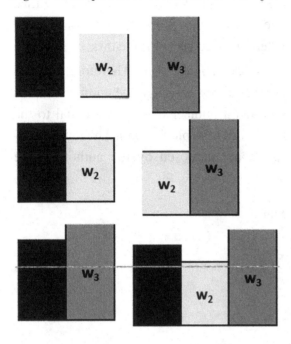

$$A = \begin{pmatrix} 1 & 0 & 0 & 1 & 0 \\ 0 & 1 & 0 & 1 & 1 \\ 0 & 0 & 1 & 0 & 1 \end{pmatrix}$$

The first optimal partition consists of the first and the fifth block in Figure 2 while the second optimal partition contains the third and the fourth block.

The number of servers used by both the two partitions is equal to 2. In particular, in the first partition, the block that contains w_1 is assigned to one server while the block that contains w_2 and w_3 is assigned to the other. On the other hand, in the second partition, the block that contains w_3 is assigned to one server while the block that contains w_1 and w_2 is assigned to the other.

In addition, after experimenting with the mathematical model, the authors propose to generate only medium size blocks since they will be selected with higher probability.

Alternatively, they propose a column generation based solution approach. We refer the interested readers to the work of (Borovskiy, Wust, Schwarz, Koch, & Zeier, 2011) for a study on the solution approaches.

By assuming that the number of the available homogeneous servers is equal to k, the problem could be also modeled by introducing the binary decision variable $y_j, j = 1, ..., k$ equal to 1 if the server j is used, 0 otherwise and the binary decision variable $x_{ij}, i = 1, ..., n \; j = 1, ..., k$ equal to 1 if the task i is processed by the server j, 0 otherwise:

Min

for each block) and 3 constraints (one for each task):

Min

$$y_1 + y_2 + y_3 + y_4 + y_5$$

$$y_1 + y_4 = 1$$

$$y_2 + y_4 + y_5 = 1$$

$$y_3 + y_5 = 1$$

$$y_j \in \{0,1\} \; \forall j = 1, ..., 5$$

The matrix A is indicated in the following:

$$\sum_{j=1}^{k} y_j$$

subject to

$$\sum_{i=1}^{n} w_i x_{ij} \leq C y_j \quad \forall j = 1, ..., k$$

$$\sum_{j=1}^{k} x_{ij} = 1 \quad \forall i = 1, ..., n$$

$$y_j \in \{0,1\} \quad \forall j = 1, ..., k$$

$$x_{ij} \in \{0,1\} \quad \forall i = 1, ..., n \quad \forall j = 1, ..., k$$

where the first group of constraints imposes that the total capacity of each server is never exceeded while the second group assures that each task is processed by only one server (unique assignment constraint). The objective function to be minimized represents the total number of selected servers.

A lower bound ($\underline{k}$) on the total number of servers that have to be used can be found as in the following:

$$\underline{k} = \left\lceil \frac{\sum_{i=1}^{n} w_i}{C} \right\rceil$$

In this model, more constraints can be included in order to better assist the decision makers to control the final solutions. For instance, a decision maker, interested in finding solutions in which a task i cannot be processed by the same server of the task t, will include the following group of constraints:

$$x_{ij} + x_{tj} \leq 1 \forall j = 1, ..., k$$

Moreover, under the hypothesis that the capacity could vary from a server to another, the related constraint is modified as in the following:

$$\sum_{i=1}^{n} w_i x_{ij} \leq C_j y_j \quad \forall j = 1, ..., k$$

where C_j denotes the capacity of the server j. In this case, it could be more reasonable to consider a different cost for each server j such as δ_j. Therefore, the mathematical formulation is in the following:

Min

$$\sum_{j=1}^{k} \delta_j y_j$$

subject to

$$\sum_{i=1}^{n} w_i x_{ij} \leq C_j y_j \quad \forall j = 1, ..., k$$

$$\sum_{j=1}^{k} x_{ij} = 1 \quad \forall i = 1, ..., n$$

$$y_j \in \{0,1\} \quad \forall j = 1, ..., k$$

$$x_{ij} \in \{0,1\} \quad \forall i = 1, ..., n \quad \forall j = 1, ..., k$$

3.3 Virtual Machine Allocation Problem

A big issue in cloud computing is to decide how to map the virtual machines onto the physical servers since the workloads can dynamically vary. Virtualization technology as well as consolidation play a key role in this context since several jobs can be run on the physical machines, can share a pool of resources and can migrate from a machine to another. The major benefit of this dynamic management is a considerable reduction of the idleness with a consequent reduction of the total power consumption.

One of the widely used modeling approaches for solving the *Virtual Machines Allocation Problem* is to see it as a *Bin Packing Problem*. The readers interested to have more details on this specific class of optimization problems are referred to Seiden (2002). It is assumed that the "bins" are the physical machines (with the same or different capacity) and the "items" to load are the virtual machines with specific "weights" (requirements). Therefore, the problem consists in determining how to assign the "items" to the "bins" with the aim of minimizing the total number of used "bins." The problem is solved under capacity constraints and unique assignment constraints such as each "item" assigned to only one "bin."

In literature, several scientific contributions have been proposed and described with regard to the problem under investigation in this section. However, since a complete treatment of this topic is beyond the scope of the chapter, a few of them are described in the following.

In Speitkamp and Bichler (2010), the *static server consolidation problem* is modeled by introducing a cost associated to each physical server that can denote the purchasing cost and/or the power consumption. Therefore, the objective function, to be minimized, denotes the total cost/consumption. On the contrary, under the hypothesis that the physical machines are identical, the problem aims to optimize the total number of used machines. The imposed constraints assure that each virtual machine is assigned to one server and that each assignment satisfies the capacity of the server. The authors also derive several variants and/or extensions of the model by including several realistic constraints such as an upper bound on the number of virtual machines assigned to a server. In addition, they illustrate how to change the proposed formulation in the more realistic situation in which the requirements vary over time. We refer the readers to this work for more details.

The static server consolidation problem basically aims to map the virtual machines onto physical servers by considering the average workload picks in order to certainly avoid overloading situations. However, idleness situations could not be avoided.

For this purpose, in Ferreto, Netto, Calheiros, and De Rose (2011), the problem is addressed as a *dynamic server consolidation problem* by also allowing a migration of the virtual machines according to the workload variabilities. It means that, for example, a physical server can be turn off, at a consolidation stage, if its virtual machines can be re-allocated to other servers. The authors solve this problem by allowing a *periodi-*

cal consolidation step. Each consolidation step depends on the mapping found at the previous one.

For the sake of clarity, in the following, the set S contains the s services (such as the virtual machines that have to be mapped), the set M identifies the m servers and the set R contains the r available resources. In addition, for each resource i, it is known that the server j has an capacity q_{ij}. For each service k and resource i, z_{ik} is the amount of i required for the service k. The problem under investigation selects the servers to be used by specifying the following decision variables: $y_j, j \in M$ equal to 1 if the server j is used, 0 otherwise and $x_{kj}, k \in S, j \in M$ equal to 1 if the service k is assigned to the server j and 0 otherwise. Then, (Ferreto, Netto, Calheiros, & De Rose, 2011) include two types of additional information in their formulation. The former is related to the mapping found at the previous consolidation stage (i.e., $\tilde{x}_{kj}, k \in S, j \in M$) while the latter ($\lambda_k, k \in S$) indicates if the demand of the service k is changed ($\lambda_k = 1$) or not ($\lambda_k = 0$). The model proposed by (Ferreto, Netto, Calheiros, & De Rose, 2011) is the following:

Min

$$\sum_{j=1}^{m} y_j$$

$$\sum_{j=1}^{m} x_{kj} = 1 \ \forall k = 1, \dots, s$$

$$\sum_{k=1}^{s} z_{ik} x_{kj} \le q_{ij} y_j \ \forall j = 1, \dots, m \ \ \forall i = 1, \dots, r$$

$$-\lambda_k + \tilde{x}_{kj} \le x_{kj} \le \lambda_k + \tilde{x}_{kj} \forall k = 1, \dots, s \ \ \forall j = 1, \dots, m$$

$$y_j \in \{0,1\} \ \ \forall j = 1, \dots, m$$

$$x_{kj} \in \{0,1\} \ \forall k = 1, \dots, s \ \forall j = 1, \dots, m$$

The objective function to be minimized denotes the total number of physical servers used. Beyond the classic unique assignment and capacity constraints (first and second group), the third group assures that if the demand of the service k is changed (such as $\lambda_k = 1$), then the new mapping x_{kj} could change at the next consolidation stage while it has to remain the same in the opposite situation (such as $\lambda_k = 0$). It is worth noting that, at the first consolidation stage, Ferreto, Netto, Calheiros, and De Rose (2011) propose to solve the static server consolidation problem while the additional constraints are added only from the beginning of the second consolidation step.

Indeed, these considerations highlight that the problem in cloud environments is usually more complex than the traditional bin packing problem and additional constraints should be included in the mathematical formulations in order to take into account some significant aspects. In Beaumont, Eyraud-Dubois, Pesneau, and Renaud-Goud (2013), for example, the authors take into consideration the *Service Level Agreement* (SLA) between the cloud provider and the user. In other words, each user of the platform expresses the minimum number of service instances that has to be alive at the end of the day, with a specific reliability. Then, the problem consists in determining an allocation, at minimum cost, of the virtual machines under both the packing constraints and the reliability constraints (imposed for each required service). In their scientific contribution, the problem is modeled as a non-linear optimization model under the assumption to have only a single service.

However, in its general form, the problem could become a *multi-dimensional bin packing problem* under the assumption that each virtual machine has a requirement for each resource type and, at the same time, each physical machine has a specific availability for each resource type.

Together with mathematical models, the problem has been also studied and analyzed from a methodological point of view. In fact, several scientific contributions describe and present heuristic approaches for solving it under different conditions.

From a general point of view, for addressing the traditional bin packing problem, a lot of heuristic approaches have been proposed in literature (see Galambos and Woeginger (1995) and Coffman, Garey, and Johnson (1997)). Among these, for example:

First Fit Heuristic (FF): Aims to allocate an "item" to the first open "bin" with remaining capacity not less than the "weight" of the item itself. If a such bin does not exist, a new bin is open and the item is allocated to it;

Best Fit Heuristic (BF): Aims to allocate an "item" to the open "bin" with the smallest remaining capacity that is also not less than the "weight" of the item itself. If a such bin does not exist, a new bin is open and the item is allocated to it.

Both the two heuristics are designed for an *on-line bin packing problem* that arises when only some items to be allocated are available from the beginning. Otherwise, the problem becomes an *off-line bin packing problem*. In this case, before starting to allocate the items, it is possible to sort them by no increasing "weights" (*First Fit Decreasing* heuristic, for example).

As already noted, in cloud computing environments, the bin packing problem cannot be addressed and solved in a static manner due to the variabilities. In addition, the process of reallocating the virtual machines requires high overheads since we need to store their status on their current servers, to transmit the required information to the new servers and then, to start them on the new servers (Ho, Liu, & Wu, 2011).

In order to provide a good mapping that is a reasonable trade-off between the minimization of the number of used servers (such as the *power consumption*) and the minimization of the *overheads* (such as the number of the virtual machines that change their mapping), Ho, Liu, and Wu (2011) propose a new heuristic approach, *Heaviest First Reallocation*. In this case, the proposed algorithm looks for the heaviest "bin" *B*. Then, for each "bin" different from *B*, an "item" is individuated that can be allocated to *B*. Then, some "bins" could become empty and therefore, they can be considered not used. We refer the readers to this work for more details and for some numerical results.

By following the observations of Ho, Liu, and Wu (2011), the mathematical model proposed in Ferreto, Netto, Calheiros, and De Rose (2011) could be extended to the multi-objective case. Beyond the minimization of the power consumption, it could be also possible to minimize the number of the virtual machines that change their allocation at the new consolidation stage (such as to minimize the overheads).

Other heuristic approaches have been proposed in literature for the problem under investigation. For example, in Bobroff, Kochut, and Beaty (2007), the authors solve the problem with the aim of determining the minimum number of physical machines without violating the SLA constraints. In particular, the main steps of this procedure consist of firstly collecting the resource data and of forecasting the future resource demands. Then, a new allocation is heuristically determined and the virtual machines are migrated consequently. For determining a new allocation, with the aim of minimizing the number of physical machines, the authors propose to use the First Fit heuristic. These steps are performed at each time interval.

In Li, Li, Huai, Wo, Li, and Zhong (2009), the authors propose a novel approach by taking into consideration the energy efficiency. For this purpose, they firstly abstract the problem

as a bin packing problem, and then, propose an energy-aware heuristic.

In addition, genetic algorithms have been also proposed in literature for heuristically solving the problem under investigation.

As already noted, in a cloud computing environment, the resource requirements are usually not known in advance and therefore, the problem could be formulated as a stochastic programming model. In Chaisiri, Lee, and Niyato (2009), for example, the authors highlight that in a cloud computing environment, the providers can offer two different payment plans: *reservation plan* and *on-demand plan*, each characterized by a specific cost (usually, reservation plan is the cheapest one). However, the limit in the reservation plan is that it has to be acquired in advance and it could not satisfy the future demands. Therefore, the authors assume that, as soon as the demands exceed the availability (reserved resources), additional resources can be acquired according to an on-demand plan. Then, they formulate the problem as a stochastic integer programming model in order to find allocations at minimum total cost (cost for reservations plus cost for on-demand plans), under the hypothesis of uncertainty of demand and prices. Their decision process mainly consists of two stages (Stochastic Programming with recourse). The first stage is related to the number of reserved resources while the second one to both the actual number of required resources and the prices applied by the provider.

Other versions of the problem have been proposed in literature and we refer the interested readers to these specific scientific contributions.

3.4 A Multi-Objective Job Scheduling Problem

The job scheduling problem in the cloud has been recently formulated also as a multi-objective optimization model by (Grandinetti, Pisacane, & Sheikhalishahi, 2013). The authors consider a homogeneous platform and formalize the problem with the aim to minimize the total average waiting time of the jobs, the average waiting time of the jobs that belong to the longest working schedule (such as the *makespan*) and the required number of hosts.

In literature, few contributions address this topic. For example, in Wieczorek, Hoheisel, and Prodan (2009), the authors propose some taxonomies of the multi-objective grid workflow scheduling while in Stevens et al. (2009), the authors describe some multi-objective algorithms with the aim of finding the starting times for data transmission and jobs execution. In the scientific contribution of Lucas-Simarro, Moreno-Vozmediano, Montero, and Llorente (2013), the authors highlight a modular broker architecture by considering different scheduling strategies with the aim of optimally deploying virtual services across multiple clouds. Instead, in Pandey, Wu, Guru, and Buyya (2010), the authors describe and outline a particle swarm optimization based heuristic for the job scheduling problem in the cloud and they also include both the computing and the data transmission costs.

One of the most used multi-objective optimization methodologies is based on the ϵ-*constraint method*. The readers are referred to the work of Ehrgott and Gandibleux (2000) for a detailed survey on multi-objective combinatorial optimization. In the work of Boulif and Atif (2006), for instance, this innovative framework is applied to the manufacturing cell formation problem for minimizing both the intercellular movements and the workload unbalance; in Esmaili, Amjady, and Shayanfar (2011), it is successfully applied to the multi-objective congestion management problem for optimizing the congestion management cost, the voltage and the dynamic security. Other significant scientific contributions emphasize the relevance of this solution approach. An approximate ϵ-constraint based heuristic, for instance, is also proposed for the multi-objective undirected capacitated arc routing problem (Grandinetti, Guerriero, Laganà, & Pisacane, 2012).

Recently, in Grandinetti, Pisacane, and Sheikhalishahi (2013), the authors have proposed an ϵ-constraint based approach for solving the multi-objective job scheduling problem in the cloud. The set of n jobs is denoted by J while H represents the set of m homogeneous hosts. Moreover, w_j is the workload of the job j and, under the assumption of a homogeneous cloud, the capacity of each host is denoted by u. Finally, t_j represents the processing time required by the job j on any machine. Both the workload and the host capacity are expressed in the same unit (in terms of CPU time, for example). A working schedule, executed on a host, is feasible if the capacity constraint is satisfied.

The proposed approach heuristically generates all the feasible working schedules and populates a set Ω. Then, the following mathematical multi-objective model is formulated by the authors:

Min

δ

Min

$$\sum_{\omega \in \Omega} c_\omega x_\omega$$

Min

$$\sum_{\omega \in \Omega} x_\omega$$

subject to

$$\sum_{\omega \in \Omega} a_{j\omega} x_\omega = 1 \quad \forall j \in J$$

$$\delta \geq c_\omega x_\omega \quad \forall \omega \in \Omega$$

$$\delta \geq 0$$

$$x_\omega \in \{0,1\}, \forall \omega \in \Omega$$

where, x_ω is a binary decision variable equal to 1 if the feasible schedule ω belongs to the solution and 0 otherwise. Moreover, each entry $a_{j\omega}$ of the $|J| \times |\Omega|$ binary matrix A is equal to 1 if the job j belongs to the feasible

schedule ω and 0 otherwise. The total average waiting time of the jobs in the feasible schedule ω is properly computed by the authors and it is denoted by c_ω.

The three objectives to minimize are the makespan (δ), the total average waiting time and the number of used hosts, respectively. The first group of constraints guarantees that each job j belongs to only one schedule and the second group imposes that δ has to be greater or equal to the total average waiting time of each feasible schedule.

The upper bound U_H on the number of used hosts is set to the number of the submitted jobs, under the assumption that each host exactly processes one job: $U_H = |J|$. Instead, the lower bound L_H of the used hosts is computed by the authors by the following formula:

$$L_H = \lceil \frac{\sum_{j \in J} w_j}{u} \rceil$$

The resulting three-objectives formulation is transformed into a bi-objective model with the aim of minimizing δ and the total average waiting time while the number of used hosts $\bar{m}$ is varied in $[L_H, U_H]$.

The proposed approach, for each $\bar{m} \in [L_H, U_H]$, solves two ϵ-constraint problems where each of them optimizes one objective function at a time constraining the remaining one. In particular, the first model minimizes the total average waiting time and imposes an upper bound ϵ_2 on δ while the second formulation minimizes δ and imposes an upper bound ϵ_1 on the total average waiting time. In both the two models, the following constraint is introduced in order to control the number of used hosts:

$$\sum_{\omega \in \Omega} x_\omega \leq \overline{m}.$$

The feasible ranges for the two parameters ϵ_1 and ϵ_2 are opportunely determined. In particular, a single objective formulation is solved for minimizing the total average waiting time and let be t_1 the optimal value and δ_1 the makespan associated to it. Then, a single objective model is solved for minimizing δ and let be δ_2 the optimal value and t_2 the total average waiting time associated to it.

These values are logically related to each other by the following conditions: $t_1 \leq t_2$ and $\delta_1 \geq \delta_2$. Therefore, by varying $\epsilon_1 \in \left[t_1, t_2\right]$ and $\epsilon_2 \in \left[\delta_2, \delta_1\right]$, it is possible to determine Pareto efficient solutions that are then proposed to the decision makers.

The readers are referred to the work of (Grandinetti, Pisacane, & Sheikhalishahi, 2013) for assumptions, definitions, numerical comparisons, evaluations and conclusions.

3.5 Partner Provider Selection Problem

In some critical situations (a natural disaster, for example), a provider has to discharge the user demands to a set of partners that have been properly selected (Iyoob, Zarifoglu, & Dieker, 2013).

This problem could share some features with one of the most frequent optimization problems that arises especially in logistic contexts: the *Supplier Selection Problem*. In order to design an efficient supply chain, in fact, the suppliers have to be selected according to some criteria properly defined. These criteria strongly depend on the goals of the managers/providers such as to minimize costs and/or to maximize reliability.

In some cases, they are interested in finding a set of partners in order to optimize more than one criterion at a time. Therefore, this problem refers to multi-objective models for which the *Weighting Sum Method* could be a possible solution approach. Readers are referred to (Cohon, 1978) for the multi-objective programming.

As already noted, the problem could share some features with the supplier selection problem that has been extensively investigated in literature (see Mendoza, Santiago, and Ravindran, (2008) for example). Therefore, a possible way to address it could be to adopt a solution approach based on a multi-criteria decision making technique, the *Analytic Hierarchy Process* (AHP), developed and introduced in literature by the mathematician Thomas L. Saaty (Saaty (1980) and Saaty (1990), for example).

In the following, a possible adaptation of the solution approach proposed in Mendoza, Santiago, and Ravindran (2008) for the supplier selection is described with regard to the case under investigation in this section:

Step 1: Define the criteria and the sub-criteria in order to build a hierarchy. At the top, we have the *goal of the problem*.

The *criteria* and the *sub-criteria* are in the middle of this structure. At the bottom, the *alternatives* are presented (i.e., the potential partners). In this way, it is possible to break down a more complex decision problem into a hierarchy of criteria, sub-criteria and alternatives. The criteria and the sub-criteria will be properly used for selecting the best alternatives. In some cases, a pre-screening phase is performed with the aim to remove the dominated alternatives (Mendoza, Santiago, & Ravindran, 2008). It aims to reduce the number of the potential alternatives (i.e., the set of the potential partners P) since the AHP will compare each partner with the set of all the criteria and the sub-criteria. For the sake of simplicity, in the rest of the section, we will assume to have only η main criteria (see Figure 3, for example);

Step 2: Compute the weight of each criterion;

Step 3: Evaluate the score of each potential partner;

Step 4: Select the partners in order to maximize the total score *TW*, for instance.

It is worth noting that Step 2 requires to build an $\eta \times \eta$ pairwise comparison matrix A. Each its entry a_{ij} denotes the importance of the criterion i with regard to the criterion j such that $a_{ii} = 1, \forall i = 1, ..., \eta$ and $a_{ji} = \frac{1}{a_{ij}}, \forall i = 1, ..., \eta \, j = 1, ..., \eta$ and $i \neq j$.

The relative importance a_{ij} of a criterion i with regard to another j is usually set to one of these possible values: $\{1, 3, 5, 7, 9\}$ (Saaty, 1980). In particular, if $a_{ij} = 1$, the two crite-

ria have the same importance. In the four remaining cases, the criterion i is, *weakly*, *strongly*, *very* and *absolutely* more important than j, respectively.

For deriving the weights of the involved criteria, several methods have been presented in literature. In the following, two of them are described (see (Saaty, 1980) for more details).

1. Compute the sum s_j of each column j:

$$s_j = \sum_{k=1}^{\eta} a_{kj} \quad \forall j = 1 ..., \eta;$$

2. Divide each entry a_{ij} of A by the sum of the related column:

$$\bar{a}_{ij} = \frac{a_{ij}}{s_j} \quad \forall i, j = 1 ..., \eta;$$

3. Then, set the weight of the criterion i to the following value:

$$w_i = \frac{\sum_{j=1}^{\eta} \bar{a}_{ij}}{\eta} \quad \forall i = 1 ..., \eta.$$

An alternative method, based on the geometric mean, is in the following:

1. For each row i of A, multiply its elements together:

$$p_i = \prod_{j=1}^{\eta} a_{ij} \quad \forall i = 1 ..., \eta;$$

2. For each row i of A, compute the ηth root of p_i:

Table 1. Relative importance of the selected criteria

	Reliability	Flexibility	Price	Security
Reliability	1	5	7	1
Flexibility	1/5	1	3	1/5
Price	1/7	1/3	1	1/9
Security	1	5	9	1

$$\tilde{p}_i = \sqrt[\eta]{p_i} \quad \forall i = 1\ldots,\eta;$$

3. Then, set the weight of the criterion i to the following value:

$$w_i = \frac{\tilde{p}_i}{\sum_{k=1}^{\eta}\tilde{p}_k} \quad \forall i = 1\ldots,\eta.$$

In the case in which there are also sub-criteria, this step is performed for each sub-level of criteria and sub-criteria (Mendoza, Santiago, & Ravindran, 2008).

A cloud provider has in mind to select the partners by considering the following main criteria: *reliability*, *flexibility*, *price* and *security*. The relative importances are shown in Table 1 as well as the related matrix A.

$$A = \begin{pmatrix} 1.000 & 5.000 & 7.000 & 1.000 \\ 0.200 & 1.000 & 3.000 & 0.200 \\ 0.143 & 0.333 & 1.000 & 0.111 \\ 1.000 & 5.000 & 9.000 & 1.000 \end{pmatrix}$$

In order to derive the weights, we firstly compute the sum s_j of each column $j = 1,\ldots,\eta$ (in bold in Table 2).

Then, we divide each element of A by the sum of its column:

$$\bar{A} = \begin{pmatrix} 0.427 & 0.441 & 0.350 & 0.433 \\ 0.085 & 0.088 & 0.150 & 0.087 \\ 0.061 & 0.029 & 0.050 & 0.048 \\ 0.427 & 0.441 & 0.450 & 0.433 \end{pmatrix}$$

Finally, we compute the average value of each row and this results in the column in bold in Table 3.

It is worth noting that by construction:

Table 2. Sum of each column

	Reliability	Flexibility	Price	Security
Reliability	1	5	7	1
Flexibility	1/5	1	3	1/5
Price	1/7	1/3	1	1/9
Security	1	5	9	1
Total	**2.343**	**11.333**	**20.000**	**2.311**

Table 3. Weight of each criterion computed by adopting the first method

	Reliability	Flexibility	Price	Security	w
Reliability	0.427	0.441	0.350	0.433	**0.413**
Flexibility	0.085	0.088	0.150	0.087	**0.103**
Price	0.061	0.029	0.050	0.048	**0.047**
Security	0.427	0.441	0.450	0.433	**0.438**

Table 4. Weight of each criterion computed by adopting the second method

	Reliability	Flexibility	Price	Security	p	$\tilde{p}$	w
Reliability	1.000	5.000	7.000	1.000	**35.000**	**2.432**	**0.414**
Flexibility	0.200	1.000	3.000	0.200	**0.120**	**0.589**	**0.100**
Price	0.143	0.333	1.000	0.111	**0.005**	**0.270**	**0.046**
Security	1.000	5.000	9.000	1.000	**45.000**	**2.590**	**0.440**
						5.881	

$$\sum_{i=1}^{\eta} w_i = 1$$

$$CI = \frac{\lambda - \eta}{\eta - 1}$$

The reader can easily verify that the weights obtained by applying the second method are the ones shown in Table 4.

According to the numerical results, in both the two cases, *Security* contains the highest percentage of the total importance.

After determining the weights, the AHP yields a way for measuring the level of the (eventual) inconsistency of the matrix A since its entries could be affected by some judgment errors. For this purpose, Saaty defines the *Consistency Ratio* (*CR*) as in the following:

$$CR = CI / RI$$

where CI is the *Consistency Index*, defined as in the following:

in which λ denotes the *maximum eigenvalue* of A.

Instead, RI denotes a *Random Index* whose values are reported in Saaty (1980) for several η. If CR is less or equal than 0.1, Saaty accepts A as consistent.

In order to select the partners, each of them has to be ranked by making a comparison with regard to each criterion and the score of each of them has to be determined. By assuming to know the evaluation (σ_{ip}) of each partner p with respect to each criterion i, the score associated to p *is* computed as in the following:

$$score_p = \sum_{i=1}^{\eta} w_i \sigma_{ip} \quad p \in P.$$

In the case in which only one partner has to be selected, without considering specific constraints, the provider sorts the partners by decreasing scores and then, choices the first one (i.e., the one with the highest score).

The cloud provider of the previous example has to evaluate the score of each partner (P_1, P_2, P_3). The relative evaluations ($\sigma_{ip}, \forall i = 1, \ldots, 4\, p = 1, \ldots, 3$) are known and shown in Table 5. Figure 3 shows the hierarchy related to this example.

Therefore, according to the weights shown in Table 3, the following values are determined for each potential partner:

$$score_1 = \sum_{i=1}^{4} w_i \sigma_{i1} = 8.503$$

$$score_2 = \sum_{i=1}^{4} w_i \sigma_{i2} = 7.883$$

$$score_3 = \sum_{i=1}^{4} w_i \sigma_{i3} = 6.387.$$

The selected partner is P_1.

Table 5. Values of σ for each couple (criterion, partner)

	P_1	P_2	P_3
Reliability	9	7	5
Flexibility	5	7	9
Price	7	7	7
Security	9	9	7

Figure 3. Hierarchy of the proposed example

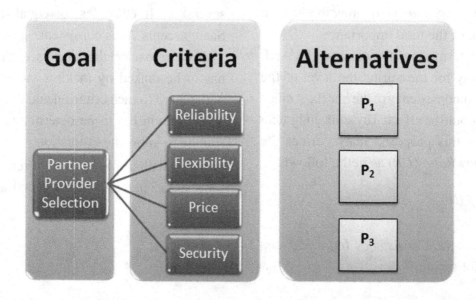

In the cases in which the provider includes some specific constraints during the decision process and/or he/she is interested in choosing more than one partner, appropriate mathematical models can be formulated and solved. With refer to cloud computing environments, for instance, the partners could be selected under constraints on the service levels and on the outage risks (see Iyoob, Zarifoglu, and Dieker (2013) for details).

4. SIMULATION-BASED OPTIMIZATION AND CLOUD COMPUTING

Simulation represents one of the widely used techniques of OR and it basically aims to emulate the behavior of a real process or system. In order to simulate the system of interest, we need to integrate an appropriate model of the system itself (*simulation model*) into a computer program. In this way, the decision maker can study the effects produced by actions done on the system or he/she can estimate the performances of alternative designs.

Simulation is used especially in the presence of complex real systems since it could be impossible (sometimes also dangerous) to directly experiment their behavior. Moreover, it is also used in all the cases in which high costs have to be incurred to build the system prototype.

However, by using a simulation model, the decision maker can only perform a *what-if* analysis to establish in advance the impact of his/her choices. This analysis is very useful in the contexts in which an exhaustive comparison among (few) possible alternative designs is practicable. On the contrary, by a *what-is-best* analysis, the decision maker identifies the best choice with regard to a performance measure.

A branch of OR, known as *Simulation-Optimization*, aims to perform a *what-is-best* analysis by properly integrating simulation with optimization. Therefore, simulation-based optimization approaches are characterized by:

1. An *optimizer* that identifies a solution that is candidate to be optimal;
2. A *simulator* that receives this solution and estimates the performance measure.

In the case of a very complex system, the candidate solution can be individuated heuristically. Therefore, the two-step approach is generalized as in the following: the optimizer heuristically determines a candidate solution. The simulator estimates the related performance measure. If the target is reached, the algorithm ends. Otherwise, the simulator communicates to the optimizer the violations and the optimizer looks for a new candidate solution by including the information on the violations (see Figure 4). If the decision maker is interested in finding the solutions that only partially satisfy the target, the approach ends when a fixed time limit is reached.

With refer to cloud computing environments, a simulation-based optimization approach could be applied for solving the task scheduling problem in the presence of stochastic scenarios, for instance. In these cases, among the other things, jobs are assumed to randomly arrive according to stochastic

Figure 4. A general simulation-based optimization approach

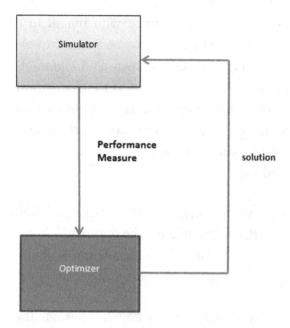

processes and their duration is also random. A simulation optimization approach could be defined by implementing a simulation model of the dynamics of a cloud and by invoking an optimizer suitable to individuate candidate solutions for the problem under investigation.

Regarding the possibility to simulate cloud computing systems, in Calheiros, Ranjan, Beloglazov, De Rose, and Buyya (2011), the authors describe a toolkit that supports both the modeling and simulation of the components of a cloud system such as data centers, virtual machines and resource providing policies.

Moreover, in literature, some significant scientific contributions have been proposed also with the aim to show how simulation optimization approaches can be efficiently run on a cloud. In Luo and Hong (2011), for instance, the authors describe how *Ranking and Selection* (R&S) procedures can be run on a cloud. They are commonly used for

selecting the best configuration among a set of feasible alternatives (Swisher, Hyden, Jacobson, & Schruben, 2004). However, in the presence of a large number of alternatives, these procedures become computationally impracticable. As highlighted in Luo and Hong (2011), in fact, in the presence of cases with more than 1,000 feasible alternatives, they are seldom used. A possible way to overcome this limitation is to solve them as simulation optimization problems. The authors discuss how R&S problems and their simulation optimization counterparts can be successfully solved on a cloud.

5. CONCLUSION

This chapter was devoted to show how some classes of optimization problems can be efficiently solved on a cloud, especially in terms of storage capacity and computing power. For this purpose, the most significant optimization algorithms were described and reconsidered with reference to their scalable distributed versions.

On the other hand, the chapter aimed to show how some issues in designing and in managing a cloud can be efficiently addressed by adopting the methods and by adapting the models provided by OR. For this purpose, some scientific contributions were described in detail. Some numerical examples were also presented and solved.

Finally, the last two paragraphs were devoted to address the *Partner Provider Selection Problem* and to discuss about the relation between cloud computing and *Simulation-based Optimization*.

REFERENCES

Aida, Natsume, & Futakata. (2003). Distributed computing with hierarchical master-worker paradigm for parallel branch and bound algorithm. In *Proceedings of 3rd IEEE/ACM International Symposium on Cluster Computing and the Grid*. IEEE/ACM.

Beaumont, O., Eyraud-Dubois, L., Pesneau, P., & Renaud-Goud, P. (2013). Reliable service allocation in clouds with memory and capacity constraints. In *Proceedings of Resilience 2013*. Retrieved from http://hal.inria.fr/hal-00850125/PDF/resilience.pdf

Bendjoudi, Melab, & Talbi. (2012). Hierarchical branch and bound algorithm for computational grids. *Future Generation Computer Systems, 28*(8), 1168–1176. doi:10.1016/j.future.2012.03.001

Beraldi, Grandinetti, Musmanno, & Triki. (2000). Parallel algorithms to solve two-stage stochastic linear programs with robustness constraints. *Parallel Computing, 26*(1314), 1889–1908. doi:10.1016/S0167-8191(00)00057-0

Bobroff, N., Kochut, A., & Beaty, K. (2007). Dynamic placement of virtual machines for managing SLA violations. In *Proceedings of 10th IFIP/IEEE International Symposium on Integrated Network Management* (IM '07). IEEE.

Borovskiy, Wust, Schwarz, Koch, & Zeier. (2011). A linear programming approach for optimizing workload distribution in a cloud. In *Cloud computing*. Academic Press.

Boulif & Atif. (2006). An exact multiobjective epsilon-constraint approach for the manufacturing cell formation problem. In *Proceedings of 2006 International Conference on Service Systems and Service Management*, (vol. 2, pp. 883–888). Academic Press.

Calheiros, Ranjan, & Beloglazov, De Rose, & Buyya. (2011). Cloudsim: A toolkit for modeling and simulation of cloud computing environments and evaluation of resource provisioning algorithms. *Software, Practice & Experience, 41*(1), 23–50. doi:10.1002/spe.995

Coffman, Garey, & Johnson. (1997). Approximation algorithms for NP-hard problems. PWS Publishing Co.

Chaisiri, Lee & Niyato, D. (2009). Optimal virtual machine placement across multiple cloud providers. In *Proceedings of Services Computing Conference*. IEEE.

Cohon. (1978). *Multiobjective programming and planning*. London: Elsevier.

Dantzig. (2004). Linear programming under uncertainty. *Management Science, 50*, 1764–1769.

Drummond, Uchoa, & Gonçalves, Silva, Santos, & de Castro. (2006). A grid-enabled distributed branch-and-bound algorithm with application on the steiner problem in graphs. *Parallel Computing, 32*(9), 629–642. doi:10.1016/j.parco.2005.09.006

Ehrgott & Gandibleux. (2000). A survey and annotated bibliography of multiobjective combinatorial optimization. *OR-Spektrum, 22*(4), 425–460. doi:10.1007/s002910000046

Esmaili, Amjady, & Shayanfar. (2011). Multi-objective congestion management by modified augmented ïµ-constraint method. *Applied Energy*, *88*(3), 755–766. doi:10.1016/j.apenergy.2010.09.014

Ferreto, Netto, Calheiros, & De Rose. (2011). Server consolidation with migration control for virtualized data centers. *Future Generation Computer Systems*, *27*(8), 1027–1034. doi:10.1016/j.future.2011.04.016

Galambos & Woeginger. (1995). On-line bin packing - A restricted survey. *ZOR: Zeitschrift Fuer Operations Research*, *42*(1), 25.

Grandinetti, Guerriero, Laganà, & Pisacane. (2012). An optimization-based heuristic for the multi-objective undirected capacitated arc routing problem. *Computers & Operations Research*, *39*, 2300–2309. doi:10.1016/j.cor.2011.12.009

Grandinetti, Pisacane, & Sheikhalishahi. (2013). An approximate ε-constraint method for a multi-objective job scheduling in the cloud. *Future Generation Computer Systems*, *29*(8), 1901–1908. doi:10.1016/j.future.2013.04.023

Greenberg, Hamilton, Maltz, & Patel. (2008). The cost of a cloud: Research problems in data center networks. *ACM SIGCOMM Computer Communication Review, 39*(1), 68–73.

Ho, Liu, & Wu. (2011). Server consolidation algorithms with bounded migration cost and performance guarantees in cloud computing. In *Proceedings of IEEE International Conference on Utility and Cloud Computing*. IEEE.

Iyoob, Zarifoglu, & Dieker. (2013). Cloud computing operations research. *Service Science*, *5*(2), 88–101. doi:10.1287/serv.1120.0038

Kreinovich. (2013). Towards optimizing cloud computing: An example of optimization under uncertainty. In *Scalable computing and communications: Theory and practice*. New York: John Wiley & Sons and IEEE Computer Science Press.

Langer, Venkataraman, Palekar, Kale, & Baker. (2012). Performance optimization of a parallel, two stage stochastic linear program. In *Proceedings of 2012 IEEE 18th International Conference on Parallel and Distributed Systems*, (pp. 676–683). IEEE.

Latorre, Cerisola, Ramos, & Palacios. (2009). Analysis of stochastic problem decomposition algorithms in computational grids. *Annals of Operations Research*, *166*(1), 355–373. doi:10.1007/s10479-008-0476-1

Leukel, Kirn, & Schlegel. (2011). Supply chain as a service: A cloud perspective on supply chain systems. *IEEE Systems Journal*, 16–27.

Li, B., Li, J., Huai, J., Wo, T., Li, Q., & Zhong, L. (2009). EnaCloud: An energy-saving application live placement approach for cloud computing environments. In *Proceedings of IEEE International Conference on Cloud Computing*. IEEE. Retrieved from http://ieeexplore.ieee.org/stamp/stamp.jsp?tp=&arnumber=5284078&isnumber=5283545

Li. (2011). The impact of cloud computing-based information sharing on supply chain. In *Proceedings of 2011 International Conference on Management of e-Commerce and e-Government*. Academic Press.

Linderoth & Wright. (2003). Decomposition algorithms for stochastic programming on a computational grid. *Computational Optimization and Applications, 24*(2-3), 207–250.

Love, Morris, & Wesolowsky. (1988). *Facility location*. New York: Elsevier.

Lubin, Martin, Petra, & Sandikçi. (2013). On parallelizing dual decomposition in stochastic integer programming. *Operations Research Letters, 41*(3), 252–258. doi:10.1016/j.orl.2013.02.003

Lucas-Simarro, Moreno-Vozmediano, Montero, & Llorente. (2013). Scheduling strategies for optimal service deployment across multiple clouds. *Future Generation Computer Systems, 29*(6), 1431–1441. doi:10.1016/j.future.2012.01.007

Luo & Hong. (2011). Large-scale ranking and selection using cloud computing. In *Proceedings of the Winter Simulation Conference*, (pp. 4051–4061). Winter Simulation Conference.

Mendoza, Santiago, & Ravindran. (2008). A three-phase multicriteria method to the supplier selection problem. *International Journal of Industrial Engineering: Theory. Applications and Practice, 15*(2), 195–210.

Mirchandani & Francis. (1990). *Discrete location theory*. New York: Wiley.

Pandey, W. Guru, & Buyya. (2010). A particle swarm optimization-based heuristic for scheduling workflow applications in cloud computing environments. In *Proceedings of 24th IEEE International Conference on Advanced Information Networking and Applications*. IEEE.

Povidaiko, F. Moreira, & Filho. (2010). A java router based on real time traffic congestion information. In *Proceedings of 40th International Conference on Computers and Industrial Engineering*. Academic Press.

Rossetti & Chen. (2012). A cloud computing architecture for supply chain network simulation. In *Proceedings of the 2012 Winter Simulation Conference*. Academic Press.

Saaty. (1980). *The analytic hierarchy process: Planning, priority setting, resource, allocation*. New York: McGraw-Hill.

Saaty. (1990). How to make a decision: The analytic hierarchy process. *European Journal of Operational Research, 48*(1), 9 – 26.

Seiden. (2002). On the online bin packing problem. *Journal of the ACM, 49*(5), 640–671.

Speitkamp & Bichler. (2010). A mathematical programming approach for server consolidation problems in virtualized data centers. *IEEE Transactions on Services Computing, 3*(4), 266–278. doi:10.1109/TSC.2010.25

Stevens, De Leenheer, Develder, Dhoedt, & Christodoulopoulos, Kokkinos, & Varvarigos. (2009). Multi-cost job routing and scheduling in grid networks. *Future Generation Computer Systems, 25*(8), 912–925. doi:10.1016/j.future.2008.08.004

Swisher, Hyden, Jacobson, & Schruben. (2004). A survey of recent advances in discrete input parameter discrete-event simulation optimization. *IIE Transactions*, *36*(6), 591–600. doi:10.1080/07408170490438726

Triki & Grandinetti. (2001). Computational grids to solve large scale optimization problems with uncertain data. In *Proceedings of International Workshop on Intelligent Data Acquisition and Advanced Computing Systems: Technology and Applications*. Academic Press.

Wang, Ren, & Wang. (2011). Secure and practical outsourcing of linear programming in cloud computing. In *Proceedings of INFOCOM*. IEEE.

Wieczorek, Hoheisel, & Prodan. (2009). Towards a general model of the multi-criteria workflow scheduling on the grid. *Future Generation Computer Systems*, *25*(3), 237–256. doi:10.1016/j.future.2008.09.002

Yarmish & Van Slyke. (2009). A distributed, scaleable simplex method. *The Journal of Supercomputing*, *49*(3), 373–381. doi:10.1007/s11227-008-0253-6

KEY TERMS AND DEFINITIONS

Analytical Hierarchy Process: A multi-criteria decision making technique introduced and developed by the mathematician Thomas L. Saaty.

Operations Research: Aims to define theoretical foundation and mathematical methods for modeling and simulation of complex, challenging optimization, organization, management planning problems and to devise the relevant computational algorithms and software for their numerical solution.

Stochastic Programming: A branch of Operations Research that allows to explicitly deal with the random nature that characterizes a lot of the real world applications.

Chapter 11
Cloud Computing and Healthcare

ABSTRACT

This chapter discusses the adoption of cloud computing in healthcare. First, the advantages are explored; then, the disadvantages, such as data security issues that still limit the diffusion of cloud computing in this sector, are also explored. In addition, the Vitaever® Cloud product, developed by the Italian company Nethical S.r.l., is detailed and presented as a case study with reference to homecare. Finally, the intersection of cloud computing with mobile technologies for providing advanced healthcare services is investigated.

1. INTRODUCTION

The progressive aging population can be seen as one of the main causes of an increasing demand for medical cares. ICT plays a key role to support the health organizations in managing these increasing demands. They can offer more advanced applications, significant cost savings, more collaborative environments, and efficient medical devices to name a few.

The introduction of the surface computing in this sector, for example, can better represent the inclination of the ICT to design advanced healthcare applications. However, these applications would provide more capabilities if they were offered as services.

Cloud computing represents an opportunity for healthcare by enabling the organizations to use advanced applications as services. It guarantees flexibility, elasticity, scalability, significant reduction of medical errors that are mainly due to a poor communication among

DOI: 10.4018/978-1-4666-4683-4.ch011

the specialists, an improved information sharing and big data analysis.

Healthcare significantly contributes to the big data growth. A huge amount of data means higher analysis quality. Healthcare organizations have a big source of information but they do not often have advanced services to access data. Cloud systems represent a significant support to data access and can offer scalable healthcare analytics services. *Data classification*, *text* and *process mining* can be offered as services. This is a big advantage in healthcare since it is possible to predict and to manage pandemic risks more accurately, to estimate the mortality rate, to analyze the effectiveness of vaccines, etc. Then, healthcare becomes more reactive and can efficiently manage emergencies. In addition, each single data mining process is combined in complex analysis applications that can take advantage from a cloud in terms of storage and computational resources. Thus, a more accurate clinical data analysis, a more effective data aggregation, and a significant reduction of redundancies can be achieved. Specially, medical data aggregation plays a key role for a better information sharing among the specialists, the organizations, and the practitioners.

Nonetheless, the adoption of cloud computing in healthcare is still limited by some challenging issues such as data security and interoperability among different systems. In the following two sections, benefits as well as criticisms of adopting cloud-based healthcare solutions will be explored.

Then, Vitaever® will be described as an interesting case study with reference to homecare.

2. CLOUD COMPUTING FOR HEALTHCARE

In the traditional healthcare systems, medical records are on paper and therefore their "use" is very limited. An effective and efficient collaboration as well as information sharing among organizations, practitioners and specialists cannot be achieved.

Nowadays, many healthcare organizations are adopting electronic medical record systems. In the following, the main concepts are introduced:

- **Electronic Medical Record (EMR):** Represents the legal documentation managed and owned by a healthcare organization. It basically aims to describe what happened to a patient during an encounter. It contains information that can be shared among laboratories and staff that belong to the organization;
- **Electronic Health Record (EHR):** Integrates data and information generated from the different healthcare organizations involved in the patient's care. It contains information that can be shared among the authorized stakeholders and clinicians and the patient him/herself;
- **Personal Health Record (PHR):** Denotes the health documentation managed and populated by an individual. It aims to give a comprehensive view on the health and medical history of an individual. Data is gathered from different sources (EHRs and EMRs) and it is accessible to only those have permissions.

It could be extremely complex to share medical information among different organizations. However, data aggregation becomes a big concern especially in the presence of patients that have different health providers.

A cloud platform supports healthcare not only in terms of cost savings but also in efficiently sharing medical information. Cloud computing provides a centralized platform in order to access data, get information, analyze clinical reports, etc. Then, more accurate diagnosis can be made.

The cloud computing models together with the related services can support a healthcare organization for different purposes at different levels. For example, an organization can adopt a cloud infrastructure for data recovery (IaaS). Then, it maintains a data repository and "purchase" storage and network services in order to send a copy of data to the cloud provider. It can remotely use software applications by a Web browser (SaaS) for processing clinical images while it will adopt a cloud platform in order to develop a local electronic medical record.

Infrastructure, platforms and applications can be offered as services on demand to healthcare, easily used by the organizations without specific technical skills. In addition, in a private cloud, infrastructure is offered to a health organization. In this case, the provider guarantees security mechanisms in order to protect data stored in the EMRs. In a community cloud, infrastructure is shared among different healthcare organizations while in a public cloud, infrastructure is offered to the general public. In this last case, the developers of the healthcare applications have to protect patient's data. However, it is usually adopted a hybrid cloud as a good compromise between the private and the public solution.

A cloud-based solution offers also significant advantages in terms of an improved health delivery to rural and developing countries that can use "services" at lower costs. In addition, cloud computing enables the health organizations to offer services with only minimum downtimes.

From a high level perspective, a cloud-based healthcare platform can be seen as a natural solution for satisfying different requirements. In fact, it enables the healthcare organizations to share the infrastructure and the services while the experts to share the information on both patients and pathologies.

In critical situations, in which some vital parameters of a patient present anomalies, it is fundamental that the specialists monitor them and then select the best medical practices. The cloud healthcare solution described in Fan, He, Cai, and Li (2012) provides advanced tools for a more effective analysis of these vital parameters. For example, it offers the possibility for an on-line analysis of electrocardiogram. The large and heterogeneous ECG data are stored on a cloud where they are properly processed and analyzed. In the presence of anomalous data, the system quickly generates a warning message. Then, the specialists can constantly monitor patients.

Telemedicine plays a significant and relevant role in providing good quality services especially to those live in rural and developing countries. However, it could be often impossible to easily use the applications due to inadequate bandwidth, for example (Matlani

& Londhe, 2013). Therefore, it can take big advantage from the adoption of cloud computing especially in terms of advanced application software offered as services. Remote medical consultations and shared medical imaging services to name a few. Clinical data can be remotely acquired and then transmitted to a cloud where it can be properly processed. For instance, cloud-based solutions can be adopted for collecting and processing patient's data (Rolim et al., 2010). The patient's vital parameters can be collected via a sensors network connected to the medical equipments. Then, they are transmitted to a cloud where they can be stored, analyzed and delivered. As a consequence, the possibility to make errors is reduced since data is automatically registered and entered (see Rolim et al. (2010) for more details).

The advent of the cloud computing represents also a significant support to the mobile heath devices that present a limited computational capacity and short life batteries. In an integrated architecture, the complex computational algorithms applied for properly processing the data are run on the cloud platform and the final results are sent to the device. Data storage is offered as a service and therefore, the medical images can be stored in specific cloud databases. In addition, to move the intensive tasks (like the images processing) from the mobile devices to the clouds assures also a considerable reduction of the battery consumption.

The use of the traditional outdoor devices is another example of mobile device affected by the limited computational resources. For this purpose, in Angin (2011), the authors propose a mobile cloud approach for the context-aware blind navigation. In their architecture, the modern and advanced mobile devices are properly combined with the computational resources available on a cloud.

Also, the diabetic patients need to constantly measure their glucose level in order to avoid inappropriate insulin injections. They usually write these values in a daily diary. Nowadays, a lot of electronic programs available also on mobile devices provide advanced services. An integration of these programs with a cloud could easily support both the patients and the experts.

3. SECURITY AND INTEROPERABILITY

Confidential and private information on remote data centers provided by third parties causes some challenging issues related to data security and privacy. One possible solution is to adopt a private cloud. But, it is usually very expensive. Another possibility could be to adopt cloud solutions that are basically *"patient-centric."*

On the other hand, a way to protect patient data is to combine *encryption mechanisms* with other techniques such as *authenticity* and *authorization*. For example, in M. Li, Yu, Zheng, Ren, and Lou (2013), authors propose a framework with the aim of guaranteeing the secure by sharing of the PHRs in cloud computing. In Löhr, Sadeghi, and Winandy (2010), the authors propose a solution for a secure and advanced e-health cloud based on a *Trusted Virtual Domain* model.

Moreover, providing trusted data in healthcare is essential since they are "re-used" by specialists for making diagnosis and assigning therapies. For this purpose, to standard the documents that usually come from different archives and to verify the digital signs are key steps.

In Lounis, Hadjidj, Bouabdallah, and Challal (2012), the authors propose a cloud-based architecture that collects and provides the medical data generated from sensor networks.

In Zhang and Liu (2010), the authors address the security and privacy issues with reference to the access and management of EHRs in the context of healthcare clouds. They highlight the main requirements and propose an advanced EHR security reference model. The interested readers are referred to their work for details.

Interoperability represents another big issue when medical data is moved to a cloud. We cannot have data aggregation without interoperability among the systems the data comes from. Healthcare systems can use different protocols, different operating systems and different programming languages, and therefore they are often *incompatible*. Then, the first fundamental requirement is that they integrate their already existing systems and standardize their processes.

The standards play an essential role in order to guarantee interoperability among different software systems and they are usually defined at different levels according to the specific purposes. From a general point of view, they define the format followed by the *communication messages*, exchanged among different systems according to the

principle that the messages have to be both easily produced by the sender and easily understood by the receiver. Each message usually presents some optional fields that guarantee a more flexible structure. In addition, the type of a message is also a relevant information. In Hammond and Cimino (2006), the main stages for defining the standards are highlighted. The first identifies the reasons beyond the standard definition (*Identification Stage*). The second defines, among the other things, the functions and the characteristics of the standard (*Conceptualization Stage*). Then, the experts that concur to the standard definition establish its content together with the critical issues that have to be managed (*Discussion Stage*). Among the other features, the standards have also to guarantee *Abstraction* and *Representation*. The information is usually made abstract with the aim to reduce its content to the only useful data while the data representation is seen as a comprehensive perspective that includes as many details as possible (Hammond & Cimino, 2006). Thus, they are both extremely important in health contexts. In the case in which a patient has to make a specific test, it is not necessary to access to the whole medical record but it is sufficient to get the useful information for the analysis.

An international standard for medical images and related information is DICOM® (*Digital Imaging and COmmunication in Medicine* (http://medical.nema.org/Dicom/about-DICOM.html). It defines the formats for medical images that can be exchanged with data. It is currently implemented in almost every radiology, cardiology imaging and radiotherapy device and therefore, it is considered one of the most important healthcare messaging standards in the world.

It is mainly based on the *Entity-Relationship Model* according to which a set of *Entities* (like Patient, Image and, etc.) is defined together with a set of *Relationships* among entities. The entities are represented as *Objects* with specific *Attributes*.

According to this object-oriented structure, the DICOM® services are organized in some service classes that support, among the other functionalities, the activities for storing and searching data, for printing images and etc.

The readers are referred to http://medical.nema.org/dicom/presents.html to get more details on the main services and functionalities provided by DICOM® (Website http://medical.nema.org/Dicom/).

4. CASE STUDY: VITAEVER CLOUD INFRASTRUCTURE

This section illustrates the case study authored by the Italian company Nethical s.r.l. (www.nethical.net) and is intended solely for use in the context of the present chapter.

Nethical s.r.l exploits the cloud technology in order to innovate healthcare, to assist medical organizations that provide homecare services, to optimize processes and to reduce operating costs.

As an innovating company, it got several successful achievements not only at national but also at international level. More information and a detailed profile of the company can be found on the following Websites www.nethical.net and www.vitaever.com.

4.1 The Context

The increasing demand for care to manage the aging population together with the increasing number of chronic or terminal diseases is causing very high costs in health-care and this burden is expected to increase if no action is taken to curb the trend. The *Home Care Assistance* generates substantial savings for the national health system. However, it is necessary to develop new paradigms to ensure the same quality and the therapeutic efficiency that characterize the traditional hospitals.

The set of the health services offered at home is called *Integrated Home Care* (IHC) that is characterized by the integration of various services offered by multidisciplinary professionals such as doctors, nurses, psychologists, physiotherapists, pharmacists, social workers and caregivers who share objectives, responsibilities and resources to ensure *Patients* continuity of care. Such a kind of home care includes different type of assistance and therefore, it requires a system that can manage them in a complete, easy and intuitive way, giving importance to various factors such as the greater or lesser intensity of the disease, the specific professional competence and the operating territory. Home care, from an economic point of view, is also an opportunity to start new business models supporting the *Public Health System*. A key factor for supporting these new care models is the availability of technologies that facilitate communication and interaction between professionals involved in a context of home care and can improve relationship between the practitioners and the *Patients*.

In summary, all these considerations have pushed Nethical S.r.l., in collaboration with the ANT Foundation (www.ant.it) and with the contribution of the Department of Informatics, Science and Engineering, University of Bologna (www.unibo.it), to apply the cloud technologies in order to create a service suitable to both support and promote the home care paradigm: Vitaever®.

The readers are also referred to the work of Casadio et al. (2010) and Bracci, Corradi, and Foschini (2012).

4.2 The Project

Vitaever is a cloud technology that combines the software and the hardware, flexible and reliable, which you pay as you go, in order to manage in an efficient and intuitive way the home care services.

Distributed as a Service (SaaS), Vitaever allows the hospital unit to organize the daily activities, facilitates communication and information sharing among practitioners and optimizes the displacements around the territory. Moreover, thanks to reports and dashboards, it makes a real time analysis of all the activities and used resources.

Vitaever was designed to meet two main requirements:

- To provide a simple and powerful tool to efficiently manage home care contexts, and then, to take costs under control;
- To offer health and social services to the citizens, facilitating the communication and the interaction among all the professionals involved in a context of integrated home care.

Vitaever uses the technical and economic potential of the cloud computing model guaranteeing great savings: no installation, maintenance, upgrading costs for both the software and the hardware infrastructure. The cost is proportional to the organization's size, according to the number of the Patients, of the performed activities or of the involved *Operators*. This allows organizations of any size to adopt a fully functional software to run efficiently their daily jobs. Moreover, Vitaever is not only a useful tool for the organizations but also for the Patient himself/herself who has access to the system and can share his/her data with specialists involved in the healthcare process.

Vitaever is addressed mainly to the organizations and the structures that carry out home care activities, such as those that provide social services at home, distributed medical services or childcare. It can support professional studies, consortia and cooperatives, associations, pharmacies and home care organizations in their activities.

Vitaever is already used in different contexts such as *Social care Services*, *Palliative care*, *Auto-infusion therapy*, *Physiotherapy*, *Educational services*, *Logistic Services* and medical supplies.

4.3 The Cloud Infrastructure

Before analyzing Vitaever Cloud infrastructure, the most important components used in this project are described in the following.

Amazon Web Services™ (AWS™) is a set of Web services that compose a cloud computing platform. Launched in July 2002, it provides on-line services to other Web sites or client-side applications. Vitaever currently is deployed on Amazon™ Cloud and does not require any software installation on client side but only a common Web browser. The used data center is placed in Ireland.

Regarding Web connection, SSL protocol is used for encrypted connection, using AES 256 (256-bit keys). For software design and implementation, MVC pattern was used. The architecture (Figure 1) can be divided into three levels: Monitoring/Load Balancing level, Web Service level and Storage/Archivation level.

Regarding Web Service and Storage level, it is possible to observe that the architecture used for Vitaever SaaS consists of both permanent instances and a variable number of on-demand instances.

In monitoring level, there are two key services for EC2™: the Amazon™ Elastic Load Balancing and Amazon™ scaling service. In Web Service level, among the persistent resources, there are two instances of Elastic Compute Cloud™ (EC2™) type m1.small with a bandwidth of 250mbit/s in/out. They implement two Web servers and are load-balanced through Amazon™ Elastic Load Balancing service (ELB, in Monitoring/Load Balancing layer). The number of EC2™ on-demand instances varies depending on the workload: they are used to replicate the two permanent Web-server instances and are managed by Amazon™ scaling service. Within Storage/Archivation layer, a EC2™ instance is used as File Server, and the Amazon Elastic Block Store™ service (EBS) provides a shared storage with 50GB of persistent memory.

A EC2™ Large instance is also used for DMBS management through Amazon

Figure 1. Vitaever modules on Amazon™. (© [2013] [Nethical s.r.l.]. Used with permission).

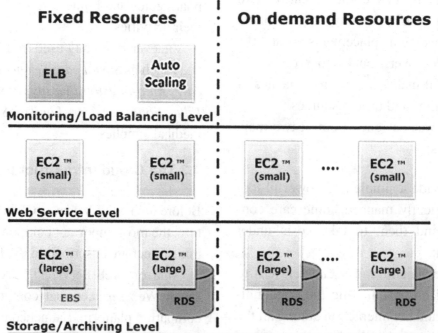

Relational Database Service™ (RDS). This service provides additional features, including automatic database backup. In this layer, some additional instances can be used in the case of increased workload.

4.4 The Deployment Architecture

Starting from Figure 1, it is possible to redesign Vitaever cloud computing architecture integrating the relations among the various instances. In particular, the Web Server, the File Server and the Database service (Figure 2) are described in the following.

4.4.1 Web Server

EC2 instances are created with a single Amazon™ AMI image. Web Servers receive requests from Web browsers: it is actually the Amazon™ Elastic Load Balancing layer that receives requests and sends them to one of the Web Servers available.

4.4.2 File Server

The File Server hosts Vitaever engine (SaaS Vitaever). This framework is the same for all licenses and requires small space on the hard drive.

Figure 2. Vitaever Architecture on Amazon™. (© [2013] [Nethical s.r.l.]. Used with permission).

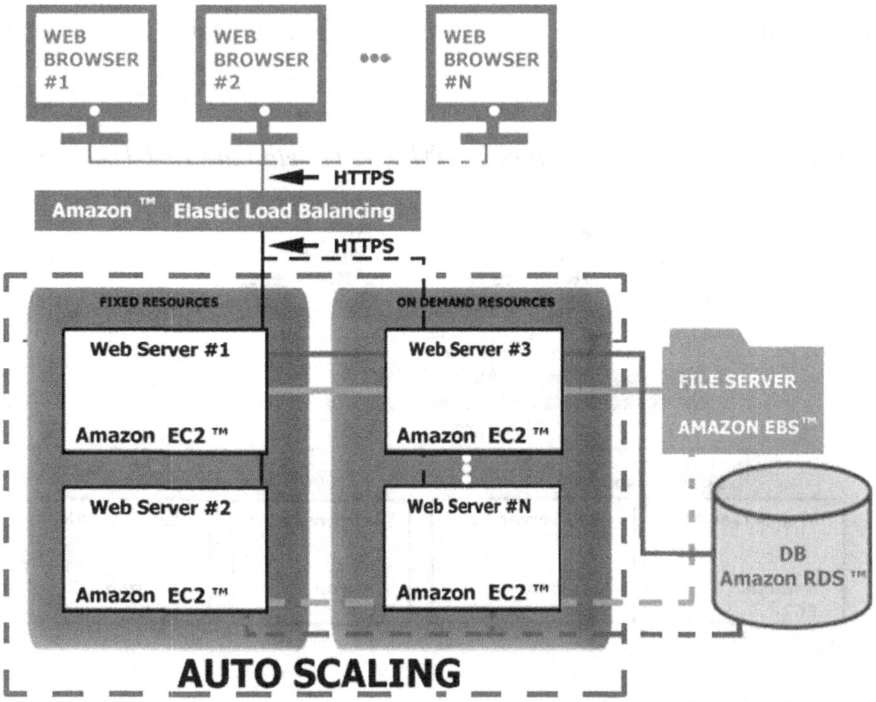

Figure 3 shows a development already in place. The File Server is removed and the code is moved to the Web servers. This eliminates the bottleneck represented by the File Server.

4.4.3 Database Service

Database is implemented using Amazon Relational Database Service™ (Amazon RDS™) that provides DB-ready Instance. It is Amazon RDS™ responsibility to ensure database security (from a reliability, availability and service ability, but not privacy point of view). Amazon RDS™ allows to schedule the creation of backup instances, creating an image of the entire instance. This feature makes easy to start new instances, always EC2™, containing not only the database but also the instance best configuration.

4.4.4 Security Server: Security and Key Management

With reference to the encryption strategy, the security of the encrypted data depends on: cryptographic algorithm, size of the encryption key and protection of the encryption key. In order to select the appropriate encryption algorithm, the following aspects have been taken into consideration: repetitive patterns, updates, massive volume of encrypted data. Moreover, the protection mechanism has to be effective so that the data can be valid for a very long period (such as several years). Another fundamental issue concerns the protection of the encryption keys.

In particular, the encryption keys location together with the access restrictions are particularly important. The choice was to move

Figure 3. Vitaever Architecture in development. (© [2013] [Nethical s.r.l.]. Used with permission).

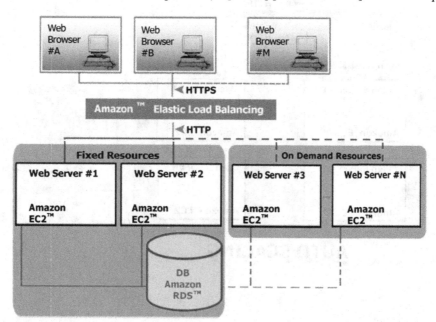

the security operations to separate software running on a separate server (physical), called the Security Server, as shown in Figure 4. The Security Server manages the users, the roles, the privileges, the policies and the encryption keys. Inside the DBMS, a security module communicates with the Security Server in order to authenticate the users, to control the privileges and to encrypt or decrypt data. The encryption keys can then be connected to either the users or the user privileges.

4.5 The Cloud Architecture with Encryption

Vitaever ensures data security and integrity by using secure protocols and individual encrypted password. Only authorized persons are allowed to view and edit personal and confidential information. Finally, thanks to technology developed in collaboration with the University of Bologna, Vitaever runs up the encryption of all the sensitive data by using private keys on an individual license. This guarantees data integrity even against third party suppliers and makes Vitaever Cloud a secure technology also for health field applications.

The final architecture is composed by two main modules (Figure 5):

- Vitaever Amazon™ AWS™ that contains all the AWS™ resources used to realize Vitaever Cloud. The necessary changes to implement the encryption do not alter the basic structure of the cloud currently in use but only of a small part of Vitaever code;

- Key Manager that is the critical component for guaranteeing security since it manages the encryption keys. It also allows to storage and retrieval all the encryption keys in the system and contains the Security Server that is the service dedicated to manage all the encryption keys.

A hierarchy has been introduced and the encryption keys have been associated to the system's groups. In fact, it is not only possible to encrypt all columns that contain sensitive data but also to use different encryption keys (Figure 6). This component has been created by a LDAP (Lightweight Directory Access Protocol) service that has the intrinsic properties compatible to the required ones: the hierarchy, including the encryption keys and the system's groups, has been easily implemented by a tree structure such as LDAP (Figure 7). The Key Manager, then, becomes the key component for the Vitaever implementation on a public cloud..

4.5.1 System Access Groups

The profiles, or groups, define the data to which you may access and the operations that can be performed. The user can configure and customize the permissions, at both group and individual user level, ensuring the granularity required.

System administrator: System administrators are responsible for configuring and customizing the system: they can, for instance, enable or disable modules, customize the list of services, add new services' categories, create personalized care plans, manage various

Figure 4. Key Management. (© [2013] [Nethical s.r.l.]. Used with permission).

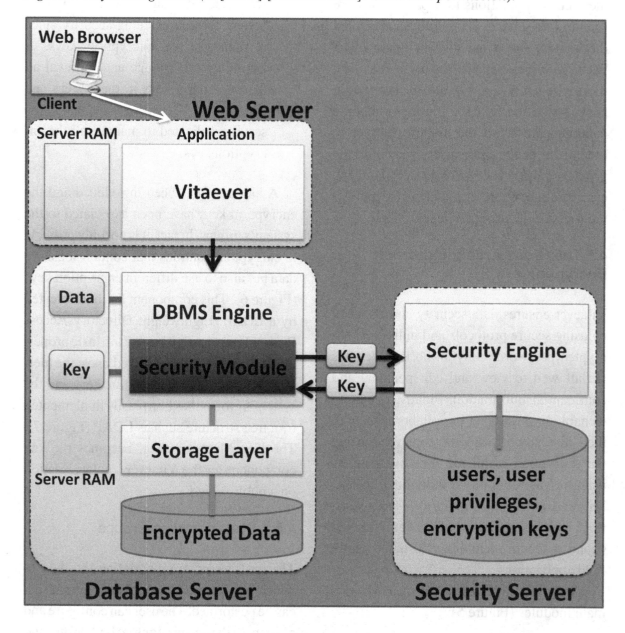

types of attachments, create and customize printing templates, add users and customize profiles and categories of billing.

Patient: Each authorized Patient can access the system for consulting and sharing his/her clinical data. This allows to fully involve him/her in the home care process, promoting greater awareness of his/her own clinical situation.

Operator: Medical staff belongs to the Operators group and is distinguished into some categories according to the role and job profile. Each operator is enabled to plan his/her own agenda, display data from all Patients, write

Figure 5. Vitaever cloud architecture with encryption. (© [2013] [Nethical s.r.l.]. Used with permission).

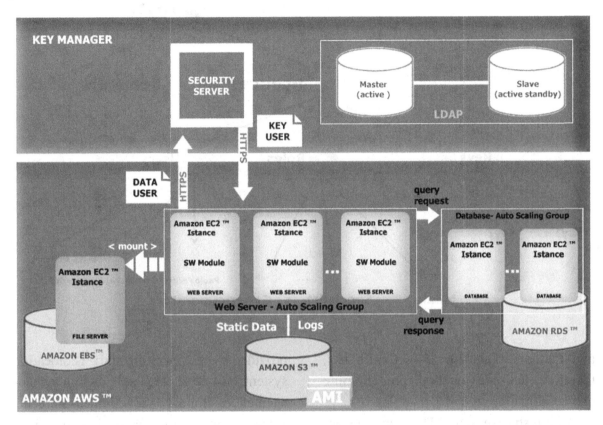

Figure 6. Example of multiple encryption keys. (© [2013] [Nethical s.r.l.]. Used with permission).

Key1		Key2	Key3
Name	**Surname**	**Date of Birth**	**ZIP Code**
AxhYMiwC	byQXKITB	S4/aSfGaSf5NSWCC	T8nuS4bC
gl6qnIwC	bx6X+xTzMbCC	S4PaSfbaSf5NT/CC	R4sSfaC
fihsKIwC	bxcJ0IHyKbCC	S8GaS8WaSf5NTbCC	W3nuS8/C

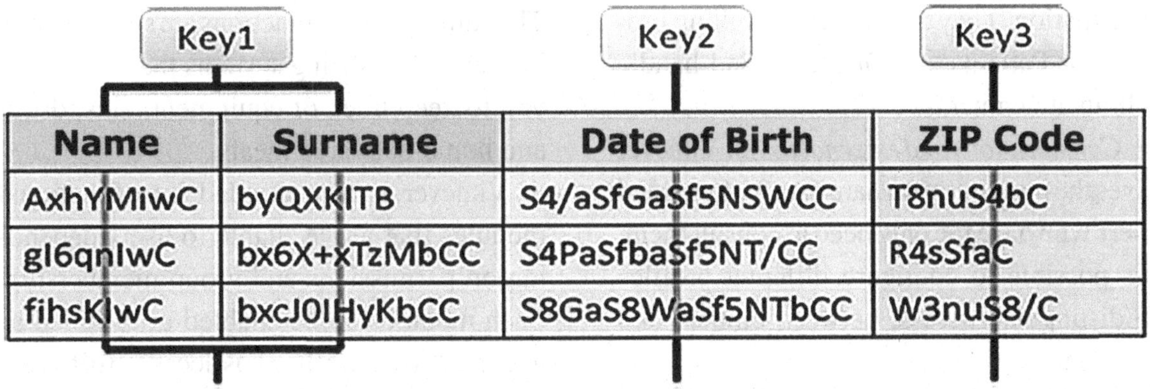

and edit Patient's diaries. Operators can see clinical data, agenda, the list of performance included in the home care plan and display the temporal evolution of each symptom (such as pain, performance status, temperature, etc.).

Operating centre: They can view and edit each user personal information, health parameters, insert and update Patient clinical records, monitor activities carried out through reports and manage reporting for Operators

Figure 7. Example of LDAP structure. (© [2013] [Nethical s.r.l.]. Used with permission).

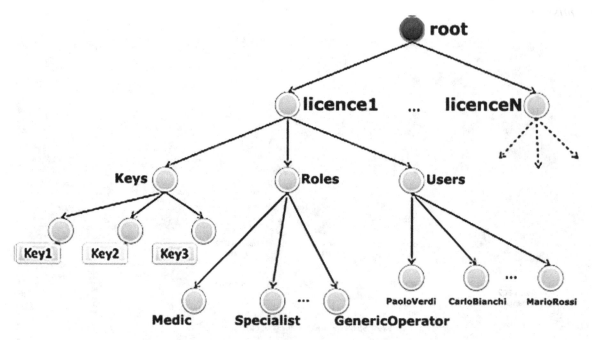

and Patients. The Operating Centre has, therefore, activities on both programming and coordination.

Administrative staff: They manage accounting and administrative activities. They can consult but not change Patient's personal information. They can also create billing profiles for Patients and Operators and handle billing attachments.

Consultations and external users: Vitaever gives the possibility to share data with enabled users who have the only need to consult them. It's possible to configure different profiles to distinguish access, between clinical and personal data.

4.6 The Main Features

Vitaever provides effective tools that allow to organize the assistance activities and services

provided by the operating staff: geolocation system, best route calculator, complete management of clinical data with measurements signature and history, care plans based on the list of performances available, internal message system, shared calendars and more. The administrative functions are simplified by billing and reporting systems that also allow you to keep track of equipment, aids, drugs and home-delivered meals.

Vitaever is also divided into functional modules that are available to users depending on permissions and group membership. Each module can be enabled or disabled as needed. Each user then has access to different resources depending on their profile.

4.6.1 Master Data Management

Vitaever manages complete personal profiles for Patients, Operators and Users (Figure 8). It is possible to assign Patients to departments witch the structure is divided into and Operators can work on multiple departments simultaneously. These Operators, depending on the group/s to which they belong, can perform different actions on system data, from a full management to a simple consultation. It is possible to get updated lists of system users, enable or disable access and customize access permissions to resources. In addition, the system provides import and export procedures to ensure interoperability with other software.

4.6.2 Assistance Management

One or more assistance periods (assistances) are associated to each Patient. The assistances identify the periods within which Operators may carry out activities on Patients. Different information can be associated to any assistance (level of care, Regional Public Health Unit and district of reference, etc.). These data allows specifying and defining a precise period of the clinical history of the Patient. Vitaever, thanks to a punctual management of assistance periods, ensures a proper reporting and a more accurate analysis of the collected data.

Figure 8. Personal data. (© [2013] [Nethical s.r.l.]. Used with permission).

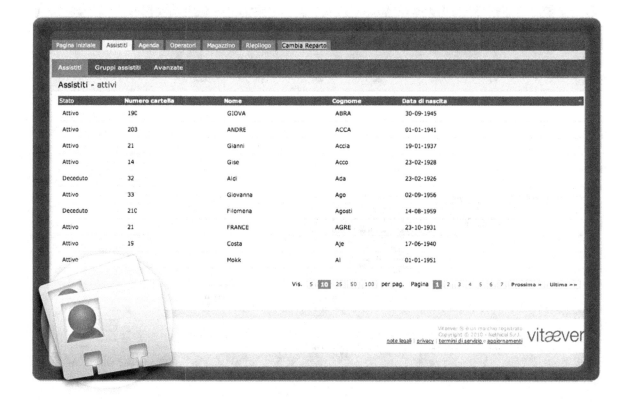

4.6.3 Planning and Activities Management

Each Operator has a personal agenda that can be shared with Patients and other Operators in order to manage in a fast and complete way the assistance programs (Figure 9). Through the agenda, the Operator can organize various kinds of activities such as external events like the activities for individual Patients, interior appointments like the activities not related to Patients and group appointments like any activity that involves Patients organized into groups.

It is possible to request the support of other Operators, to export the agenda in a standard format, to set appointments with daily, weekly, monthly or yearly repetitions and to easily replicate an agenda period into another.

4.6.4 Clinical Data

Vitaever manages the organizational aspects of daily work but it is also used to store in a secure way different clinical aspects of Patients (Figure 10). It is possible to compile Patients clinical records (medical history, social welfare sheets, etc.), symptoms (pain, vomit, hematuria, performance status hemoptysis,

Figure 9. Agenda. (© [2013] [Nethical s.r.l.]. Used with permission).

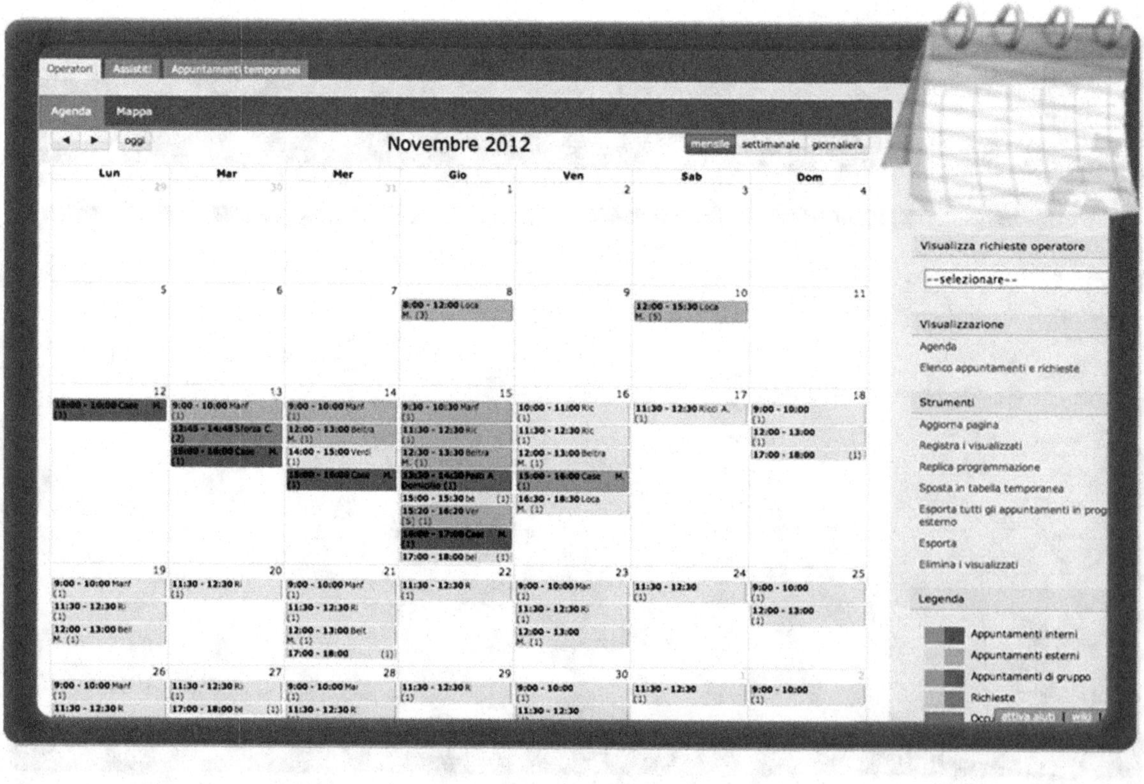

Figure 10. Clinical data. (© [2013] [Nethical s.r.l.]. Used with permission).

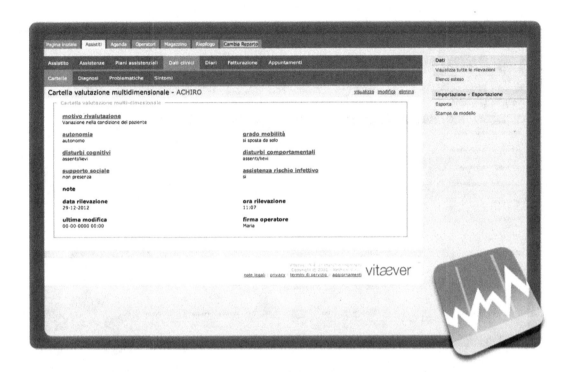

etc.), ongoing problems (breathing, mobility, nutrition, sleep therapy management, etc.) and to keep track of the examinations, treatments and ongoing diagnosis. The system keeps track of who changes the data and allows to track the history of all changes.

4.6.5 Geolocation

Activities geolocation service is very useful in the daily work on the territory. The system is able to calculate the best route to reach the Patient's home, providing the related road directions. The possibility to plan the various displacements to be made allows to save time and to take under control the fuel consumption with a consequent reduction of the costs and a positive ecological impact.

4.6.6 Billing and Reporting

Vitaever provides the necessary tools for managing the process of reporting and billing activities (Figure 11). The ability to configure, for each and every Operator or Assisted, a custom billing profile, allows to generate detailed summaries of all costs related to provided or received services.

4.6.7 Reports and Dashboards

Reports and dashboards allow you to monitor at any time Operators' activity, used resources, provided services and costs (Figure 12). By using filters and export functions, it is possible to process data also by third part tools. For instance, the user can export the details

Figure 11 Billing. (© [2013] [Nethical s.r.l.]. Used with permission).

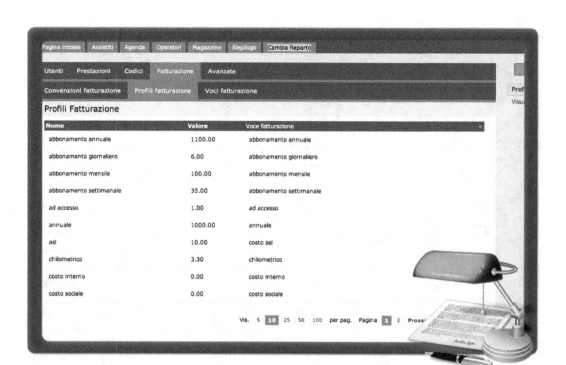

Figure 12. Report. (© [2013] [Nethical s.r.l.]. Used with permission).

of the performed services together with the hours of assistance. In addition, it is also possible to export the details of a specific provided service, the updated Patients' lists and the billing reports. Finally, it is possible to analyze the organization efficiency by the differences between the planned and the performed activities.

4.6.8 Access with Mobile Devices

The user can access the system by any device connected to the Internet and this allows to use Vitaever functionalities either through a personal computer or through mobile devices such as mobile phones, smartphone or tablet (Figure 13). In this way, without additional costs and the need of buying specific hardware, the Operator is able to always get the latest information on the status of the Patient.

4.7 The ANT ITALIA Case Study

ANT Foundation is an Italian leading no profit organization which successfully developed the largest EU home based cancer hospital with over 4,000 Patients assisted every day at home and organized by 21 regional clusters throughout Italy. Since 1985, ANT assists over 95,000 Patients in the advanced stages of cancer together with their families and offers free of charge professional medical assistance,

Figure 13. Mobile. (© [2013] [Nethical s.r.l.]. Used with permission).

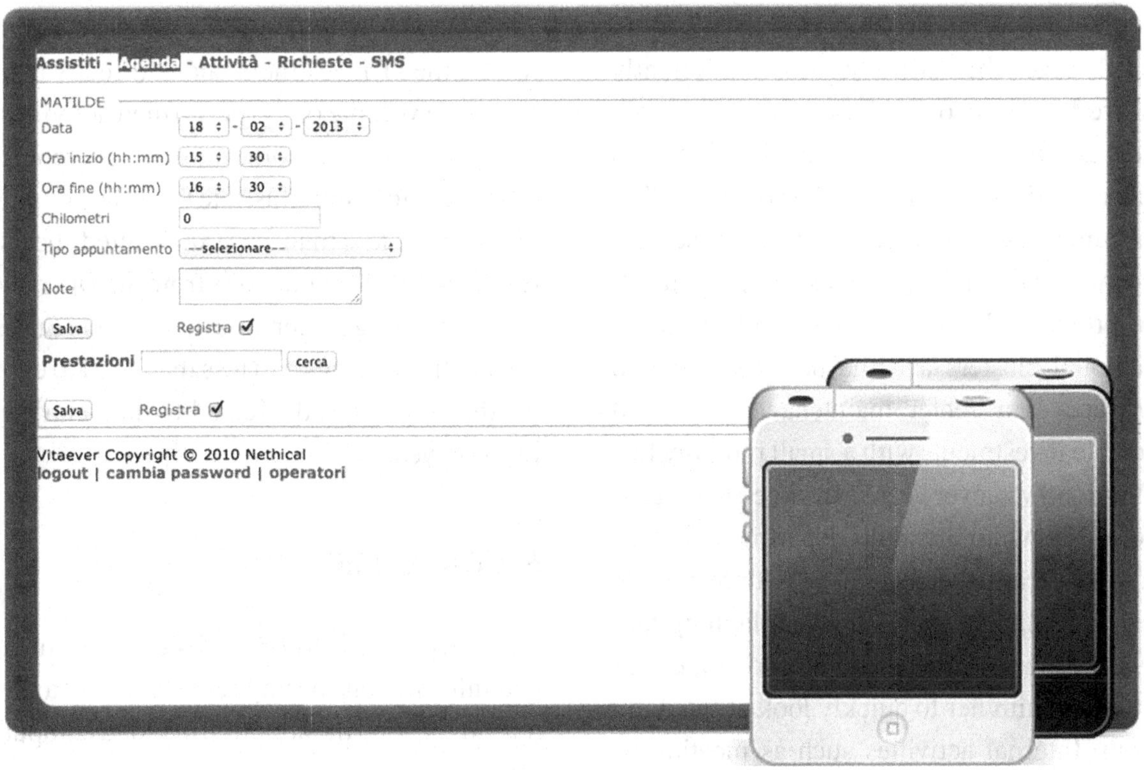

drugs, food and psychology consultancy as well as disease prevention and screening programs. The ANT Hospital involves around 350 medical professionals, and 1,300 volunteers in support roles. This amounts to a complex system that is fast growing and everyday pointing out new organization and data sharing limits. Moreover ANT was required to report its activity to the local healthcare authority within a really short time by the end of every month. Vitaever cloud technology helps ANT to leverage its fast growing and complex model, thereby to keep offering the same care, benefits and efficiency of traditional healthcare services. Vitaever provides ANT with a cutting edge smart technology to track, manage and optimize distribution of personnel, assets and goods in a mobile environment. In particularly the project have addressed the following ANT needs: to optimize people and resources scheduling, to easily reach the Patient houses, to efficiently share health records and notes, to track assets and drugs, to monitor the activities and measure the performance, to produce billing documents within 24 hours, to replace several software with a unique fast scaling platform, to provide a "plug and play" tool to the 21 regional clusters and the new ones and to replace data center maintenance cost and update investments with a small monthly fee. A unique Vitaever license has been generated for ANT while the multi department feature allows creating dedicated environments for each regional cluster. Vitaever planning features provide an agenda for each Operator and help him/her to quickly look at the daily plan. Internal activities such as meeting or

briefings are also included. The map interface supports the movements in order to reach the houses of several Patients in one day, saving time and reducing the Operator stress. On the medical side, reports and notes help to share data among the Operators that hardly meet each other.

Mobile phones allows ANT personnel to access Vitaever and to instantly update Patients records and their activity logs. This makes possible to generate within a few hours documents for billing or reporting purpose.

Vitaever is currently adopted in all ANT regional clusters. The ANT IT team has been partially converted from infrastructure manager to service manager and it is currently supporting an even bigger user community with less efforts. Vitaever, distributed as a service, let ANT cut several costs such as for software installation and maintenance as well as for server hardware. This allows ANT to reduce the IT investment and to directly bind its cost to volume of the performed activities.

In the following, some numbers are reported in order to better illustrate the potentialities of Vitaever: less than 700,000 printed sheets, less than 40,000 phone calls from the Operator to the operating center, less than 90,000 Euros for supplying drugs and less than 80,000 euro for the employees dedicated to data entry in just one year.

5. CONCLUSION

Elasticity, scalability, big data management and information sharing represent only a few reasons beyond the adoption of cloud computing in healthcare.

It gives to healthcare the possibility to use more advanced analysis tools, data storage and computational resources as services, to have a comprehensive view on the patient health history, to develop new models, to discover new medical facts and to experiment new therapies. A more collaborative environment in which the costs are shared among the users and paid according to the real consume.

Cloud computing can "reinvent" healthcare services, improve efficiency and productivity.

However, especially the security issues still limit the adoption of cloud computing in this sector. To implement, in fact, security mechanisms becomes a must since medical data are mostly confidential and private information. In addition, to use standards is crucial and significant in order to guarantee data aggregation.

REFERENCES

Angin. (2011). Real-time mobile-cloud computing for context- aware blind navigation. *International Journal of Next Generation Computing, 2*(2).

Bracci, F., Corradi, A., & Foschini, L. (2012). Database security management for healthcare SaaS in the Amazon AWS cloud. In *Proceedings of 2012 IEEE Symposium on Computers and Communications* (ISCC). IEEE.

Casadio, M., Biasco, G., Abernethy, A., Bonazzi, V., Pannuti, R., & Pannuti, F. (2010). The national tumor association foundation (ANT): A 30 year old model of home palliative care. *BMC Palliative Care, 9*(12). PMID:20529310

Fan, H. Cai, & Li. (2012). HCloud: A novel application-oriented cloud platform for preventive healthcare. In *Proceedings of 2012 IEEE 4th International Conference on Cloud Computing Technology and Science* (Cloud-Com), (pp. 705–710). IEEE.

Hammond & Cimino. (2006). Standards in biomedical informatics. In *Biomedical informatics, health informatics*. New York: Springer.

Li, Yu, Zheng, Ren, & Lou. (2013). Scalable and secure sharing of personal health records in cloud computing using attribute-based encryption. *IEEE Transactions on Parallel and Distributed Systems, 24*(1), 131–143. doi:10.1109/TPDS.2012.97

Löhr. Sadeghi, & Winandy. (2010). Securing the e-health cloud. In *Proceedings of the 1st ACM International Health Informatics Symposium*. ACM.

Lounis, H. Bouabdallah, & Challal. (2012). Secure and scalable cloud-based architecture for e-health wireless sensor networks. In *Proceedings of International Conference on Computer Communications and Networks*. ICCCN.

Matlani & Londhe. (2013). A cloud computing based telemedicine service. In *Point-of-care healthcare technologies (PHT)*. IEEE.

Rolim, K., & Westphall, W. Fracalossi, & Salvador. (2010). A cloud computing solution for patient's data collection in health care institutions. In *Proceedings of Second International Conference on eHealth, Telemedicine, and Social Medicine*, (pp. 95–99). Academic Press.

Zhang & Liu. (2010). Security models and requirements for healthcare application clouds. In *Proceedings of IEEE 3rd International Conference on Cloud Computing* (CLOUD), (pp. 268–275). IEEE.

KEY TERMS AND DEFINITIONS

Electronic Health Record (EHR): Integrates data and information generated from the different healthcare organizations involved in the patient's care. It contains information that can be shared among the authorized stakeholders and clinicians and the patients themselves.

Electronic Medical Record (EMR): The legal documentation managed and owned by a healthcare organization. It basically aims to describe what happened to a patient during an encounter. It contains information that can be shared among laboratories and staff that belong to the organization.

Integrated Home Care (IHC): Characterized by the integration of various services offered by multidisciplinary professionals such as doctors, nurses, psychologists, physiotherapists, pharmacists, social workers, and caregivers who share objectives, responsibilities, and resources to ensure patients' continuity of care.

Personal Health Record (PHR): Denotes the health documentation managed and populated by an individual. It aims to give a comprehensive view on the health and medical history of an individual. Data is gathered from different sources and it is accessible to only those have permissions.

Vitaever ®: A cloud technology, developed by Nethical s.r.l., in collaboration with the ANT Foundation and with the contribution of the Department of Informatics, Science and Engineering, University of Bologna, that combines the software and the hardware, flexible and reliable, which you pay as you go, in order to manage in an efficient and intuitive way the home care services.

Chapter 12
Green Computing:
A Dual Technology for HPC and Cloud Computing

ABSTRACT

Green computing is a contemporary research topic to address climate and energy challenges. In this chapter, the authors envision the duality of green computing with technological trends in other fields of computing such as High Performance Computing (HPC) and cloud computing on one hand and economy and business on the other hand. For instance, in order to provide electricity for large-scale cloud infrastructures and to reach exascale computing, we need huge amounts of energy. Thus, green computing is a challenge for the future of cloud computing and HPC. Alternatively, clouds and HPC provide solutions for green computing and climate change. In this chapter, the authors discuss this proposition by looking at the technology in detail.

1. INTRODUCTION

Climate change and global warming are the two most important challenging problems for the earth. These problems pertain to a general increase in world temperatures caused by increased amounts of carbon dioxide around the earth. Researchers in various fields of science and technology in recent years started to carry out research in order to address these problems by developing environmentally friendly solutions. Green IT and in particular green computing are two new terms introduced mainly in ICT community to address the aforementioned problems.

DOI: 10.4018/978-1-4666-4683-4.ch012

With the explosive growth of Internet-enabled cloud computing and HPC centers of all types, IT's energy consumption and sustainability impact are expected to continue climbing well into the future. Green IT recognizes this problem and efforts are under way in both industry and academia to address it. Green IT denotes energy efficiency in all components of computing systems to make the use of computers and the Internet as energy efficient as possible.

As computing and communication continue to grow, servers, networks and data centers consume more and more energy. For example, IT resources in the US consume more than 1.5% of the total electricity consumption. The power consumption of the data centers in the US in 2006 was 1.5% of the total energy consumed at a cost of more than $4.5B. With the expected 30-fold increase in data traffic over the next decade, the overall power consumption of data centers and networks will become an issue of vital importance to the IT and telecommunications industries.

While computing and information technologies consume energy, they also enable productivity enhancements and directly contribute to energy efficiency. Some even argue that computing and information technologies are vital, significant and critical in moving towards a low-carbon future (Smart 2020: Enabling the Low Carbon Economy in the Information Age, 2010).

In this chapter, we envision the duality of green computing with technological trends in other fields of computing such as HPC, cloud computing, business, and economy.

2. PROPOSITION

Our proposition in this chapter is that green computing is a dual technology for computing and communication technologies such as HPC and cloud computing. This means that green computing solutions will drive the development of HPC and cloud computing; on the other hand, HPC solutions and cloud computing solutions will drive the development of green computing. Therefore, we may say these technologies are dual to each other, thus we envision green computing as a dual technology for HPC and cloud computing.

On the other hand, HPC provides solutions for green computing and climate change. Complicated processes of new sources of energy, need exascale computing for modeling and simulation.

In addition, these contemporary technologies are moving toward Intelligent Computation in order to optimize resource and energy consumption without losing performance. Intelligent Computations are done with the techniques and mechanisms of new computing technologies such as hardware and software co-design, application profiling, and virtual machine consolidation to optimize resource consumption, and pay-as-you-go business model to reduce costs, etc.

In sum, if we solve the challenges and problems of HPC and exascale, we would implicitly solve many challenges in green computing such as access to new sources of energy, etc. Similarly, if we solve green computing challenges, we would solve HPC and cloud computing challenges such as the challenge of exascale power and building huge cloud data centers. This is the duality theorem we observe among energy efficiency, green computing and other technological trends in computing and communication technologies. This proposition is illustrated in Figure 1.

In the remainder of this chapter, we go over some research work at the intersection of cloud computing and HPC with green computing to realize our observation and proposition of duality.

3. CLOUD COMPUTING

In the cloud computing world, IT capabilities are delivered on the fly and on-demand through the Internet when the need arises instead of drawing from desktop computers. Many design and architectural patterns (Armbrust et al., 2010) are emerging around cloud computing that makes it difficult to fit everything into a prefect definition.

In a formal definition, we denote cloud computing as an extreme specialization (hyperspecialization) and at the same time a general purpose model of information technology to digest the flux of future IT. More specifically, we connote the real definition of cloud computing as the convergence of the following essential and ideal characteristics of various distributed computing technologies:

1. **Infinity:** Large scale data centers;

Figure 1. Green computing: A dual technology for computing and communication technologies

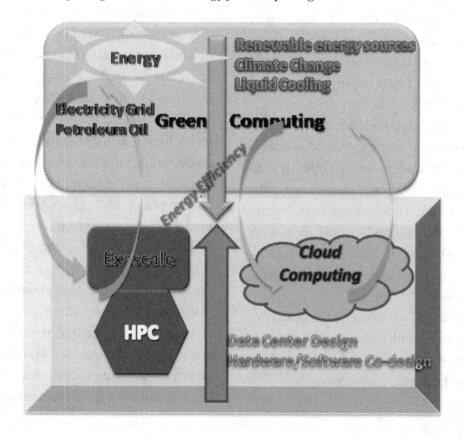

2. **Outsourcing:** Remote, over the Internet;
3. **Utility:** Pay per use;
4. **Economy of scale;**
5. **Self-Service:** Self-provisioning, on the fly;
6. **Multi-tenancy**
7. **On-demand;**
8. **Elasticity:** Scalability, autoscaling;
9. ***-abilities:** Availability, reliability, scalability, sustainability, etc.

The nature and the anatomy of cloud computing is totally green. From the users' point of view, cloud computing makes their IT life easier. They can access IT services without spending too much effort and energy, compared to the other IT models (that are dedicated). On the other hand, from the scientific point of view, the characteristics of cloud computing and deployment models make it a ubiquitous green IT paradigm.

In the following, we review cloud's characteristics and cloud deployment options to highlight that they are cost-, and energy-effective. In addition, from this highlight we observe green computing contribution to cloud computing.

3.1 Infinity

Clouds approach infinity (Armbrust et al., 2009); we observe this character from many statistics about computing. Statistics demonstrate that power requirement and power management become a major challenge in massive scale systems infrastructures such as cloud computing data centers. For instance, currently Microsoft and Google have data centers with 48 MW and 85 MW power requirement, respectively.

In sum, we conclude that green computing contributes to the development of cloud computing. Green computing's goal is to provide energy and to increase energy efficiency and reduce resource consumption of the cloud infrastructures.

3.2 Outsourcing: Remote, Over the Internet

Cloud computing is often represented with a diagram that contains a cloud-like shape indicating a layer where the responsibility for a service goes from user to provider. This is outsourcing of a service from the user side to the provider side. It is similar to the electrical power we receive each day, cloud computing provides subscribers and users with access to provisioned services.

This feature makes users' life to get access to services easier and without any effort. Outsourcing implicitly contributes to energy efficiency and green computing.

3.3 Utility: Pay Per Use

In cloud computing, payment of resource consumption is just like utilities that are paid for by the hour. In other words, service consumption is metered or measured.

When demand for a service varies with time, and when demand is unknown in advance, the utility character of a cloud will definitely make it economically cost-saving.

In the traditional computing models, provisioning a data center for the peak load that it must sustain a few days per month leads to under utilization at other times that is not energy efficient. Instead, cloud computing lets an organization pay by the hour for computing resources, potentially leading to cost savings even if the hourly rate to rent a machine from a cloud provider is higher than the rate to own one.

In addition, with the cost associativity of cloud computing, computations can finish faster, since using 1000 EC2 machines for 1 hour costs the same as using 1 machine for 1000 hours.

3.4 Economy of Scale

Cloud providers purchase data center infrastructure equipments such as hardware, network, and bandwidth much cheaper than a regular business. The construction and operation of extremely large-scale, commodity-computer datacenters at low-cost locations is the key necessary enabler of cloud computing (Armbrust et al., 2009).

The cost of electricity, network bandwidth, operations, software, and hardware is decreased in the factors of 5 to 7 at very large economies of scale. These factors, combined with statistical multiplexing to increase utilization compared to a private cloud, meant that cloud computing could offer services below the costs of a medium-sized data center and yet still make a good profit (Armbrust et al., 2009).

Economies of scale for consumers means if you need more storage, it is just a matter of upping your subscription costs with your provider, instead of buying new equipment. If you need more computational cycles, you need not buy more servers; rather you just buy more from your cloud provider.

Economy of scale is cost-effective and directly contributes to energy efficiency and green computing.

3.5 Self Service: Self-Provisioning, on the Fly

User self-provisioning is one the greatest benefits of the cloud. With that, you have the ability to get applications up and running in a fraction of the time you would need in a conventional scenario.

In a cloud, users prepare their resources on the fly by themselves. On the other hand, infrastructure is adapted to the applications. Theoretically, Amazon Web Services (AWS) makes it possible for anyone with an Internet connection and a credit card to access the same kind of world class computing systems that Amazon uses to run its multi-billion per year retail operation. On the other hand, the number of VMs instantiated on Amazon is limited. Users have a limit for on-demand service, however, they can request more using an online request form. Thus, massive self-provisioning of cloud resources on the fly is limited.

This cloud's characteristic significantly reduces time to solutions and access to services, thus it is energy efficient and green.

3.6 Multi-Tenancy

In traditional data centers, computing systems suffer from under utilization of computing power and networking bandwidth. Multi-tenant is a business model that provides a secure, exclusive virtualized computing environment in which servers, databases, and other resources are shared by multiple user companies in a cloud environment.

Public cloud is hosted, operated and managed by a third-party vendor from one or more data centers. Since the services are offered to multiple customers with the aforementioned characters, it is multiple tenants over a common infrastructure.

With virtualization and multi-tenant feature, the resources in the cloud are not devoted to specific usages and users. At one time, a cloud resource can be used for an application by a user, and at another time it can be used for another diverse application by the same user or another user.

Virtualization and shared hosting technologies coupled with multicore servers are the enablers of cloud infrastructures to support a large number of disparate applications running simultaneously on multicore servers. Moreover, these technologies enable VM consolidation, infrastructure-adapted-to-applications (Intelligent Computation), and other resource optimization techniques.

This multi-usage feature of cloud addresses energy efficiency and green computing challenges by significantly improving resource utilization and minimizing resource waste.

3.7 Public Cloud

When a cloud is made available in a pay-as-you-go manner to the public, we call it a public cloud (Armbrust et al., 2009); the service being sold is Utility Computing. Public cloud resembles the Internet; current examples of public Utility Computing include AWS, Google App Engine, and Microsoft Azure.

Institutions rely on public clouds for providing their services. This is a high level perspective of Green IT. Public clouds refer to infrastructure provided to the general public by a large industry selling cloud services. Amazon's cloud offering would fall in this category. These services are on a pay-as-you-go basis and can usually be purchased using a credit card.

In public cloud, everything is outsourced to outside of a corporation administrative domain such as security management and day to day operations. These outsourced tasks are handled by the provider of public cloud service offering. Hence, the customer of the public cloud service offering has much lower degree of control and oversight of the physical and logical security aspects of a private cloud.

Public cloud providers optimize energy consumption as a way to offer competitive prices. This is Green IT at a low level powered by market rules. Moreover, some public cloud providers could relay to other public cloud providers for certain services.

HPC applications in public cloud is an economic and green approach. In Vazquez-Poletti, Barderas, Llorente, and Romero (2012), an astronomy application with a parameter sweep profile from the next mission to Planet Mars is ported to a public cloud environment. This application requires a big quantity of computing resources in a short term with punctual situations. Authors proposed a model for optimal execution of that application on a public cloud infrastructure in terms of time and cost metrics.

3.8 Cloud Federation and Hybrid Cloud

Hybrid clouds refer to two or more cloud infrastructures that operate independently but are bound together by technology compliance to enable application portability.

With hybrid cloud and cloud federation, we can build green services. For each service, we should find the most green cloud provider, that is, a provider that consumes the least amount of energy to provide a service.

These deployment models are energy efficient and directly contribute to green computing challenges by improving energy consumption.

4. HIGH PERFORMANCE COMPUTING

HPC is the use of advanced parallel processing systems (usually, above a teraflop or 1012 floating-point operations per second) for running complicated and huge processes quickly, efficiently, and reliably.

The energy (power), cooling, and data center design are the three most prominent challenges of future HPC systems. Power has become the pre-eminent design constraint for future HPC systems. Moreover, the energy cost becomes an increasingly important factor.

We believe green and performance objectives converge to the same point. In this direction, HPC provides solutions for green computing. We cite some research work on the areas of energy and climate that are at the intersection of HPC and green computing.

HPC is used to provide energy, and vice versa energy is required to operate HPC systems. In particular, as exascale systems are emerging, they would need huge amounts of electricity to sustain. HPC systems of today need about 10MW power requirement. For instance, Sequoia, the IBM BlueGene/Q system installed at the Department of Energy Lawrence Livermore National Laboratory, is on the top of the Top500 list with 16.32 petaflop/s (The Top500, 2012). It is also one of the most energy efficient systems on the list with 7890kW power requirement. In addition, the target for the future exascale systems' power requirement is 20MW.

ExxonMobil (Exxonmobil, 2012) predicts the outlook for energy enabled with supercomputing, ExxonMobil's global energy outlook projects through 2040. The projections indicate that, at that time, the world's population will be 8 billion, roughly 25% higher than today. Along with this population rise will be continuing economic growth. This combination of population and economic growth will increase energy demand by over 50% versus 2000.

HPC drives the process of finding new sources of energy. Effective technology solutions to the energy challenges rely on modeling complicated processes and that in turn will lead to a strong need for supercomputing. Two examples of the supercomputing need in the oil business are seismic approaches for finding petroleum and petroleum reservoir fluid-flow modeling (also known as "reservoir simulation").

HPC and exascale systems are the main tools to solve climate change challenges. HPC will become an even more critical resource to help the broader research community to develop solutions to potential environmental impacts.

On the electricity grid front, power grid applications are exploiting HPC and networking. The first workshop (1st International Workshop on High Performance Computing, Networking and Analytics for the Power Grid, 2010) on this challenge discussed the use of HPC and networking for power grid applications. Technological and policy changes make this an urgent priority.

From the new hardware technologies point of view, Nvidia evolutionary systems, i.e. GPUs, Flash technology, and special-purpose hardware systems drive the development of green and energy efficient architecture and systems.

From the processing technologies point of view, Nvidia evolutionary systems, i.e. GPUs, will be among the main building blocks of future exascale systems. Accelerator-based supercomputers now occupy the top eight slots of the most recent the Green500 list (The Green500, 2012), so we observe that heterogeneous computing is extensively examined as a means for achieving computing system energy efficiency.

Hardware and software co-design, that we call Intelligent Computation, is another key solution for green computing and energy efficiency. For instance, GreenFlash (LBL, 2010) is a radically new approach to application-driven hardware and software co-design inspired by design principles from the consumer electronics marketplace. The GreenFlash system addresses some aspects of green computing and exascale system for specific applications. In addition, it significantly reduces cost and accelerates the development cycle of exascale systems. The application that is the target of GreenFlash is "The Earth's Atmosphere at Kilometer Scales."

In Mohiyuddin et al. (2009), the authors presented a hardware and software co-tuning (Intelligent Computation) as a novel approach for HPC system design. In this research, in order to substantially improve hardware area and power efficiency, traditional architecture space exploration is tightly coupled with software auto-tuning. Their approach demonstrates that co-tuning would be considered as a key driver for the next generation HPC system design.

In the past decades of HPC design, the performance and speed were the main metrics in supercomputer design. This focus on performance as the ultimate metric has caused other metrics such as energy consumption, reliability, sustainability, availability, and usability to be largely ignored. In addition, this particular emphasis has led to the emergence of supercomputers that consume huge amounts of electrical power and produce so much heat that overpriced cooling facilities must be constructed to ensure proper operation. Therefore, there has been an extraordinary increase in the total cost of ownership (TCO) of a supercomputer.

To that end, the Green500 (The Green500, 2012) is developed to encourage sustainable supercomputing by raising awareness to the energy efficiency of such systems. The purpose of the Green500 is to provide a ranking of the most energy efficient supercomputers in the world.

5. GREEN COMPUTING

Green computing is a growing research topic in recent years to address climate and energy challenges. In this section, we review green computing solutions such as liquid cooling that address HPC and cloud computing challenges. In addition, green computing duality with economy and business is envisioned.

5.1 Liquid Cooling

Liquid cooling is a heat removal method based on liquids as the heat conductor, as opposed to air cooling that uses air for heat removal. The main mechanism for liquid cooling is convective heat transfer. Liquid cooling is used for cooling large industrial equipments in grid power plants, petroleum stations and recent computer systems. The thermal energy that the water extracts from the equipment can be reused for heating purposes.

In recent years, liquid cooling is used to develop cost-effective cooling mechanism of computing systems. In particular, large computer systems like big data centers and supercomputers such as Eurotech's HPC offering will exploit this cooling mechanism to reduce cooling and operational costs, and reduce construction space.

Aurora is an innovative system of Eurotech's HPC offering (Eurotech, 2012). Aurora exploits liquid cooling to design a high density system, that leads to a high energy efficient HPC system. Such a high density is achieved with extensive usage of liquid cooling, carried out with metal plates coupled to all Aurora boards, having coolant flow inside them. Aurora modules have no moving parts, no attached modules, and are hot-replaceable, being connected with miniaturized couplings to the heat removal hydraulic infrastructure. In addition, it features Intel's latest generation processors and chipsets.

Hardcore Computer company (Solutions, 2012) has a patented product called Liquid Blade. Liquid Blade is designed to operate in almost any environment and does not require costly, overly-complicated environmental control systems. According to Hardcore Computer, Liquid Blade can deliver up to an 80% reduction in data center cooling costs and reduce construction and on-going operating costs by up to 25%. Liquid Blade has a significant, undeniable and immediate reduction in TCO.

5.2 Renewable Energy Sources

On the renewable energy sources front, the demand for clean energy generation is driving the use of non-dispatchable power sources such as solar and wind (World's #1 Renewable Energy Network, 2012). According to a survey by (World's #1 Renewable Energy Network, 2012), 85 percent of survey respondents voted for more renewable energy options. With 49 percent saying they would have no problem digging deeper into their pockets to support companies committed to renewable energy in the product manufacturing process. Renewable energy sources such as solar and geothermal energies may be used to power on large data centers like HPC data centers.

5.3 Intelligent Computation

In green world, research on minimizing energy and resource consumption through algorithmic and software techniques such as monitoring, power-aware consolidation, scheduling as well as user/application profiling and debugging are other aspects of addressing energy efficiency. These solutions are the facets of Intelligent Computation.

Contemporary computing technologies, HPC and in particular cloud, are moving toward Intelligent Computation in order to optimize resource and energy consumption without losing performance. The other aspects of Intelligent Computation are hardware and software co-design, infrastructure-adapted-to-applications, virtual machine consolidation, and pay-as-you-go business model.

Hardware and software co-design is mostly being used for exascale development. It implies user/vendor development for a particular application space. Hw/sw co-design is a facet of HPC Intelligent Computation.

On the other hand, in the cloud computing world, infrastructure is adapted to the applications by the means of enabling technologies i.e virtualization and shared hosting technologies coupled with multicore processors.

While hardware and software co-design from HPC and Infrastructure-adapted-to-applications from cloud are different approaches, they both contribute to energy efficiency. This observation demonstrates how different technologies develop different mechanisms.

5.4 Economy and Business

Green computing and climate change have a direct and significant impact on economy and business as well.

More and more companies consider green policy and climate change risks as part of their business policy and strategy. One of the main reasons is that companies with long-term climate change risks and opportunities in their business policy will gain strategic advantage over their competitors (BARRINGER, 2012).

In addition, investors fund businesses and companies that consider the environmental policies and the environmental risks as part of their business strategies. For instance, there were floods in Thailand last year with the total cost of $15 billion to $20 billion that had big impact on the sell and services of companies. The floods had negative impact on the automotive supply industry such as the automaker Daimler. In addition, the floods resulted in shortages of critical IT components and materials of Hewlett-Packard and Dell.

Last but not the least, insurance companies have to take into account climate change risks in their risk analysis and calculations. They supply investors with information about potential environmental risks, costs and benefits.

Similarly, good economy contributes to the development of green computing and climate change solutions.

6. CONCLUSION

In this section, we summarize our thesis statement and supporting evidence by highlighting all the main findings in the previous sections about cloud computing and HPC. We close this chapter by a set of conclusions and implications about future research.

In this chapter, we have envisioned the duality of green computing with HPC and cloud computing, business, and economy. Green computing solutions drive the development of HPC, cloud computing, economy, and business and vice versa.

Cloud computing as an extreme specialization (hyperspecialization) and as a general purpose model of information technology has a green anatomy. The essential characteristics of cloud computing i.e., infinity, outsourcing, utility business model, elasticity, on-demand, self-provisioning, multi-tenancy, and *-abilities, and deployment models make it an ideal and ubiquitous green IT paradigm. In summary, cloud significantly reduces effort, energy and resource consumptions.

HPC is used to provide energy, and vice versa energy is required to operate HPC systems. In particular, as exascale systems are emerging, they would need huge amounts of electricity (20MW) to sustain. In addition, HPC drives the process of finding new sources of energy.

On the other hand, HPC and exascale systems are the main tools to solve climate change challenges. HPC will become an even more critical resource to help the broader research community to develop solutions to potential environmental impacts.

By all means, contemporary technologies are moving toward Intelligent Computation in order to optimize resource and energy consumption.

In addition, green computing and climate change have a direct impact on economy and business. Green policy and climate change risks are a part of companies' business policy and strategy. In addition, investors fund businesses and companies that consider the environmental policies and the environmental risks as part of their business strategies.

Energy consumption is a suitable metric to measure how much a technology, a system, etc. are green. Figure 2 illustrates the green duality gap based on energy metric. The difference between supplied energy, i.e. real energy consumption, and demanded energy is part of this gap. In addition to this difference, all the parameters, and factors we have mentioned in this chapter (as technology advantages) should be reflected in the green duality gap formulation. Technology disadvantages have a negative impact on green gap.

As much as a technology's or a system's green gap approaches to zero, it becomes greener. The future research in green computing would need to address this gap.

Figure 2. Duality gap between green energy and real energy consumption of a system

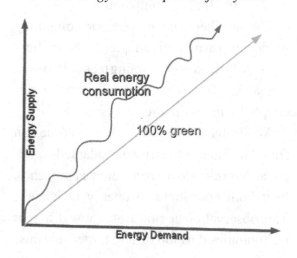

REFERENCES

Armbrust, M., Fox, A., Griffith, R., Joseph, A. D., Katz, R., Konwinski, A., & Zaharia, M. (2010). A view of cloud computing. *Communications of the ACM, 53*(4), 50–58. doi:10.1145/1721654.1721672

Armbrust, M., Fox, A., Griffith, R., Joseph, A. D., Katz, R. H., Konwinski, A., & Zaharia, M. (2009). *Above the clouds: A Berkeley view of cloud computing* (Tech. Rep. No. UCB/EECS-2009-28). EECS Department, University of California, Berkeley. Retrieved from http://www.eecs.berkeley.edu/Pubs/TechRpts/2009/EECS-2009-28.html

Barringer, F. (2012). *Corporations slow to act on climate change.* Retrieved from http://green.blogs.nytimes.com/2012/09/12/corporations-slow-to-act-onclimate-change-report-says/more-147625

Eurotech. (2012). *Hot water cooled supercomputer.* Retrieved from http://www.eurotech.com/en/hpc/hpc+solutions/liquid+cooling

Exxonmobil. (2012). *The outlook for energy.* Retrieved from http://www.exxonmobil.com/Corporate/energyoutlook.aspx

First International Workshop on High Performance Computing, Networking and Analytics for the Power Grid. (2010). Retrieved from http://gridoptics.pnnl.gov/sc11/

LBL. (2010). *Green flash.* Retrieved from http://www.lbl.gov/cs/html/greenflash.html

Mohiyuddin, M., Murphy, M., Oliker, L., Shalf, J., Wawrzynek, J., & Williams, S. (2009). A design methodology for domain-optimized power-efficient supercomputing. In *Proceedings of the Conference on High Performance Computing Networking, Storage and Analysis* (pp. 12:1–12:12). Academic Press.

Smart 2020: Enabling the Low Carbon Economy in the Information Age. (2010). Retrieved from http://www.smart2020.org/

Solutions, L. (2012). *Liquidcool solutions.* Retrieved from http://www.liquidcoolsolutions.com/

The green500. (2012). Retrieved from http://www.green500.org/

(2012).. . *Top (Madrid), 500,* Retrieved from http://www.top500.org/

Vazquez-Poletti, J., Barderas, G., Llorente, I., & Romero, P. (2012). A model for efficient onboard actualization of an instrumental cyclogram for the mars metnet mission on a public cloud infrastructure. In *Proceedings of para2010: State of the Art in Scientific and Parallel Computing* (Vol. 7133, pp. 33–42). Berlin: Springer Verlag. doi:10.1007/978-3-642-28151-8_4

World's #1 Renewable Energy Network. (2012). Retrieved from http://www.renewableenergyworld.com/

KEY TERMS AND DEFINITIONS

Climate Change and Global Warming: The two most important challenging problems for the earth. These problems pertain to a general increase in world temperatures caused by increased amounts of carbon dioxide around the earth. Researchers in various fields of science and technology in recent years started to carry out research in order to address these problems by developing environmentally friendly solutions.

Energy Efficiency: Green IT denotes energy efficiency in all components of computing systems to make the use of computers and the Internet as energy efficient as possible.

Green Computing: A contemporary research topic in recent years to address climate and energy challenges of the world.

Green IT: And in particular green computing are two new terms introduced mainly in ICT community to address climate change and global warming.

Hardware and Software Co-Design: Mostly used for exascale development. It implies user/vendor collaborative development for a particular application space.

Infrastructure-Adapted-to-Applications: In the cloud computing world, infrastructure is adapted to the applications by the means of enabling technologies i.e virtualization and shared hosting technologies coupled with multicore processors.

Intelligent Computation: Done with the techniques and mechanisms of new computing technologies such as hardware and software co-design, application profiling, and virtual machine consolidation to optimize resource consumption, and pay-as-you-go business model to reduce costs, etc.

Liquid Cooling: A heat removal method based on liquids as the heat conductor, as opposed to air cooling that uses air for heat removal. The main mechanism for liquid cooling is convective heat transfer.

Nvidia GPUs: Among the main building blocks of future exascale systems. Accelerator-based supercomputers now occupy the top eight slots of the most recent the Green500 list.

Renewable Energy Sources: The demand for clean energy generation is driving the use of non-dispatchable power sources such as solar and wind.

Glossary

Amazon EC2 Interface: A de facto standard in IaaS cloud while it was not designed as an industry-standard API.

Amazon EC2's Spot Instance Mechanism: Shares many similarities with the standard uniform price auction mechanism. The provider assigns resources to bidders in decreasing order of their bids until all available resources have been allocated or all resource requests have been satisfied.

Amazon Web Services (AWS): A public cloud infrastructure made available to the public users in a pay-as-you-go model. AWS is the most popular and the first public utility computing.

Analytical Hierarchical Process: Multi-criteria decision making technique, introduced and developed by the mathematician Thomas L. Saaty.

Big Data: Large data set that is a data set with size greater than the capacity of the traditional databases.

Climate Change and Global Warming: The two most important challenging problems for the earth. These problems pertain to a general increase in world temperatures caused by increased amounts of carbon dioxide around the earth. Researchers in various fields of science and technology in recent years started to carry out research in order to address these problems by developing environmentally friendly solutions.

Cloud Industrialization: The anatomy and ubiquity of cloud computing make it a key technology to advance and accelerate innovations in industry and manufacturing sectors.

Cloud Manufacturing: The manufacturing version of cloud computing. In cloud manufacturing, distributed resources are encapsulated as cloud services and managed in a centralized way. Users can use cloud services according to their requirements. They can request services ranging from product design, manufacturing, testing, to management, and all other stages of a product life cycle.

Cloud Security Alliance: A not-for-profit organization with a mission to promote the use of best practices for providing security assurance within cloud computing, and to provide education on the uses of cloud computing to help secure all other forms of computing.

Cloud Standardization: Will bring interoperability, integration and portability to the cloud computing landscape. With these three features, the main elements of IT, i.e., computation and data, can move from one cloud provider to another.

Clustering: A data mining technique that mainly aims to group the data/objects into clusters according to their similarities and features.

Cumulus: An Open Source Storage Cloud for Science; it is like Amazon S3.

Data Mining: The process of analyzing databases with the aim of extracting the relevant and useful information.

Data Privacy: Multi-tenancy feature of public clouds introduces data privacy concerns.

Database Management System: Software system to handle an organized collection of intercorrelated data (database).

Deployment Options: Categorized as public, private, community, and hybrid. A cloud is deployed as one of them, depending on how the cloud infrastructure is operated.

Distributed Database Management System: Provides the mechanisms for accessing and managing the distributed databases.

Distributed Database: A database with storage services distributed on a computer network.

Dynamic Sharing and Collaboration: Specific security issues emerge during dynamic sharing and collaboration across multiple clouds. Particularly, trust, policy, and privacy concerns pertain to multi-cloud models.

Economic Denial of Sustainability (EDoS): A specific type of attack for cloud computing. The elasticity of cloud computing allows users to scale servers up and up in order to service request demands. This opens a new avenue of approach for attackers, which originally was labeled an economic denial of sustainability attack. This type of attack is directly connected with a DoS attack, but its target is to inflate the cloud services budget.

Economies of Scale: A resource gets shared and the volume of service is huge, it will always be better than own infrastructure.

Elasticity: With elasticity, users can rapidly increase or decrease the capacity of their resources, companies can ramp capacity up and down.

Electronic Health Record (EHR): Integrates data and information generated from the different healthcare organizations involved in the patient's care. It contains information that can be shared among the authorized stakeholders and clinicians and the patients him/herself.

Electronic Medical Record (EMR): The legal documentation managed and owned by a healthcare organization. It basically aims to describe what happened to a patient during an encounter. It contains information that can be shared among laboratories and staff that belong to the organization.

Energy Efficiency: Green IT denotes energy efficiency in all components of computing systems to make the use of computers and the Internet as energy efficient as possible.

Extensible Messaging and Presence Protocol (XMPP): The next generation of HTTP for cloud computing. XMPP is not based on HTTP, thus there is doubt about its widespread adoption.

Federated Cloud: The management, interconnection, interoperation, deployment, and coordination of multiple public and private cloud computing services to function as a single entity, and to match business needs and spikes in demand.

Globus Online: A hosted service to automate the tasks associated with moving files between sites. It does not require custom infrastructure, Globus Online is software-as-a-service that can be used today without building these features yourself.

Google AppEngine: An application development environment and deployment container without the cost of deploying infrastructure.

Green Computing: Climate change and global warming are the two most important challenging problems for the earth. These problems pertain to a general increase in world temperatures caused by increased amounts of carbon dioxide around the earth. Researchers in various fields of science and technology in recent years started to carry out research in order to address these problems by developing environmentally friendly solutions. Green IT and in particular green computing are two new terms introduced mainly in ICT community to address these problems.

Green IT: Green IT and, in particular green computing, are two new terms introduced mainly in ICT community to address climate change and global warming.

Grid Computing: Coordinated resource sharing and problem solving in dynamic, multi-institutional virtual organization. Grids have been the center of attention from scientific and High Performance Computing communities (HPC), especially for the distributed and large scale scientific applications, and also in collaborative style of work.

Hardware and Software Co-Design: Mostly being used for exascale development. It implies user/vendor collaborative development for a particular application space.

HelixNebula: A recent cloud computing project for Science Clouds; it has been launched by some of Europe's biggest research such as CERN along with European IT companies.

High Performance Computing (HPC): The use of advanced parallel processing systems (usually, above a teraflop or 1012 floating-point operations per second) for running complicated and huge processes quickly, efficiently, and reliably.

Homomorphic Encryption: This security scheme allows data to be processed without being decrypted. This is a huge advancement in cryptography, and it will have a significant positive impact on cloud computing as soon as it moves into deployment.

Hybrid Cloud: A deployment model, as a composition of both public and private clouds. A hybrid cloud consists of multiple internal and external providers.

Infrastructure Security: The scope of infrastructure security in public cloud is limited to the layers of infrastructure that are outsourced to third-party service providers, that is moved beyond the organization's control and into the hands of service providers.

Infrastructure-Adapted-to-Applications: In the cloud computing world, infrastructure is adapted to the applications by the means of enabling technologies i.e virtualization and shared hosting technologies coupled with multicore processors.

Integrated Home Care (IHC): Characterized by the integration of various services offered by multidisciplinary professionals such as doctors, nurses, psychologists, physiotherapists, pharmacists, social workers and caregivers who share objectives, responsibilities and resources to ensure Patients continuity of care.

Intelligent Computation: Done with the techniques and mechanisms of new computing technologies such as hardware and software co-design, application profiling, and virtual machine consolidation to optimize resource consumption, and pay-as-you-go business model to reduce costs, etc.

Internet of Things: Another breakthrough, omnipresent and transformative technology with a futuristic vision perhaps over a span of one thousand years. It is predicted that 50 to 100 billion things will be electronically connected by 2020. This Internet of Things (IoT) will fuel technology innovation by creating the means for machines to communicate many different types of information with one another.

Interoperability: Minimize cloud fragmentation. We need interoperability and portability to achieve cloud federation and to build hybrid cloud.

Liquid Cooling: A heat removal method based on liquids as the heat conductor, as opposed to air cooling that uses air for heat removal. The main mechanism for liquid cooling is convective heat transfer.

Magellan: One of the first projects to conduct an exhaustive evaluation of the use of cloud computing for science in the US. The Magellan project is funded through the U.S. Department of Energy (DOE) Office of Advanced Scientific Computing Research (ASCR).

Managed Security Services (MSSs): MSS provider (MSSP) assigns security personnel to its clients to administer the security mechanisms, in particular related to cloud services using a pay-per-use model. With this, the customer is in charge of the security policies and it is his responsibility to monitor the efficiency of the services provided by the MSSP.

Manufacturing Industry: Cloud computing is emerging as one of the major enablers for the manufacturing industry to transform the traditional manufacturing business model.

Microsoft Windows Azure: Provides a development, service hosting, and service management environment. Windows Azure provides on-demand compute and storage resources for hosting applications to scale costs.

Multicore Processors: A single physical processor of multicore design type contains the core logic of more than one processor. The multicore design puts several cores (multicore) together and packages them as a single physical processor. The main goal is to enable a system to run more tasks simultaneously and thereby achieve greater overall system performance.

Multi-Tenancy: A business model that provides a secure, exclusive virtualized computing environment in which servers, databases, and other resources are shared by multiple users in a cloud environment.

National Institute of Standards and Technology (NIST): A non-regulatory federal agency whose mission is to promote U.S. innovation and industrial competitiveness by advancing measurement science, standards, and technology. NIST has started a program to develop a set of cloud computing standards, with the first results being already published as NIST Cloud Computing Program.

Network Overlay: Categorized as part of network virtualization in cloud computing. It provides facilities to build a network on top of another network. For example, many peer-to-peer networks are overlay networks on top of the Internet and dial-up Internet is an overlay upon the telephone network.

Network Virtualization: Virtual device adapter (Ethernet adapters), VLANs, and virtual switches. A VM can be configured with one or more virtual Ethernet adapters with their own IP addresses and MAC addresses. As a result, VMs have the same properties as physical machines from a networking point of view.

Networked Manufacturing (NM): Cloud manufacturing is a multi-disciplinary domain and a computing and service oriented manufacturing model developed from existing advanced manufacturing technologies and models such as networked manufacturing (NM), virtual manufacturing, agile manufacturing (AM), Application Service Provider (ASP), Manufacturing Grid (MGrid), and enterprise information technologies under the support of cloud computing, Internet of Things (IoT), virtualization, service oriented technologies, and advanced computing technologies.

Nimbus Infrastructure: An open source EC2/S3-compatible Infrastructure-as-a-Service implementation specifically targeting features of interest to the scientific community such as support for proxy credentials, batch schedulers, best-effort allocations and others.

Nimbus Toolkit: An Infrastructure-as-a-Service cloud computing for science. Nimbus platform is an integrated set of tools that deliver the power and versatility of infrastructure clouds to scientific users. Nimbus platform allows you to combine Nimbus, OpenStack, Amazon, and other clouds.

Non-Disclosure Agreement (NDA): Under a non-disclosure agreement (NDA), customers can request information related to the provider's security practices. This information encompasses design, architecture, development, black- and white-box application security testing, and release management.

Nvidia GPUs: Will be among the main building blocks of future exascale systems. Accelerator-based supercomputers now occupy the top eight slots of the most recent the Green500 list.

On-Demand: Users can provision cloud infrastructure components such as servers and networks with little human intervention and through automation whenever they want.

Open Cloud Computing Interface (OCCI): A general-purpose set of specifications for cloud-based interactions with resources in a way that is explicitly vendor-independent, platform-neutral and can be extended to solve a broad variety of problems in cloud computing.

Open Grid Forum (OGF): A leading standards development organization operating in the areas of grid, cloud and related forms of advanced distributed computing. The OGF community pursues these technologies through an open process for development, creation and promotion of relevant specifications and use cases.

Open Virtualization Format (OVF): Describes an open, secure, portable, efficient and extensible format for the packaging and distribution of software to be run in virtual machines.

Operations Research: Aims to define theoretical foundation and mathematical methods for modeling and simulation, of complex, challenging optimization, organization, management, planning problems and to devise the relevant computational algorithms and software for their numerical solution.

Organization for the Advancement of Structured Information Standards: Drives the development, convergence and adoption of open standards for the global information society. OASIS as the source of many of the foundational standards in use today sees cloud computing as a natural extension of SOA and network management models.

Outsourcing: Software companies are rapidly moving more and more of their services, software, and applications to cloud computing due to users' radical, urgent, growing, fluctuating, seasonal, competing, enormous, and economic demands.

Over-Provisioning: Cloud computing transfers the risks of over-provisioning or under-provisioning to the cloud provider, who mitigates that risk by statistical multiplexing over a much larger set of users and who offers relatively low prices due to better utilization and from the economy of purchasing at a larger scale.

Pay Per Use: Payment of resource consumption is like utilities that are paid for by the hour. With pay per use model, service consumption is metered and measured.

Personal Health Record (PHR): Denotes the health documentation managed and populated by an individual. It aims to give a comprehensive view on the health and medical history of an individual. Data is gathered from different sources and it is accessible to only those have permissions.

Private Cloud: Operated for an organization. It may be managed by the organization or a third party and may exist on premise or off premise. A private cloud is an offering of cloud computing on private sector.

Public Cloud: The main cloud computing model. Public cloud is hosted, operated and managed by a third-party vendor from one or more data centers. The service is offered to multiple customers, that is called multiple tenants over a common infrastructure.

Public Cloud Security: In this deployment option, some security aspects are provided by cloud providers while the rest have to be provided by the customers. Public cloud security address and incorporate how an organization's existing network topology interacts with public cloud provider's network topology.

Renewable Energy Sources: The demand for clean energy generation is driving the use of non-dispatchable power sources such as solar and wind.

Salesforce.com: One of the best Software as a Service (SaaS) provider. It is a classic example of cloud computing. Salesforce.com has made cloud computing a reality by offering Customer Relationship Management (CRM) as a SaaS.

Science Clouds: Have been emerged as a result of scientific application needs for outsourced compute and storage infrastructures. Science Clouds provided by Open Source Nimbus Toolkit, and Commercial Amazon Elastic Compute Cloud (EC2) that provide computational capabilities for computing are often referred as IaaS. They provide compute cycles in the cloud for scientific communities using Nimbus.

Seal-Bid Uniform Price Auction: A truthful auction, providing the supply level is adjustable ex post, i.e., after the bids have been decided.

Secure Socket Layer (SSL): Provides standard encryption and authentication for the communication.

Security Groups: The traditional model of network zones and tiers has been replaced in public cloud computing with security groups, security domains, and virtual data centers. They have logical separation between tiers but are less precise and afford less protection than the formerly established model.

Service Delivery: Cloud offerings are typically categorized as Infrastructure as a Service (IaaS), Platform as a Service (PaaS), and Software as a Service (SaaS). These are three main service delivery models in cloud computing.

Smart City: Makes a conscious effort to use innovative ICT based solutions to improve conditions of living and working and to support a more inclusive and sustainable urban environment.

Smart Grid: Emerging to address the electricity grid challenges. The smart grid is an intelligent electricity grid network to deliver sustainable, reliable, storage, ubiquitous, decentralized, flexible, economic, autonomic and secure electricity supplies.

Spot Markets: Amazon EC2 runs one spot market for each VM type in each availability zone. All spot markets share the free data center capacity, which is the remaining capacity after serving all the guaranteed instances.

Spot Price: Based on the provider's spot pricing policy, the selling price, i.e. the spot price, is equal to the lowest winning bid, or the selling price depends on the supply and the demand. You get the instance only when your bid exceeds the spot price.

Stochastic Programming: A branch of Operations Research that allows to explicitly deal with the random nature that characterizes a lot of the real world applications.

Supply Chain: A network of interdependent trading partners who are geographically dispersed. Each trading partner has many upstream and downstream trading partners with whom they need to coordinate plans, schedules, deliveries, etc.

UberCloud Experiment: Has brought together four categories of participants: the industry end-users, the computing and storage resource providers, the software providers, and the experts. Participants have voluntary contribution to their individual teams and thus to the whole Experiment. This is an experimental research and study to address roadblocks on the way of transitioning to cloud solutions for industries.

Vendor and Technology Lock-In: Standardization eliminates vendor and technology lock-in that is one of the barriers in cloud adoption.

VENUS-C (Virtual Multidisciplinary EnviroNments USing Cloud Infrastructures): Aims to develop, test and deploy an industry-quality, highly-scalable and flexible cloud infrastructure to empower researchers through the easy deployment of end-user services.

Virtual Firewall: Network firewall service or appliance running entirely within a virtualized environment and which provides the usual packet filtering and monitoring provided via a physical network firewall.

Virtual Machine Hypervisor Interfaces (VMHI): A framework of interfaces based on virtualization products to accelerate the development of open standards in a neutral way.

Virtual Private Network (VPN): A private network that uses a public network such as the Internet to connect remote networks, sites, and users together. It uses virtual connections through the public network, instead of using dedicated connections such as leased or owned lines to connect private networks via tunneling and/or encryption over the public Internet, thus resulting in a much lower cost.

Virtualization: The primary enabler for cloud computing. Virtualization technology provides techniques and conditions to run multiple Virtual Machines (VMs) on top of a single physical machine.

Vitaever ®: A cloud technology, developed by Nethical s.r.l., in collaboration with the ANT Foundation and with the contribution of the Department of Informatics, Science and Engineering, University of Bologna, that combines the software and the hardware, flexible and reliable, which you pay as you go, in order to manage in an efficient and intuitive way the home care services.

Web Services: Executed on a remote system hosting the requested service. Interaction between services, resources and agents in a heterogeneous environment that is based on Web Services Technologies would be more interoperable. SOA is highly based on Web Services technologies.

TRADEMARKS NOTICE

Amazon Web Services, AWS, Amazon EC2, EC2, Amazon Elastic Compute Cloud, Amazon Virtual Private Cloud, Amazon VPC, Amazon SimpleDB, SimpleDB, Amazon S3, Amazon Simple Storage Service, Amazon CloudFront, CloudFront, Amazon SQS, SQS, Amazon Simple Queue Service, Amazon Elastic Block Store, Amazon EBS, Amazon Simple Email Service, Amazon Elastic Beanstalk, Amazon Simple Notification Service, Amazon Route 53, Amazon RDS, Amazon Relational Database, Amazon CloudWatch, AWS Premium Support, AWS Import/Export, Amazon FPS, Amazon Flexible Payments Service, Amazon DevPay, DevPay, Amazon Mechanical Turk, Mechanical Turk, Alexa Web Search, Alexa Web Information Service, Alexa Top Sites, Alexa Site Thumbnail, Amazon FWS, Amazon Fulfillment Web Service, Amazon Associates Web Service, and service names are trademarks, registered trademarks or trade dress of AWS in the U.S. and/or other countries.

The following is an illustrative, non-exhaustive list of trademarks owned by Google Inc. as well as suggested generic terms for those trademarks.

Art, Copy Code™ marketing project
Chrome™ browser
Chrome OS™ operating system
Gmail™ webmail service
Google App Engine™ platform
Google Apps™ service
Google Compute Engine™ service
Google Docs™ program
Google Drive™ online storage service
Google Earth™ mapping service
Google Finance™ financial information service
Google Groups™ discussion forums
Google Maps™ mapping service
Google MapReduce™
Google Street View™ mapping service
Google™ search or search engine
Go™ programming language
Nexus One™ mobile phone
Nexus S™ mobile phone
Nexus™ family of marks for mobile devices and peripherals
Pagerank™ algorithm
Street View™ images

Microsoft, Windows, HealthVault, Internet Explorer, SQL Azure, SQL Server, Surface, Windows Azure, Windows XP, and MSN are either registered trademarks or trademarks of Microsoft Corporation in the United States and/or other countries.

The below software product and project names are considered trademarks of the ASF. Typically, each Top Level Project (TLP) managed by a Project Management Committee (PMC) provides a named software product for public use.

Apache Hadoop, Hadoop Apache Hadoop is a software product that provides a distributed computing platform for sharing large amounts of data and processing it.

Apache Cassandra, Cassandra Apache Cassandra is a software product.

Apache CouchDB, CouchDB Apache CouchDB is a document-oriented database that can be queried and indexed in a MapReduce fashion using JavaScript.

Apache Hbase, Hbase Apache Hbase is a software product.

Related References

To continue our tradition of advancing information science and technology research, we have compiled a list of recommended IGI Global readings. These references will provide additional information and guidance to further enrich your knowledge and assist you with your own research and future publications.

Aalmink, J., von der Dovenmühle, T., & Gómez, J. M. (2013). Enterprise tomography: Maintenance and root-cause-analysis of federated erp in enterprise clouds. In P. Ordóñez de Pablos, H. Nigro, R. Tennyson, S. Gonzalez Cisaro, & W. Karwowski (Eds.), *Advancing information management through semantic web concepts and ontologies* (pp. 133–153). Hershey, PA: Information Science Reference.

Abu, S. T., & Tsuji, M. (2011). The development of ICT for envisioning cloud computing and innovation in South Asia. [IJIDE]. *International Journal of Innovation in the Digital Economy*, 2(1), 61–72. doi:10.4018/jide.2011010105

Abu, S. T., & Tsuji, M. (2012). The development of ICT for envisioning cloud computing and innovation in South Asia. In I. Management Association (Ed.), Grid and cloud computing: Concepts, methodologies, tools and applications (pp. 453-465). Hershey, PA: Information Science Reference. doi: doi:10.4018/978-1-4666-0879-5.ch207

Abu, S. T., & Tsuji, M. (2013). The development of ICT for envisioning cloud computing and innovation in South Asia. In I. Oncioiu (Ed.), *Business innovation, development, and advancement in the digital economy* (pp. 35–47). Hershey, PA: Business Science Reference. doi:10.4018/978-1-4666-2934-9.ch003

Adams, R. (2013). The emergence of cloud storage and the need for a new digital forensic process model. In K. Ruan (Ed.), *Cybercrime and cloud forensics: Applications for investigation processes* (pp. 79–104). Hershey, PA: Information Science Reference.

Adeyeye, M. (2013). Provisioning converged applications and services via the cloud. In D. Kanellopoulos (Ed.), *Intelligent multimedia technologies for networking applications: Techniques and tools* (pp. 248–269). Hershey, PA: Information Science Reference.

Aggarwal, A. (2013). A systems approach to cloud computing services. In A. Bento, & A. Aggarwal (Eds.), *Cloud computing service and deployment models: Layers and management* (pp. 124–136). Hershey, PA: Business Science Reference.

Ahmed, K., Hussain, A., & Gregory, M. A. (2013). An efficient, robust, and secure SSO architecture for cloud computing implemented in a service oriented architecture. In X. Yang, & L. Liu (Eds.), *Principles, methodologies, and service-oriented approaches for cloud computing* (pp. 259–282). Hershey, PA: Business Science Reference. doi:10.4018/978-1-4666-2854-0.ch011

Ahuja, S. P., & Mani, S. (2013). Empirical performance analysis of HPC benchmarks across variations in cloud computing. [IJCAC]. *International Journal of Cloud Applications and Computing*, 3(1), 13–26. doi:10.4018/ijcac.2013010102

Ahuja, S. P., & Rolli, A. C. (2011). Survey of the state-of-the-art of cloud computing. [IJCAC]. *International Journal of Cloud Applications and Computing*, *1*(4), 34–43. doi:10.4018/ijcac.2011100103

Ahuja, S. P., & Rolli, A. C. (2013). Survey of the state-of-the-art of cloud computing. In S. Aljawarneh (Ed.), *Cloud computing advancements in design, implementation, and technologies* (pp. 252–262). Hershey, PA: Information Science Reference.

Ahuja, S. P., & Sridharan, S. (2012). Performance evaluation of hypervisors for cloud computing. [IJCAC]. *International Journal of Cloud Applications and Computing*, *2*(3), 26–67. doi:10.4018/ijcac.2012070102

Akyuz, G. A., & Rehan, M. (2013). A generic, cloud-based representation for supply chains (SC's). [IJCAC]. *International Journal of Cloud Applications and Computing*, *3*(2), 12–20. doi:10.4018/ijcac.2013040102

Al-Aqrabi, H., & Liu, L. (2013). IT security and governance compliant service oriented computing in cloud computing environments. In X. Yang, & L. Liu (Eds.), *Principles, methodologies, and service-oriented approaches for cloud computing* (pp. 143–163). Hershey, PA: Business Science Reference. doi:10.4018/978-1-4666-2854-0.ch006

Al-Zoube, M., & Wyne, M. F. (2012). Building integrated e-learning environment using cloud services and social networking sites. In Q. Jin (Ed.), *Intelligent learning systems and advancements in computer-aided instruction: Emerging studies* (pp. 214–233). Hershey, PA: Information Science Reference.

Alam, N., & Karmakar, R. (2014). Cloud computing and its application to information centre. In S. Dhamdhere (Ed.), *Cloud computing and virtualization technologies in libraries* (pp. 63–76). Hershey, PA: Information Science Reference.

Alhaj, A., Aljawarneh, S., Masadeh, S., & Abu-Taieh, E. (2013). A secure data transmission mechanism for cloud outsourced data. [IJCAC]. *International Journal of Cloud Applications and Computing*, *3*(1), 34–43. doi:10.4018/ijcac.2013010104

Alharbi, S. T. (2012). Users' acceptance of cloud computing in Saudi Arabia: An extension of technology acceptance model. [IJCAC]. *International Journal of Cloud Applications and Computing*, *2*(2), 1–11. doi:10.4018/ijcac.2012040101

Ali, S. S., & Khan, M. N. (2013). ICT infrastructure framework for microfinance institutions and banks in Pakistan: An optimized approach. [IJOM]. *International Journal of Online Marketing*, *3*(2), 75–86. doi:10.4018/ijom.2013040105

Aljawarneh, S. (2011). Cloud security engineering: Avoiding security threats the right way. [IJCAC]. *International Journal of Cloud Applications and Computing*, *1*(2), 64–70. doi:10.4018/ijcac.2011040105

Aljawarneh, S. (2013). Cloud security engineering: Avoiding security threats the right way. In S. Aljawarneh (Ed.), *Cloud computing advancements in design, implementation, and technologies* (pp. 147–153). Hershey, PA: Information Science Reference.

Alshattnawi, S. (2013). Utilizing cloud computing in developing a mobile location-aware tourist guide system. [IJAPUC]. *International Journal of Advanced Pervasive and Ubiquitous Computing*, *5*(2), 9–18. doi:10.4018/japuc.2013040102

Alsmadi, I. (2013). Software development methodologies for cloud computing. In K. Buragga, & N. Zaman (Eds.), *Software development techniques for constructive information systems design* (pp. 110–117). Hershey, PA: Information Science Reference. doi:10.4018/978-1-4666-3679-8.ch006

Anand, V. (2013). Survivable mapping of virtual networks onto a shared substrate network. In X. Yang, & L. Liu (Eds.), *Principles, methodologies, and service-oriented approaches for cloud computing* (pp. 325–343). Hershey, PA: Business Science Reference. doi:10.4018/978-1-4666-2854-0.ch014

Antonova, A. (2013). Green, sustainable, or clean: What type of IT/IS technologies will we need in the future? In P. Ordóñez de Pablos (Ed.), *Green technologies and business practices: An IT approach* (pp. 151–162). Hershey, PA: Information Science Reference. doi:10.4018/978-1-4666-4852-4.ch021

Ardissono, L., Bosio, G., Goy, A., Petrone, G., Segnan, M., & Torretta, F. (2011). Collaboration support for activity management in a personal cloud environment. [IJDST]. *International Journal of Distributed Systems and Technologies, 2*(4), 30–43. doi:10.4018/jdst.2011100103

Ardissono, L., Bosio, G., Goy, A., Petrone, G., Segnan, M., & Torretta, F. (2013). Collaboration support for activity management in a personal cloud environment. In N. Bessis (Ed.), *Development of distributed systems from design to application and maintenance* (pp. 199–212). Hershey, PA: Information Science Reference.

Argiolas, M., Atzori, M., Dessì, N., & Pes, B. (2012). Dataspaces enhancing decision support systems in clouds. [IJWP]. *International Journal of Web Portals, 4*(2), 35–55. doi:10.4018/jwp.2012040103

Arinze, B., & Anandarajan, M. (2012). Factors that determine the adoption of cloud computing: A global perspective. In M. Tavana (Ed.), *Enterprise Information Systems and Advancing Business Solutions: Emerging Models* (pp. 210–223). Hershey, PA: Business Science Reference. doi:10.4018/978-1-4666-1761-2.ch012

Arinze, B., & Sylla, C. (2012). Conducting research in the cloud. In L. Chao (Ed.), *Cloud computing for teaching and learning: Strategies for design and implementation* (pp. 50–63). Hershey, PA: Information Science Reference. doi:10.4018/978-1-4666-0957-0.ch004

Arshad, J., Townend, P., & Xu, J. (2011). An abstract model for integrated intrusion detection and severity analysis for clouds. [IJCAC]. *International Journal of Cloud Applications and Computing, 1*(1), 1–16. doi:10.4018/ijcac.2011010101

Arshad, J., Townend, P., & Xu, J. (2013). An abstract model for integrated intrusion detection and severity analysis for clouds. In S. Aljawarneh (Ed.), *Cloud computing advancements in design, implementation, and technologies* (pp. 1–17). Hershey, PA: Information Science Reference.

Arshad, J., Townend, P., Xu, J., & Jie, W. (2012). Cloud computing security: Opportunities and pitfalls. [IJGHPC]. *International Journal of Grid and High Performance Computing, 4*(1), 52–66. doi:10.4018/jghpc.2012010104

Baars, T., & Spruit, M. (2012). Designing a secure cloud architecture: The SeCA model. [IJISP]. *International Journal of Information Security and Privacy, 6*(1), 14–32. doi:10.4018/jisp.2012010102

Bai, X., Gao, J. Z., & Tsai, W. (2013). Cloud scalability measurement and testing. In S. Tilley, & T. Parveen (Eds.), *Software testing in the cloud: Perspectives on an emerging discipline* (pp. 356–381). Hershey, PA: Information Science Reference.

Baldini, G., & Stirparo, P. (2014). A cognitive access framework for security and privacy protection in mobile cloud computing. In J. Rodrigues, K. Lin, & J. Lloret (Eds.), *Mobile networks and cloud computing convergence for progressive services and applications* (pp. 92–117). Hershey, PA: Information Science Reference.

Balduf, S., Balke, T., & Eymann, T. (2012). Cultural differences in managing cloud computing service level agreements. In I. Management Association (Ed.), Grid and cloud computing: Concepts, methodologies, tools and applications (pp. 1237-1263). Hershey, PA: Information Science Reference. doi: doi:10.4018/978-1-4666-0879-5.ch512

Banerjee, S., Sing, T. Y., Chowdhury, A. R., & Anwar, H. (2013). Motivations to adopt green ICT: A tale of two organizations. [IJGC]. *International Journal of Green Computing, 4*(2), 1–11. doi:10.4018/jgc.2013070101

Barreto, J., Di Sanzo, P., Palmieri, R., & Romano, P. (2013). Cloud-TM: An elastic, self-tuning transactional store for the cloud. In D. Kyriazis, A. Voulodimos, S. Gogouvitis, & T. Varvarigou (Eds.), *Data intensive storage services for cloud environments* (pp. 192–224). Hershey, PA: Business Science Reference. doi:10.4018/978-1-4666-3934-8.ch013

Belalem, G., & Limam, S. (2011). Fault tolerant architecture to cloud computing using adaptive checkpoint. [IJCAC]. *International Journal of Cloud Applications and Computing, 1*(4), 60–69. doi:10.4018/ijcac.2011100105

Belalem, G., & Limam, S. (2013). Fault tolerant architecture to cloud computing using adaptive checkpoint. In S. Aljawarneh (Ed.), *Cloud computing advancements in design, implementation, and technologies* (pp. 280–289). Hershey, PA: Information Science Reference.

Ben Belgacem, M., Abdennadher, N., & Niinimaki, M. (2012). Virtual EZ grid: A volunteer computing infrastructure for scientific medical applications. [IJHCR]. *International Journal of Handheld Computing Research*, *3*(1), 74–85. doi:10.4018/jhcr.2012010105

Bhatt, S., Chaudhary, S., & Bhise, M. (2013). Migration of data between cloud and non-cloud datastores. In A. Ionita, M. Litoiu, & G. Lewis (Eds.), *Migrating legacy applications: Challenges in service oriented architecture and cloud computing environments* (pp. 206–225). Hershey, PA: Information Science Reference.

Biancofiore, G., & Leone, S. (2014). Google apps as a cloud computing solution in Italian municipalities: Technological features and implications. In S. Leone (Ed.), *Synergic integration of formal and informal e-learning environments for adult lifelong learners* (pp. 244–274). Hershey, PA: Information Science Reference.

Bibi, S., Katsaros, D., & Bozanis, P. (2012). How to choose the right cloud. In I. Management Association (Ed.), Grid and cloud computing: Concepts, methodologies, tools and applications (pp. 1530-1552). Hershey, PA: Information Science Reference. doi: doi:10.4018/978-1-4666-0879-5.ch701

Bibi, S., Katsaros, D., & Bozanis, P. (2012). How to choose the right cloud. In X. Liu, & Y. Li (Eds.), *Advanced design approaches to emerging software systems: Principles, methodologies and tools* (pp. 219–240). Hershey, PA: Information Science Reference.

Bitam, S., Batouche, M., & Talbi, E. (2012). A bees life algorithm for cloud computing services selection. In S. Ali, N. Abbadeni, & M. Batouche (Eds.), *Multidisciplinary computational intelligence techniques: Applications in business, engineering, and medicine* (pp. 31–46). Hershey, PA: Information Science Reference. doi:10.4018/978-1-4666-1830-5.ch003

Bittencourt, L. F., Madeira, E. R., & da Fonseca, N. L. (2014). Communication aspects of resource management in hybrid clouds. In H. Mouftah, & B. Kantarci (Eds.), *Communication infrastructures for cloud computing* (pp. 409–433). Hershey, PA: Information Science Reference.

Bonelli, L., Giudicianni, L., Immediata, A., & Luzzi, A. (2013). Compliance in the cloud. In D. Kyriazis, A. Voulodimos, S. Gogouvitis, & T. Varvarigou (Eds.), *Data intensive storage services for cloud environments* (pp. 109–131). Hershey, PA: Business Science Reference. doi:10.4018/978-1-4666-3934-8.ch008

Boniface, M., Nasser, B., Surridge, M., & Oliveros, E. (2012). Securing real-time interactive applications in federated clouds. In I. Management Association (Ed.), Grid and cloud computing: Concepts, methodologies, tools and applications (pp. 1822-1835). Hershey, PA: Information Science Reference. doi: doi:10.4018/978-1-4666-0879-5.ch806

Boukhobza, J. (2013). Flashing in the cloud: Shedding some light on NAND flash memory storage systems. In D. Kyriazis, A. Voulodimos, S. Gogouvitis, & T. Varvarigou (Eds.), *Data intensive storage services for cloud environments* (pp. 241–266). Hershey, PA: Business Science Reference. doi:10.4018/978-1-4666-3934-8.ch015

Bracci, F., Corradi, A., & Foschini, L. (2014). Cloud standards: Security and interoperability issues. In H. Mouftah, & B. Kantarci (Eds.), *Communication infrastructures for cloud computing* (pp. 465–495). Hershey, PA: Information Science Reference.

Brown, A. W. (2013). Experiences with cloud technology to realize software testing factories. In S. Tilley, & T. Parveen (Eds.), *Software testing in the cloud: Perspectives on an emerging discipline* (pp. 1–27). Hershey, PA: Information Science Reference.

Calcavecchia, N. M., Celesti, A., & Di Nitto, E. (2012). Understanding decentralized and dynamic brokerage in federated cloud environments. In M. Villari, I. Brandic, & F. Tusa (Eds.), *Achieving federated and self-manageable cloud infrastructures: Theory and practice* (pp. 36–56). Hershey, PA: Business Science Reference. doi:10.4018/978-1-4666-1631-8.ch003

Calero, J. M., König, B., & Kirschnick, J. (2012). Cross-layer monitoring in cloud computing. In H. Rashvand, & Y. Kavian (Eds.), *Using cross-layer techniques for communication systems* (pp. 328–348). Hershey, PA: Information Science Reference. doi:10.4018/978-1-4666-0960-0.ch014

Cardellini, V., Casalicchio, E., & Silvestri, L. (2012). Service level provisioning for cloud-based applications service level provisioning for cloud-based applications. In A. Pathan, M. Pathan, & H. Lee (Eds.), *Advancements in distributed computing and internet technologies: Trends and issues* (pp. 363–385). Hershey, PA: Information Science Publishing. doi:10.4018/978-1-4666-0879-5.ch611

Cardellini, V., Casalicchio, E., & Silvestri, L. (2012). Service level provisioning for cloud-based applications service level provisioning for cloud-based applications. In I. Management Association (Ed.), Grid and cloud computing: Concepts, methodologies, tools and applications (pp. 1479-1500). Hershey, PA: Information Science Reference. doi: doi:10.4018/978-1-4666-0879-5.ch611

Carlin, S., & Curran, K. (2013). Cloud computing security. In K. Curran (Ed.), *Pervasive and ubiquitous technology innovations for ambient intelligence environments* (pp. 12–17). Hershey, PA: Information Science Reference.

Carlton, G. H., & Zhou, H. (2011). A survey of cloud computing challenges from a digital forensics perspective. [IJITN]. *International Journal of Interdisciplinary Telecommunications and Networking*, *3*(4), 1–16. doi:10.4018/jitn.2011100101

Carlton, G. H., & Zhou, H. (2012). A survey of cloud computing challenges from a digital forensics perspective. In I. Management Association (Ed.), Grid and cloud computing: Concepts, methodologies, tools and applications (pp. 1221-1236). Hershey, PA: Information Science Reference. doi: doi:10.4018/978-1-4666-0879-5.ch511

Carlton, G. H., & Zhou, H. (2013). A survey of cloud computing challenges from a digital forensics perspective. In M. Bartolacci, & S. Powell (Eds.), *Advancements and innovations in wireless communications and network technologies* (pp. 213–228). Hershey, PA: Information Science Reference.

Carpen-Amarie, A., Costan, A., Leordeanu, C., Basescu, C., & Antoniu, G. (2012). Towards a generic security framework for cloud data management environments. [IJDST]. *International Journal of Distributed Systems and Technologies*, *3*(1), 17–34. doi:10.4018/jdst.2012010102

Casola, V., Cuomo, A., Villano, U., & Rak, M. (2012). Access control in federated clouds: The cloudgrid case study. In M. Villari, I. Brandic, & F. Tusa (Eds.), *Achieving Federated and Self-Manageable Cloud Infrastructures: Theory and Practice* (pp. 395–417). Hershey, PA: Business Science Reference. doi:10.4018/978-1-4666-1631-8.ch020

Casola, V., Cuomo, A., Villano, U., & Rak, M. (2013). Access control in federated clouds: The cloudgrid case study. In I. Management Association (Ed.), IT policy and ethics: Concepts, methodologies, tools, and applications (pp. 148-169). Hershey, PA: Information Science Reference. doi: doi:10.4018/978-1-4666-2919-6.ch008

Celesti, A., Tusa, F., & Villari, M. (2012). Toward cloud federation: Concepts and challenges. In M. Villari, I. Brandic, & F. Tusa (Eds.), *Achieving federated and self-manageable cloud infrastructures: Theory and practice* (pp. 1–17). Hershey, PA: Business Science Reference. doi:10.4018/978-1-4666-1631-8.ch001

Chaka, C. (2013). Virtualization and cloud computing: Business models in the virtual cloud. In A. Loo (Ed.), *Distributed computing innovations for business, engineering, and science* (pp. 176–190). Hershey, PA: Information Science Reference.

Chang, J. (2011). A framework for analysing the impact of cloud computing on local government in the UK. [IJCAC]. *International Journal of Cloud Applications and Computing*, *1*(4), 25–33. doi:10.4018/ijcac.2011100102

Chang, J. (2013). A framework for analysing the impact of cloud computing on local government in the UK. In S. Aljawarneh (Ed.), *Cloud computing advancements in design, implementation, and technologies* (pp. 243–251). Hershey, PA: Information Science Reference.

Chang, J., & Johnston, M. (2012). Cloud computing in local government: From the perspective of four London borough councils. [IJCAC]. *International Journal of Cloud Applications and Computing*, *2*(4), 1–15. doi:10.4018/ijcac.2012100101

Chang, K., & Wang, K. (2012). Efficient support of streaming videos through patching proxies in the cloud. [IJGHPC]. *International Journal of Grid and High Performance Computing*, *4*(4), 22–36. doi:10.4018/jghpc.2012100102

Chang, R., Liao, C., & Liu, C. (2013). Choosing clouds for an enterprise: Modeling and evaluation. [IJEEI]. *International Journal of E-Entrepreneurship and Innovation, 4*(2), 38–53. doi:10.4018/ijeei.2013040103

Chang, V., De Roure, D., Wills, G., & Walters, R. J. (2011). Case studies and organisational sustainability modelling presented by cloud computing business framework. [IJWSR]. *International Journal of Web Services Research, 8*(3), 26–53. doi: doi:10.4018/jwsr.2011070102

Chang, V., Li, C., De Roure, D., Wills, G., Walters, R. J., & Chee, C. (2011). The financial clouds review. [IJCAC]. *International Journal of Cloud Applications and Computing, 1*(2), 41–63. doi:10.4018/ijcac.2011040104

Chang, V., Li, C., De Roure, D., Wills, G., Walters, R. J., & Chee, C. (2013). The financial clouds review. In S. Aljawarneh (Ed.), *Cloud computing advancements in design, implementation, and technologies* (pp. 125–146). Hershey, PA: Information Science Reference.

Chang, V., Walters, R. J., & Wills, G. (2012). Business integration as a service. [IJCAC]. *International Journal of Cloud Applications and Computing, 2*(1), 16–40. doi:10.4018/ijcac.2012010102

Chang, V., & Wills, G. (2013). A University of Greenwich case study of cloud computing: Education as a service. In D. Graham, I. Manikas, & D. Folinas (Eds.), *E-logistics and e-supply chain management: Applications for evolving business* (pp. 232–253). Hershey, PA: Business Science Reference. doi:10.4018/978-1-4666-3914-0.ch013

Chang, V., Wills, G., Walters, R. J., & Currie, W. (2012). Towards a structured cloud ROI: The University of Southampton cost-saving and user satisfaction case studies. In W. Hu, & N. Kaabouch (Eds.), *Sustainable ICTs and management systems for green computing* (pp. 179–200). Hershey, PA: Information Science Reference. doi:10.4018/978-1-4666-1839-8.ch008

Chang, Y., Lee, Y., Juang, T., & Yen, J. (2013). Cost evaluation on building and operating cloud platform. [IJGHPC]. *International Journal of Grid and High Performance Computing, 5*(2), 43–53. doi:10.4018/jghpc.2013040103

Chao, L. (2012). Cloud computing solution for internet based teaching and learning. In L. Chao (Ed.), *Cloud computing for teaching and learning: Strategies for design and implementation* (pp. 210–235). Hershey, PA: Information Science Reference. doi:10.4018/978-1-4666-0957-0.ch015

Chao, L. (2012). Overview of cloud computing and its application in e-learning. In L. Chao (Ed.), *Cloud computing for teaching and learning: Strategies for design and implementation* (pp. 1–16). Hershey, PA: Information Science Reference. doi:10.4018/978-1-4666-0957-0.ch001

Chauhan, S., Raman, A., & Singh, N. (2013). A comparative cost analysis of on premises IT infrastructure and cloud-based email services in an Indian business school. [IJCAC]. *International Journal of Cloud Applications and Computing, 3*(2), 21–34. doi:10.4018/ijcac.2013040103

Chen, C., Chao, H., Wu, T., Fan, C., Chen, J., Chen, Y., & Hsu, J. (2011). IoT-IMS communication platform for future internet. [IJARAS]. *International Journal of Adaptive, Resilient and Autonomic Systems, 2*(4), 74–94. doi:10.4018/jaras.2011100105

Chen, C., Chao, H., Wu, T., Fan, C., Chen, J., Chen, Y., & Hsu, J. (2013). IoT-IMS communication platform for future internet. In V. De Florio (Ed.), *Innovations and approaches for resilient and adaptive systems* (pp. 68–86). Hershey, PA: Information Science Reference.

Chen, C. C. (2013). Cloud computing in case-based pedagogy: An information systems success perspective. [IJDTIS]. *International Journal of Dependable and Trustworthy Information Systems, 2*(3), 1–16. doi:10.4018/jdtis.2011070101

Cheney, A. W., Riedl, R. E., Sanders, R., & Tashner, J. H. (2012). The new company water cooler: Use of 3D virtual immersive worlds to promote networking and professional learning in organizations. In I. Management Association (Ed.), *Organizational learning and knowledge: Concepts, methodologies, tools and applications* (pp. 2848-2861). Hershey, PA: Business Science Reference. doi: doi:10.4018/978-1-60960-783-8.ch801

Chiang, C., & Yu, S. (2013). Cloud-enabled software testing based on program understanding. In S. Tilley, & T. Parveen (Eds.), *Software testing in the cloud: Perspectives on an emerging discipline* (pp. 54–67). Hershey, PA: Information Science Reference.

Chou, Y., & Oetting, J. (2011). Risk assessment for cloud-based IT systems. [IJGHPC]. *International Journal of Grid and High Performance Computing*, *3*(2), 1–13. doi:10.4018/jghpc.2011040101

Chou, Y., & Oetting, J. (2012). Risk assessment for cloud-based IT systems. In I. Management Association (Ed.), Grid and cloud computing: Concepts, methodologies, tools and applications (pp. 272-285). Hershey, PA: Information Science Reference. doi: doi:10.4018/978-1-4666-0879-5.ch113

Chou, Y., & Oetting, J. (2013). Risk assessment for cloud-based IT systems. In E. Udoh (Ed.), *Applications and developments in grid, cloud, and high performance computing* (pp. 1–14). Hershey, PA: Information Science Reference.

Cohen, F. (2013). Challenges to digital forensic evidence in the cloud. In K. Ruan (Ed.), *Cybercrime and cloud forensics: Applications for investigation processes* (pp. 59–78). Hershey, PA: Information Science Reference.

Cossu, R., Di Giulio, C., Brito, F., & Petcu, D. (2013). Cloud computing for earth observation. In D. Kyriazis, A. Voulodimos, S. Gogouvitis, & T. Varvarigou (Eds.), *Data intensive storage services for cloud environments* (pp. 166–191). Hershey, PA: Business Science Reference. doi:10.4018/978-1-4666-3934-8.ch012

Costa, J. E., & Rodrigues, J. J. (2014). Mobile cloud computing: Technologies, services, and applications. In J. Rodrigues, K. Lin, & J. Lloret (Eds.), *Mobile networks and cloud computing convergence for progressive services and applications* (pp. 1–17). Hershey, PA: Information Science Reference.

Creaner, G., & Pahl, C. (2013). Flexible coordination techniques for dynamic cloud service collaboration. In G. Ortiz, & J. Cubo (Eds.), *Adaptive web services for modular and reusable software development: Tactics and solutions* (pp. 239–252). Hershey, PA: Information Science Reference.

Crosbie, M. (2013). Hack the cloud: Ethical hacking and cloud forensics. In K. Ruan (Ed.), *Cybercrime and cloud forensics: Applications for investigation processes* (pp. 42–58). Hershey, PA: Information Science Reference.

Curran, K., Carlin, S., & Adams, M. (2012). Security issues in cloud computing. In L. Chao (Ed.), *Cloud computing for teaching and learning: Strategies for design and implementation* (pp. 200–208). Hershey, PA: Information Science Reference. doi:10.4018/978-1-4666-0957-0.ch014

Dahbur, K., & Mohammad, B. (2011). Toward understanding the challenges and countermeasures in computer anti-forensics. [IJCAC]. *International Journal of Cloud Applications and Computing*, *1*(3), 22–35. doi:10.4018/ijcac.2011070103

Dahbur, K., Mohammad, B., & Tarakji, A. B. (2011). Security issues in cloud computing: A survey of risks, threats and vulnerabilities. [IJCAC]. *International Journal of Cloud Applications and Computing*, *1*(3), 1–11. doi:10.4018/ijcac.2011070101

Dahbur, K., Mohammad, B., & Tarakji, A. B. (2012). Security issues in cloud computing: A survey of risks, threats and vulnerabilities. In I. Management Association (Ed.), Grid and cloud computing: Concepts, methodologies, tools and applications (pp. 1644-1655). Hershey, PA: Information Science Reference. doi: doi:10.4018/978-1-4666-0879-5.ch707

Dahbur, K., Mohammad, B., & Tarakji, A. B. (2013). Security issues in cloud computing: A survey of risks, threats and vulnerabilities. In S. Aljawarneh (Ed.), *Cloud computing advancements in design, implementation, and technologies* (pp. 154–165). Hershey, PA: Information Science Reference.

Daim, T., Britton, M., Subramanian, G., Brenden, R., & Intarode, N. (2012). Adopting and integrating cloud computing. In E. Eyob, & E. Tetteh (Eds.), *Customer-oriented global supply chains: Concepts for effective management* (pp. 175–197). Hershey, PA: Information Science Reference. doi:10.4018/978-1-4666-0246-5.ch011

Davis, M., & Sedsman, A. (2012). Grey areas: The legal dimensions of cloud computing. In C. Li, & A. Ho (Eds.), *Crime prevention technologies and applications for advancing criminal investigation* (pp. 263–273). Hershey, PA: Information Science Reference. doi:10.4018/978-1-4666-1758-2.ch017

De Coster, R., & Albesher, A. (2013). The development of mobile service applications for consumers and intelligent networks. In I. Lee (Ed.), *Mobile services industries, technologies, and applications in the global economy* (pp. 273–289). Hershey, PA: Information Science Reference.

De Filippi, P. (2014). Ubiquitous computing in the cloud: User empowerment vs. user obsequity. In J. Pelet, & P. Papadopoulou (Eds.), *User behavior in ubiquitous online environments* (pp. 44–63). Hershey, PA: Information Science Reference.

De Silva, S. (2013). Key legal issues with cloud computing: A UK law perspective. In A. Bento, & A. Aggarwal (Eds.), *Cloud computing service and deployment models: Layers and management* (pp. 242–256). Hershey, PA: Business Science Reference.

Deed, C., & Cragg, P. (2013). Business impacts of cloud computing. In A. Bento, & A. Aggarwal (Eds.), *Cloud computing service and deployment models: Layers and management* (pp. 274–288). Hershey, PA: Business Science Reference.

Deng, M., Petkovic, M., Nalin, M., & Baroni, I. (2013). Home healthcare in cloud computing. In M. Cruz-Cunha, I. Miranda, & P. Gonçalves (Eds.), *Handbook of research on ICTs and management systems for improving efficiency in healthcare and social care* (pp. 614–634). Hershey, PA: Medical Information Science Reference. doi:10.4018/978-1-4666-3990-4.ch032

Desai, A. M., & Mock, K. (2013). Security in cloud computing. In A. Bento, & A. Aggarwal (Eds.), *Cloud computing service and deployment models: Layers and management* (pp. 208–221). Hershey, PA: Business Science Reference.

Deshpande, R. M., Patle, B. V., & Bhoskar, R. D. (2014). Planning and implementation of cloud computing in NIT's in India: Special reference to VNIT. In S. Dhamdhere (Ed.), *Cloud computing and virtualization technologies in libraries* (pp. 90–106). Hershey, PA: Information Science Reference.

Dhamdhere, S. N., & Lihitkar, R. (2014). The university cloud library model and the role of the cloud librarian. In S. Dhamdhere (Ed.), *Cloud computing and virtualization technologies in libraries* (pp. 150–161). Hershey, PA: Information Science Reference.

Di Martino, S., Ferrucci, F., Maggio, V., & Sarro, F. (2013). Towards migrating genetic algorithms for test data generation to the cloud. In S. Tilley, & T. Parveen (Eds.), *Software testing in the cloud: Perspectives on an emerging discipline* (pp. 113–135). Hershey, PA: Information Science Reference.

Di Sano, M., Di Stefano, A., Morana, G., & Zito, D. (2013). FSaaS: Configuring policies for managing shared files among cooperating, distributed applications. [IJWP]. *International Journal of Web Portals*, 5(1), 1–14. doi:10.4018/jwp.2013010101

Dippl, S., Jaeger, M. C., Luhn, A., Shulman-Peleg, A., & Vernik, G. (2013). Towards federation and interoperability of cloud storage systems. In D. Kyriazis, A. Voulodimos, S. Gogouvitis, & T. Varvarigou (Eds.), *Data intensive storage services for cloud environments* (pp. 60–71). Hershey, PA: Business Science Reference. doi:10.4018/978-1-4666-3934-8.ch005

Distefano, S., & Puliafito, A. (2012). The cloud@home volunteer and interoperable cloud through the future internet. In M. Villari, I. Brandic, & F. Tusa (Eds.), *Achieving federated and self-manageable cloud infrastructures: Theory and practice* (pp. 79–96). Hershey, PA: Business Science Reference. doi:10.4018/978-1-4666-1631-8.ch005

Djoleto, W. (2013). Cloud computing and ecommerce or ebusiness: "The now it way" – An overview. In *Electronic commerce and organizational leadership: perspectives and methodologies* (pp. 239–254). Hershey, PA: Business Science Reference. doi:10.4018/978-1-4666-2982-0.ch010

Dollmann, T. J., Loos, P., Fellmann, M., Thomas, O., Hoheisel, A., Katranuschkov, P., & Scherer, R. (2011). Design and usage of a process-centric collaboration methodology for virtual organizations in hybrid environments. [IJIIT]. *International Journal of Intelligent Information Technologies*, *7*(1), 45–64. doi:10.4018/jiit.2011010104

Dollmann, T. J., Loos, P., Fellmann, M., Thomas, O., Hoheisel, A., Katranuschkov, P., & Scherer, R. (2013). Design and usage of a process-centric collaboration methodology for virtual organizations in hybrid environments. In V. Sugumaran (Ed.), *Organizational efficiency through intelligent information technologies* (pp. 45–64). Hershey, PA: Information Science Reference.

Dreher, P., & Vouk, M. (2012). Utilizing open source cloud computing environments to provide cost effective support for university education and research. In L. Chao (Ed.), *Cloud computing for teaching and learning: Strategies for design and implementation* (pp. 32–49). Hershey, PA: Information Science Reference. doi:10.4018/978-1-4666-0957-0.ch003

Drum, D., Becker, D., & Fish, M. (2013). Technology adoption in troubled times: A cloud computing case study. [JCIT]. *Journal of Cases on Information Technology*, *15*(2), 57–71. doi:10.4018/jcit.2013040104

Dunaway, D. M. (2013). Creating virtual collaborative learning experiences for aspiring teachers. In R. Hartshorne, T. Heafner, & T. Petty (Eds.), *Teacher education programs and online learning tools: Innovations in teacher preparation* (pp. 167–180). Hershey, PA: Information Science Reference.

Dykstra, J. (2013). Seizing electronic evidence from cloud computing environments. In K. Ruan (Ed.), *Cybercrime and cloud forensics: Applications for investigation processes* (pp. 156–185). Hershey, PA: Information Science Reference.

El-Refaey, M., & Rimal, B. P. (2012). Grid, SOA and cloud computing: On-demand computing models. In I. Management Association (Ed.), *Grid and cloud computing: Concepts, methodologies, tools and applications* (pp. 12–51). Hershey, PA: Information Science Reference. doi: doi:10.4018/978-1-4666-0879-5.ch102

El-Refaey, M., & Rimal, B. P. (2012). Grid, SOA and cloud computing: On-demand computing models. In N. Preve (Ed.), *Computational and data grids: Principles, applications and design* (pp. 45–85). Hershey, PA: Information Science Reference. doi:10.4018/978-1-4666-0879-5.ch102

Elnaffar, S., Maamar, Z., & Sheng, Q. Z. (2013). When clouds start socializing: The sky model. [IJEBR]. *International Journal of E-Business Research*, *9*(2), 1–7. doi:10.4018/jebr.2013040101

Elwood, S., & Keengwe, J. (2012). Microbursts: A design format for mobile cloud computing. [IJICTE]. *International Journal of Information and Communication Technology Education*, *8*(2), 102–110. doi:10.4018/jicte.2012040109

Emeakaroha, V. C., Netto, M. A., Calheiros, R. N., & De Rose, C. A. (2012). Achieving flexible SLA and resource management in clouds. In M. Villari, I. Brandic, & F. Tusa (Eds.), *Achieving federated and self-manageable cloud infrastructures: Theory and practice* (pp. 266–287). Hershey, PA: Business Science Reference. doi:10.4018/978-1-4666-1631-8.ch014

Etro, F. (2013). The economics of cloud computing. In A. Bento, & A. Aggarwal (Eds.), *Cloud computing service and deployment models: Layers and management* (pp. 296–309). Hershey, PA: Business Science Reference.

Ezugwu, A. E., Buhari, S. M., & Junaidu, S. B. (2013). Virtual machine allocation in cloud computing environment. [IJCAC]. *International Journal of Cloud Applications and Computing*, *3*(2), 47–60. doi:10.4018/ijcac.2013040105

Fauzi, A. H., & Taylor, H. (2013). Secure community trust stores for peer-to-peer e-commerce applications using cloud services. [IJEEI]. *International Journal of E-Entrepreneurship and Innovation*, *4*(1), 1–15. doi:10.4018/jeei.2013010101

Ferguson-Boucher, K., & Endicott-Popovsky, B. (2013). Forensic readiness in the cloud (FRC): Integrating records management and digital forensics. In K. Ruan (Ed.), *Cybercrime and cloud forensics: Applications for investigation processes* (pp. 105–128). Hershey, PA: Information Science Reference.

Ferraro de Souza, R., Westphall, C. B., dos Santos, D. R., & Westphall, C. M. (2013). A review of PACS on cloud for archiving secure medical images. [IJPHIM]. *International Journal of Privacy and Health Information Management, 1*(1), 53–62. doi:10.4018/ijphim.2013010104

Firdhous, M., Hassan, S., & Ghazali, O. (2013). Statistically enhanced multi-dimensional trust computing mechanism for cloud computing. [IJMCMC]. *International Journal of Mobile Computing and Multimedia Communications, 5*(2), 1–17. doi:10.4018/jmcmc.2013040101

Formisano, C., Bonelli, L., Balraj, K. R., & Shulman-Peleg, A. (2013). Cloud access control mechanisms. In D. Kyriazis, A. Voulodimos, S. Gogouvitis, & T. Varvarigou (Eds.), *Data intensive storage services for cloud environments* (pp. 94–108). Hershey, PA: Business Science Reference. doi:10.4018/978-1-4666-3934-8.ch007

Frank, H., & Mesentean, S. (2012). Efficient communication interfaces for distributed energy resources. In E. Udoh (Ed.), *Evolving developments in grid and cloud computing: Advancing research* (pp. 185–196). Hershey, PA: Information Science Reference. doi:10.4018/978-1-4666-0056-0.ch013

Gallina, B., & Guelfi, N. (2012). Reusing transaction models for dependable cloud computing. In H. Yang, & X. Liu (Eds.), *Software reuse in the emerging cloud computing era* (pp. 248–277). Hershey, PA: Information Science Reference. doi:10.4018/978-1-4666-0897-9.ch011

Garofalo, D. A. (2013). Empires of the future: Libraries, technology, and the academic environment. In E. Iglesias (Ed.), *Robots in academic libraries: Advancements in library automation* (pp. 180–206). Hershey, PA: Information Science Reference. doi:10.4018/978-1-4666-3938-6.ch010

Gebremeskel, G. B., He, Z., & Jing, X. (2013). Semantic integrating for intelligent cloud data mining platform and cloud based business intelligence for optimization of mobile social networks. In V. Bhatnagar (Ed.), *Data mining in dynamic social networks and fuzzy systems* (pp. 173–211). Hershey, PA: Information Science Reference. doi:10.4018/978-1-4666-4213-3.ch009

Gentleman, W. M. (2013). Using the cloud for testing NOT adjunct to development. In S. Tilley, & T. Parveen (Eds.), *Software testing in the cloud: Perspectives on an emerging discipline* (pp. 216–230). Hershey, PA: Information Science Reference.

Ghafoor, K. Z., Mohammed, M. A., Abu Bakar, K., Sadiq, A. S., & Lloret, J. (2014). Vehicular cloud computing: Trends and challenges. In J. Rodrigues, K. Lin, & J. Lloret (Eds.), *Mobile networks and cloud computing convergence for progressive services and applications* (pp. 262–274). Hershey, PA: Information Science Reference.

Giannakaki, M. (2012). The "right to be forgotten" in the era of social media and cloud computing. In C. Akrivopoulou, & N. Garipidis (Eds.), *Human rights and risks in the digital era: Globalization and the effects of information technologies* (pp. 10–24). Hershey, PA: Information Science Reference. doi:10.4018/978-1-4666-0891-7.ch002

Gillam, L., Li, B., & O'Loughlin, J. (2012). Teaching clouds: Lessons taught and lessons learnt. In L. Chao (Ed.), *Cloud computing for teaching and learning: Strategies for design and implementation* (pp. 82–94). Hershey, PA: Information Science Reference. doi:10.4018/978-1-4666-0957-0.ch006

Gonsowski, D. (2013). Compliance in the cloud and the implications on electronic discovery. In K. Ruan (Ed.), *Cybercrime and cloud forensics: Applications for investigation processes* (pp. 230–250). Hershey, PA: Information Science Reference.

Gonzalez-Sanchez, J., Conley, Q., Chavez-Echeagaray, M., & Atkinson, R. K. (2012). Supporting the assembly process by leveraging augmented reality, cloud computing, and mobile devices. [IJCBPL]. *International Journal of Cyber Behavior, Psychology and Learning, 2*(3), 86–102. doi:10.4018/ijcbpl.2012070107

Gopinath, R., & Geetha, B. (2013). An e-learning system based on secure data storage services in cloud computing. [IJITWE]. *International Journal of Information Technology and Web Engineering, 8*(2), 1–17. doi:10.4018/jitwe.2013040101

Gossin, P. C., & LaBrie, R. C. (2013). Data center waste management. In P. Ordóñez de Pablos (Ed.), *Green technologies and business practices: An IT approach* (pp. 226–235). Hershey, PA: Information Science Reference.

Goswami, V., Patra, S. S., & Mund, G. B. (2012). Performance analysis of cloud computing centers for bulk services. [IJCAC]. *International Journal of Cloud Applications and Computing*, 2(4), 53–65. doi:10.4018/ijcac.2012100104

Goswami, V., & Sahoo, C. N. (2013). Optimal resource usage in multi-cloud computing environment. [IJCAC]. *International Journal of Cloud Applications and Computing*, 3(1), 44–57. doi:10.4018/ijcac.2013010105

Gräuler, M., Teuteberg, F., Mahmoud, T., & Gómez, J. M. (2013). Requirements prioritization and design considerations for the next generation of corporate environmental management information systems: A foundation for innovation. [IJITSA]. *International Journal of Information Technologies and Systems Approach*, 6(1), 98–116. doi:10.4018/jitsa.2013010106

Grieve, G. P., & Heston, K. (2012). Finding liquid salvation: Using the cardean ethnographic method to document second life residents and religious cloud communities. In N. Zagalo, L. Morgado, & A. Boa-Ventura (Eds.), *Virtual worlds and metaverse platforms: New communication and identity paradigms* (pp. 288–305). Hershey, PA: Information Science Reference.

Grispos, G., Storer, T., & Glisson, W. B. (2012). Calm before the storm: The challenges of cloud computing in digital forensics. [IJDCF]. *International Journal of Digital Crime and Forensics*, 4(2), 28–48. doi:10.4018/jdcf.2012040103

Grispos, G., Storer, T., & Glisson, W. B. (2013). Calm before the storm: The challenges of cloud computing in digital forensics. In C. Li (Ed.), *Emerging digital forensics applications for crime detection, prevention, and security* (pp. 211–233). Hershey, PA: Information Science Reference. doi:10.4018/978-1-4666-4006-1.ch015

Guster, D., & Lee, O. F. (2011). Enhancing the disaster recovery plan through virtualization. [JITR]. *Journal of Information Technology Research*, 4(4), 18–40. doi:10.4018/jitr.2011100102

Hanawa, T., & Sato, M. (2013). D-Cloud: Software testing environment for dependable distributed systems using cloud computing technology. In S. Tilley, & T. Parveen (Eds.), *Software testing in the cloud: Perspectives on an emerging discipline* (pp. 340–355). Hershey, PA: Information Science Reference.

Hardy, J., Liu, L., Lei, C., & Li, J. (2013). Internet-based virtual computing infrastructure for cloud computing. In X. Yang, & L. Liu (Eds.), *Principles, methodologies, and service-oriented approaches for cloud computing* (pp. 371–389). Hershey, PA: Business Science Reference. doi:10.4018/978-1-4666-2854-0.ch016

Hashizume, K., Yoshioka, N., & Fernandez, E. B. (2013). Three misuse patterns for cloud computing. In D. Rosado, D. Mellado, E. Fernandez-Medina, & M. Piattini (Eds.), *Security engineering for cloud computing: Approaches and tools* (pp. 36–53). Hershey, PA: Information Science Reference.

Hassan, Q. F., Riad, A. M., & Hassan, A. E. (2012). Understanding cloud computing. In H. Yang, & X. Liu (Eds.), *Software reuse in the emerging cloud computing era* (pp. 204–227). Hershey, PA: Information Science Reference. doi:10.4018/978-1-4666-0897-9.ch009

Hasselmeyer, P., Katsaros, G., Koller, B., & Wieder, P. (2012). Cloud monitoring. In M. Villari, I. Brandic, & F. Tusa (Eds.), *Achieving federated and self-manageable cloud infrastructures: Theory and practice* (pp. 97–116). Hershey, PA: Business Science Reference. doi:10.4018/978-1-4666-1631-8.ch006

Hertzler, B. T., Frost, E., Bressler, G. H., & Goehring, C. (2011). Experience report: Using a cloud computing environment during Haiti and Exercise24. [IJISCRAM]. *International Journal of Information Systems for Crisis Response and Management*, 3(1), 50–64. doi:10.4018/jiscrm.2011010104

Hertzler, B. T., Frost, E., Bressler, G. H., & Goehring, C. (2013). Experience report: Using a cloud computing environment during Haiti and Exercise24. In M. Jennex (Ed.), *Using social and information technologies for disaster and crisis management* (pp. 52–66). Hershey, PA: Information Science Reference. doi:10.4018/978-1-4666-2788-8.ch004

Ho, R. (2013). Cloud computing and enterprise migration strategies. In A. Loo (Ed.), *Distributed computing innovations for business, engineering, and science* (pp. 156–175). Hershey, PA: Information Science Reference.

Hobona, G., Jackson, M., & Anand, S. (2012). Implementing geospatial web services for cloud computing. In I. Management Association (Ed.), Grid and cloud computing: Concepts, methodologies, tools and applications (pp. 615-636). Hershey, PA: Information Science Reference. doi: doi:10.4018/978-1-4666-0879-5.ch305

Hochstein, L., Schott, B., & Graybill, R. B. (2011). Computational engineering in the cloud: Benefits and challenges. [JOEUC]. *Journal of Organizational and End User Computing, 23*(4), 31–50. doi:10.4018/joeuc.2011100103

Hochstein, L., Schott, B., & Graybill, R. B. (2013). Computational engineering in the cloud: Benefits and challenges. In A. Dwivedi, & S. Clarke (Eds.), *Innovative strategies and approaches for end-user computing advancements* (pp. 314–332). Hershey, PA: Information Science Reference.

Honarvar, A. R. (2013). Developing an elastic cloud computing application through multi-agent systems. [IJCAC]. *International Journal of Cloud Applications and Computing, 3*(1), 58–64. doi:10.4018/ijcac.2013010106

Hossain, S. (2013). Cloud computing terms, definitions, and taxonomy. In A. Bento, & A. Aggarwal (Eds.), *Cloud computing service and deployment models: Layers and management* (pp. 1–25). Hershey, PA: Business Science Reference.

Hudzia, B., Sinclair, J., & Lindner, M. (2013). Deploying and running enterprise grade applications in a federated cloud. In I. Association (Ed.), *Supply chain management: Concepts, methodologies, tools, and applications* (pp. 1350–1370). Hershey, PA: Business Science Reference.

Hung, S., Shieh, J., & Lee, C. (2011). Migrating android applications to the cloud. [IJGHPC]. *International Journal of Grid and High Performance Computing, 3*(2), 14–28. doi:10.4018/jghpc.2011040102

Hung, S., Shieh, J., & Lee, C. (2013). Migrating android applications to the cloud. In E. Udoh (Ed.), *Applications and developments in grid, cloud, and high performance computing* (pp. 307–322). Hershey, PA: Information Science Reference.

Islam, S., Mouratidis, H., & Weippl, E. R. (2013). A goal-driven risk management approach to support security and privacy analysis of cloud-based system. In D. Rosado, D. Mellado, E. Fernandez-Medina, & M. Piattini (Eds.), *Security engineering for cloud computing: Approaches and tools* (pp. 97–122). Hershey, PA: Information Science Reference.

Itani, W., Kayssi, A., & Chehab, A. (2013). Hardware-based security for ensuring data privacy in the cloud. In D. Rosado, D. Mellado, E. Fernandez-Medina, & M. Piattini (Eds.), *Security engineering for cloud computing: Approaches and tools* (pp. 147–170). Hershey, PA: Information Science Reference.

Jackson, A., & Weiland, M. (2013). Cloud computing for scientific simulation and high performance computing. In X. Yang, & L. Liu (Eds.), *Principles, methodologies, and service-oriented approaches for cloud computing* (pp. 51–70). Hershey, PA: Business Science Reference. doi:10.4018/978-1-4666-2854-0.ch003

Jaeger, M. C., & Hohenstein, U. (2013). Content centric storage and current storage systems. In D. Kyriazis, A. Voulodimos, S. Gogouvitis, & T. Varvarigou (Eds.), *Data intensive storage services for cloud environments* (pp. 27–46). Hershey, PA: Business Science Reference. doi:10.4018/978-1-4666-3934-8.ch003

James, J. I., Shosha, A. F., & Gladyshev, P. (2013). Digital forensic investigation and cloud computing. In K. Ruan (Ed.), *Cybercrime and cloud forensics: Applications for investigation processes* (pp. 1–41). Hershey, PA: Information Science Reference.

Jena, R. K. (2013). Green computing to green business. In P. Ordóñez de Pablos (Ed.), *Green technologies and business practices: An IT approach* (pp. 138–150). Hershey, PA: Information Science Reference.

Jeyarani, R., & Nagaveni, N. (2012). A heuristic meta scheduler for optimal resource utilization and improved QoS in cloud computing environment. [IJCAC]. *International Journal of Cloud Applications and Computing, 2*(1), 41–52. doi:10.4018/ijcac.2012010103

Jeyarani, R., Nagaveni, N., & Ram, R. V. (2011). Self adaptive particle swarm optimization for efficient virtual machine provisioning in cloud. [IJIIT]. *International Journal of Intelligent Information Technologies*, *7*(2), 25–44. doi:10.4018/jiit.2011040102

Jeyarani, R., Nagaveni, N., & Ram, R. V. (2013). Self adaptive particle swarm optimization for efficient virtual machine provisioning in cloud. In V. Sugumaran (Ed.), *Organizational efficiency through intelligent information technologies* (pp. 88–107). Hershey, PA: Information Science Reference.

Jeyarani, R., Nagaveni, N., Sadasivam, S. K., & Rajarathinam, V. R. (2011). Power aware meta scheduler for adaptive VM provisioning in IaaS cloud. [IJCAC]. *International Journal of Cloud Applications and Computing*, *1*(3), 36–51. doi:10.4018/ijcac.2011070104

Jeyarani, R., Nagaveni, N., Sadasivam, S. K., & Rajarathinam, V. R. (2013). Power aware meta scheduler for adaptive VM provisioning in IaaS cloud. In S. Aljawarneh (Ed.), *Cloud computing advancements in design, implementation, and technologies* (pp. 190–204). Hershey, PA: Information Science Reference.

Jiang, J., Huang, X., Wu, Y., & Yang, G. (2013). Campus cloud storage and preservation: From distributed file system to data sharing service. In X. Yang, & L. Liu (Eds.), *Principles, methodologies, and service-oriented approaches for cloud computing* (pp. 284–301). Hershey, PA: Business Science Reference. doi:10.4018/978-1-4666-2854-0.ch012

Jing, S. (2012). The application exploration of cloud computing in information technology teaching. [IJAPUC]. *International Journal of Advanced Pervasive and Ubiquitous Computing*, *4*(4), 23–27. doi:10.4018/japuc.2012100104

Johansson, D., & Wiberg, M. (2012). Conceptually advancing "application mobility" towards design: Applying a concept-driven approach to the design of mobile IT for home care service groups. [IJACI]. *International Journal of Ambient Computing and Intelligence*, *4*(3), 20–32. doi:10.4018/jaci.2012070102

Jorda, J., & M'zoughi, A. (2013). Securing cloud storage. In D. Rosado, D. Mellado, E. Fernandez-Medina, & M. Piattini (Eds.), *Security engineering for cloud computing: Approaches and tools* (pp. 171–190). Hershey, PA: Information Science Reference.

Juiz, C., & Alexander de Pous, V. (2014). Cloud computing: IT governance, legal, and public policy aspects. In I. Portela, & F. Almeida (Eds.), *Organizational, legal, and technological dimensions of information system administration* (pp. 139–166). Hershey, PA: Information Science Reference.

Kaisler, S. H., Money, W., & Cohen, S. J. (2013). Cloud computing: A decision framework for small businesses. In A. Bento, & A. Aggarwal (Eds.), *Cloud computing service and deployment models: Layers and management* (pp. 151–172). Hershey, PA: Business Science Reference.

Kanamori, Y., & Yen, M. Y. (2013). Cloud computing security and risk management. In A. Bento, & A. Aggarwal (Eds.), *Cloud computing service and deployment models: Layers and management* (pp. 222–240). Hershey, PA: Business Science Reference.

Karadsheh, L., & Alhawari, S. (2011). Applying security policies in small business utilizing cloud computing technologies. [IJCAC]. *International Journal of Cloud Applications and Computing*, *1*(2), 29–40. doi:10.4018/ijcac.2011040103

Karadsheh, L., & Alhawari, S. (2013). Applying security policies in small business utilizing cloud computing technologies. In S. Aljawarneh (Ed.), *Cloud computing advancements in design, implementation, and technologies* (pp. 112–124). Hershey, PA: Information Science Reference.

Kaupins, G. (2012). Laws associated with mobile computing in the cloud. [IJWNBT]. *International Journal of Wireless Networks and Broadband Technologies*, *2*(3), 1–9. doi:10.4018/ijwnbt.2012070101

Kemp, M. L., Robb, S., & Deans, P. C. (2013). The legal implications of cloud computing. In A. Bento, & A. Aggarwal (Eds.), *Cloud computing service and deployment models: Layers and management* (pp. 257–272). Hershey, PA: Business Science Reference.

Khan, N., Ahmad, N., Herawan, T., & Inayat, Z. (2012). Cloud computing: Locally sub-clouds instead of globally one cloud. [IJCAC]. *International Journal of Cloud Applications and Computing*, 2(3), 68–85. doi:10.4018/ijcac.2012070103

Khan, N., Noraziah, A., Ismail, E. I., Deris, M. M., & Herawan, T. (2012). Cloud computing: Analysis of various platforms. [IJEEI]. *International Journal of E-Entrepreneurship and Innovation*, 3(2), 51–59. doi:10.4018/jeei.2012040104

Khansa, L., Forcade, J., Nambari, G., Parasuraman, S., & Cox, P. (2012). Proposing an intelligent cloud-based electronic health record system. [IJBDCN]. *International Journal of Business Data Communications and Networking*, 8(3), 57–71. doi:10.4018/jbdcn.2012070104

Kierkegaard, S. (2012). Not every cloud brings rain: Legal risks on the horizon. In M. Gupta, J. Walp, & R. Sharman (Eds.), *Strategic and practical approaches for information security governance: Technologies and applied solutions* (pp. 181–194). Hershey, PA: Information Science Reference. doi:10.4018/978-1-4666-0197-0.ch011

Kifayat, K., Shamsa, T. B., Mackay, M., Merabti, M., & Shi, Q. (2013). Real time risk management in cloud computation. In D. Rosado, D. Mellado, E. Fernandez-Medina, & M. Piattini (Eds.), *Security engineering for cloud computing: Approaches and tools* (pp. 123–145). Hershey, PA: Information Science Reference.

King, T. M., Ganti, A. S., & Froslie, D. (2013). Towards improving the testability of cloud application services. In S. Tilley, & T. Parveen (Eds.), *Software testing in the cloud: Perspectives on an emerging discipline* (pp. 322–339). Hershey, PA: Information Science Reference.

Kipp, A., Schneider, R., & Schubert, L. (2013). Encapsulation of complex HPC services. In C. Rückemann (Ed.), *Integrated information and computing systems for natural, spatial, and social sciences* (pp. 153–176). Hershey, PA: Information Science Reference.

Kldiashvili, E. (2012). The cloud computing as the tool for implementation of virtual organization technology for ehealth. [JITR]. *Journal of Information Technology Research*, 5(1), 18–34. doi:10.4018/jitr.2012010102

Kldiashvili, E. (2013). Implementation of telecytology in georgia for quality assurance programs. [JITR]. *Journal of Information Technology Research*, 6(2), 24–45. doi:10.4018/jitr.2013040102

Kosmatov, N. (2013). Concolic test generation and the cloud: deployment and verification perspectives. In S. Tilley, & T. Parveen (Eds.), *Software testing in the cloud: Perspectives on an emerging discipline* (pp. 231–251). Hershey, PA: Information Science Reference.

Kotamarti, R. M., Thornton, M. A., & Dunham, M. H. (2012). Quantum computing approach for alignment-free sequence search and classification. In S. Ali, N. Abbadeni, & M. Batouche (Eds.), *Multidisciplinary computational intelligence techniques: Applications in business, engineering, and medicine* (pp. 279–300). Hershey, PA: Information Science Reference. doi:10.4018/978-1-4666-1830-5.ch017

Kremmydas, D., Petsakos, A., & Rozakis, S. (2012). Parametric optimization of linear and non-linear models via parallel computing to enhance web-spatial DSS interactivity. [IJDSST]. *International Journal of Decision Support System Technology*, 4(1), 14–29. doi:10.4018/jdsst.2012010102

Krishnadas, N., & Pillai, R. R. (2013). Cloud computing diagnosis: A comprehensive study. In X. Yang, & L. Liu (Eds.), *Principles, methodologies, and service-oriented approaches for cloud computing* (pp. 1–18). Hershey, PA: Business Science Reference. doi:10.4018/978-1-4666-2854-0.ch001

Kübert, R., & Katsaros, G. (2011). Using free software for elastic web hosting on a private cloud. [IJCAC]. *International Journal of Cloud Applications and Computing*, 1(2), 14–28. doi:10.4018/ijcac.2011040102

Kübert, R., & Katsaros, G. (2013). Using free software for elastic web hosting on a private cloud. In S. Aljawarneh (Ed.), *Cloud computing advancements in design, implementation, and technologies* (pp. 97–111). Hershey, PA: Information Science Reference.

Kumar, P. S., Ashok, M. S., & Subramanian, R. (2012). A publicly verifiable dynamic secret sharing protocol for secure and dependable data storage in cloud computing. [IJCAC]. *International Journal of Cloud Applications and Computing*, 2(3), 1–25. doi:10.4018/ijcac.2012070101

Lasluisa, S., Rodero, I., & Parashar, M. (2013). Software design for passing sarbanes-oxley in cloud computing. In C. Rückemann (Ed.), *Integrated information and computing systems for natural, spatial, and social sciences* (pp. 27–42). Hershey, PA: Information Science Reference. doi:10.4018/978-1-4666-4301-7.ch080

Lasluisa, S., Rodero, I., & Parashar, M. (2014). Software design for passing sarbanes-oxley in cloud computing. In I. Management Association (Ed.), Software design and development: Concepts, methodologies, tools, and applications (pp. 1659-1674). Hershey, PA: Information Science Reference. doi: doi:10.4018/978-1-4666-4301-7.ch080

Lee, W. N. (2013). An economic analysis of cloud: "Software as a service" (saas) computing and "virtual desktop infrastructure" (VDI) models. In A. Bento, & A. Aggarwal (Eds.), *Cloud computing service and deployment models: Layers and management* (pp. 289–295). Hershey, PA: Business Science Reference.

Levine, K., & White, B. A. (2011). A crisis at hafford furniture: Cloud computing case study. [JCIT]. *Journal of Cases on Information Technology*, *13*(1), 57–71. doi:10.4018/jcit.2011010104

Levine, K., & White, B. A. (2013). A crisis at Hafford furniture: Cloud computing case study. In M. Khosrow-Pour (Ed.), *Cases on emerging information technology research and applications* (pp. 70–87). Hershey, PA: Information Science Reference.

Li, J., Meng, L., Zhu, Z., Li, X., Huai, J., & Liu, L. (2013). CloudRank: A cloud service ranking method based on both user feedback and service testing. In X. Yang, & L. Liu (Eds.), *Principles, methodologies, and service-oriented approaches for cloud computing* (pp. 230–258). Hershey, PA: Business Science Reference. doi:10.4018/978-1-4666-2854-0.ch010

Liang, T., Lu, F., & Chiu, J. (2012). A hybrid resource reservation method for workflows in clouds. [IJGHPC]. *International Journal of Grid and High Performance Computing*, *4*(4), 1–21. doi:10.4018/jghpc.2012100101

Lorenz, M., Rath-Wiggins, L., Runde, W., Messina, A., Sunna, P., & Dimino, G. et al. (2013). Media convergence and cloud technologies: Smart storage, better workflows. In D. Kyriazis, A. Voulodimos, S. Gogouvitis, & T. Varvarigou (Eds.), *Data intensive storage services for cloud environments* (pp. 132–144). Hershey, PA: Business Science Reference. doi:10.4018/978-1-4666-3934-8.ch009

M., S. G., & G., S. K. (2012). An enterprise mashup integration service framework for clouds. *International Journal of Cloud Applications and Computing (IJCAC)*, *2*(2), 31-40. doi:10.4018/ijcac.2012040103

Maharana, S. K., P., G. P., & Bhati, A. (2012). A study of cloud computing for retinal image processing through MATLAB. [IJCAC]. *International Journal of Cloud Applications and Computing*, *2*(2), 59–69. doi:10.4018/ijcac.2012040106

Maharana, S. K., Mali, P. B., & Prabhakar, G., J, S., & Kumar, V. (2011). Cloud computing applied for numerical study of thermal characteristics of SIP. [IJCAC]. *International Journal of Cloud Applications and Computing*, *1*(3), 12–21. doi:10.4018/ijcac.2011070102

Maharana, S. K., Mali, P. B., & Prabhakar, G. J, S., & Kumar, V. (2013). Cloud computing applied for numerical study of thermal characteristics of SIP. In S. Aljawarneh (Ed.), Cloud computing advancements in design, implementation, and technologies (pp. 166-175). Hershey, PA: Information Science Reference. doi: doi:10.4018/978-1-4666-1879-4.ch012

Maharana, S. K., & Prabhakar, P. G., & Bhati, A. (2013). A study of cloud computing for retinal image processing through MATLAB. In I. Association (Ed.), Image processing: Concepts, methodologies, tools, and applications (pp. 101-111). Hershey, PA: Information Science Reference. doi: doi:10.4018/978-1-4666-3994-2.ch006

Mahesh, S., Landry, B. J., Sridhar, T., & Walsh, K. R. (2011). A decision table for the cloud computing decision in small business. [IRMJ]. *Information Resources Management Journal*, *24*(3), 9–25. doi:10.4018/irmj.2011070102

Mahesh, S., Landry, B. J., Sridhar, T., & Walsh, K. R. (2013). A decision table for the cloud computing decision in small business. In M. Khosrow-Pour (Ed.), *Managing information resources and technology: Emerging Applications and theories* (pp. 159–176). Hershey, PA: Information Science Reference. doi:10.4018/978-1-4666-3616-3.ch012

Marquezan, C. C., Metzger, A., Pohl, K., Engen, V., Boniface, M., Phillips, S. C., & Zlatev, Z. (2013). Adaptive future internet applications: Opportunities and challenges for adaptive web services technology. In G. Ortiz, & J. Cubo (Eds.), *Adaptive web services for modular and reusable software development: Tactics and solutions* (pp. 333–353). Hershey, PA: Information Science Reference.

Marshall, P. J. (2012). Cloud computing: Next generation education. In L. Chao (Ed.), *Cloud computing for teaching and learning: Strategies for design and implementation* (pp. 180–185). Hershey, PA: Information Science Reference. doi:10.4018/978-1-4666-0957-0.ch012

Martinez-Ortiz, A. (2012). Open cloud technologies. In L. Vaquero, J. Cáceres, & J. Hierro (Eds.), *Open source cloud computing systems: Practices and paradigms* (pp. 1–17). Hershey, PA: Information Science Reference. doi:10.4018/978-1-4666-0098-0.ch001

Massonet, P., Michot, A., Naqvi, S., Villari, M., & Latanicki, J. (2013). Securing the external interfaces of a federated infrastructure cloud. In I. Management Association (Ed.), IT policy and ethics: Concepts, methodologies, tools, and applications (pp. 1876-1903). Hershey, PA: Information Science Reference. doi: doi:10.4018/978-1-4666-2919-6.ch082

Mavrogeorgi, N., Gogouvitis, S. V., Voulodimos, A., & Alexandrou, V. (2013). SLA management in storage clouds. In D. Kyriazis, A. Voulodimos, S. Gogouvitis, & T. Varvarigou (Eds.), *Data intensive storage services for cloud environments* (pp. 72–93). Hershey, PA: Business Science Reference. doi:10.4018/978-1-4666-3934-8.ch006

Mehta, H. K. (2013). Cloud selection for e-business a parameter based solution. In K. Tarnay, S. Imre, & L. Xu (Eds.), *Research and development in e-business through service-oriented solutions* (pp. 199–207). Hershey, PA: Business Science Reference.

Mehta, H. K., & Gupta, E. (2013). Economy based resource allocation in IaaS cloud. [IJCAC]. *International Journal of Cloud Applications and Computing*, 3(2), 1–11. doi:10.4018/ijcac.2013040101

Miah, S. J. (2012). Cloud-based intelligent DSS design for emergency professionals. In S. Ali, N. Abbadeni, & M. Batouche (Eds.), *Multidisciplinary computational intelligence techniques: Applications in business, engineering, and medicine* (pp. 47–60). Hershey, PA: Information Science Reference. doi:10.4018/978-1-4666-1830-5.ch004

Miah, S. J. (2013). Cloud-based intelligent DSS design for emergency professionals. In I. Association (Ed.), *Data mining: Concepts, methodologies, tools, and applications* (pp. 991–1003). Hershey, PA: Information Science Reference.

Mikkilineni, R. (2012). Architectural resiliency in distributed computing. [IJGHPC]. *International Journal of Grid and High Performance Computing*, 4(4), 37–51. doi:10.4018/jghpc.2012100103

Millham, R. (2012). Software asset re-use: Migration of data-intensive legacy system to the cloud computing paradigm. In H. Yang, & X. Liu (Eds.), *Software reuse in the emerging cloud computing era* (pp. 1–27). Hershey, PA: Information Science Reference. doi:10.4018/978-1-4666-0897-9.ch001

Mircea, M. (2011). Building the agile enterprise with service-oriented architecture, business process management and decision management. [IJEEI]. *International Journal of E-Entrepreneurship and Innovation*, 2(4), 32–48. doi:10.4018/jeei.2011100103

Modares, H., Lloret, J., Moravejosharieh, A., & Salleh, R. (2014). Security in mobile cloud computing. In J. Rodrigues, K. Lin, & J. Lloret (Eds.), *Mobile networks and cloud computing convergence for progressive services and applications* (pp. 79–91). Hershey, PA: Information Science Reference.

Moedjiono, S., & Mas'at, A. (2012). Cloud computing implementation strategy for information dissemination on meteorology, climatology, air quality, and geophysics (MKKuG). [JITR]. *Journal of Information Technology Research*, 5(3), 71–84. doi:10.4018/jitr.2012070104

Moiny, J. (2012). Cloud based social network sites: Under whose control? In A. Dudley, J. Braman, & G. Vincenti (Eds.), *Investigating cyber law and cyber ethics: Issues, impacts and practices* (pp. 147–219). Hershey, PA: Information Science Reference.

Moreno, I. S., & Xu, J. (2011). Energy-efficiency in cloud computing environments: Towards energy savings without performance degradation. [IJCAC]. *International Journal of Cloud Applications and Computing, 1*(1), 17–33. doi:10.4018/ijcac.2011010102

Moreno, I. S., & Xu, J. (2013). Energy-efficiency in cloud computing environments: Towards energy savings without performance degradation. In S. Aljawarneh (Ed.), *Cloud computing advancements in design, implementation, and technologies* (pp. 18–36). Hershey, PA: Information Science Reference.

Muñoz, A., Maña, A., & González, J. (2013). Dynamic security properties monitoring architecture for cloud computing. In D. Rosado, D. Mellado, E. Fernandez-Medina, & M. Piattini (Eds.), *Security engineering for cloud computing: Approaches and tools* (pp. 1–18). Hershey, PA: Information Science Reference.

Mvelase, P., Dlodlo, N., Williams, Q., & Adigun, M. O. (2011). Custom-made cloud enterprise architecture for small medium and micro enterprises. [IJCAC]. *International Journal of Cloud Applications and Computing, 1*(3), 52–63. doi:10.4018/ijcac.2011070105

Mvelase, P., Dlodlo, N., Williams, Q., & Adigun, M. O. (2012). Custom-made cloud enterprise architecture for small medium and micro enterprises. In I. Management Association (Ed.), Grid and cloud computing: Concepts, methodologies, tools and applications (pp. 589-601). Hershey, PA: Information Science Reference. doi: doi:10.4018/978-1-4666-0879-5.ch303

Mvelase, P., Dlodlo, N., Williams, Q., & Adigun, M. O. (2013). Custom-made cloud enterprise architecture for small medium and micro enterprises. In S. Aljawarneh (Ed.), *Cloud computing advancements in design, implementation, and technologies* (pp. 205–217). Hershey, PA: Information Science Reference.

Naeem, M. A., Dobbie, G., & Weber, G. (2014). Big data management in the context of real-time data warehousing. In W. Hu, & N. Kaabouch (Eds.), *Big data management, technologies, and applications* (pp. 150–176). Hershey, PA: Information Science Reference.

Ofosu, W. K., & Saliah-Hassane, H. (2013). Cloud computing in the education environment for developing nations. [IJITN]. *International Journal of Interdisciplinary Telecommunications and Networking, 5*(3), 54–62. doi:10.4018/jitn.2013070106

Oliveros, E., Cucinotta, T., Phillips, S. C., Yang, X., Middleton, S., & Voith, T. (2012). Monitoring and metering in the cloud. In D. Kyriazis, T. Varvarigou, & K. Konstanteli (Eds.), *Achieving real-time in distributed computing: From grids to clouds* (pp. 94–114). Hershey, PA: Information Science Reference.

Orton, I., Alva, A., & Endicott-Popovsky, B. (2013). Legal process and requirements for cloud forensic investigations. In K. Ruan (Ed.), *Cybercrime and cloud forensics: Applications for investigation processes* (pp. 186–229). Hershey, PA: Information Science Reference.

Pakhira, A., & Andras, P. (2013). Leveraging the cloud for large-scale software testing – A case study: Google Chrome on Amazon. In S. Tilley, & T. Parveen (Eds.), *Software testing in the cloud: Perspectives on an emerging discipline* (pp. 252–279). Hershey, PA: Information Science Reference.

Pal, K., & Karakostas, B. (2013). The use of cloud computing in shipping logistics. In D. Graham, I. Manikas, & D. Folinas (Eds.), *E-logistics and e-supply chain management: Applications for evolving business* (pp. 104–124). Hershey, PA: Business Science Reference. doi:10.4018/978-1-4666-3914-0.ch006

Pal, S. (2013). Cloud computing: Security concerns and issues. In A. Bento, & A. Aggarwal (Eds.), *Cloud computing service and deployment models: Layers and management* (pp. 191–207). Hershey, PA: Business Science Reference.

Pal, S. (2013). Storage security and technical challenges of cloud computing. In D. Kyriazis, A. Voulodimos, S. Gogouvitis, & T. Varvarigou (Eds.), *Data intensive storage services for cloud environments* (pp. 225–240). Hershey, PA: Business Science Reference. doi:10.4018/978-1-4666-3934-8.ch014

Palanivel, K., & Kuppuswami, S. (2014). A cloud-oriented reference architecture to digital library systems. In S. Dhamdhere (Ed.), *Cloud computing and virtualization technologies in libraries* (pp. 230–254). Hershey, PA: Information Science Reference.

Paletta, M. (2012). Intelligent clouds: By means of using multi-agent systems environments. In L. Chao (Ed.), *Cloud computing for teaching and learning: Strategies for design and implementation* (pp. 254–279). Hershey, PA: Information Science Reference. doi:10.4018/978-1-4666-0957-0.ch017

Pallot, M., Le Marc, C., Richir, S., Schmidt, C., & Mathieu, J. (2012). Innovation gaming: An immersive experience environment enabling co-creation. In M. Cruz-Cunha (Ed.), *Handbook of research on serious games as educational, business and research tools* (pp. 1–24). Hershey, PA: Information Science Reference. doi:10.4018/978-1-4666-0149-9.ch001

Pankowska, M. (2011). Information technology resources virtualization for sustainable development. [IJAL]. *International Journal of Applied Logistics*, *2*(2), 35–48. doi:10.4018/jal.2011040103

Pankowska, M. (2013). Information technology resources virtualization for sustainable development. In Z. Luo (Ed.), *Technological solutions for modern logistics and supply chain management* (pp. 248–262). Hershey, PA: Business Science Reference. doi:10.4018/978-1-4666-2773-4.ch016

Parappallil, J. J., Zarvic, N., & Thomas, O. (2012). A context and content reflection on business-IT alignment research. [IJITBAG]. *International Journal of IT/Business Alignment and Governance*, *3*(2), 21–37. doi:10.4018/jitbag.2012070102

Parashar, V., Vishwakarma, M. L., & Parashar, R. (2014). A new framework for building academic library through cloud computing. In S. Dhamdhere (Ed.), *Cloud computing and virtualization technologies in libraries* (pp. 107–123). Hershey, PA: Information Science Reference.

Pendyala, V. S., & Holliday, J. (2012). Cloud as a computer. In X. Liu, & Y. Li (Eds.), *Advanced design approaches to emerging software systems: Principles, methodologies and tools* (pp. 241–249). Hershey, PA: Information Science Reference.

Petruch, K., Tamm, G., & Stantchev, V. (2012). Deriving in-depth knowledge from IT-performance data simulations. [IJKSR]. *International Journal of Knowledge Society Research*, *3*(2), 13–29. doi:10.4018/jksr.2012040102

Philipson, G. (2011). A framework for green computing. [IJGC]. *International Journal of Green Computing*, *2*(1), 12–26. doi:10.4018/jgc.2011010102

Philipson, G. (2013). A framework for green computing. In K. Ganesh, & S. Anbuudayasankar (Eds.), *International and interdisciplinary studies in green computing* (pp. 12–26). Hershey, PA: Information Science Reference.

Phythian, M. (2013). The 'cloud' of unknowing – What a government cloud may and may not offer: A practitioner perspective. [IJT]. *International Journal of Technoethics*, *4*(1), 1–10. doi:10.4018/jte.2013010101

Pym, D., & Sadler, M. (2012). Information stewardship in cloud computing. In I. Management Association (Ed.), Grid and cloud computing: Concepts, methodologies, tools and applications (pp. 185-202). Hershey, PA: Information Science Reference. doi: doi:10.4018/978-1-4666-0879-5.ch109

Pym, D., & Sadler, M. (2012). Information stewardship in cloud computing. In S. Galup (Ed.), *Technological applications and advancements in service science, management, and engineering* (pp. 52–69). Hershey, PA: Business Science Reference. doi:10.4018/978-1-4666-1583-0.ch004

Qiu, J., Ekanayake, J., Gunarathne, T., Choi, J. Y., Bae, S., & Ruan, Y. … Tang, H. (2013). Data intensive computing for bioinformatics. In I. Management Association (Ed.), Bioinformatics: Concepts, methodologies, tools, and applications (pp. 287-321). Hershey, PA: Medical Information Science Reference. doi: doi:10.4018/978-1-4666-3604-0.ch016

Rabaey, M. (2012). A public economics approach to enabling enterprise architecture with the government cloud in Belgium. In P. Saha (Ed.), *Enterprise architecture for connected e-government: Practices and innovations* (pp. 467–493). Hershey, PA: Information Science Reference. doi:10.4018/978-1-4666-1824-4.ch020

Rabaey, M. (2013). A complex adaptive system thinking approach of government e-procurement in a cloud computing environment. In P. Ordóñez de Pablos, J. Lovelle, J. Gayo, & R. Tennyson (Eds.), *E-procurement management for successful electronic government systems* (pp. 193–219). Hershey, PA: Information Science Reference.

Rabaey, M. (2013). Holistic investment framework for cloud computing: A management-philosophical approach based on complex adaptive systems. In A. Bento, & A. Aggarwal (Eds.), *Cloud computing service and deployment models: Layers and management* (pp. 94–122). Hershey, PA: Business Science Reference.

Rak, M., Ficco, M., Luna, J., Ghani, H., Suri, N., Panica, S., & Petcu, D. (2012). Security issues in cloud federations. In M. Villari, I. Brandic, & F. Tusa (Eds.), *Achieving federated and self-manageable cloud infrastructures: Theory and practice* (pp. 176–194). Hershey, PA: Business Science Reference. doi:10.4018/978-1-4666-1631-8.ch010

Ramanathan, R. (2013). Extending service-driven architectural approaches to the cloud. In R. Ramanathan, & K. Raja (Eds.), *Service-driven approaches to architecture and enterprise integration* (pp. 334–359). Hershey, PA: Information Science Reference. doi:10.4018/978-1-4666-4193-8.ch013

Ramírez, M., Gutiérrez, A., Monguet, J. M., & Muñoz, C. (2012). An internet cost model, assignment of costs based on actual network use. [IJWP]. *International Journal of Web Portals*, 4(4), 19–34. doi:10.4018/jwp.2012100102

Rashid, A., Wang, W. Y., & Tan, F. B. (2013). Value co-creation in cloud services. In A. Lin, J. Foster, & P. Scifleet (Eds.), *Consumer information systems and relationship management: Design, implementation, and use* (pp. 74–91). Hershey, PA: Business Science Reference. doi:10.4018/978-1-4666-4082-5.ch005

Ratten, V. (2012). Cloud computing services: Theoretical foundations of ethical and entrepreneurial adoption behaviour. [IJCAC]. *International Journal of Cloud Applications and Computing*, 2(2), 48–58. doi:10.4018/ijcac.2012040105

Ratten, V. (2013). Exploring behaviors and perceptions affecting the adoption of cloud computing. [IJIDE]. *International Journal of Innovation in the Digital Economy*, 4(3), 51–68. doi:10.4018/jide.2013070104

Ravi, V. (2012). Cloud computing paradigm for indian education sector. [IJCAC]. *International Journal of Cloud Applications and Computing*, 2(2), 41–47. doi:10.4018/ijcac.2012040104

Rawat, A., Kapoor, P., & Sushil, R. (2014). Application of cloud computing in library information service sector. In S. Dhamdhere (Ed.), *Cloud computing and virtualization technologies in libraries* (pp. 77–89). Hershey, PA: Information Science Reference.

Reich, C., Hübner, S., & Kuijs, H. (2012). Cloud computing for on-demand virtual desktops and labs. In L. Chao (Ed.), *Cloud computing for teaching and learning: strategies for design and implementation* (pp. 111–125). Hershey, PA: Information Science Reference. doi:10.4018/978-1-4666-0957-0.ch008

Rice, R. W. (2013). Testing in the cloud: Balancing the value and risks of cloud computing. In S. Tilley, & T. Parveen (Eds.), *Software testing in the cloud: Perspectives on an emerging discipline* (pp. 404–416). Hershey, PA: Information Science Reference.

Ruan, K. (2013). Designing a forensic-enabling cloud ecosystem. In K. Ruan (Ed.), *Cybercrime and cloud forensics: Applications for investigation processes* (pp. 331–344). Hershey, PA: Information Science Reference.

Sabetzadeh, F., & Tsui, E. (2011). Delivering knowledge services in the cloud. [IJKSS]. *International Journal of Knowledge and Systems Science*, 2(4), 14–20. doi:10.4018/jkss.2011100102

Sabetzadeh, F., & Tsui, E. (2013). Delivering knowledge services in the cloud. In G. Yang (Ed.), *Multidisciplinary studies in knowledge and systems science* (pp. 247–254). Hershey, PA: Information Science Reference.

Saedi, A., & Iahad, N. A. (2013). Future research on cloud computing adoption by small and medium-sized enterprises: A critical analysis of relevant theories. [IJAN-TTI]. *International Journal of Actor-Network Theory and Technological Innovation, 5*(2), 1–16. doi:10.4018/jantti.2013040101

Saha, D., & Sridhar, V. (2011). Emerging areas of research in business data communications. [IJBDCN]. *International Journal of Business Data Communications and Networking, 7*(4), 52–59. doi: doi:10.4018/ijbdcn.2011100104

Saha, D., & Sridhar, V. (2013). Platform on platform (PoP) model for meta-networking: A new paradigm for networks of the future. [IJBDCN]. *International Journal of Business Data Communications and Networking, 9*(1), 1–10. doi:10.4018/jbdcn.2013010101

Sahlin, J. P. (2013). Cloud computing: Past, present, and future. In X. Yang, & L. Liu (Eds.), *Principles, methodologies, and service-oriented approaches for cloud computing* (pp. 19–50). Hershey, PA: Business Science Reference. doi:10.4018/978-1-4666-2854-0.ch002

Salama, M., & Shawish, A. (2012). Libraries: From the classical to cloud-based era. [IJDLS]. *International Journal of Digital Library Systems, 3*(3), 14–32. doi:10.4018/jdls.2012070102

Sánchez, C. M., Molina, D., Vozmediano, R. M., Montero, R. S., & Llorente, I. M. (2012). On the use of the hybrid cloud computing paradigm. In M. Villari, I. Brandic, & F. Tusa (Eds.), *Achieving federated and self-manageable cloud infrastructures: Theory and practice* (pp. 196–218). Hershey, PA: Business Science Reference. doi:10.4018/978-1-4666-1631-8.ch011

Sasikala, P. (2011). Architectural strategies for green cloud computing: Environments, infrastructure and resources. [IJCAC]. *International Journal of Cloud Applications and Computing, 1*(4), 1–24. doi:10.4018/ijcac.2011100101

Sasikala, P. (2011). Cloud computing in higher education: Opportunities and issues. [IJCAC]. *International Journal of Cloud Applications and Computing, 1*(2), 1–13. doi:10.4018/ijcac.2011040101

Sasikala, P. (2011). Cloud computing towards technological convergence. [IJCAC]. *International Journal of Cloud Applications and Computing, 1*(4), 44–59. doi:10.4018/ijcac.2011100104

Sasikala, P. (2012). Cloud computing and e-governance: Advances, opportunities and challenges. [IJCAC]. *International Journal of Cloud Applications and Computing, 2*(4), 32–52. doi:10.4018/ijcac.2012100103

Sasikala, P. (2012). Cloud computing in higher education: Opportunities and issues. In I. Management Association (Ed.), Grid and cloud computing: Concepts, methodologies, tools and applications (pp. 1672-1685). Hershey, PA: Information Science Reference. doi: doi:10.4018/978-1-4666-0879-5.ch709

Sasikala, P. (2012). Cloud computing towards technological convergence. In I. Management Association (Ed.), Grid and cloud computing: Concepts, methodologies, tools and applications (pp. 1576-1592). Hershey, PA: Information Science Reference. doi: doi:10.4018/978-1-4666-0879-5.ch703

Sasikala, P. (2013). Architectural strategies for green cloud computing: Environments, infrastructure and resources. In S. Aljawarneh (Ed.), *Cloud computing advancements in design, implementation, and technologies* (pp. 218–242). Hershey, PA: Information Science Reference.

Sasikala, P. (2013). Cloud computing in higher education: Opportunities and issues. In S. Aljawarneh (Ed.), *Cloud computing advancements in design, implementation, and technologies* (pp. 83–96). Hershey, PA: Information Science Reference.

Sasikala, P. (2013). Cloud computing towards technological convergence. In S. Aljawarneh (Ed.), *Cloud computing advancements in design, implementation, and technologies* (pp. 263–279). Hershey, PA: Information Science Reference.

Sasikala, P. (2013). New media cloud computing: Opportunities and challenges. [IJCAC]. *International Journal of Cloud Applications and Computing, 3*(2), 61–72. doi:10.4018/ijcac.2013040106

Schrödl, H., & Wind, S. (2013). Requirements engineering for cloud application development. In A. Bento, & A. Aggarwal (Eds.), *Cloud computing service and deployment models: Layers and management* (pp. 137–150). Hershey, PA: Business Science Reference.

Sclater, N. (2012). Legal and contractual issues of cloud computing for educational institutions. In L. Chao (Ed.), *Cloud computing for teaching and learning: Strategies for design and implementation* (pp. 186–199). Hershey, PA: Information Science Reference. doi:10.4018/978-1-4666-0957-0.ch013

Sen, J. (2014). Security and privacy issues in cloud computing. In A. Ruiz-Martinez, R. Marin-Lopez, & F. Pereniguez-Garcia (Eds.), *Architectures and protocols for secure information technology infrastructures* (pp. 1–45). Hershey, PA: Information Science Reference.

Shah, B. (2013). Cloud environment controls assessment framework. In I. Management Association (Ed.), IT policy and ethics: Concepts, methodologies, tools, and applications (pp. 1822-1847). Hershey, PA: Information Science Reference. doi: doi:10.4018/978-1-4666-2919-6.ch080

Shah, B. (2013). Cloud environment controls assessment framework. In S. Tilley, & T. Parveen (Eds.), *Software testing in the cloud: Perspectives on an emerging discipline* (pp. 28–53). Hershey, PA: Information Science Reference.

Shang, X., Zhang, R., & Chen, Y. (2012). Internet of things (IoT) service architecture and its application in e-commerce. [JECO]. *Journal of Electronic Commerce in Organizations, 10*(3), 44–55. doi:10.4018/jeco.2012070104

Shankararaman, V., & Kit, L. E. (2013). Integrating the cloud scenarios and solutions. In A. Bento, & A. Aggarwal (Eds.), *Cloud computing service and deployment models: Layers and management* (pp. 173–189). Hershey, PA: Business Science Reference.

Sharma, A., & Maurer, F. (2013). A roadmap for software engineering for the cloud: Results of a systematic review. In X. Wang, N. Ali, I. Ramos, & R. Vidgen (Eds.), *Agile and lean service-oriented development: Foundations, theory, and practice* (pp. 48–63). Hershey, PA: Information Science Reference.

Sharma, A., & Maurer, F. (2014). A roadmap for software engineering for the cloud: Results of a systematic review. In I. Management Association (Ed.), Software design and development: Concepts, methodologies, tools, and applications (pp. 1-16). Hershey, PA: Information Science Reference. doi: doi:10.4018/978-1-4666-4301-7.ch001

Sharma, S. C., & Bagoria, H. (2014). Libraries and cloud computing models: A changing paradigm. In S. Dhamdhere (Ed.), *Cloud computing and virtualization technologies in libraries* (pp. 124–149). Hershey, PA: Information Science Reference.

Shawish, A., & Salama, M. (2013). Cloud computing in academia, governments, and industry. In X. Yang, & L. Liu (Eds.), *Principles, methodologies, and service-oriented approaches for cloud computing* (pp. 71–114). Hershey, PA: Business Science Reference. doi:10.4018/978-1-4666-2854-0.ch004

Shebanow, A., Perez, R., & Howard, C. (2012). The effect of firewall testing types on cloud security policies. [IJSITA]. *International Journal of Strategic Information Technology and Applications, 3*(3), 60–68. doi:10.4018/jsita.2012070105

Sheikhalishahi, M., Devare, M., Grandinetti, L., & Incutti, M. C. (2012). A complementary approach to grid and cloud distributed computing paradigms. In I. Management Association (Ed.), Grid and cloud computing: Concepts, methodologies, tools and applications (pp. 1929-1942). Hershey, PA: Information Science Reference. doi:doi:10.4018/978-1-4666-0879-5.ch811

Sheikhalishahi, M., Devare, M., Grandinetti, L., & Incutti, M. C. (2012). A complementary approach to grid and cloud distributed computing paradigms. In N. Preve (Ed.), *Computational and data grids: Principles, applications and design* (pp. 31–44). Hershey, PA: Information Science Reference. doi:10.4018/978-1-4666-0879-5.ch811

Shen, Y., Li, Y., Wu, L., Liu, S., & Wen, Q. (2014). Cloud computing overview. In Y. Shen, Y. Li, L. Wu, S. Liu, & Q. Wen (Eds.), *Enabling the new era of cloud computing: Data security, transfer, and management* (pp. 1–24). Hershey, PA: Information Science Reference.

Shen, Y., Li, Y., Wu, L., Liu, S., & Wen, Q. (2014). Main components of cloud computing. In Y. Shen, Y. Li, L. Wu, S. Liu, & Q. Wen (Eds.), *Enabling the new era of cloud computing: Data security, transfer, and management* (pp. 25–50). Hershey, PA: Information Science Reference.

Shen, Y., Yang, J., & Keskin, T. (2014). Impact of cultural differences on the cloud computing ecosystems in the USA and China. In Y. Shen, Y. Li, L. Wu, S. Liu, & Q. Wen (Eds.), *Enabling the new era of cloud computing: Data security, transfer, and management* (pp. 269–283). Hershey, PA: Information Science Reference.

Shetty, S., & Rawat, D. B. (2013). Cloud computing based cognitive radio networking. In N. Meghanathan, & Y. Reddy (Eds.), *Cognitive radio technology applications for wireless and mobile ad hoc networks* (pp. 153–164). Hershey, PA: Information Science Reference. doi:10.4018/978-1-4666-4221-8.ch008

Shi, Z., & Beard, C. (2014). QoS in the mobile cloud computing environment. In J. Rodrigues, K. Lin, & J. Lloret (Eds.), *Mobile networks and cloud computing convergence for progressive services and applications* (pp. 200–217). Hershey, PA: Information Science Reference.

Shuster, L. (2013). Enterprise integration: Challenges and solution architecture. In R. Ramanathan, & K. Raja (Eds.), *Service-driven approaches to architecture and enterprise integration* (pp. 43–66). Hershey, PA: Information Science Reference.

Siahos, Y., Papanagiotou, I., Georgopoulos, A., Tsamis, F., & Papaioannou, I. (2012). An architecture paradigm for providing cloud services in school labs based on open source software to enhance ICT in education. [IJCEE]. *International Journal of Cyber Ethics in Education, 2*(1), 44–57. doi:10.4018/ijcee.2012010105

Simon, E., & Estublier, J. (2013). Model driven integration of heterogeneous software artifacts in service oriented computing. In A. Ionita, M. Litoiu, & G. Lewis (Eds.), *Migrating legacy applications: Challenges in service oriented architecture and cloud computing environments* (pp. 332–360). Hershey, PA: Information Science Reference.

Singh, J., & Kumar, V. (2013). Compliance and regulatory standards for cloud computing. In R. Khurana, & R. Aggarwal (Eds.), *Interdisciplinary perspectives on business convergence, computing, and legality* (pp. 54–64). Hershey, PA: Business Science Reference. doi:10.4018/978-1-4666-4209-6.ch006

Singh, V. V. (2012). Software development using service syndication based on API handshake approach between cloud-based and SOA-based reusable services. In H. Yang, & X. Liu (Eds.), *Software reuse in the emerging cloud computing era* (pp. 136–157). Hershey, PA: Information Science Reference. doi:10.4018/978-1-4666-0897-9.ch006

Smeitink, M., & Spruit, M. (2013). Maturity for sustainability in IT: Introducing the MITS. [IJITSA]. *International Journal of Information Technologies and Systems Approach, 6*(1), 39–56. doi:10.4018/jitsa.2013010103

Smith, P. A., & Cockburn, T. (2013). Socio-digital technologies. In *Dynamic leadership models for global business: Enhancing digitally connected environments* (pp. 142–168). Hershey, PA: Business Science Reference. doi:10.4018/978-1-4666-2836-6.ch006

Sneed, H. M. (2013). Testing web services in the cloud. In S. Tilley, & T. Parveen (Eds.), *Software testing in the cloud: Perspectives on an emerging discipline* (pp. 136–173). Hershey, PA: Information Science Reference.

Solomon, B., Ionescu, D., Gadea, C., & Litoiu, M. (2013). Geographically distributed cloud-based collaborative application. In A. Ionita, M. Litoiu, & G. Lewis (Eds.), *Migrating legacy applications: Challenges in service oriented architecture and cloud computing environments* (pp. 248–274). Hershey, PA: Information Science Reference.

Song, W., & Xiao, Z. (2013). An infrastructure-as-a-service cloud: On-demand resource provisioning. In X. Yang, & L. Liu (Eds.), *Principles, methodologies, and service-oriented approaches for cloud computing* (pp. 302–324). Hershey, PA: Business Science Reference. doi:10.4018/978-1-4666-2854-0.ch013

Sood, S. K. (2013). A value based dynamic resource provisioning model in cloud. [IJCAC]. *International Journal of Cloud Applications and Computing, 3*(1), 1–12. doi:10.4018/ijcac.2013010101

Sotiriadis, S., Bessis, N., & Antonopoulos, N. (2012). Exploring inter-cloud load balancing by utilizing historical service submission records. [IJDST]. *International Journal of Distributed Systems and Technologies, 3*(3), 72–81. doi:10.4018/jdst.2012070106

Soyata, T., Ba, H., Heinzelman, W., Kwon, M., & Shi, J. (2014). Accelerating mobile-cloud computing: A survey. In H. Mouftah, & B. Kantarci (Eds.), *Communication infrastructures for cloud computing* (pp. 175–197). Hershey, PA: Information Science Reference.

Spyridopoulos, T., & Katos, V. (2011). Requirements for a forensically ready cloud storage service. [IJDCF]. *International Journal of Digital Crime and Forensics, 3*(3), 19–36. doi:10.4018/jdcf.2011070102

Spyridopoulos, T., & Katos, V. (2013). Data recovery strategies for cloud environments. In K. Ruan (Ed.), *Cybercrime and cloud forensics: Applications for investigation processes* (pp. 251–265). Hershey, PA: Information Science Reference.

Srinivasa, K. G., S., H. R., H., M. K., & Venkatesh, N. (2012). MeghaOS: A framework for scalable, interoperable cloud based operating system. [IJCAC]. *International Journal of Cloud Applications and Computing, 2*(1), 53–70. doi:10.4018/ijcac.2012010104

Stantchev, V., & Stantcheva, L. (2012). Extending traditional IT-governance knowledge towards SOA and cloud governance. [IJKSR]. *International Journal of Knowledge Society Research, 3*(2), 30–43. doi:10.4018/jksr.2012040103

Stantchev, V., & Tamm, G. (2012). Reducing information asymmetry in cloud marketplaces. [IJHCITP]. *International Journal of Human Capital and Information Technology Professionals, 3*(4), 1–10. doi:10.4018/jhcitp.2012100101

Steinbuß, S., & Weißenberg, N. (2013). Service design and process design for the logistics mall cloud. In X. Yang, & L. Liu (Eds.), *Principles, methodologies, and service-oriented approaches for cloud computing* (pp. 186–206). Hershey, PA: Business Science Reference. doi:10.4018/978-1-4666-2854-0.ch008

Stender, J., Berlin, M., & Reinefeld, A. (2013). XtreemFS: A file system for the cloud. In D. Kyriazis, A. Voulodimos, S. Gogouvitis, & T. Varvarigou (Eds.), *Data intensive storage services for cloud environments* (pp. 267–285). Hershey, PA: Business Science Reference. doi:10.4018/978-1-4666-3934-8.ch016

Sticklen, D. J., & Issa, T. (2011). An initial examination of free and proprietary software-selection in organizations. [IJWP]. *International Journal of Web Portals, 3*(4), 27–43. doi:10.4018/jwp.2011100103

Sun, Y., White, J., Gray, J., & Gokhale, A. (2012). Model-driven automated error recovery in cloud computing. In I. Management Association (Ed.), Grid and cloud computing: Concepts, methodologies, tools and applications (pp. 680-700). Hershey, PA: Information Science Reference. doi: doi:10.4018/978-1-4666-0879-5.ch308

Sun, Z., Yang, Y., Zhou, Y., & Cruickshank, H. (2014). Agent-based resource management for mobile cloud. In J. Rodrigues, K. Lin, & J. Lloret (Eds.), *Mobile networks and cloud computing convergence for progressive services and applications* (pp. 118–134). Hershey, PA: Information Science Reference.

Sutherland, S. (2013). Convergence of interoperability of cloud computing, service oriented architecture and enterprise architecture. [IJEEI]. *International Journal of E-Entrepreneurship and Innovation, 4*(1), 43–51. doi:10.4018/jeei.2013010104

Takabi, H., & Joshi, J. B. (2013). Policy management in cloud: Challenges and approaches. In D. Rosado, D. Mellado, E. Fernandez-Medina, & M. Piattini (Eds.), *Security engineering for cloud computing: Approaches and tools* (pp. 191–211). Hershey, PA: Information Science Reference.

Takabi, H., & Joshi, J. B. (2013). Policy management in cloud: Challenges and approaches. In I. Management Association (Ed.), IT policy and ethics: Concepts, methodologies, tools, and applications (pp. 814-834). Hershey, PA: Information Science Reference. doi: doi:10.4018/978-1-4666-2919-6.ch037

Takabi, H., Joshi, J. B., & Ahn, G. (2013). Security and privacy in cloud computing: Towards a comprehensive framework. In X. Yang, & L. Liu (Eds.), *Principles, methodologies, and service-oriented approaches for cloud computing* (pp. 164–184). Hershey, PA: Business Science Reference. doi:10.4018/978-1-4666-2854-0.ch007

Takabi, H., Zargar, S. T., & Joshi, J. B. (2014). Mobile cloud computing and its security and privacy challenges. In D. Rawat, B. Bista, & G. Yan (Eds.), *Security, privacy, trust, and resource management in mobile and wireless communications* (pp. 384–407). Hershey, PA: Information Science Reference.

Teixeira, C., Pinto, J. S., Ferreira, F., Oliveira, A., Teixeira, A., & Pereira, C. (2013). Cloud computing enhanced service development architecture for the living usability lab. In R. Martinho, R. Rijo, M. Cruz-Cunha, & J. Varajão (Eds.), *Information systems and technologies for enhancing health and social care* (pp. 33–53). Hershey, PA: Medical Information Science Reference. doi:10.4018/978-1-4666-3667-5.ch003

Thimm, H. (2012). Cloud-based collaborative decision making: Design considerations and architecture of the GRUPO-MOD system. [IJDSST]. *International Journal of Decision Support System Technology*, 4(4), 39–59. doi:10.4018/jdsst.2012100103

Thomas, P. (2012). Harnessing the potential of cloud computing to transform higher education. In L. Chao (Ed.), *Cloud computing for teaching and learning: Strategies for design and implementation* (pp. 147–158). Hershey, PA: Information Science Reference. doi:10.4018/978-1-4666-0957-0.ch010

T.M. K., & Gopalakrishnan, S. (2014). Green economic and secure libraries on cloud. In S. Dhamdhere (Ed.), Cloud computing and virtualization technologies in libraries (pp. 297-315). Hershey, PA: Information Science Reference. doi: doi:10.4018/978-1-4666-4631-5.ch017

Toka, A., Aivazidou, E., Antoniou, A., & Arvanitopoulos-Darginis, K. (2013). Cloud computing in supply chain management: An overview. In D. Graham, I. Manikas, & D. Folinas (Eds.), *E-logistics and e-supply chain management: Applications for evolving business* (pp. 218–231). Hershey, PA: Business Science Reference. doi:10.4018/978-1-4666-3914-0.ch012

Torrealba, S. M., Morales P., M., Campos, J. M., & Meza S., M. (2013). A software tool to support risks analysis about what should or should not go to the cloud. In D. Rosado, D. Mellado, E. Fernandez-Medina, & M. Piattini (Eds.) Security engineering for cloud computing: Approaches and tools (pp. 72-96). Hershey, PA: Information Science Reference. doi: doi:10.4018/978-1-4666-2125-1.ch005

Trivedi, M., & Suthar, V. (2013). Cloud computing: A feasible platform for ICT enabled health science libraries in India. [IJUDH]. *International Journal of User-Driven Healthcare*, 3(2), 69–77. doi:10.4018/ijudh.2013040108

Truong, H., Pham, T., Thoai, N., & Dustdar, S. (2012). Cloud computing for education and research in developing countries. In L. Chao (Ed.), *Cloud computing for teaching and learning: Strategies for design and implementation* (pp. 64–80). Hershey, PA: Information Science Reference. doi:10.4018/978-1-4666-0957-0.ch005

Tsirmpas, C., Giokas, K., Iliopoulou, D., & Koutsouris, D. (2012). Magnetic resonance imaging and magnetic resonance spectroscopy cloud computing framework. [IJRQEH]. *International Journal of Reliable and Quality E-Healthcare*, 1(4), 1–12. doi:10.4018/ijrqeh.2012100101

Turner, H., White, J., Reed, J., Galindo, J., Porter, A., Marathe, M., et al. (2013). Building a cloud-based mobile application testbed. In I. Management Association (Ed.), IT policy and ethics: Concepts, methodologies, tools, and applications (pp. 879-899). Hershey, PA: Information Science Reference. doi: doi:10.4018/978-1-4666-2919-6.ch040

Turner, H., White, J., Reed, J., Galindo, J., Porter, A., & Marathe, M. et al. (2013). Building a cloud-based mobile application testbed. In S. Tilley, & T. Parveen (Eds.), *Software testing in the cloud: Perspectives on an emerging discipline* (pp. 382–403). Hershey, PA: Information Science Reference.

Tusa, F., Paone, M., & Villari, M. (2012). CLEVER: A cloud middleware beyond the federation. In M. Villari, I. Brandic, & F. Tusa (Eds.), *Achieving federated and self-manageable cloud infrastructures: Theory and practice* (pp. 219–241). Hershey, PA: Business Science Reference. doi:10.4018/978-1-4666-1631-8.ch012

Udoh, E. (2012). Technology acceptance model applied to the adoption of grid and cloud technology. [IJGHPC]. *International Journal of Grid and High Performance Computing, 4*(1), 1–20. doi:10.4018/jghpc.2012010101

Vannoy, S. A. (2011). A structured content analytic assessment of business services advertisements in the cloud-based web services marketplace. [IJDTIS]. *International Journal of Dependable and Trustworthy Information Systems, 2*(1), 18–49. doi:10.4018/jdtis.2011010102

Vaquero, L. M., Cáceres, J., & Morán, D. (2011). The challenge of service level scalability for the cloud. [IJCAC]. *International Journal of Cloud Applications and Computing, 1*(1), 34–44. doi:10.4018/ijcac.2011010103

Vaquero, L. M., Cáceres, J., & Morán, D. (2013). The challenge of service level scalability for the cloud. In S. Aljawarneh (Ed.), *Cloud computing advancements in design, implementation, and technologies* (pp. 37–48). Hershey, PA: Information Science Reference.

Venkatraman, R., Venkatraman, S., & Asaithambi, S. P. (2013). A practical cloud services implementation framework for e-businesses. In K. Tarnay, S. Imre, & L. Xu (Eds.), *Research and development in e-business through service-oriented solutions* (pp. 167–198). Hershey, PA: Business Science Reference.

Venkatraman, S. (2013). Software engineering research gaps in the cloud. [JITR]. *Journal of Information Technology Research, 6*(1), 1–19. doi: doi:10.4018/jitr.2013010101

Vijaykumar, S., Rajkarthick, K. S., & Priya, J. (2012). Innovative business opportunities and smart business management techniques from green cloud TPS. [IJABIM]. *International Journal of Asian Business and Information Management, 3*(4), 62–72. doi:10.4018/jabim.2012100107

Wang, C., Lam, K. T., & Kui Ma, R. K. (2012). A computation migration approach to elasticity of cloud computing. In J. Abawajy, M. Pathan, M. Rahman, A. Pathan, & M. Deris (Eds.), *Network and traffic engineering in emerging distributed computing applications* (pp. 145–178). Hershey, PA: Information Science Reference. doi:10.4018/978-1-4666-1888-6.ch007

Wang, D., & Wu, J. (2014). Carrier-grade distributed cloud computing: Demands, challenges, designs, and future perspectives. In H. Mouftah, & B. Kantarci (Eds.), *Communication infrastructures for cloud computing* (pp. 264–281). Hershey, PA: Information Science Reference.

Wang, H., & Philips, D. (2012). Implement virtual programming lab with cloud computing for web-based distance education. In L. Chao (Ed.), *Cloud computing for teaching and learning: Strategies for design and implementation* (pp. 95–110). Hershey, PA: Information Science Reference. doi:10.4018/978-1-4666-0957-0.ch007

Warneke, D. (2013). Ad-hoc parallel data processing on pay-as-you-go clouds with nephele. In A. Loo (Ed.), *Distributed computing innovations for business, engineering, and science* (pp. 191–218). Hershey, PA: Information Science Reference.

Wei, Y., & Blake, M. B. (2013). Adaptive web services monitoring in cloud environments. [IJWP]. *International Journal of Web Portals, 5*(1), 15–27. doi:10.4018/jwp.2013010102

White, S. C., Sedigh, S., & Hurson, A. R. (2013). Security concepts for cloud computing. In X. Yang, & L. Liu (Eds.), *Principles, methodologies, and service-oriented approaches for cloud computing* (pp. 116–142). Hershey, PA: Business Science Reference. doi:10.4018/978-1-4666-2854-0.ch005

Williams, A. J. (2013). The role of emerging technologies in developing and sustaining diverse suppliers in competitive markets. In I. Association (Ed.), *Enterprise resource planning: Concepts, methodologies, tools, and applications* (pp. 1550–1560). Hershey, PA: Business Science Reference. doi:10.4018/978-1-4666-4153-2.ch082

Williams, A. J. (2013). The role of emerging technologies in developing and sustaining diverse suppliers in competitive markets. In J. Lewis, A. Green, & D. Surry (Eds.), *Technology as a tool for diversity leadership: Implementation and future implications* (pp. 95–105). Hershey, PA: Information Science Reference. doi:10.4018/978-1-4666-4153-2.ch082

Wilson, L., Goh, T. T., & Wang, W. Y. (2012). Big data management challenges in a meteorological organisation. [IJEA]. *International Journal of E-Adoption, 4*(2), 1–14. doi:10.4018/jea.2012040101

Wu, R., Ahn, G., & Hu, H. (2012). Towards HIPAA-compliant healthcare systems in cloud computing. [IJC-MAM]. *International Journal of Computational Models and Algorithms in Medicine, 3*(2), 1–22. doi:10.4018/jcmam.2012040101

Xiao, J., Wang, M., Wang, L., & Zhu, X. (2013). Design and implementation of C-iLearning: A cloud-based intelligent learning system. [IJDET]. *International Journal of Distance Education Technologies, 11*(3), 79–97. doi:10.4018/jdet.2013070106

Xing, R., Wang, Z., & Peterson, R. L. (2011). Redefining the information technology in the 21st century. [IJSITA]. *International Journal of Strategic Information Technology and Applications, 2*(1), 1–10. doi:10.4018/jsita.2011010101

Xu, L., Huang, D., Tsai, W., & Atkinson, R. K. (2012). V-lab: A mobile, cloud-based virtual laboratory platform for hands-on networking courses. [IJCBPL]. *International Journal of Cyber Behavior, Psychology and Learning, 2*(3), 73–85. doi:10.4018/ijcbpl.2012070106

Xu, Y., & Mao, S. (2014). Mobile cloud media: State of the art and outlook. In J. Rodrigues, K. Lin, & J. Lloret (Eds.), *Mobile networks and cloud computing convergence for progressive services and applications* (pp. 18–38). Hershey, PA: Information Science Reference.

Xu, Z., Yan, B., & Zou, Y. (2013). Beyond hadoop: Recent directions in data computing for internet services. In S. Aljawarneh (Ed.), *Cloud computing advancements in design, implementation, and technologies* (pp. 49–66). Hershey, PA: Information Science Reference.

Yan, Z. (2014). Trust management in mobile cloud computing. In *Trust management in mobile environments: Autonomic and usable models* (pp. 54–93). Hershey, PA: Information Science Reference.

Yang, D. X. (2012). QoS-oriented service computing: Bringing SOA into cloud environment. In X. Liu, & Y. Li (Eds.), *Advanced design approaches to emerging software systems: Principles, methodologies and tools* (pp. 274–296). Hershey, PA: Information Science Reference. doi:10.4018/978-1-4666-0879-5.ch706

Yang, H., Huff, S. L., & Tate, M. (2013). Managing the cloud for information systems agility. In A. Bento, & A. Aggarwal (Eds.), *Cloud computing service and deployment models: Layers and management* (pp. 70–93). Hershey, PA: Business Science Reference.

Yang, M., Kuo, C., & Yeh, Y. (2011). Dynamic rightsizing with quality-controlled algorithms in virtualization environments. [IJGHPC]. *International Journal of Grid and High Performance Computing, 3*(2), 29–43. doi:10.4018/jghpc.2011040103

Yang, X. (2012). QoS-oriented service computing: Bringing SOA into cloud environment. In I. Management Association (Ed.), Grid and cloud computing: Concepts, methodologies, tools and applications (pp. 1621-1643). Hershey, PA: Information Science Reference. doi: doi:10.4018/978-1-4666-0879-5.ch706

Yang, Y., Chen, J., & Hu, H. (2012). The convergence between cloud computing and cable TV. [IJTD]. *International Journal of Technology Diffusion, 3*(2), 1–11. doi:10.4018/jtd.2012040101

Yassein, M. O., Khamayseh, Y. M., & Hatamleh, A. M. (2013). Intelligent randomize round robin for cloud computing. [IJCAC]. *International Journal of Cloud Applications and Computing, 3*(1), 27–33. doi:10.4018/ijcac.2013010103

Yau, S. S., An, H. G., & Buduru, A. B. (2012). An approach to data confidentiality protection in cloud environments. [IJWSR]. *International Journal of Web Services Research, 9*(3), 67–83. doi:10.4018/jwsr.2012070104

Yu, W. D., Adiga, A. S., Rao, S., & Panakkel, M. J. (2012). A SOA based system development methodology for cloud computing environment: Using uhealthcare as practice. [IJEHMC]. *International Journal of E-Health and Medical Communications, 3*(4), 42–63. doi:10.4018/jehmc.2012100104

Yu, W. D., & Bhagwat, R. (2011). Modeling emergency and telemedicine heath support system: A service oriented architecture approach using cloud computing. [IJEHMC]. *International Journal of E-Health and Medical Communications, 2*(3), 63–88. doi:10.4018/jehmc.2011070104

Yu, W. D., & Bhagwat, R. (2013). Modeling emergency and telemedicine health support system: A service oriented architecture approach using cloud computing. In J. Rodrigues (Ed.), *Digital advances in medicine, e-health, and communication technologies* (pp. 187–213). Hershey, PA: Medical Information Science Reference. doi:10.4018/978-1-4666-2794-9.ch011

Yuan, D., Lewandowski, C., & Zhong, J. (2012). Developing a private cloud based IP telephony laboratory and curriculum. In L. Chao (Ed.), *Cloud computing for teaching and learning: Strategies for design and implementation* (pp. 126–145). Hershey, PA: Information Science Reference. doi:10.4018/978-1-4666-0957-0.ch009

Yuvaraj, M. (2014). Cloud libraries: Issues and challenges. In S. Dhamdhere (Ed.), *Cloud computing and virtualization technologies in libraries* (pp. 316–338). Hershey, PA: Information Science Reference.

Zaman, M., Simmers, C. A., & Anandarajan, M. (2013). Using an ethical framework to examine linkages between "going green" in research practices and information and communication technologies. In B. Medlin (Ed.), *Integrations of technology utilization and social dynamics in organizations* (pp. 243–262). Hershey, PA: Information Science Reference.

Zapata, B. C., & Alemán, J. L. (2013). Security risks in cloud computing: An analysis of the main vulnerabilities. In D. Rosado, D. Mellado, E. Fernandez-Medina, & M. Piattini (Eds.), *Security engineering for cloud computing: Approaches and tools* (pp. 55–71). Hershey, PA: Information Science Reference.

Zapata, B. C., & Alemán, J. L. (2014). Security risks in cloud computing: An analysis of the main vulnerabilities. In I. Management Association (Ed.), Software design and development: Concepts, methodologies, tools, and applications (pp. 936-952). Hershey, PA: Information Science Reference. doi: doi:10.4018/978-1-4666-4301-7.ch045

Zardari, S., Faniyi, F., & Bahsoon, R. (2013). Using obstacles for systematically modeling, analysing, and mitigating risks in cloud adoption. In I. Mistrik, A. Tang, R. Bahsoon, & J. Stafford (Eds.), *Aligning enterprise, system, and software architectures* (pp. 275–296). Hershey, PA: Business Science Reference.

Zech, P., Kalb, P., Felderer, M., & Breu, R. (2013). Threatening the cloud: Securing services and data by continuous, model-driven negative security testing. In S. Tilley, & T. Parveen (Eds.), *Software testing in the cloud: Perspectives on an emerging discipline* (pp. 280–304). Hershey, PA: Information Science Reference.

Zhang, F., Cao, J., Cai, H., & Wu, C. (2011). Provisioning virtual resources adaptively in elastic compute cloud platforms. [IJWSR]. *International Journal of Web Services Research, 8*(3), 54–69. doi:10.4018/jwsr.2011070103

Zhang, G., Li, C., Xue, S., Liu, Y., Zhang, Y., & Xing, C. (2012). A new electronic commerce architecture in the cloud. [JECO]. *Journal of Electronic Commerce in Organizations, 10*(4), 42–56. doi:10.4018/jeco.2012100104

Zhang, J., Yao, J., Chen, S., & Levy, D. (2011). Facilitating biodefense research with mobile-cloud computing. [IJSSOE]. *International Journal of Systems and Service-Oriented Engineering, 2*(3), 18–31. doi:10.4018/jssoe.2011070102

Zhang, J., Yao, J., Chen, S., & Levy, D. (2013). Facilitating biodefense research with mobile-cloud computing. In D. Chiu (Ed.), *Mobile and web innovations in systems and service-oriented engineering* (pp. 318–332). Hershey, PA: Information Science Reference.

Zheng, S., Chen, F., Yang, H., & Li, J. (2013). An approach to evolving legacy software system into cloud computing environment. In X. Yang, & L. Liu (Eds.), *Principles, methodologies, and service-oriented approaches for cloud computing* (pp. 207–229). Hershey, PA: Business Science Reference. doi:10.4018/978-1-4666-2854-0.ch009

Zhou, J., Athukorala, K., Gilman, E., Riekki, J., & Yliantila, M. (2012). Cloud architecture for dynamic service composition. [IJGHPC]. *International Journal of Grid and High Performance Computing, 4*(2), 17–31. doi:10.4018/jghpc.2012040102

Compilation of References

(2012)... *Top (Madrid)*, *500*, Retrieved from http://www.top500.org/

Abidi, Abidi, & Armani. (2012). Cloud libraries: A novel application of cloud computing. In *Proceedings of 2012 International Conference on Education and e-Learning Innovations*. IEEE.

Addis, M., Ferris, J., Greenwood, M., Li, P., Marvin, D., Oinn, T., & Wipat, A. (2003). Experiences with e-science workflow specification and enactment in bioinformatics. In *All hands meeting*. Academic Press.

Agrawal & Srikant. (1994). Fast algorithms for mining association rules in large databases. In *Proceedings of the 20th International Conference on Very Large Data Bases*. Morgan Kaufmann Publishers Inc.

Ahronovitz, M. (2012). *The memories of a product manager: Amazon or self-hosted?* Retrieved from http://my-inner-voice.blogspot.it/2012/02/amazon-or-selfhosted.html

Aida, Natsume, & Futakata. (2003). Distributed computing with hierarchical master-worker paradigm for parallel branch and bound algorithm. In *Proceedings of 3rd IEEE/ACM International Symposium on Cluster Computing and the Grid*. IEEE/ACM.

Alpaydin. (2010). *Introduction to machine learning* (2nd ed.). Cambridge, MA: The MIT Press.

Amazon Elastic Compute Cloud. (2012). Retrieved from http://aws.amazon.com/ec2

Amazon Virtual Private Cloud (Amazon VPC). (2012). Retrieved from http://aws.amazon.com/vpc/

Amazon. (2010). *Amazon ec2 spot instances*. Retrieved from http://aws.amazon.com/

Amazon: Hey Spammers, Get Off My Cloud ! (2008). Retrieved from http://voices.washingtonpost.com/securityfix/2008/07/

AMPL. (2011). Retrieved from http://www.ampl.com

Angin. (2011). Real-time mobile-cloud computing for context- aware blind navigation. *International Journal of Next Generation Computing*, *2*(2).

Armbrust, M., Fox, A., Griffith, R., Joseph, A. D., Katz, R. H., Konwinski, A., & Zaharia, M. (2009). *Above the clouds: A Berkeley view of cloud computing* (Tech. Rep. No. UCB/EECS-2009-28). EECS Department, University of California, Berkeley. Retrieved from http://www.eecs.berkeley.edu/Pubs/TechRpts/2009/EECS-2009-28.html

Armbrust, M., Fox, A., Griffith, R., Joseph, A. D., Katz, R., Konwinski, A., & Zaharia, M. (2010). A view of cloud computing. *Communications of the ACM*, *53*(4), 50–58. http://doi.acm.org/10.1145/1721654.1721672 doi:10.1145/1721654.1721672

Ashton, K. (2010). That 'internet of things' thing. *RFID Journal*, *53*(4), 50–58.

Avanade. (2010). *Global survey: The business impact of big data*. Academic Press.

Bakshi, K. (2012). *Cisco cloud computing - Data center strategy, architecture, and solutions*. Cisco Systems Inc.

Barham, P., et al. (2003). Xen and the art of virtualization. In *Proceedings of SOSP '03*. SOSP.

Barr, J. (2012). *Amazon ec2 spot price history*. Retrieved from http://aws.typepad.com/aws/2011/07/ec2-spot-pricing-now-specific-toeach-availability-zone.html

Barringer, F. (2012). *Corporations slow to act on climate change.* Retrieved from http://green.blogs.nytimes.com/2012/09/12/corporations-slow-to-act-onclimate-change-report-says/more-147625

Beaumont, O., Eyraud-Dubois, L., Pesneau, P., & Renaud-Goud, P. (2013). Reliable service allocation in clouds with memory and capacity constraints. In *Proceedings of Resilience 2013*. Retrieved from http://hal.inria.fr/hal-00850125/PDF/resilience.pdf

Bendjoudi, Melab, & Talbi. (2012). Hierarchical branch and bound algorithm for computational grids. *Future Generation Computer Systems*, 28(8), 1168–1176. doi:10.1016/j.future.2012.03.001

Beraldi, Grandinetti, Musmanno, & Triki. (2000). Parallel algorithms to solve two-stage stochastic linear programs with robustness constraints. *Parallel Computing*, 26(1314), 1889–1908. doi:10.1016/S0167-8191(00)00057-0

Bobroff, N., Kochut, A., & Beaty, K. (2007). Dynamic placement of virtual machines for managing SLA violations. In *Proceedings of 10th IFIP/IEEE International Symposium on Integrated Network Management* (IM '07). IEEE.

Boothe, P., Hiebert, J., & Bush, R. (2006). Short-lived prefix hijacking on the internet. In *Proceedings of NANOG 36*. NANOG.

Borovskiy, Wust, Schwarz, Koch, & Zeier. (2011). A linear programming approach for optimizing workload distribution in a cloud. In *Cloud computing*. Academic Press.

Boulif & Atif. (2006). An exact multiobjective epsilon-constraint approach for the manufacturing cell formation problem. In *Proceedings of 2006 International Conference on Service Systems and Service Management*, (vol. 2, pp. 883–888). Academic Press.

Bracci, F., Corradi, A., & Foschini, L. (2012). Database security management for healthcare SaaS in the Amazon AWS cloud. In *Proceedings of 2012 IEEE Symposium on Computers and Communications* (ISCC). IEEE.

Bu-Sung Lee Chaisiri, S., & Niyato, D. (2009). Optimal virtual machine placement across multiple cloud providers. In *Proceedings of Services Computing Conference*. IEEE.

Buyya, R., Yeo, C. S., & Venugopal, S. (2008). Market-oriented cloud computing: Vision, hype, and reality for delivering it services as computing utilities. In *Proceedings of HPCC* (pp. 5-13). HPCC.

Calheiros, Ranjan, & Beloglazov, De Rose, & Buyya. (2011). Cloudsim: A toolkit for modeling and simulation of cloud computing environments and evaluation of resource provisioning algorithms. *Software, Practice & Experience*, 41(1), 23–50. doi:10.1002/spe.995

Caminero, A. C., Robles-Gomez, A., Ros, S., Hernandez, R., Pastor, R., Oliva, N., & Castro, M. (2011). Harnessing clouds for e-learning: New directions followed by UNED. In *Proceedings of Global Engineering Education Conference (EDUCON)*. IEEE.

Casadio, M., Biasco, G., Abernethy, A., Bonazzi, V., Pannuti, R., & Pannuti, F. (2010). The national tumor association foundation (ANT): A 30 year old model of home palliative care. *BMC Palliative Care*, 9(12). PMID:20529310

Cattell, R. (2011). Scalable SQL and NOSQL data stores. *SIGMOD Record*, 39(4), 12–27. doi:10.1145/1978915.1978919

CERN - The Large Hadron Collider. (2012). Retrieved from http://public.Web.cern.ch/public/en/LHC/LHC-en.html

Chang, V., Wills, G., & Walters, R. (2011). The positive impacts offered by healthcare cloud and 3D bioinformatics. In *Proceedings of 10th E-Science all Hands Meeting 2011*. Academic Press.

Charlton, S. (2012). *Cloud computing and the next generation of enterprise architecture.* Retrieved from http://www.slideshare.net/StuC/cloud-computing-and-thenextgeneration-of-enterprise-architecture-cloud-computing-expo-2008-presentation

Chun, B. N., Buonadonna, P., Auyoung, A., Ng, C., Parkes, D. C., Shneidman, J., & Vahdat, A. (2005). Mirage: A microeconomic resource allocation system for sensornet testbeds. In *Proceedings of the 2nd IEEE Workshop on Embedded Networked Sensors*. IEEE.

Chun, B. N., Buonadonna, P., Auyoung, A., Ng, C., Parkes, D. C., Shneidman, J., & Vahdat, A. (2005). Mirage: A microeconomic resource allocation system for sensornet testbeds. In *Proceedings of the 2nd IEEE Workshop on Embedded Networked Sensors*. IEEE. *CRM at salesforce. com, Inc.* (2012). Retrieved from http://www.salesforce. com

Cloud Architecture Reference Models: A Survey. (2011, January 25). (DRAFT NIST CCRATWG 004 v2).

Cloud Computing Expo. (2012). Retrieved from http:// www.cloudcomputingexpo.com

Cloud Security Alliance . (2012). Retrieved from http:// www.CloudSecurityAlliance.org

Cloud Storage for Cloud Computing . (2012). Retrieved from www.snia.org/cloud/CloudStorageForCloudComputing.pdf

Coffman, J. Garey, & Johnson. (1997). Approximation algorithms for NP-hard problems. PWS Publishing Co.

Cohon. (1978). *Multiobjective programming and planning*. London: Elsevier.

Computational Infrastructure for Operations Research . (2011). Retrieved from http://www.coinor.org

CRM. (2012). Retrieved from http://www.salesforce.com

Czyzyk, J., Mesnier, M. P., & Mor'e, J. J. (1998). The neos server. *IEEE Computational Science & Engineering*, *5*, 68–75. doi:10.1109/99.714603

Dantzig. (2004). Linear programming under uncertainty. *Management Science, 50*, 1764–1769.

Dean & Ghemawat. (2008). Mapreduce: Simplified data processing on large clusters. *Communications of the ACM*, *51*(1), 107–113. doi:10.1145/1327452.1327492

Drummond, Uchoa, & Gonçalves, Silva, Santos, & de Castro. (2006). A grid-enabled distributed branch-and-bound algorithm with application on the steiner problem in graphs. *Parallel Computing*, *32*(9), 629–642. doi:10.1016/j.parco.2005.09.006

Dudley, J. T., Pouliot, Y., Chen, R., Morgan, A. A., & Butte, A. J. (2010). Translational bioinformatics in the cloud: An affordable alternative. *Genome Medicine*, *2*(8), 51. doi:10.1186/gm172 PMID:20691073

Ehrgott & Gandibleux. (2000). A survey and annotated bibliography of multiobjective combinatorial optimization. *OR-Spektrum*, *22*(4), 425–460. doi:10.1007/s002910000046

Ekanayake, J., Gunarathne, T., & Qiu, J. (2010). *Cloud technologies for bioinformatics applications*. Academic Press.

Ene, Im, & Moseley. (2011). Fast clustering using mapreduce. In *Proceedings of the 17th ACM SIGKDD International Conference on Knowledge Discovery and Data Mining*. ACM.

Esmaili, Amjady, & Shayanfar. (2011). Multi-objective congestion management by modified augmented ïμ-constraint method. *Applied Energy*, *88*(3), 755–766. doi:10.1016/j.apenergy.2010.09.014

European Grid Initiative . (2012). Retrieved from http:// www.egi.eu/

Eurotech. (2012). *Hot water cooled supercomputer*. Retrieved from http://www.eurotech.com/en/hpc/hpc+solutions/liquid+cooling

Exxonmobil. (2012). *The outlook for energy*. Retrieved from http://www.exxonmobil.com/Corporate/energy-outlook.aspx

Fan, H. Cai, & Li. (2012). HCloud: A novel application-oriented cloud platform for preventive healthcare. In *Proceedings of 2012 IEEE 4th International Conference on Cloud Computing Technology and Science* (CloudCom), (pp. 705–710). IEEE.

Ferreto, Netto, Calheiros, & De Rose. (2011). Server consolidation with migration control for virtualized data centers. *Future Generation Computer Systems*, *27*(8), 1027–1034. doi:10.1016/j.future.2011.04.016

First International Workshop on High Performance Computing, Networking and Analytics for the Power Grid. (2010). Retrieved from http://gridoptics.pnnl.gov/sc11/

Foster, I., Kesselman, C., & Tuecke, S. (2001). The anatomy of the grid – Enabling scalable virtual organizations. *The International Journal of Supercomputer Applications*, *15*, 200–222. doi:10.1177/109434200101500302

Fourer, R., Ma, J., & Martin, R. K. (2010). Optimization services: A framework for distributed optimization. *Operations Research, 58*(6), 1624–1636. doi:10.1287/opre.1100.0880

Fox, G. C., & Pierce, M. (2009). *Web 2.0, cloud computing, and earthquake forecasting.* Retrieved from http://grids.ucs.indiana.edu/ptliupages/publications/CloudWeb20Quakesim.pdf

Freeman. (1977). A set of measures of centrality based on betweenness. *Sociometry, 40*(1), 35–41.

Future Grid Portal. (2012). Retrieved from https://portal.futuregrid.org/

Galambos & Woeginger. (1995). On-line bin packing - A restricted survey. *ZOR: Zeitschrift Fuer Operations Research, 42*(1), 25.

Gams. (2011). Retrieved from http://www.gams.com

Gelogo & Lee. (2012). Database management system as a cloud service. *International Journal of Future Generation Communication and Networking, 5*(2), 71–76.

Gentzsch, W., & Yenier, B. (2012). *HPC experiment - Final report of round 2.*

Gentzsch, W., & Yenier, B. (2012a). *CAE in the cloud-New business opportunities for manufacturers and ISVS.* Retrieved from http://www.hpcinthecloud.com/hpccloud/2012-07-19/cae-in-the-cloud

Gentzsch, W., Grandinetti, L., & Joubert, G. (2010). *High speed and large scale scientific computing.* IOS Press Inc. Retrieved from http://books.google.it/books?id=c6xcnhMXSsC

Gentzsch, W., & Yenier, B. (2012). *HPC experiment - Final report of round 1.* The UberCloud LLC.

Gentzsch, W., & Yenier, B. (2012b). *HPC experiment - Final report of round 2.* The UberCloud LLC.

Getov, V. (2012). Security as a service in smart clouds - Opportunities and concerns. In *Proceedings of COMPSAC* (pp. 373-379). COMPSAC.

Ghazizadeh. (2012). Cloud computing benefits and architecture in e-learning. In *Proceedings of 17th IEEE International Conference on Wireless, Mobile and Ubiquitous Technology in Education.* IEEE.

Globus Online Project. (2011). Retrieved from http://www.globusonline.org/

Google App. Engine, Google Code Official Portal Site. (2012). Retrieved from http://code.google.com/appengine/

Google Apps for Business. (2012). Retrieved from http://www.google.com/enterprise/apps/business/pricing.html

Grandinetti, L. (2008). *High performance computing and grids in action.* IOS Press Inc. Retrieved from http://books.google.it/books?id=zNmZLutAXA8C

Grandinetti, Guerriero, Laganà, & Pisacane. (2012). An optimization-based heuristic for the multi-objective undirected capacitated arc routing problem. *Computers & Operations Research, 39*, 2300–2309. doi:10.1016/j.cor.2011.12.009

Grandinetti, Pisacane, & Sheikhalishahi. (2013). An approximate $_p$-constraint method for a multi-objective job scheduling in the cloud. *Future Generation Computer Systems, 29*(8), 1901–1908. doi:10.1016/j.future.2013.04.023

Greenberg, Hamilton, Maltz, & Patel. (2008). The cost of a cloud: Research problems in data center networks. *ACM SIGCOMM Computer Communication Review, 39*(1), 68–73.

Hammond & Cimino. (2006). Standards in biomedical informatics. In *Biomedical informatics, health informatics.* New York: Springer.

Han. (2005). *Data mining: Concepts and techniques.* San Francisco: Morgan Kaufmann Publishers Inc.

Hao, Walden, & Trenkamp. (2013). Accelerating e-commerce sites in the cloud. In *Proceedings of 2013 IEEE 10th Consumer Communications and Networking Conference.* IEEE.

Hartigan. (1972). Direct clustering of a data matrix. *Journal of the American Statistical Association, 67*(337), 123–129.

Helixnebula Project for Science Cloud. (2012). Retrieved from http://www.HelixNebula.org

Ho, Liu, & Wu. (2011). Server consolidation algorithms with bounded migration cost and performance guarantees in cloud computing. In *Proceedings of IEEE International Conference on Utility and Cloud Computing*. IEEE.

IDIGI Device Cloud. (2012). Retrieved from http://www.idigi.com

IEEE Standards Association . (2012). Retrieved from http://www.standardsinsight.com/ieeenews/iotworkshop-2

Intel. (2010). Retrieved from http://www.intel.com/support/processors/xeon/sb/cs012641.htm

Interoperable Clouds White Paper . (2009). Retrieved from http://www.dmtf.org/about/cloud-incubator/DSPIS01011.0.0.pdf

Italian Grid Infrastructure. (2012). Retrieved from http://www.italiangrid.org/

Iyoob, Zarifoglu, & Dieker. (2013). Cloud computing operations research. *Service Science*, 5(2), 88–101. doi:10.1287/serv.1120.0038

Keahey. (2008). Science clouds: Early experiences in cloud computing for scientific applications. In *Proceedings of Cloud Computing and its Applications 2008 (CCA-08)*. Chicago, IL: CCA.

Kelem, N. L., & Feiertag, R. J. (1991). A separation model for virtual machine monitors. In *Proceedings of IEEE Symposium on Security and Privacy* (pp. 78-86). IEEE.

Khasnabish, B., JunSheng, C., SuAn, M., So, N., Unbehagen, P., Morrow, M.,...Yu, M. (2012). *Cloud reference framework*. IETF Internet-draft.

Kim, J., Pratt, M. J., Iyer, R. G., & Sriram, R. D. (2008). Standardized data exchange of CAD models with design intent. *Computer Aided Design*, 40(7), 760–777. doi:10.1016/j.cad.2007.06.014

Kreinovich. (2013). Towards optimizing cloud computing: An example of optimization under uncertainty. In *Scalable computing and communications: Theory and practice*. New York: John Wiley & Sons and IEEE Computer Science Press.

Langer, Venkataraman, Palekar, Kale, & Baker. (2012). Performance optimization of a parallel, two stage stochastic linear program. In *Proceedings of 2012 IEEE 18th International Conference on Parallel and Distributed Systems*, (pp. 676–683). IEEE.

Latorre, Cerisola, Ramos, & Palacios. (2009). Analysis of stochastic problem decomposition algorithms in computational grids. *Annals of Operations Research*, 166(1), 355–373. doi:10.1007/s10479-008-0476-1

LBL. (2010). *Green flash*. Retrieved from http://www.lbl.gov/cs/html/greenflash.html

Lee & Hong. (2011). Pervasive forensic analysis based on mobile cloud computing. In *Proceedings of 2011 Third International Conference on Multimedia Information Networking and Security*. MINES.

Leukel, Kirn, & Schlegel. (2011). Supply chain as a service: A cloud perspective on supply chain systems. *IEEE Systems Journal*, 16–27.

Li & Zhang. (2011). The strategy of mining association rule based on cloud computing. In *Proceedings of 2011 International Conference on Business Computing and Global Informatization (BCGIN)*. BCGIN.

Li, B., Li, J., Huai, J., Wo, T., Li, Q., & Zhong, L. (2009). EnaCloud: An energy-saving application live placement approach for cloud computing environments. In *Proceedings of IEEE International Conference on Cloud Computing*. IEEE. Retrieved from http://ieeexplore.ieee.org/stamp/stamp.jsp?tp=&arnumber=5284078&isnumber=5283545

Li. (2011). The impact of cloud computing-based information sharing on supply chain. In *Proceedings of 2011 International Conference on Management of e-Commerce and e-Government*. Academic Press.

Liang. (2012). Government cloud: Enhancing efficiency of e-government and providing better public services. In *Proceedings of 2012 International Joint Conference on Service Sciences (IJCSS)*. IJCSS.

Linderoth & Wright. (2003). Decomposition algorithms for stochastic programming on a computational grid. *Computational Optimization and Applications*, 24(2-3), 207–250.

Linux Containers Project Official Portal Site . (2012). Retrieved from http://lxc.sourceforge.net/

Li, Yu, Zheng, Ren, & Lou. (2013). Scalable and secure sharing of personal health records in cloud computing using attribute-based encryption. *IEEE Transactions on Parallel and Distributed Systems*, *24*(1), 131–143. doi:10.1109/TPDS.2012.97

Löhr. Sadeghi, & Winandy. (2010). Securing the e-health cloud. In *Proceedings of the 1st ACM International Health Informatics Symposium*. ACM.

Lounis, H. Bouabdallah, & Challal. (2012). Secure and scalable cloud-based architecture for e-health wireless sensor networks. In *Proceedings of International Conference on Computer Communications and Networks*. ICCCN.

Love, Morris, & Wesolowsky. (1988). *Facility location*. New York: Elsevier.

Lubin, Martin, Petra, & Sandikçi. (2013). On parallelizing dual decomposition in stochastic integer programming. *Operations Research Letters*, *41*(3), 252–258. doi:10.1016/j.orl.2013.02.003

Lucas-Simarro, Moreno-Vozmediano, Montero, & Llorente. (2013). Scheduling strategies for optimal service deployment across multiple clouds. *Future Generation Computer Systems*, *29*(6), 1431–1441. doi:10.1016/j.future.2012.01.007

Luo & Hong. (2011). Large-scale ranking and selection using cloud computing. In *Proceedings of the Winter Simulation Conference*, (pp. 4051–4061). Winter Simulation Conference.

Magrassi, P., & Berg, T. (2002). *A world of smart objects*. Retrieved from http://www.renewableenergyworld.com/

Mallegan Project. (2012). Retrieved from http://magellan.alcf.anl.gov/architecture/

Marit, S. (2010, October 5). *Open days workshop 05a34 smart sustainable cities and regions*. Retrieved from http://ec.europa.eu/regional policy/conferences/od2010/

Mathur, Mathur, & Upadhyay. (2011). Cloud based distributed databases: The future ahead. *International Journal on Computer Science and Engineering*, *3*(6), 2477–2481.

Matlani & Londhe. (2013). A cloud computing based telemedicine service. In *Point-of-care healthcare technologies (PHT)*. IEEE.

Matsunaga, A., Tsugawa, M., & Fortes, J. (2008). CloudBLAST: Combining MapReduce and virtualization on distributed resources for bioinformatics applications. In *Proceedings of IEEE International Conference on eScience*. IEEE.

Mendoza, Santiago, & Ravindran. (2008). A three-phase multicriteria method to the supplier selection problem. *International Journal of Industrial Engineering: Theory. Applications and Practice*, *15*(2), 195–210.

Mirchandani & Francis. (1990). *Discrete location theory*. New York: Wiley.

Mohiyuddin, M., Murphy, M., Oliker, L., Shalf, J., Wawrzynek, J., & Williams, S. (2009). A design methodology for domain-optimized power-efficient supercomputing. In *Proceedings of the Conference on High Performance Computing Networking, Storage and Analysis* (pp. 12:1–12:12). Academic Press.

Nebula, O. (2010). *Opennebula cloud toolkit*. Retrieved from http://OpenNebula.org/

Nee, A. Y. C. (2009). *Advanced design and manufacturing based on step*. London: Springer London.

Network Overlay Definition . (2012). Retrieved from http://en.wikipedia.org/wiki/Overlay network

Nimbits: Free, Social and Open Source Internet of Things. (2012). Retrieved from http://www.nimbits.com

Nimbus Toolkit Project . (2010). Retrieved from http://nimbusproject.org/

Numa: Definition and Additional Resources from zdnet . (2012). Retrieved from http://dictionary.zdnet.com/definition/NUMA.html

Nurmi, D. et al. (2008). The eucalyptus open-source cloud-computing system. In *Proceedings of Cloud Computing and its Applications'08*. Academic Press.

Oberheide, J., Cooke, E., & Jahanian, F. (2008). Cloudav: N-version antivirus in the network cloud. In *Proceedings of the 17th Conference on Security Symposium* (pp. 91–106). Berkeley, CA: USENIX Association. Retrieved from http://dl.acm.org/citation.cfm?id=1496711.1496718

OGC Abstract Specification. (2012). Retrieved from http://www.opengeospatial.org/standards/as

Open Cloud Computing Interface (OCCI) . (2012). Retrieved from http://occi-wg.org/

Open Security Architecture. (2012). Retrieved from http://www.opensecurityarchitecture.org/cms/

Openflow. (2012). Retrieved from http://www.openflow.org/

OpenNebula. (2010). *Opennebula cloud toolkit*. Retrieved from http://OpenNebula.org/

Pandey, W. Guru, & Buyya. (2010). A particle swarm optimization-based heuristic for scheduling workflow applications in cloud computing environments. In *Proceedings of 24th IEEE International Conference on Advanced Information Networking and Applications*. IEEE.

Papadimitriou & Sun. (2008). Disco: Distributed co-clustering with map-reduce: A case study towards petabyte-scale end-to-end mining. In *Proceedings of Eighth IEEE International Conference on Data Mining*. IEEE.

Parker, R. (2011). *Business strategy: Cloud computing in manufacturing*. Academic Press.

Percival, C. (2012). *AWS signature version 1 is insecure*. Retrieved from http://www.daemonology.net/blog/2008-12-18-AWS-signature-version-1-is-insecure.html

Phankokkruad. (2012). Implement of cloud computing for e-learning system. In *Proceedings of Computer Information Science (ICCIS)*. ICCIS.

Photo Sharing (Flicker) . (2012). Retrieved from http://www.Flicker.com

Povidaiko, F. Moreira, & Filho. (2010). A java router based on real time traffic congestion information. In *Proceedings of 40th International Conference on Computers and Industrial Engineering*. Academic Press.

Practical Guide for Service Level Agreements. (2012). Retrieved from http://www.cloudcouncil.org/04102012.htm

Rajendran & Veilumuthu. (2011). A cost-effective cloud service for e-learning video on demand. *European Journal of Scientific Research*, 55, 569–579.

Redekopp, Simmhan, & Prasanna. (2011). Performance analysis of vertex-centric graph algorithms on the azure cloud platform. In *Proceedings of Workshop on Parallel Algorithms and Software for Analysis of Massive Graphs*. Academic Press.

Rekhter., et al. (1996). *RFC 1918: Address allocation for private internets*. Retrieved from http://tools.ietf.org/html/rfc1918

Reservoir Project . (2012). Retrieved from http://www.reservoir-fp7.eu/

Rizvandi, B. Kamyabpour, & Zomaya. (2011). Mapreduce implementation of prestack kirchhoff time migration (PKTM) on seismic data. In Proceedings of Parallel and Distributed Computing, Applications and Technologies. PDCAT.

Rolim, K., & Westphall, W. Fracalossi, & Salvador. (2010). A cloud computing solution for patient's data collection in health care institutions. In *Proceedings of Second International Conference on eHealth, Telemedicine, and Social Medicine*, (pp. 95–99). Academic Press.

Rossetti & Chen. (2012). A cloud computing architecture for supply chain network simulation. In *Proceedings of the 2012 Winter Simulation Conference*. Academic Press.

Saaty. (1980). *The analytic hierarchy process: Planning, priority setting, resource, allocation*. New York: McGraw-Hill.

Saaty. (1990). How to make a decision: The analytic hierarchy process. *European Journal of Operational Research, 48*(1), 9 – 26.

Science Clouds Project . (2012). Retrieved from http://www.scienceclouds.org/

Seiden. (2002). On the online bin packing problem. *Journal of the ACM, 49*(5), 640–671.

Shima, K., Ishida, W., & Sekiya, Y. (2012). Design, implementation, and operation of ipv6-only iaas system with ipv4-ipv6 translator for transition toward the future internet datacenter. In *Proceedings of Closer 2012-2nd International Conference on Cloud Computing and Services Science* (pp. 306-314). Closer.

Smart 2020: Enabling the Low Carbon Economy in the Information Age . (2010). Retrieved from http://www.smart2020.org/

Smart Grid / Department of Energy. (2012). Retrieved from http://energy.gov/oe/technologydevelopment/

Smith, M. S. (2011). Nuclear data for astrophysics research: A new online paradigm. *Journal of the Korean Physical Society, 59*(2), 761–766.

Social Networking (Facebook) . (2012). Retrieved from http://www.facebook.com

Solutions, L. (2012). *Liquidcool solutions.* Retrieved from http://www.liquidcoolsolutions.com/

Sotomayor, B. (2010). *Haizea.* Retrieved from http://haizea.cs.uchicago.edu/

Sotomayor, B., Montero, R., Llorente, I., & Foster, I. (2009). Virtual infrastructure management in private and hybrid clouds. *IEEE Internet Computing, 13*(5), 14–22. doi:10.1109/MIC.2009.119

Speitkamp & Bichler. (2010). A mathematical programming approach for server consolidation problems in virtualized data centers. *IEEE Transactions on Services Computing, 3*(4), 266–278. doi:10.1109/TSC.2010.25

Srirama, Batrashev, Jakovits, & Vainikko. (2011). Scalability of parallel scientific applications on the cloud. *Science Progress, 19*(2-3), 91–105.

Stevens, De Leenheer, Develder, Dhoedt, & Christodoulopoulos, Kokkinos, & Varvarigos. (2009). Multi-cost job routing and scheduling in grid networks. *Future Generation Computer Systems, 25*(8), 912–925. doi:10.1016/j.future.2008.08.004

Stratosphere Inc . (2012). Retrieved from http://gl.accesscompany.com/newsevent/archives/2012/20120405 iij/

Swisher, Hyden, Jacobson, & Schruben. (2004). A survey of recent advances in discrete input parameter discrete-event simulation optimization. *IIE Transactions, 36*(6), 591–600. doi:10.1080/07408170490438726

Teragrid. (2012). Retrieved from http://www.teragrid.org/

The green500 . (2012). Retrieved from http://www.green500.org/

The Star Collaboration . (2012). Retrieved from http://www.star.bnl.gov

Trick, M. (2008). *Operations research blog: Don Ratliff at IFORS.* Retrieved from http://mat.tepper.cmu.edu/blog/?p=301

Triki & Grandinetti. (2001). Computational grids to solve large scale optimization problems with uncertain data. In *Proceedings of International Workshop on Intelligent Data Acquisition and Advanced Computing Systems: Technology and Applications.* Academic Press.

Tudoran, Costan, Da Mota, Antoniu, & Thirion. (2012). A-brain: Using the cloud to understand the impact of genetic variability on the brain. In *CloudFutures.* Berkeley, CA: Microsoft.

V'azquez-Poletti, J. L., Moreno-Vozmediano, R., & Llorente, I. M. (2011). Comparison of admission control policies for service provision in public clouds. In K. D. Bosschere, E. H. D'Hollander, G. R. Joubert, D. A. Padua, F. J. Peters, & M. Sawyer (Eds.), *Parco* (Vol. 22, pp. 19–28). IOS Press.

Vance, A. (2011, March). The power of the cloud. *Bloomberg Business Week,* 68–75.

Vazquez-Poletti, J., Barderas, G., Llorente, I., & Romero, P. (2012). A model for efficient onboard actualization of an instrumental cyclogram for the mars metnet mission on a public cloud infrastructure. In *Proceedings of para2010: State of the Art in Scientific and Parallel Computing* (Vol. 7133, pp. 33–42). Berlin: Springer Verlag. doi:10.1007/978-3-642-28151-8_4

Vmware Infrastructure 3 . (2012). Retrieved from http://www.vmware.com/products/vi/overview.html

VMware. (2010). *Vmware dynamic resource scheduler.* Retrieved from http://www.vmware.com/files/pdf/drs datasheet.pdf

Wall, D., Kudtarkar, P., Fusaro, V., Pivovarov, R., Patil, P., & Tonellato, P. (2010). Cloud computing for comparative genomics. *BMC Bioinformatics*, *11*(1), 259. doi:10.1186/1471-2105-11-259 PMID:20482786

Walmart. (2012). *Amazon.com hit with denial of service attack*. Retrieved from http://www.techflash.com/seattle/2009/12/

Wang, Ren, & Wang. (2011). Secure and practical outsourcing of linear programming in cloud computing. In *Proceedings of INFOCOM*. IEEE.

Watson, P., Lord, P., Gibson, F., Periorellis, P., & Pitsilis, G. (2008). Cloud computing for e-science with Carmen. In *Proceedings of 2nd Iberian Grid Infrastructure Conference* (pp. 3–14). Academic Press.

Web Services Architecture. (2012). Retrieved from http://www.w3.org/TR/ws-arch/#whatis/

Weng, C., Li, M., Lu, X., & Deng, Q. (2005). An economic-based resource management framework in the grid context. In *Proceedings of the Fifth IEEE International Symposium on Cluster Computing and the Grid* (pp. 542–549). Washington, DC: IEEE Computer Society. Retrieved from http://dl.acm.org/citation.cfm?id=1169222.1169513

Weng, C., Li, M., Lu, X., & Deng, Q. (2005). An economic-based resource management framework in the grid context. In *Proceedings of the Fifth IEEE International Symposium on Cluster Computing and the Grid*. IEEE.

Wieczorek, Hoheisel, & Prodan. (2009). Towards a general model of the multi-criteria workflow scheduling on the grid. *Future Generation Computer Systems*, *25*(3), 237–256. doi:10.1016/j.future.2008.09.002

Wittmann, A. (2012). *Why infrastructure as a service is a bad deal*. Retrieved from http://www.informationweek.com/cloud-computing/infrastructure/whyinfrastructure-as-a-service-is-a-bad/232601889

World's #1 Renewable Energy Network. (2012). Retrieved from http://www.renewableenergyworld.com/

Wyld. (2010). The cloudy future of government it: Cloud computing and the public sector around the world. *International Journal of Web & Semantic Technology*, *1*(1), 1–20.

Xen Paravirtualization Official Portal Site . (2012). Retrieved from http://www.xen.org/about/paravirtualization.html

Xu, X. (2011, July). From cloud computing to cloud manufacturing. *Robotics and Computer-integrated Manufacturing*, 1–12. doi: doi:10.1016/j.rcim.2011.07.002

Yarmish & Van Slyke. (2009). A distributed, scaleable simplex method. *The Journal of Supercomputing*, *49*(3), 373–381. doi:10.1007/s11227-008-0253-6

Zhang & Liu. (2010). Security models and requirements for healthcare application clouds. In *Proceedings of IEEE 3rd International Conference on Cloud Computing (CLOUD)*, (pp. 268–275). IEEE.

Zhang & Zhang. (2002). *Association rule mining: models and algorithms*. Berlin: Springer-Verlag.

Zheng, Z., Zhu, J., & Lyu, M. R. (2013). Service-generated big data and big data-as-a-service: An overview. In *Proceedings of 2013 IEEE International Congress on Big Data (BigData Congress)* (pp. 403–410). IEEE. doi:10.1109/BigData.Congress.2013.60

About the Authors

Lucio Grandinetti is Professor Emeritus at the Department of Computer Engineering, Electronics, and Systems of University of Calabria (UNICAL), Italy. At the same University, he holds the position of Vice Rector. He graduated from the University of Pisa, Italy and the University of California at Berkeley. He has been a post-doc fellow at University of Southern California, Los Angeles and Research Fellow at the University of Dundee, Scotland. He was a member of the IEEE Committee on Parallel Processing, and European Editor of the MIT Press book series on Advanced Computational Methods and Engineering. Currently he is a member of the Editorial Board of four international journals. He is author of many research papers in well-established international journals and Editor or co-Editor of several books on algorithms, software, applications of Parallel Computing, HPC, Grids, and Clouds. He has been the recipient and scientific leader of many European Commission-funded projects since 1993 (e.g., Molecular Dynamics Simulations by MPP Systems, EUROMED, HPC Finance, WADI, and BEINGRID). Currently, he is Director of the Centre of Excellence on HPC established at the University of Calabria by the Italian government and Co-managing director of a Supercomputing Centre jointly established by the University of Calabria and NEC Corporation.

Ornella Pisacane obtained her Laurea degree in Computer Engineering from the University of Calabria (UNICAL) with the maximum score of 110/110 with honors and defending a thesis on *Parallel Algorithms of Simulated Annealing for Simulation-Optimization*. At the same university, she completed her Ph.D. in Operations Research, defending a thesis on *Agent Scheduling in a Multiskill Call Center*. During her Ph.D. course, she also conducted research activities at the Département d'Informatique et de Recherche Opérationnelle, Université De Montréal (Canada). She was a research fellow at the Department of Electronics, Informatics, and Systems of UNICAL and teaching assistant in some courses of Optimization and Logistics at the same university. Currently, she is research fellow at the Information Engineering Department of the Università Politecnica delle Marche, where she also teaches a course on mathematical models for production management. Her scientific research area mainly concerns the definition of optimization models and solution approaches for addressing problems that arise in Grid/Cloud environments, in Logistics, and in Transportation (such as (Electric) Vehicle Routing). She is co-author of international journal papers, conference proceedings, and book chapters.

Mehdi Sheikhalishahi has 12 years of experience in Web technology, network security, and distributed computing technologies. Mehdi is currently a research fellow in the Computer Science and Engineering Department at University of Calabria in Italy after completing his PhD studies and PhD thesis on energy efficient computing at the same department. In this position, he is doing research on cloud, green computing, and application of cloud computing in futuristic "Internet of Things." In addition, he is currently collaborating with the Energy Efficient HPC Working Group (EE HPC WG), which is an international group with participants mostly from the United States, to drive implementation of energy conservation measures and energy efficient design in high performance computing (HPC). Also, Mehdi is a collaborator in an HPC cloud experiment, i.e., The Uber-Cloud Experiment. This experiment aims at exploring remote computing services for the future. While cloud computing in general is moving fast, there are still some hurdles to overcome when it comes to more sophisticated services such as HPC and engineering simulations in the cloud. During his PhD studies, he has conducted research on challenges of energy efficiency in cloud computing infrastructures, in particular focusing on resource management and scheduling components of a cloud system. He spent his abroad research at Distributed Systems Architecture Research Group, Complutense University of Madrid in Madrid, Spain. He was a research visitor at the cloud group of the same department from September, 2010 until February, 2011. Under supervision of Prof. Ignacio M. Llorente, he carried out research on challenges of energy optimization in cloud computing infrastructures. In particular, he developed efficient energy aware consolidation policies. Prior to that, he gained experience and conducted research on HPC and grid computing during his Master studies. Previously, he worked in the network security field, developing security systems such as firewalls and Public Key Infrastructure products. In addition, he was involved in Web development of e-Commerce systems such as online store during the first stage of his career. Mehdi is a co-author of several scientific papers on grid, cloud computing, and energy efficiency, and he was reviewer of several conferences and journals such as *Journal of Optimization Methods and Software*, and *A Special Issue of IEEE Transactions on Parallel and Distributed Systems (TPDS) on Many Task Computing*. He taught several computer science courses (programming and HPC programming) in Iran. Mehdi is a founding member and technical advisor to a spin-off company on emerging computing technologies in Italy. All in all, Mehdi has high-profile global roles in network, computing, and information security architecture, engineering, operations, product management, and marketing with a passion for cloud computing.

Index